Praise for *Building Multi-Tenant SaaS Architectures*

For anyone looking to build, sustain, and thrive in the software-as-a-service business, the guidance in this book is invaluable. Not only is it grounded in real-world solutions for common challenges, but the patterns and practices will stand the test of time.

—*Adrian De Luca, Director of Cloud Acceleration, AWS*

A complete reference of SaaS concepts that goes deep detailing real-world architecture patterns that address security, tenant isolation, scalability, and more. A must-have companion for anyone building multi-tenant SaaS solutions.

—*Tony Pallas, Chief Commercial and Technology Officer,*
ShyTouch Technology

This book focuses brilliantly on the crucial domain concepts and levers that you need to master to put together a successful SaaS, or PaaS, product.

—*Russ Miles, Platform Engineer, Clear.Bank*

Tod's many years of real-world experience working with a wide variety of customers really shines through in this book. It will be a great resource for those who want to build scalable and secure SaaS solutions, particularly on AWS.

—*Anubhav Sharma, Principal Solutions Architect, AWS*

With his conversational style and practical examples, Tod Golding demystifies the complex world of building SaaS applications on AWS. He breaks down complicated technical concepts into easy-to-grasp explanations that builders of all levels can understand. Whether you're new to SaaS or a seasoned pro, Tod's real-world insights and hard-won best practices will help you architect robust and scalable SaaS solutions. This book is an indispensable guidebook for anyone looking to successfully deliver their SaaS software on AWS.

—*Toby Buckley, Sr. Solutions Architect, AWS*

Tod is the mastermind behind the multi-tenant architecture we've implemented at Stedi. He is years ahead of the market, and we have realized tremendous advantages by adopting his framework early. This book is a goldmine.

—*Zack Kanter, Founder and CEO, Stedi*

Building Multi-Tenant SaaS Architectures
Principles, Practices, and Patterns Using AWS

Tod Golding

Beijing · Boston · Farnham · Sebastopol · Tokyo

Building Multi-Tenant SaaS Architectures

by Tod Golding

Published by O'Reilly Media, Inc., 1005 Gravenstein Highway North, Sebastopol, CA 95472.

O'Reilly books may be purchased for educational, business, or sales promotional use. Online editions are also available for most titles (*http://oreilly.com*). For more information, contact our corporate/institutional sales department: 800-998-9938 or *corporate@oreilly.com*.

Acquisitions Editor: Louise Corrigan	**Indexer:** nSight, Inc.
Development Editor: Melissa Potter	**Interior Designer:** David Futato
Production Editor: Gregory Hyman	**Cover Designer:** Karen Montgomery
Copyeditor: Charles Roumeliotis	**Illustrator:** Kate Dullea
Proofreader: Tove Innis	

May 2024:   First Edition

Revision History for the First Edition
2024-04-24:   First Release

See *http://oreilly.com/catalog/errata.csp?isbn=9781098140649* for release details.

978-1-098-14064-9

[LSI]

Table of Contents

Preface

When I first started digging into the software-as-a-service (SaaS) domain, I expected to find plenty of existing best practices guidance. After all, SaaS certainly wasn't a new concept. There were multiple examples of successful SaaS companies and a general sentiment that SaaS was establishing itself as the preferred mode of delivery for many companies. To me, this meant I'd mostly be absorbing and applying an existing set of patterns and strategies. Surprisingly, it didn't go that way.

The more I wandered into customers' solutions and the more I scanned the industry for guidance, the more I began to realize just how little clarity there was around what it meant to design, build, and operate SaaS environments. I think part of this was the byproduct of the natural ambiguity that comes with attaching a label to any technology. The lack of absolutes has created lots of room for competing definitions and opinions about what SaaS is meant to look like. This has opened the door for companies with fundamentally different implementations and approaches to brand themselves as SaaS. In fact, I continue to see a number of companies setting off on their journey to SaaS with wildly different, misaligned views about what it means for them to adopt a SaaS delivery model.

There's nothing inherently wrong with this. It's fine to have different ideas about what it means to be SaaS. This, however, becomes a bigger problem when you need to work with customers that are looking to you as *the* SaaS expert. As the expert, you can't just tell customers to build whatever they want. Vagueness doesn't work for teams that are relying on you to point them at proven best practices strategies and patterns. To do my job, I really needed to be able to enter our discussion with a clear point of view around what it means to build a best practices SaaS architecture and business. I needed to be able to bring more definition to the SaaS landscape in a way that would help teams understand the trade-offs, architecture patterns, and operational considerations that would directly shape their multi-tenant architecture. Getting there meant I would need to create a clear taxonomy of SaaS principles and strategies that could span a range of domains, workloads, customer profiles, and so on. In many respects, this was also about intentionally moving away from wide-open notions of what it meant to be a SaaS solution, defining a more specific set of guard-rails that could help organizations plot their path forward.

It was this fundamental need that set me off on a multiyear path to better define the SaaS architecture landscape. What started with a few blog posts was followed by a stream of whitepapers, webinars, podcasts, training videos, and conference presentations. Along the way, I noticed that the concepts and principles that I was advocating were grabbing hold in more settings and being applied more widely. This had me thinking that it may be time to write a book that could assemble all of the key elements of this guidance into one end-to-end experience.

With this book, I'm hoping I can bring more definition to the SaaS discussion, establishing a framework for how to think about SaaS and how to connect these concepts to real-world constructs. The goal is to be sure we have alignment on the foundational principles and then illustrate how those principles are realized across different use cases and technology stacks. By connecting these concepts to specific technologies (Kubernetes, serverless, and so on), you'll be able to see how the nuances of individual technologies can have a significant influence on the overall footprint of your multi-tenant architecture.

Along the way, I'll create a clear taxonomy of the core elements of any SaaS environment, defining a vocabulary for SaaS that allows us to have a more universal approach to how we categorize and describe the moving parts of a SaaS architecture. I'll look at the full range of SaaS-specific architecture mechanisms, including tenant isolation, onboarding, tiering, identity, metrics, billing, and data partitioning. For each of these areas, we'll look at examples of how they might be applied in different settings.

The book would also be incomplete without exploring the operational elements of SaaS. As you'll discover, the architecture of SaaS environments is directly shaped by core operational business goals (agility, innovation, cost efficiency). We'll look at this strong correlation throughout the book, outlining the operational considerations that will influence the footprint of your SaaS environment.

Overall, I see this book representing a good starting point for the SaaS architecture discussion. It sets out to create a clearer view of how we define what it means to be SaaS, highlighting key principles, constructs, and strategies that are core to shaping how you'll approach building a best practices SaaS architecture.

An Evolving Landscape

The early multi-tenant solutions I worked on had a very simple notion of what it meant to be SaaS. These environments typically employed a model where customers shared one compute cluster and stored each customer's data in a separate database. I suspect there are still plenty of systems that are using this model today—especially in environments where teams are hosting and managing their own SaaS infrastructure.

Now, when the cloud came along, it brought an all-new dimension of possibilities to the SaaS picture. The managed services, dynamic scaling, and pay-as-you-go nature of the cloud equipped SaaS teams with tools and mechanisms that aligned naturally with their needs. Organizations could piggyback on all the goodness of the cloud to enrich the cost, operational, and agility profile of their SaaS environments. In some cases, the appeal of the cloud was so compelling that some companies equated being in the cloud with being SaaS (which it's not).

You can imagine how the emergence of the cloud opened up an entirely new realm for SaaS architects. It provided architects with a much bigger set of tools, services, and operational mechanisms that could streamline their development of their multi-tenant environments. The cloud also allowed SaaS teams to push even more operational complexity to the cloud, reducing the friction and overhead that came with supporting and operating a SaaS business. It also provided native mechanisms that promoted scale, high availability, and cost/operational efficiency.

This natural fit between SaaS and the cloud contributed significantly to the broader overall appeal and rapid adoption of the SaaS delivery model. New SaaS companies have been able to leverage the strengths of the cloud to accelerate the development of SaaS offerings, enabling them to disrupt existing domains and market segments. Cloud-based SaaS businesses could move faster, achieve better margins, capture new markets, and innovate at a much faster pace. This, as you can imagine, motivated existing software companies to accelerate their path to SaaS, some of whom saw moving to SaaS as fundamental to their survival. It also directly shaped the behavior of software customers who began to expect and embrace the low-friction, value-focused nature of the SaaS model.

All of this activity has created an avalanche of SaaS adoption. It also created a significant need for additional insights and guidance around how these cloud constructs could be applied in a multi-tenant architecture. The convergence of these factors— the need for much broader and deeper architecture guidance, the general SaaS adoption momentum, and the influence of the cloud—drove demand for greater clarity around how SaaS solutions are designed, built, and operated.

So, what's this mean for this book? The main point is that the domain of SaaS best practices continues to be a moving target. The rapid evolution of SaaS companies and the emergence of new technologies continue to introduce new strategies, mechanisms, and constructs that may influence future guidance. It's fair to assume that SaaS best practices and strategies will continue to morph based on the shifting technology landscape.

Who's This Book For?

This book is targeted at builder, architect, and operations teams who are creating, migrating, or optimizing SaaS solutions. You might be brand new to SaaS and looking for the foundational concepts that can get you started with SaaS, or you might already be immersed in SaaS and are looking at how you might want to apply the principles outlined here to enhance an existing solution. You'll notice that I've also included operations in this list. While significant parts of this book will be more focused on the builders and architects, there is a clear need for operations teams to be equally immersed in shaping the trade-offs and strategies that will be used to define the footprint of your as-a-service experience. There's also a corresponding need for builders and architects to be more immersed in the operations experience.

I intentionally start by establishing a clear set of foundational concepts that span the entire book. Even if you have experience with SaaS, I would strongly encourage you to invest in starting with these foundational concepts. The ideas that are established in the early stages of the book challenge some of the classic notions of what it means to be SaaS, introducing terminology and mindsets that influence every aspect of how you design and build a SaaS environment. The examples that show up later in this book illustrate how these design choices and patterns are realized and applied. Having this foundation in place and having good alignment around these core principles will directly influence how you approach the decomposition of microservices, the deployment model of your solution, the identity model you adopt, and so on. My point is that, as you move more into the details of implementation, you'll see a strong connection between the core principles and the underlying implementation strategies that you might adopt. Being grounded in a common set of guiding principles will allow you and your teams to apply a common set of values throughout the design, development, and operation of your SaaS environment.

There is also a level at which this SaaS content will have value for SaaS leaders and stakeholders. While they may be less interested in the technical details, they are likely to lean on the foundational elements of the book to refine and crystalize their SaaS vision. There are cultural, metric, and team dynamic considerations that come with adopting SaaS, and the success of your organization's SaaS strategy will rely heavily on having leaders that are rooted in a common set of values. This is often one of the most overlooked aspects of building a best-of-breed SaaS business. For the same reasons, you can imagine how product owners and others connected to the SaaS vision will extract value out of having a firm grasp of these fundamental SaaS principles.

A Foundation—Not a Bible

The principles that I will be covering in this book are the byproduct of my experiences working with a large number of SaaS providers, spanning a number of domains, target experiences, industries, and so on. This book represents the themes, patterns, and guidance that emerged from those projects. I've also been fortunate to be surrounded by teams and people that have helped mature this vision.

What's important to note, though, is that this book is not meant to serve as the de facto bible of all things SaaS. The strategies and patterns for building SaaS architectures covered here were created as a starting point to bring more clarity and definition to the universe of multitenant design and architecture. In many respects, I've seen myself as filling a void, finding a way to better describe and characterize the nature of SaaS solutions, knowing that alternate strategies may exist or might emerge in the future.

My hope is that this will bring more visibility to these concepts, drawing more builders and architects into a broader discussion that better align others around these principles.

 Much of my experience in the SaaS domain has come through my direct work and experience with the AWS stack of services and tools. This means that, as we get more into the specifics, I'll naturally gravitate to AWS tools and strategies. However, the majority of the principles and strategies are not unique to the AWS stack. In fact, they should map well to most environments. I should also note that the strategies and principles I'll be covering represent my own perspectives, opinions, and views. Much of what we'll be exploring is certainly influenced by the knowledge and practices that I've been developing during my time at AWS. However, what finally landed in this book should not be viewed as AWS-endorsed guidance.

What's Not in This Book

SaaS is a broad topic that has lots of threads. As you look at the table of contents for this book, you'll see that I cover a significant span of the SaaS universe, exploring a pretty wide spectrum of design, development, and implementation perspectives—including business topics. In fact, you'll see example after example where I emphasize the connection between SaaS business and technology strategies. I make it clear that builders and architects must have a vested interest in using SaaS business parameters to shape the footprint of their solution.

While these business elements are a core part of the SaaS story, you'll also notice that I've intentionally avoided going deeper into specific aspects of the business space. There are entire books that explore SaaS sales, marketing, go-to-market, business modeling, journey mapping, metrics, and so on. To me, these topics stand on their own and apply more generally to the SaaS domain. While I have moderate exposure to these areas, I feel like they are better addressed as separate standalone topics. I'd certainly suggest that organizations get ramped on the SaaS concepts as part of building out a robust SaaS business; I just won't be covering them here.

It's also worth noting that this book is not trying to include every permutation of SaaS. There are many business-to-consumer (B2C) commercial solutions that people think of when they think of SaaS. While they may be most familiar to the everyday person, they are also designed and built around a model that, for most, is atypical. Most SaaS builders aren't trying to support millions of users. Generally, B2C environments will employ their own unique design strategies that are often hyper-optimized around a specialized set of scaling challenges. In contrast, a business-to-business (B2B) SaaS company that's supporting hundreds to thousands of businesses is likely to take a different approach to how they design and architect their multi-tenant environment. I think the B2C space is interesting, and I think the concepts of B2C will have plenty of overlap with the core set of principles I'll be covering. At the same time, I also need to acknowledge that there are areas where B2B and B2C strategies can diverge significantly. Offering tenants dedicated infrastructure, for example, is a completely valid option in a B2B setting. That same approach is unlikely to be viable in most B2C environments.

Conventions Used in This Book

The following typographical conventions are used in this book:

Italic
> Indicates new terms, URLs, email addresses, filenames, and file extensions.

`Constant width`
> Used for program listings, as well as within paragraphs to refer to program elements such as variable or function names, databases, data types, environment variables, statements, and keywords.

 This element signifies a general note.

Using Code Examples

Code examples from Chapters 10 and 11 are available for download at *https://oreil.ly/ saas-ch10-code* and *https://oreil.ly/saas-ch11-code*, respectively. Links are also provided in those chapters.

If you have a technical question or a problem using the code examples, please send email to *support@oreilly.com*.

This book is here to help you get your job done. In general, if example code is offered with this book, you may use it in your programs and documentation. You do not need to contact us for permission unless you're reproducing a significant portion of the code. For example, writing a program that uses several chunks of code from this book does not require permission. Selling or distributing examples from O'Reilly books does require permission. Answering a question by citing this book and quoting example code does not require permission. Incorporating a significant amount of example code from this book into your product's documentation does require permission.

We appreciate, but generally do not require, attribution. An attribution usually includes the title, author, publisher, and ISBN. For example: "*Building Multi-Tenant SaaS Architectures* by Tod Golding (O'Reilly). Copyright 2024 Tod Golding, 978-1-098-14064-9."

If you feel your use of code examples falls outside fair use or the permission given above, feel free to contact us at *permissions@oreilly.com*.

O'Reilly Online Learning

 For more than 40 years, *O'Reilly Media* has provided technology and business training, knowledge, and insight to help companies succeed.

Our unique network of experts and innovators share their knowledge and expertise through books, articles, and our online learning platform. O'Reilly's online learning platform gives you on-demand access to live training courses, in-depth learning paths, interactive coding environments, and a vast collection of text and video from O'Reilly and 200+ other publishers. For more information, visit *https://oreilly.com*.

How to Contact Us

Please address comments and questions concerning this book to the publisher:

O'Reilly Media, Inc.
1005 Gravenstein Highway North
Sebastopol, CA 95472
800-889-8969 (in the United States or Canada)
707-827-7019 (international or local)
707-829-0104 (fax)
support@oreilly.com
https://www.oreilly.com/about/contact.html

We have a web page for this book, where we list errata, examples, and any additional information. You can access this page at *https://oreil.ly/bldg-multitenant-saas*.

For news and information about our books and courses, visit *https://oreilly.com*.

Find us on LinkedIn: *https://linkedin.com/company/oreilly-media*

Watch us on YouTube: *https://youtube.com/oreillymedia*

Acknowledgments

I've had the good fortune of being surrounded, influenced, supported, and inspired by a great number of people that have contributed directly and indirectly to the creation of this book. The best place to start is probably at the beginning, looking at my earliest days at AWS when I was the new SaaS solutions architect hired to try to define and shape a vision for what it meant to build SaaS offerings in the cloud. It's in this time that I was lucky enough to be guided by Matt Yanchyshyn, who pushed me to dig in, move fast, and deliver results. Matt has this ability to ask a lot, give you room to operate, and inspire you to think big. His early encouragement set me off on this path and I'm not sure how or if I would have made the early progress I did without his words of wisdom.

My ability to go deep and develop my SaaS insights has also been directly connected to the experiences I've had working with SaaS companies. Being able to get in the room with organizations and go deep on their SaaS solutions exposed me to a broad range of industries, domains, business cases, and adoption scenarios. The data, patterns, and code that came out of these engagements was and continues to be priceless. I've also been fortunate to be surrounded by an amazing team of SaaS architects and business leads that have played a key role in advancing the state of SaaS and helping me continually reevaluate best practices strategies and patterns. There's too many to mention here, but I'd like to call out Craig Wicks, Seth Fox, Emily Tyack, and Michael

Schmidt for their early leadership and collaboration. Adrian De Luca was also a constant source of inspiration, providing ongoing guidance and encouragement.

Writing a book also relies heavily on a team of behind-the-scenes contributors that go down this path with you. The team at O'Reilly has been amazing throughout all phases of this book's creation. At the center of so much of my day-to-day O'Reilly interactions was Melissa Potter. Melissa was key to every bit of the book's evolution, helping me navigate the process, reviewing my first drafts, answering questions, and always being there with encouraging words of guidance. O'Reilly's Louise Corrigan was also there from the outset, guiding me during the early stages of shaping the book's structure and leaning into key decisions all along the way. I also want to thank the book's technical reviewers, Anubhav Sharma, Russell Miles, and Toby Buckley. Thanks for investing the time and sharing your insights. Your perspectives helped me refine this story and made this a better book.

Of course, at the core of every journey I take is my family. Even though they've never quite understood what it is I do, they've always been right there in my corner encouraging me along the way. My wife, Janine, has been supportive of everything I do, and this effort was no exception. Her words of encouragement always make it easier for me to keep pushing forward. Then there's my kids, Chelsea and Ryan. While they're grown now and are on their own paths, they still find ways to brighten my day and remind me just how fortunate I am.

## CHAPTER 1

The SaaS Mindset

I've worked with a number of teams that were building software-as-a-service (SaaS) solutions. When I sit down with them to map out their path to SaaS, they tend to start out with what seems like a reasonable, high-level view of what it means to be SaaS. However, as I go a layer deeper and get into the details of their solution, I often discover significant variations in their vision. Imagine, for example, someone telling you they want to construct a building. While we all have some notion of a building having walls, windows, and doors, the actual nature of these structures can vary wildly. Some teams might be envisioning a skyscraper, and others might be building a house.

It's kind of natural for there to be confusion around what SaaS looks like. As is the case in all technology realms, the SaaS universe is continually evolving. The emergence of the cloud, shifting customer needs, and the economics of the software domain are in constant motion. How we defined SaaS yesterday may not be the way we'll define it today. The other part of the challenge here is that the scope of SaaS goes well beyond the technical. It is, in many respects, a mindset that spans all the dimensions of a SaaS provider's organization.

With that in mind, the natural place to start this journey is by clarifying how I define SaaS and how I think this definition shapes our approach to architecting, designing, and building a SaaS solution. The goal in this chapter is to build a foundational mental model that will reduce some of the confusion about what it means to be SaaS. We'll move beyond some of the vague notions of SaaS and, at least for the scope of this book, attach more concrete guiding principles to the definition of SaaS that will shape the strategies that we'll explore in the coming chapters.

To get there, we'll need to look at the forces that motivated the move to SaaS and see how these forces directly influenced the resulting architectural models. Following this evolution will provide a more concrete view into the foundational principles that are used to create a SaaS solution that realizes the full value proposition of SaaS, blending the technical and business parameters that are at the core of developing modern SaaS environments. It's essential for SaaS architects to understand that SaaS is not a technology-first mindset. A SaaS architect doesn't design a multi-tenant architecture first, then figure out how the business strategy layers on top of that. Instead, the business and technology work together to find the best intersection of business goals and multi-tenant solutions that will realize those strategies. This theme will be with us throughout this book.

While you may feel comfortable with what SaaS means to you, it's possible that the foundational concepts we'll explore here might challenge your view of SaaS and the terminology we use to describe SaaS environments. So, while it may be tempting to treat this chapter as optional, it may be one of the most important chapters in the book. It's not just an introduction; it's about creating a common vocabulary and mental model that will be woven into the architecture, coding, and implementation strategies that we'll be covering throughout this book.

Where We Started

Before we can dig into defining SaaS, we need to understand where this journey started and the factors that have driven the momentum of the SaaS delivery model. Let's start by looking at how software has been traditionally built, operated, and managed. Generally, pre-SaaS systems were typically delivered in an "installed software" model where customers played a role in installation and setup of their software. The customer's IT team might install it on some vendor-provided environment or they might run it on their own infrastructure. In this mode, the management and operation of these environments, to some degree, could be pushed to the customer's IT team. A professional services team could also play some role during the installation, customization, and configuration of the customer's environment.

In this model, software development teams tended to be more removed from these delivery and setup details. They were more focused on continually building out the functional capabilities of their solutions. Delivery and operations were often on the side of the wall and handled somewhat downstream of the day-to-day development efforts.

Figure 1-1 provides a conceptual view of the footprint of the traditional software delivery model.

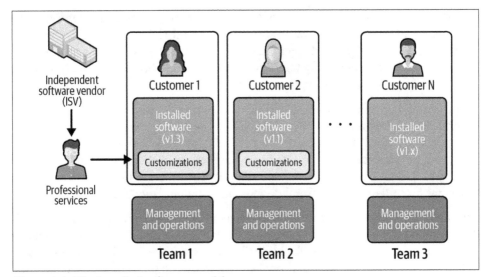

Figure 1-1. The installed software model

In the top left of Figure 1-1, you'll see I have introduced an independent software vendor (ISV) that represents the entity selling software to its customers. I've also shown two customers that currently own the ISV's software, Customers 1 and 2. Each of these customers is running specific versions of the ISV's product. As part of their onboarding, they also required one-off customizations to the product that were addressed by the ISV's professional services team. We also have other customers that may be running different versions of our product that may or may not have any customizations.

As each new customer is onboarded, the provider's operations organization may need to create focused teams that can support the day-to-day needs of these customer environments. These teams might be dedicated to an individual customer or support a cross-section of customers.

This classic mode of software delivery is a much more sales-driven model, where the business focuses on acquiring customers and handing them off to technology teams to address the specific needs of each incoming customer. You can imagine how this dynamic shapes the overall culture and development cycle of the experience. How your product is built, how new features are rolled out, how you think about customization—these are all areas influenced by the nature of this approach. The mindset here is one where landing a deal can take precedence over the need for agility, scale, and operational efficiency. These solutions are also frequently sold with long-term contracts that limit a customer's ability to easily move to any other vendor's offering.

The distributed and varying nature of these customer environments often slows the release and adoption of new features. Customers tend to have control in these settings, often dictating how and when they might upgrade to a new version. The complexity of testing and deploying these environments could become unwieldy, pushing vendors toward quarterly or semi-annual releases.

To be fair, building and delivering software using this model is and will continue to be a perfectly valid approach for some businesses. The legacy, compliance, and business realities of any given domain might align well to this model. However, for many, this mode of software delivery introduces a number of challenges. At its core, this approach focuses more on being able to sell customers whatever they need in exchange for trade-offs around scale, agility, and cost/operational efficiency.

On the surface, these trade-offs may not seem all that significant. If you have a limited number of customers and you're only landing a few a year, this model could be entirely adequate. You would still have inefficiencies, but they would be far less prominent. Consider, however, a scenario where you have a significant installed base and are looking to grow your business rapidly. In that mode, the pain points of this approach begin to represent a real problem for many software vendors.

Operational and cost efficiencies are often amongst the first areas where companies using this model start to feel the pain. The incremental overhead of supporting each new customer begins to have real impacts on the business, eroding margins and continually adding complexity to the operational profile of the business. Each new customer could require more support teams, more infrastructure, and more effort to manage the one-off variations that accompany each customer installation. In some cases, companies actually reach a point where they'll intentionally slow their growth because of the operational burdens of this model.

The bigger issue here, though, is how this model impacts agility, competition, growth, and innovation. By its very nature, this model is anything but nimble. Allowing customers to manage their own environments, supporting separate versions for each customer, enabling one-off customization—these are all areas that undermine speed and agility. Imagine what it would mean to roll out a new feature in these environments. The time between having the idea for a feature, iterating on its development, and getting it in front of all your customers is often a slow and deliberate process. By the time a new feature arrives, customer and market needs may have already shifted. This also can impact the competitive footprint of these companies, limiting their ability to rapidly react to emerging solutions that are built around a lower friction model.

While the operational and development footprint was becoming harder to scale, the needs and expectations of customers were also shifting. Customers have become less focused on retaining the ability to manage or control their environments. Instead, they're more interested in maximizing the value they can extract from their software. They are increasingly demanding lower friction experiences that can continually innovate to meet their needs, giving them more freedom to move between solutions based on the evolving needs of their businesses.

Customers are also more drawn to pricing models that better align with their value and consumption profile. In some cases, they're looking for the flexibility of subscription and/or pay-as-you-go pricing models.

You can see the natural tension that's at play here. For many, the classic delivery model simply doesn't align well with their ability to scale or grow their business and meet the evolving needs of their customers. The emergence of the cloud also played a key role here. The cloud model fundamentally altered the way companies looked at hosting, managing, and operating their software. The pay-as-you-go nature and operational model of the cloud shifted the mindset of the industry, placing a greater emphasis on agility and economies of scale. Together, these forces motivated software providers to rethink how they build, deliver, operate, and sell their solutions.

The Move to a Unified Model

By now, the basic challenges of the traditional model should be clear. While some organizations were struggling with this model, others already understood this approach would simply not scale economically or operationally. If you are a B2B ISV with thousands of customers, for example, it's unlikely that your business would be able to support a model where each customer had to be separately supported, managed, and operated.

The answer, for many, was to move to a model that unified more of the experience, reducing the complexity and cost that naturally came with supporting the per-customer model. This is where we saw teams adopting a shared infrastructure model that would allow them to scale their business and streamline their operational model more effectively.

This shift to a more unified, shared model opened a range of new opportunities for software providers. Figure 1-2 provides a conceptual view of a simplified shared infrastructure SaaS environment.

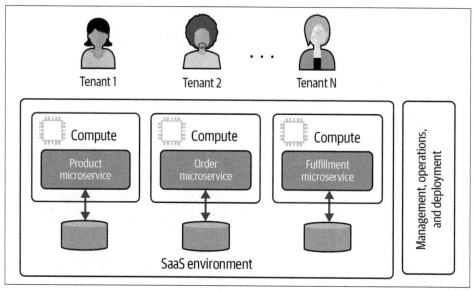

Figure 1-2. A shared infrastructure SaaS model

In Figure 1-2, you'll see a simplified view of the traditional notion of SaaS. You'll notice that we've completely moved away from the distributed, one-off, custom nature of the classic model we saw in Figure 1-1. Instead, we've shifted to a unified strategy where all the system's application services and infrastructure are shared by the customers. You'll also see that I have replaced the term "customer" with "tenant." We'll get deeper into the notion of tenancy in Chapter 2. The fundamental idea is that, as we move to this unified mindset, we look at our environment differently. It is now one set of resources that is shared and occupied by one or more consumers. The idea is that these consumers represent temporary occupants of your environment, consuming only those resources they need—hence the term "tenant."

Moving an application into a shared infrastructure model removes many of the downsides that come with having separate customer environments. Now, with every-thing being shared, we have one set of resources that can be collectively scaled, man-aged, and operated. On the righthand side of Figure 1-2, you'll see that I've added a box to represent the management, operations, and deployment of this environment. Imagine how this would simplify the deployment of updates. With shared infrastruc-ture, your deployment automation would simply deploy the update to this unified SaaS environment, and all of your tenants would immediately have access to the changes. Gone is the idea of separately deployed, versioned, managed, and operated customer environments.

The upside of shared infrastructure extends into nearly every aspect of a software business. It can streamline the aggregation and collection of operational telemetry. It can simplify the complexity of your DevOps automation. It certainly makes onboarding new tenants easier. Perhaps the biggest upside is the cost efficiencies that could come with shared infrastructure. Being able to correlate consumption of infrastructure with actual tenant activity enables teams to maximize margins and achieve economies of scale.

You can see how this model had massive appeal to those organizations that were struggling with the cost and operational challenges of the classic model. In addition to unifying the experience, it also brought a new level of agility to these environments. Built right, these environments create opportunities to release new features and capabilities at a much faster pace, allowing organizations to be more nimble in reacting and responding to customer/market needs. The nature of this model also creates new growth opportunities for some ISVs, allowing them to add new tenants at a faster pace without eroding their margins and absorbing added operational overhead. The elastic, pay-as-you-go nature of cloud infrastructure also aligns nicely with this model, supporting the pricing and scaling models that fit naturally with the elasticity of the cloud.

It's worth noting that this move to shared infrastructure also introduces a range of new challenges. As you move through this book, you'll see all the nuances and complexity that come with having shared infrastructure. Supporting shared infrastructure will directly influence the security, performance, scale, availability, and resilience profile of your SaaS environment. These factors will have a distinct impact on how you approach the design and implementation of your SaaS environment.

 This notion of having all tenants running the same *version* of your offering represents a common litmus test for SaaS environments. It is foundational to enabling many of the business benefits that are at the core of adopting a SaaS delivery model.

To create a unified experience, we must also introduce a new set of cross-cutting components that provide all the functionality that's needed to centrally manage, operate, and deploy a SaaS application. Carving out these separate components is essential to building a successful and scalable SaaS business—even if your application doesn't have shared infrastructure. In reality, these components are at the core of driving the agility, innovation, and efficiency goals of SaaS companies. To better understand this point, let's look at a slightly different view of a SaaS environment (shown in Figure 1-3).

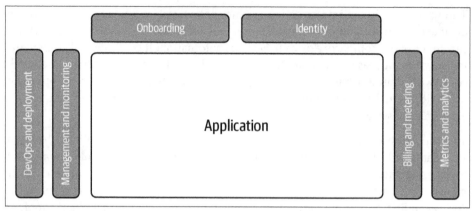

Figure 1-3. Building cross-cutting SaaS capabilities

At the center of Figure 1-3, you'll see a placeholder for your SaaS application experience. This is where the various components of your SaaS application are deployed. It's here that you would find the infrastructure of your application. Around the application are a set of components that are needed to support the broader needs of your SaaS environment. At the top, for example, I've highlighted onboarding and identity, which provide all the functionality to introduce a new tenant into your system. On the left, you'll see the placeholders for the SaaS deployment and management functionality. And, on the right, you'll see fundamental concepts like billing, metering, metrics, and analytics.

Now, for many SaaS builders, it's tempting to view these surrounding components as secondary, less critical elements of their SaaS architecture. In fact, I've worked with teams that have chosen to defer the introduction of these components/services, putting all their initial energy and effort into creating their multi-tenant applications.

While getting the application architecture right is certainly an important part of your SaaS model, the success of your SaaS business will be heavily influenced by the capabilities of these surrounding components. These capabilities are at the core of enabling much of the operational efficiency, growth, innovation, and agility goals that are motivating companies to adopt a SaaS model. So, these components—which are common to *all* SaaS environments—must be put front and center when you are building your SaaS solution. This is why I have always encouraged SaaS teams to start their SaaS development with them. It's these building blocks—which have nothing to do with the functionality of your application—that are going to have a significant influence on the SaaS footprint of your architecture, design, code, and business.

This should highlight the fact that there are multiple dimensions to the SaaS efficiency and agility story. Part of our efficiency is realized through the services that are shown here, and part of it achieved through the strategies you apply to your application architecture. If your application architecture shares infrastructure, it can add more efficiency and economies of scale to your environment. The key is that we must have these surrounding services represent the foundational elements of our unified model. Then, from there, we can think about how/if the application architecture can also be optimized to maximize efficiency and agility.

Redefining Multi-Tenancy

Up to this point, I've avoided introducing the idea of multi-tenancy. It's a term that is used heavily in the SaaS space and will appear throughout the remainder of this book. However, it's a term that we must approach gracefully. The idea of multi-tenancy comes with lots of attached baggage and, before sorting it out, I wanted to create some foundation for the fundamentals that have driven companies toward the adoption of the SaaS delivery model. The other part of the challenge here is that the notion of multi-tenancy—as we'll define it in this book—will move beyond some of the traditional definitions that are typically attached to this term.

For years, in many circles, the term "multi-tenant" was used to convey the idea that some resource was being shared by multiple tenants. This could apply in many contexts. We could say that some piece of cloud infrastructure, for example, could be deemed multi-tenant because it allows tenants to share bits of its underlying infrastructure. Many services running in the cloud may be running in a multi-tenant model to achieve their economies of scale. As a cloud consumer, this may be happening entirely outside of your view. Even in self-hosted environments, teams can build solutions where their compute, databases, and other resources are shared by tenants. This creates a very tight connection between multi-tenancy and the idea of a shared resource. In fact, in this context, this is a perfectly valid notion of multi-tenancy.

Now, as we start thinking about SaaS environments, it's entirely natural for us to bring the mapping of multi-tenancy with us. After all, SaaS environments do share infrastructure, and that sharing of infrastructure is certainly valid to label as being multi-tenant.

To better illustrate this point, let's look at a sample SaaS model that brings together the concepts that we've been discussing in this chapter. The image in Figure 1-4 provides a view of a sample multi-tenant SaaS environment.

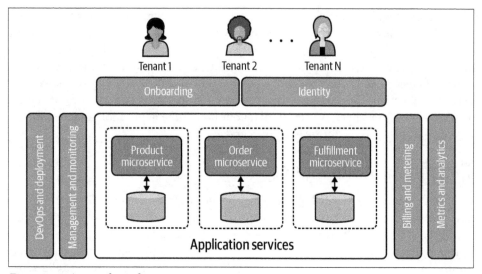

Figure 1-4. A sample multi-tenant environment

For this example, we've landed the shared infrastructure of our application services inside a surrounding set of microservices that are used to manage and operate all the moving parts of our SaaS environment. Assuming that all of our tenants are sharing their infrastructure (compute, storage, and so on), this would still fit with the classic definition of multi-tenancy, and it's not uncommon for SaaS providers to define and deliver their solution following this pattern.

The challenge is that SaaS environments don't exclusively conform to this model. Suppose, for example, I create a SaaS environment that looks like Figure 1-5.

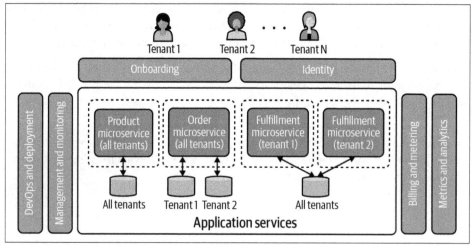

Figure 1-5. Multi-tenancy with shared and dedicated resources

Notice that we've morphed the footprint of some of our application microservices. The Product microservice is unchanged. Its compute and storage infrastructure are still shared by all tenants. However, as we move to the Order microservice, you'll see that we've mixed things up a bit. Our domain, performance, and/or security requirements may have required us to separate out the storage for each tenant. So, the compute of our Order microservice is still shared, but we have separate databases for each tenant.

Finally, our Fulfillment microservice has also shifted. Our requirements pushed us toward a model where each tenant is running dedicated compute resources. In this case, though, the database is still shared by all tenants.

This architecture has certainly added a new wrinkle to our notion of multi-tenancy. If we're sticking to the purest definition of multi-tenancy, we wouldn't really be able to say everything running here conforms to the original definition of multi-tenancy. The storage of the Order service, for example, is not sharing any infrastructure between tenants. The compute of our Fulfillment microservices is also not shared, but the database for this service is shared by all tenants.

Blurring these multi-tenant lines is common in the SaaS universe. When you're composing a SaaS environment, you're not sticking to any one absolute definition of multi-tenancy; you're picking the combinations of shared and dedicated resources that best align with the business and technical requirements of your system. This is all part of optimizing the footprint of your SaaS architecture around the needs of the business.

Even though the resources here are not shared by all tenants, the fundamentals of the SaaS principles we outlined earlier are still valid. For example, this environment would not change our application deployment approach. All tenants in this environment would still be running the same version of the product. Also, the environment would still be onboarded, operated, and managed by the same set of shared services we relied on in our prior example. This means that we're still extracting much of the operational efficiency and agility from this environment that would have been achieved in a fully shared infrastructure (with some caveats).

To drive this point home, let's look at a more extreme example. Suppose we have a SaaS architecture that resembles the model shown in Figure 1-6. In this example, the domain, market, and/or legacy requirements have required us to have all compute and storage running in a dedicated model where each tenant has a completely separate set of infrastructure resources.

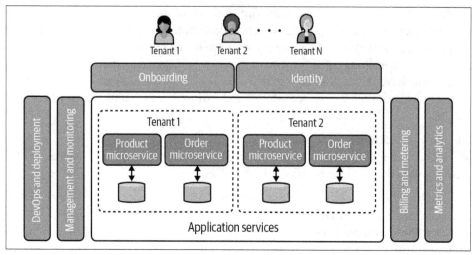

Figure 1-6. A multi-tenant environment with fully dedicated resources

While our tenants aren't sharing infrastructure in this model, you'll see that they continue to be onboarded, managed, and operated through the same set of shared capabilities that have spanned all of our examples. That means that all tenants are still running the same version of the software and they are still being managed and operated collectively.

This may seem like an unlikely scenario. However, in the wild, SaaS providers may have any number of different factors that might require them to operate in this model. Migrating SaaS providers often employ this model as a first stepping stone to SaaS. Other industries may have such extreme isolation requirements that they're not allowed to share infrastructure. There's a long list of factors that could legitimately land a SaaS provider in this model.

So, given this backdrop, it seems fair to ask ourselves how we want to define multi-tenancy in the context of a SaaS environment. Using the literal shared infrastructure definition of multi-tenancy doesn't seem to map well to the various models that can be used to deploy tenant infrastructure. Instead, these variations in SaaS models seem to demand that we evolve our definition of what it means to be multi-tenant.

For the scope of this book, at least, the term "multi-tenant" will definitely be extended to accommodate the realities outlined here. As we move forward, multi-tenant will refer to any environment that onboards, deploys, manages, and operates tenants through a single, unified experience. The sharedness of any infrastructure will have no correlation to the term "multi-tenancy."

In the ensuing chapters, we'll introduce new terminology that will help us overcome some of the ambiguity that is attached to multi-tenancy.

Avoiding the "Single-Tenant" Term

Generally, whenever architects and builders refer to something as multi-tenant, there's a natural tendency to assume there must be some corresponding notion of what it means to be single-tenant. The idea of single tenancy seems to get mapped to those environments where no infrastructure is shared by tenants.

While I follow the logic of this mindset, the term doesn't really seem to fit anywhere in the model of SaaS outlined here. If you look back to Figure 1-6, where our solution had no shared infrastructure, I noted that we would still label this a multi-tenant environment since all tenants were still running the same version and being managed or operated collectively. Labeling this a single-tenant environment would undermine the idea that we aren't somehow realizing the benefits of the SaaS model.

With this in mind, the term "single-tenant" will not be used at any point beyond this chapter. Every design and architecture we discuss will be deemed a multi-tenant architecture, and we'll attach new terms to describe the various deployment models that will still allow us to convey if and how infrastructure is being shared within a given SaaS environment. The general goal here is to disconnect the concept of multi-tenancy from the sharing of infrastructure and use it as a broader term to characterize any environment that is built, deployed, managed, and operated in a SaaS model.

This is less about what SaaS is or is not and more about establishing a vocabulary that aligns better with the concepts we'll be exploring throughout this book.

Where Are the Boundaries of SaaS?

We've laid a foundation for what it means to be SaaS, but there are lots of nuances that we haven't really talked about. For example, suppose your SaaS application requires portions of the system to be deployed in some external location, or imagine scenarios where your application has dependencies on other vendors' solutions. Maybe you are using a third-party billing system, or your data must reside in another environment. There are any number of different reasons why you may need to have parts of your overall SaaS environment hosted somewhere that may not be entirely under your control.

So, how would this more distributed footprint fit with the idea of having a single, unified experience for all of your tenants? After all, having full control over all the moving parts of your system certainly maximizes your ability to innovate and move quickly. At the same time, it's impractical to think that some SaaS providers won't face domain and technology realities that require them to support externally hosted components, tools, or technologies.

This is where we don't want to be too extreme with our definition of SaaS. To me, the boundary is more around how these external dependencies are configured, managed, and operated. If their presence is entirely hidden from your tenants and they are still managed and operated through your centralized experience, this is still SaaS to me. It may introduce new complexities, but it doesn't change the spirit of the SaaS model we're trying to build.

Where this gets more interesting is when SaaS providers rely on external resources that are in direct view of their tenants. If, for example, my SaaS solution stores data in some tenant-hosted database, that's where things get more dicey. Now, you may have a dependency on infrastructure that is not entirely under your control. Updating this database, changing its schema, managing its health—these get more complicated in this model. This is where we start to ask questions about whether this external resource is breaking the third wall of SaaS, exposing tenants to infrastructure and creating expectations or dependencies that undermine the agility, operations, and innovation of your SaaS environment.

My general rule of thumb here (with some exceptions) is that we're providing a service experience. In a service model, our tenants' view is limited to the surface of our service. The tools, technologies, and resources that are used to bring that service to life should be entirely hidden from our tenants. In many respects, this is the hard barrier that prevents our system from falling back into patterns that might lead to one-off dependencies and variations.

The Managed Service Provider Model

There's one last wrinkle that we need to address as we try to refine our view of what it means to be a multi-tenant SaaS environment. Some organizations have opted into what's referred to as a Managed Service Provider (MSP) model. In some cases, they'll categorize MSP as a variant of SaaS. This has created some confusion in the SaaS domain. To better understand the challenges here, let's start by looking at an MSP environment and see how and where it fits in this discussion. Figure 1-7 provides a conceptual view of an MSP environment.

This model resembles the classic installed software model that we outlined earlier. At the bottom of this diagram, you'll see a collection of customers that are running various versions of a software vendor's product. Each one of these customers will be running in its own infrastructure or environment.

With MSP, though, we'll try to get efficiencies and economies of scale out of moving the operations to a centralized team or entity. This is the service that these MSPs provide. They often own responsibility for installing, managing, and supporting each of these customers, attempting to extract some scale and efficiency out of tooling and mechanisms that they use to operate these customer environments.

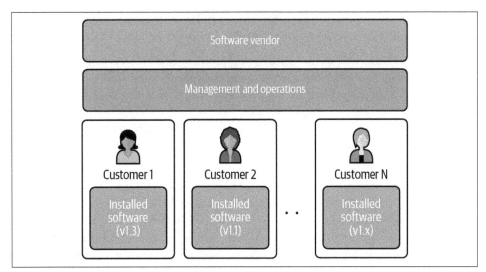

Figure 1-7. A Managed Service Provider (MSP) model

I've also represented the software vendor at the top of the diagram. This is here to convey the idea that the software provider may have third-party relationships with one or more MSPs that are managing their customer environments.

You can see how some might equate the MSP model to SaaS. After all, it does seem to be trying to provide a unified managed and operations experience for all customers. However, if you look back at the principles that we used to describe SaaS, you can see where there are substantial gaps between the MSP model and SaaS. One of the biggest differences is that customers are being allowed to run separate versions. So, while there may be some attempts to centralize management and operations, the MSP is going to have to have one-off variations in their operational experience to support the different footprints of each customer environment. This may require dedicated teams; at a minimum, it will mean having teams that can deal with the complexities of supporting the unique needs of each customer. Again, the MSP model adds lots of value and certainly creates efficiencies, but it's definitely different than having a single pane of glass that gets its efficiencies from having customers run a single version of a product and, in many cases, realizing economies of scale from sharing some or all of their infrastructure. At some level in the MSP model, you're likely to still inherit aspects of the pain that comes with one-off customer variations. MSPs can introduce some measures to offset some of the challenges, but they'll still face the operational and agility complexities that come with supporting unique, one-off needs of separate customer environments.

The other difference relates more to how SaaS teams are structured and operated. Generally, in a SaaS organization, we're attempting to avoid drawing hard lines between operations teams and the rest of the organization. We want operations, architects, product owners, and the various roles of our team working closely together to continually evaluate and refine the service experience of their offering.

This typically means that these teams are tightly connected. They're equally invested in understanding how their tenants are consuming their systems, how they're imposing load, how they're onboarding, and a host of other key insights. SaaS businesses want and need to have their fingers on the pulse of their systems. This is core to driving the success of the business and being connected more directly to the overall tenant experience. So, while this is a less concrete boundary, it still represents an important difference between SaaS and MSP.

Now, it's important to note that MSP is an entirely valid model. It often represents a good fit for some software providers. MSP can even be a stepping stone for some SaaS providers, providing access to some efficiencies while the team continues to push forward toward its SaaS delivery model. The key is that we have a clear understanding of the boundaries between SaaS and MSP and avoid viewing SaaS and MSP as somehow being synonymous.

At Its Core, SaaS Is a Business Model

By now you should have a better sense of how we characterize what it means to be SaaS. It should be clear that SaaS is very much about creating a technology, business, and operational culture that is focused squarely on driving a distinct set of business outcomes. So, while it's tempting to think about SaaS through the lens of technology patterns and strategies, you should really be viewing SaaS more as a business model.

To better understand this mindset, think about how adopting SaaS impacts the business of a SaaS provider. It directly influences and shapes how teams build, manage, operate, market, support, and sell their offerings. The principles of SaaS are ultimately woven into the culture of SaaS companies, blurring the line between the business and technology domains. With SaaS, the business strategy is focused on creating a service that can enable the business to react to current and emerging market needs without losing momentum or compromising growth.

Yes, features and functions are still important to SaaS companies. However, in a SaaS company, the features and functions are rarely introduced at the expense of agility and operational efficiency. When you're offering a multi-tenant SaaS solution, the needs of the many should always outweigh the needs of the few. Gone are the days of chasing one-off opportunities that require dedicated, one-off support at the expense of long-term success of the service.

This shift in mindset influences almost every role in a SaaS company. The role of a product owner, for example, changes significantly. Product owners must expand their view and consider operational attributes as part of constructing their backlog.

Onboarding experience, time to value, agility—these are all examples of items that must be on the radar of the product owner. They must prioritize and value these operational attributes that are essential to creating a successful SaaS business. Architects, engineers, and QA members are equally influenced by this shift. They must now think more about how the solution they're designing, building, and testing will achieve the more dynamic needs of their service experience. How your SaaS offering is marketed, priced, sold, and supported also changes. This theme of new and overlapping responsibilities is common to most SaaS organizations.

So, the question is: what are the core principles that shape and guide the business model of SaaS companies? While there might be some debate about the answer to the question, there are some key themes that seem to drive SaaS business strategies. The following outlines these key SaaS business objectives:

Agility
This term is often overloaded in the software domain. At the same time, in the SaaS universe, it is often viewed as one of the core pillars and motivating factors of a SaaS business. So many organizations that are moving to SaaS are doing so because they've become operationally crippled by their current model. Adopting SaaS is about moving to a culture and mindset that puts emphasis on speed and efficiency. Releasing new versions, reacting to market dynamics, targeting new customer segments, changing pricing models—these are amongst a long list of benefits that companies expect to extract from adopting a SaaS model. How your service is designed, how it's operated, and how it's sold are all shaped by a desire to maximize agility. A multi-tenant offering that reduced costs without realizing agility would certainly miss the broader value proposition of SaaS.

Operational efficiency
SaaS, in many respects, is about scale. In a multi-tenant environment, we're highly focused on continually growing our base of customers without requiring any specialized resources or teams to support the addition of these new customers. With SaaS, you're essentially building an operational and technological footprint that can support continual and, ideally, rapid growth. Supporting this growth means investing in building an efficient operational footprint for your entire organization. I'll often ask SaaS companies what would happen if 1,000 new customers signed up for their service tomorrow. Some would welcome this, and others cringe. This question often surfaces key questions about the operational efficiency of a SaaS company. It's important to note that operational efficiency is also about reacting and responding to customer needs. How quickly new features are released, how fast customers onboard, how quickly issues are addressed—these are all part of the operational efficiency story. Every part of the organization may play a part in building out an operationally efficient offering.

Innovation

The ability to move faster has lots of benefits for SaaS organizations. It frees them up and lets them be more open to experimenting and shifting their strategy. The investments in agility and operational efficiency allow organizations to be much more fluid and flexible. This allows them to embrace new opportunities, new market segments, new packaging/pricing strategies, and a host of other possibilities. The overall goal is to use the underlying strengths of your operational and cost model as the fuel of your innovation engine. It's this innovation that can play a big role in the broader success of your SaaS business.

Frictionless onboarding

SaaS businesses must give careful consideration to how customers get introduced into their environments. If you are trying to remain as agile and operationally efficient as possible, you must also think about how customer onboarding can be streamlined. For some SaaS businesses, this will be achieved through a classic sign-up page where customers can complete the onboarding process in an entirely self-service manner. In other environments, organizations may rely on an internal process to drive onboarding. The key is that every SaaS business must be focused on creating an onboarding experience that removes friction and enables agility and operational efficiency. For some, this will be straightforward. For others, it may take more effort to rethink how the team builds, operates, and automates its onboarding experience.

Growth

Every organization is about growth. However, SaaS organizations typically have a different notion of growth. They are investing in a model and an organizational footprint that is built to thrive on growth. Imagine building a highly efficient car factory that optimized and automated every step in the construction process. Then, imagine only asking it to produce two cars a day. Sort of pointless. With SaaS, we're building out a business footprint that streamlines the entire process of acquiring, onboarding, supporting, and managing customers. A SaaS company makes this investment with the expectation that it will help support and fuel the growth machine that ultimately influences the margins and broader success of the business. So, when we talk about growth here, we're talking about achieving a level of acceleration that couldn't be achieved without the agility, operational efficiency, and innovation that's part of SaaS. How much growth you achieve is relative. For some, growth may be adding 100 new customers, and for others it could mean adding 50,000. While the nature of your scale may vary, the goal of being growth-focused is equally essential to all SaaS businesses.

The items outlined here represent some of the core SaaS business principles. These are concepts that should be driven from the top down in a SaaS company where the leadership places clear emphasis on driving a business strategy that is focused on creating growth through investment in agility, operational efficiency, and growth goals.

Almost every dimension of your SaaS architecture and strategy is going to be derived from your business vision. The target tenant personas, the packaging, the pricing, the cost model, and a host of other factors are going to shape the architecture, operations, and management footprint of the solution you ultimately build. If you don't have clarity and alignment with the business around these points, you're unlikely to be in a position to build a SaaS offering that fully realizes your business goals.

Building a Service—Not a Product

Many software providers would view themselves as being in the business of creating products. And, in many respects, this aligns well with their business model. The mindset here is focused on a pattern where we build something, the customer acquires it, and it's, for the most part, theirs to use. There are plenty of permutations and nuances within this product-centric model, but they all gravitate toward a model that is focused on creating something more static and having customers buy it.

In this product-focused mindset, the emphasis is generally on defining the features and functions that will allow a software provider to close gaps and land new opportunities. Now, with SaaS, we shift from creating a product to creating a service. So, is this just terminology, or does it have a meaningful impact on how we approach building a SaaS offering? It turns out this is certainly more than a terminology shift.

When you offer software as a service, you think differently about what success looks like. Yes, your solution needs to meet the functional needs of your customers. That dimension of the problem doesn't go away. As a service, though, you are much more focused on the broader customer experience across all dimensions of your business.

Let's look at an example that better highlights the differences between a service and a product. A restaurant provides a good backdrop for exploring these differences. When you go out to dinner, you're certainly looking forward to the food (the product). However, the service is also a part of your experience. How fast you're greeted at the door, how soon the waiter comes to your table, how soon you get water, and how quickly your food arrives are all measures of your service experience. No matter how good the food is, your quality of service will have a lot to do with your overall impression of the restaurant.

Now, think about this through the lens of a SaaS offering. Your SaaS tenants will have similar service expectations. How easily they can onboard your solution, how long it takes to realize value, how quickly new features are released, how easily they can provide feedback, how frequently the system is down—these are all dimensions of a service that must be front and center for SaaS teams. Having a great product won't matter if the overall experience for customers does not meet their expectations.

This takes on extra meaning when software is delivered in a SaaS model, where the tenant's only view of your system is the surface of your SaaS solution. SaaS tenants have no visibility into the underlying elements of your system. They don't think about patches, updates, and infrastructure configuration. They only care that the service is providing an experience that lets them maximize the value of your solution.

In this service model, we also often see SaaS companies leveraging their operational agility to drive greater customer loyalty. These SaaS providers will get into a mode where they release new capabilities, respond to feedback, and morph their systems at a rapid pace. Seeing this constant and rapid innovation gives customers confidence that they will be benefactors of this constant evolution. In fact, this is often the tool that allows emerging SaaS companies to take business away from traditional non-SaaS market leaders. While some massive, established market leaders may have a much deeper feature set, their inability to rapidly react to market and customer needs can steer customers to nimbler SaaS-based offerings.

So, while this product versus service comparison may seem a bit pedantic, I view it as an essential part of the SaaS mental model. It connects directly to this idea that SaaS is very much a mindset that shapes how entire SaaS organizations approach their jobs and their customers. In fact, many SaaS organizations will adopt a series of metrics that measure their ability to meet their service-centric goals. It may be tempting to view this as something that can be bolted onto your service at some future date. However, many successful SaaS organizations rely on these metrics as a key pillar of their SaaS business.

The B2B and B2C SaaS Story

As teams talk about SaaS, they'll often map strategies and patterns to the business-to-consumer (B2C) and business-to-business (B2B) models. As I discussed in the preface, it's important to understand that there are clear differences in how you might approach architecting for these two models. The scale of B2C, for example, will often require highly specialized strategies that can accommodate the workload profile and cost models of these environments. At the same time, at the conceptual level, lots of topics and mechanisms discussed here could apply to B2C and BCB environments. I won't try to highlight every instance where these models might require different approaches. There are too many variables here to make absolute statements about what fits for B2C and what fits for B2B. So, for the scope of this book, let's acknowledge that being B2C or B2B can certainly influence the overall architectural model of your solution.

Defining SaaS

I've devoted the bulk of this chapter to bringing more clarity to the boundaries, scope, and nature of what it means to be SaaS. It only seems fair to take all the information we discussed here and attempt to provide an explicit definition of SaaS that, ideally, incorporates the concepts and principles that we have covered. This is the definition I think best summarizes the view of SaaS I'll be using across the rest of this book:

> SaaS is a business and software delivery model that enables organizations to offer their solutions in a low-friction, service-centric model that maximizes value for customers and providers. It relies on agility and operational efficiency as pillars of a business strategy that promotes growth, reach, and innovation.

You'll see that this definition sticks to the theme of SaaS being a business model. There's no mention of any technologies or architecture considerations. It's your job as a SaaS architect and builder to create the underlying patterns and strategies that enable the business to realize its objectives. While that may seem like the job of any architect, it should be clear that the unique blend of business and technology demands for SaaS environments will be infused directly into the design, architecture, and implementation of your SaaS solution.

Conclusion

This chapter was all about establishing the foundational elements of the SaaS mindset, providing you with a core set of concepts and terms that will be critical as we dig deeper into SaaS architecture patterns and strategies. A key part of our discussion was focused on understanding the fundamental goals of SaaS, highlighting the key elements that have motivated so many organizations to adopt a SaaS delivery model. This required us to look more closely at classic software delivery models, highlighting some of the traditional challenges associated with these models. Then, I shifted to exploring how SaaS is used to overcome these challenges, delivering efficiencies, economies of scale, and agility that can enable greater levels of growth and innovation. A key point is that SaaS architects and builders can't just be focused on creating a solid SaaS application—they must also be thinking about how their solution will solve the organization's broader operational, agility, and efficiency goals.

A big part of this chapter was also focused on aligning on some core concepts. I introduced the idea of tenants, highlighting some of the key nuances with building environments where infrastructure can be consumed in a shared model. Our discussion on shared infrastructure also highlighted some of the key differences between SaaS and traditional installed, per-customer models. At the core of this theme was the idea of creating a unified experience that would enable you to collectively manage, deploy, and operate your SaaS tenants.

It was also essential to create clearer boundaries around what's SaaS and what's not (at least for the scope of this book). It's here that I started looking at multi-tenancy and the historical baggage that's attached to this term. The goal was to create a new SaaS-aware view of multi-tenancy that moved away from the narrow, infrastructure-centric idea of multi-tenancy. I reviewed a series of SaaS deployment strategies to highlight the need for a broader definition of multi-tenancy that wasn't connected to whether we were sharing infrastructure. Having clarity around when and how the multi-tenant term is used is fundamental to how we talk about SaaS and how we describe SaaS architectures.

Finally, toward the back of the chapter, I started trying to further refine the boundaries of SaaS. I looked at the MSP model, for example, and reviewed some of the key factors that separate the MSP and SaaS models. I also looked at some of the core principles that I thought should be applied when shaping the vision for building a SaaS organization and offering. This included reviewing some of the key differences that are associated with building a service (instead of a product).

The hope is that this chapter equipped you with a better sense of how we'll be viewing SaaS throughout this book. Alignment on these principles will allow us to move through additional, more concrete concepts with a common view of what forces are shaping and guiding our architectural choices. Ideally, it also removes some of the confusion that, historically, has surrounded this topic.

Now that we have these SaaS mindset basics in place, we can start thinking about how these principles are mapped to more specific architectural patterns and constructs. In the next chapter, I'll make an end-to-end pass through all of the key SaaS architecture mechanisms and strategies without bringing in the specifics of any one solution or technology stack. This will expose a full range of the considerations that should be part of defining any SaaS architecture. Defining tenant context, discussing what common services and capabilities we need, explaining data partitioning—these are all on a much longer list of more detailed insights that we'll be covering. The goal of this chapter is to review many of the higher-level SaaS architecture constructs, explaining their role, their nuances, and where they fit into the overall SaaS architecture landscape.

Multi-Tenant Architecture Fundamentals

As you progress through this book, you'll realize that SaaS architecture comes in many shapes and sizes. There are countless permutations of multi-tenant architecture patterns and strategies that are composed to create the SaaS architecture that best aligns with the domain, compliance, and business realities of a SaaS company.

There are, however, some core themes that span all SaaS architectures. The goal of this chapter is to explore a set of architecture constructs and concepts as the most fundamental starting point for building a multi-tenant SaaS architecture. The idea is to outline the details of the core building blocks to set the table for a much deeper review of how these concepts are brought to life with specific technologies. I've intentionally tried to keep this coverage very focused on just those architectural constructs that need to be top of mind as each builder begins to define the moving parts of their SaaS environment.

We'll start this review by looking at the notion of tenancy and how tenant context is introduced into your architecture. The goal is to highlight the role tenancy plays across your entire architecture, outlining how and where it touches the different layers of a multi-tenant architecture. From there, we can then shift into looking at how we group and organize the different elements of your multi-tenant architecture. The focus will be on identifying the common moving parts of any SaaS architecture, outlining the fundamental services you'll need to support the core, horizontal services that are needed to onboard, authenticate, operate, and manage your tenants and your overall environment.

As part of this review, I'll also explore some of the core multi-tenant constructs that will show up within the implementation of your application. While each application has its own nuances, there are still a set of cross-cutting strategies that are used to implement the multi-tenant security, storage, deployment, and routing models of your SaaS implementation. The topics we'll cover will give you a better sense of how multi-tenancy influences how you design and build the moving parts of your application. To top things off, I'll explore a few of the outliers that need to be included as part of the foundation of your SaaS model. These include creating a tiered experience, provisioning and configuration of tenant resources, and building a system admin view into your environment.

Getting a firm grasp on these core SaaS architecture constructs is key to developing a solid understanding of the elements that are typically part of a multi-tenant architecture. My goal will be to give a better sense of the building blocks that should be on your radar as you begin defining the footprint of your SaaS architecture. You already likely have strong notions of what it means to scale, secure, design, and operate a robust architecture. With SaaS, our goal is to figure out how and where multi-tenancy influences and overlays these key concepts, altering how we might approach building out a multi-tenant environment.

Adding Tenancy to Your Architecture

Let's start our exploration of SaaS architecture concepts by looking at a traditional non-SaaS application. In classic applications, the environment is constructed from the ground up with the assumption that it will be installed and run by individual customers. Each customer essentially has its own dedicated footprint. Figure 2-1 provides a conceptual view of how one of these applications might be designed and built.

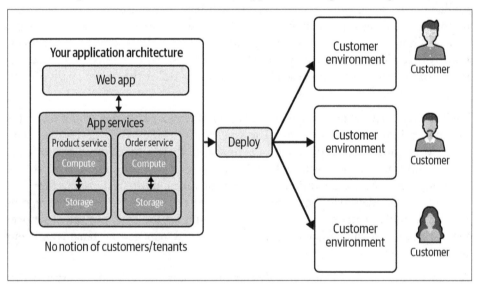

Figure 2-1. Traditional non-SaaS environments

On the left, we have a simplified view of an application. Here, this application is built and then sold to individual customers. These customers might install the software in their own environment or it might run in the cloud. This approach simplifies the entire architectural model of this environment. The choices about how customers enter the environment, how they access our resources, and how they consume the services of our environment are much simpler when we know that they will be running in an environment that is dedicated to each customer. The general mindset here is that you have a piece of software and you're just stamping out copies of it for each new customer.

Now, let's think about what it means to deliver this same application in a multi-tenant SaaS environment. Figure 2-2 provides a conceptual view of what this might look like. You see that our customers, which are now tenants, are all consuming the same application.

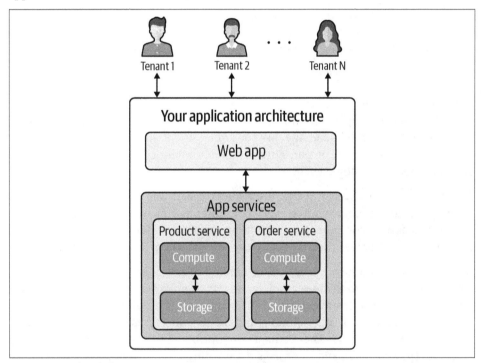

Figure 2-2. The shift to a tenant-centric experience

This shift may seem fairly simple in the diagram. However, it has a profound impact on how we design, build, secure, and manage this environment. We've essentially made the transition from a per customer dedicated model to a multi-tenant architecture. Supporting this model reaches into every dimension of the underlying implementation of your system. It affects how you implement authentication, routing, scaling, performance, storage, and, in targeted areas, how you code the application logic of your system.

You'll also notice a key shift in terminology in this figure. At the top of this diagram, you'll see that I no longer refer to the consumers of my system as customers. Instead, they are now—and will be for the entire scope of this book—referred to as tenants. Why the shift? To better understand this core concept, let's take a runtime peek inside one of our application services to see how tenants land in our environment at runtime. If I were to take separate snapshots of the product microservice at three different time intervals, I might see something resembling the image in Figure 2-3.

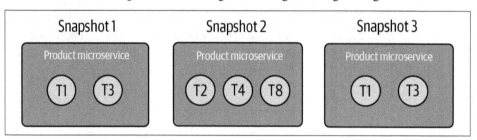

Figure 2-3. Runtime snapshot of tenancy

In snapshot 1, our product microservice has two tenants consuming our service (T1 and T3). The next snapshot has three entirely different tenants. The point is that the resource no longer belongs to any one consumer; it is a shared infrastructure that is consumed by any tenant of our system. And, in many cases, it can be consumed simultaneously by multiple tenants.

This shift to using shared infrastructure required a new way to describe how a system is being consumed. Before, when every consumer had its own dedicated infrastructure, it was easy to continue to use the term "customer." However, in a multi-tenant setting, you'll see that we describe the consumers of our environment as "tenants."

It's essential that you have a solid understanding of this concept. The notion of tenancy maps very well to the idea of an apartment complex, where you own a building and rent it out to different tenants. In this mindset, the building correlates to the shared infrastructure of your solution, and the tenants represent the different occupants of your apartments. These tenants of your building consume shared building resources (power, water, and so on). As the building owner, you manage and operate the overall building, and different tenants will come and go. The level of occupancy can vary from moment to moment.

You can see how this term better fits the SaaS model, where we are building a service that runs on shared infrastructure that can accommodate any number of tenants. Yes, tenants are still customers, but the term "tenant" lets us better characterize how they land in a SaaS environment.

As we move forward, we'll get a better sense of how and where tenancy ends up influencing the implementation of our SaaS architecture. For now, though, just know that each consumer of our environment will be referred to as a tenant. We'll use this tenant information across multiple layers of our SaaS architecture discussions. It represents one of the most fundamental elements of any SaaS architecture.

The Two Halves of Every SaaS Architecture

If we step back from the details of SaaS, we typically find that every SaaS environment—independent of its domain or design—can be broken down into two very distinct halves. In fact, across our entire discussion of SaaS across this book, we'll use these two halves as the lens through which we'll look at how a multi-tenant system is built, deployed, and operated.

Figure 2-4 provides a conceptual representation of the two halves of SaaS. On the righthand side of the diagram, you'll see what is labeled as the control plane. The control plane is where we'll place all of the cross-cutting constructs, services, and capabilities that support the foundational needs of a multi-tenant SaaS environment.

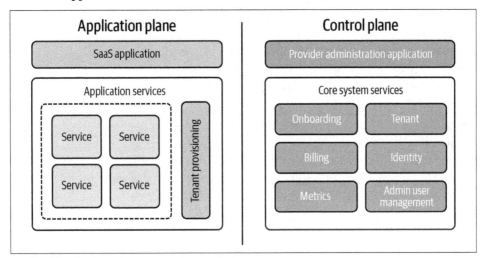

Figure 2-4. SaaS application and control planes

We often describe the control plane as the single pane of glass that is used to orchestrate and operate all the moving parts of your SaaS solution. It is at the core of enabling many of the principles that are essential to the success of your SaaS business. Concepts like tenant onboarding, billing, metrics, and a host of other services live in this control plane. You'll also see that our control plane includes an administration application. This represents the console or administration experience that is used by a SaaS provider to configure, manage, and operate their SaaS environment. This control plane correlates to the concept we saw in Chapter 1 where we had a series of components that surrounded our application.

One interesting caveat here is that the services running in the control plane are not built or designed as multi-tenant services. If you think about it, there's actually nothing multi-tenant about the capabilities of the control plane. It doesn't have functionality that supports the needs of individual tenants. Instead, it provides the services and functionality that spans all tenants.

While architects and builders are often tempted to start the SaaS discussion with the multi-tenant aspects of their application, the foundations of your SaaS architecture often start with the control plane. In many respects, the control plane serves as a forcing function, requiring engineers to inject and support the nuances of tenancy from the outset of their development.

In contrast, the application plane is where the features and functionality of your SaaS service are brought to life. This is where we see the manifestation of all the multi-tenant principles that are classically associated with SaaS environments. It's here that we focus more of our attention on how multi-tenancy will shape the design, functionality, security, and performance of our service and its underlying resources. Our time and energy in the application plane is focused squarely on identifying and choosing the technologies, application services, and architecture patterns that best align with the parameters of your environment, timelines, and business. This is where you pour your energy into building out an application footprint that embraces agility and enables the business to support a range of personas and consumption models.

It's important to note that there is no single design, architecture, or blueprint for the application plane. I tend to view the application plane as a blank canvas that gets painted based on the unique composition of services and capabilities that my SaaS service requires. Yes, there are themes and patterns we'll see that span SaaS application architectures. Still, there will always be business, domain, and legacy considerations that impose specific requirements on the footprint of your SaaS application.

This view of the two halves of SaaS aligns with the mental model of multi-tenancy that we discussed in Chapter 1. Our application plane could share all tenant infrastructure, or it could have completely dedicated infrastructure, and it wouldn't matter. As long as we have a control plane that manages and operates these tenant environments through a unified experience, then we're considering this a multi-tenant environment.

This separation of concerns also influences our mental model for how the elements of our SaaS environment are updated and evolved. The services and capabilities of the control plane typically have their own processes for versioning, updates, and deployment. They can be used across the entire lifecycle of your system, supporting a mix of operational and functional needs. Meanwhile, our application plane is being driven more by the needs and experience of the system's tenants. Here, updates and deployments are introduced to provide new features, enhance tenant performance, support new tiering strategies, and so on.

Together, these two halves of SaaS represent the most fundamental building blocks of any SaaS environment. Understanding the roles of these planes will have a significant influence on how you'll approach the architecture, design, and decomposition of your SaaS offering.

Inside the Control Plane

Now that we have a better sense of the roles of the control and application planes, let's take a high-level pass at exploring the core concepts that commonly live within the scope of the control plane. We'll dig into each of these topics in much greater detail later in this book, exploring real-world implementation and architecture strategies. At this stage, though, we need to start a level up and develop an understanding of the different components that are part of any control plane you might build. Having a higher-level grasp of these components, the roles they play, and how they are related will allow us to explore these building blocks of multi-tenancy without getting distracted by the different nuances that show up when we pivot to the specific influences of technologies, languages, and domain considerations. Having this foundational view will allow you to see the landscape of options and begin to see the different components that span all SaaS architecture models.

The following is a breakdown of the different services and capabilities that are likely to show up in the control plane of your SaaS architecture, including onboarding, identity, metrics, billing, and tenant management.

Onboarding

The control plane is responsible for managing and orchestrating all the steps needed to get a new tenant introduced into your SaaS environment. On the surface, this may seem like a simple concept. However, as you'll see in Chapter 4, there are lots of moving parts to the onboarding experience. The choices you make here, in many respects, are at the core of enabling many of the multi-tenant business and design elements of your SaaS environment.

At this stage, let's stick with a high-level view of the key elements of the onboarding experience. In Figure 2-5 you'll see a conceptualized representation of the components that play a role in the onboarding experience. I show a tenant signing up for our SaaS service and triggering the onboarding process via the control plane. After this initial request, the control plane owns the rest of the onboarding flow, creating and configuring our tenant and its corresponding identity footprint. This includes assigning a unique identifier to our tenant that will be leveraged across most of the moving parts of our multi-tenant architecture.

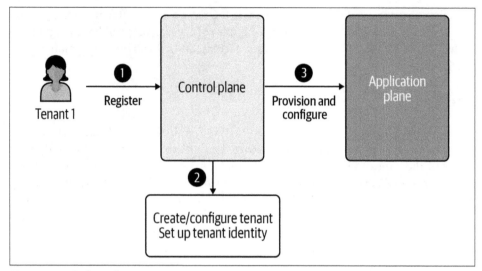

Figure 2-5. Onboarding tenants

You'll also notice that we show the control plane interacting with the application plane, provisioning and configuring any application-specific resources that may be needed for each tenant. When we get into more detailed views of sample onboarding principles, we'll see how this part of the onboarding experience can get quite involved.

While there are common themes in the onboarding experience, the actual implementation of onboarding can vary significantly based on the domain you're in, the business goals of your solution, and the footprint of your application architecture. The key, though, is that onboarding represents a foundational concept that sits at the front door of your SaaS experience. Business teams can and should take great interest in shaping and influencing how you approach building out this aspect of your system.

The higher-level takeaway is that onboarding is at the center of creating and connecting the most basic elements of a multi-tenant environment: tenants, users, identity, and tenant application resources. Onboarding weaves these concepts together and establishes the foundation for introducing tenancy to all the moving parts of your SaaS environment.

Identity

At first glance, you might wonder why identity belongs in the SaaS story. It's true that there are any number of different identity solutions that you can use to construct your SaaS solution. You could even suggest that your identity provider belongs somehow outside the scope of our control plane discussion. However, it turns out that multi-tenancy and the control plane often have a pretty tight binding to your SaaS

---

architecture. Figure 2-6 provides a simplified view of how identity is applied in multi-tenant environments.

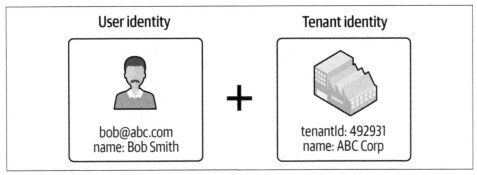

Figure 2-6. *Binding users to a tenant identity*

On the left, you'll see the classic notion of user identity that is typically associated with authentication and authorization. It's true that our SaaS user will authenticate against our SaaS system. However, in a multi-tenant environment, being able to authenticate a user is not enough. A SaaS system must know who you are as a user *and* it must also be able to bind that user to a tenant. In fact, every user that is logged into our system must be attached in some way to a tenant. I often refer to this user/tenant binding as your SaaS identity.

 This notion of mapping users to tenants fits more naturally in environments where an individual is binding to a service as part of an entity. In a B2B setting, my business *is* the tenant and I am one of possibly many users at that business. In a B2C model, the user itself could be the tenant. There is no need for a separate mapping to a tenant.

This user/tenant binding ends up adding a wrinkle to our system's overall identity experience, requiring architects and builders to develop strategies for binding these two concepts in a way that still conforms to the requirements of your overall authentication model. This gets even more complicated when we start thinking about how we might support federated identity models in multi-tenant environments. We'll see that, the more the identity experience moves outside of our control, the more complex and challenging it becomes to support this binding between users and tenants. In some cases, you may find yourself introducing constructs to stitch these two concepts together.

When we dig into onboarding and identity in Chapter 4, you'll get a better sense of the key role identity plays in the broader multi-tenant story. Getting identity right is essential to building out a crisp and efficient strategy for introducing tenants into your SaaS architecture. The policies and patterns you apply here will have a cascading impact across many of the moving parts of your design and implementation.

Metrics

When your application is running in a multi-tenant model, it becomes more difficult to create a clear picture of how your tenants are using your system. If you're sharing infrastructure, for example, it's very hard to know which tenants are currently consuming that infrastructure and how the activity of individual tenants might be impacting the scale, performance, and availability of your solution. The population of tenants that are using your system may also be constantly changing. New tenants may be added. Existing tenants might be leaving. This can make operating and supporting multi-tenant environments particularly challenging.

These factors make it especially important for SaaS companies to invest in building out a rich metrics and analytics experience as part of their control plane. The goal is to create a centralized hub for capturing and aggregating tenant activity that allows teams to monitor and analyze the usage and consumption profile of individual tenants.

The role of metrics is very wide. The data collected will be used in an operational context, allowing teams to measure and troubleshoot the health of the system. Product owners might use this data to assess the consumption of specific features. Customer success teams might use this data to measure a new customer's time to value. The idea is that successful SaaS teams will use this data to drive the business, operational, and technology success of their SaaS offering.

You can imagine how metrics will impact the architecture and implementation of many of the moving parts of your multi-tenant system. Microservice developers will need to think about how and where they'll add metrics instrumentation. Infrastructure teams will need to decide how and where they'll surface infrastructure activity. The business will need to weigh in and help capture the metrics that can measure the customer experience. These are just a few examples from a long list of areas where metrics might influence your implementation.

The tenant must be at the center of this metrics strategy. Having data on consumption and activity has significantly less value if it cannot be filtered, analyzed, and viewed through the lens of individual tenants.

Billing

Most SaaS systems have some dependency on a billing system. This could be a home-grown billing system, or it could be any one of the commercial SaaS billing systems that are available from different billing providers. Regardless of the approach, billing is a core concept that has a natural home within the control plane.

Billing has a couple of touch points within the control plane. It's typically connected to the onboarding experience, where each new tenant must be created as a "customer" within your billing system. This might include configuring the tenant's billing plan and setting up other attributes of the tenant's billing profile.

Many SaaS solutions have billing strategies that meter and measure tenant activity as part of generating a bill. This could be bandwidth consumption, number of requests, storage consumption, or any other activity-related events that are associated with a given tenant. In these models, the control plane and your billing system must provide a way for this activity data to be ingested, processed, and submitted to your billing system. This could be a direct integration with the billing system, or you could introduce your own services that process this data and send it to the billing system.

We'll get more into the details of billing integration in Chapter 14. The key here is to realize that billing will likely be part of your control plane services, and you'll likely be introducing dedicated services to orchestrate this integration.

Tenant Management

Every tenant in our SaaS system needs to be centrally managed and configured. In our control plane, this is represented by our tenant management service. Typically, this is a pretty basic service that provides all the operations needed to create and manage the state of tenants (for B2C environments, these would correlate to users). This includes tracking key attributes that associate tenants with a unique identifier, billing plans, security policies, identity configuration, and an active/inactive status.

In some cases, teams may overlook this service or combine it with other concepts (identity, for example). It's important for multi-tenant environments to have a centralized service that manages all of this tenant state. This provides a single point of tenant configuration that enables tenants to be easily managed through a centralized experience.

We'll explore the elements and permutations of implementing tenant management more in Chapter 5.

Inside the Application Plane

Now that we have a better sense of the core concepts with the control plane, let's start looking at the common areas where multi-tenancy shows up in the application plane. While the control plane typically has a consistent set of common services, the application plane is a bit more abstract. How and where multi-tenancy is applied within the application plane can vary significantly based on a wide range of factors. That being said, there are still a range of themes that will surface, albeit in different forms, within your application plane. So, even though there is variation here, every SaaS architect will need to consider how and where they will introduce these themes into the application plane of their solution.

As you dig into the application pane, you'll find that your technology stack and deployment footprint will have a significant influence on how these concepts are applied. In some cases, there may be ready-made solutions that fit your use case precisely. In other cases, you may find yourself inventing solutions to fill gaps in your technology stack. While building out something to fill these gaps may add complexity and overhead to the build of your solution, in most cases you'll want to take on this added work to ensure that your SaaS solution is not compromising on important elements of your multi-tenant architecture.

In subsequent chapters we'll look at real-world working examples that provide a more concrete view of how these constructs are realized within your application plane. For now, though, let's come up a level and establish a core set of application plane principles that should span every SaaS architecture.

Tenant Context

One of the most fundamental concepts in our application plane is the notion of tenant context. Tenant context does not map to any one specific strategy or mechanism. Instead, it's a broader concept that is meant to convey the idea that our application plane is always functioning in the context of specific tenants. This context is often represented as a token or some other construct that packages all the attributes of your tenant. A common example is a JSON Web Token (JWT), which combines your user and tenant information into one construct that is shared across all the moving parts of your multi-tenant architecture. This JWT becomes our passport for sharing tenant information (context) with any service or code that relies on this context. It's this token that is referred to as your tenant context.

Now, you'll see that this tenant context has a direct influence on how your application architecture processes tenant requests. This may affect routing, logging, metrics, data access, and a host of other constructs live within the application plane. Figure 2-7 provides a conceptual view of tenant context in action.

The flow in Figure 2-7 shows tenant context being applied across the different services and resources that are part of a multi-tenant environment. This starts on the left-hand side of the diagram where tenants authenticate against the identity that was created during onboarding and acquire their tenant context. This context is then injected into a service of the application. This same context flows into each downstream interaction of the system, enabling you to acquire and apply that context across a range of different use cases.

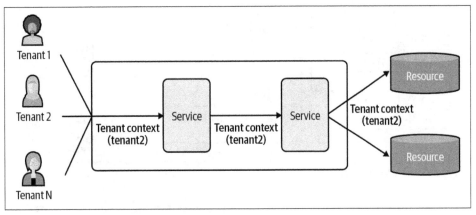

Figure 2-7. Applying tenant context

This represents one of the most fundamental differences of a SaaS environment. Our services don't just work with users—they must incorporate tenant context as part of the implementation of all the moving parts of our SaaS application. Every microservice you write will use this tenant context. It will become your job to figure out how to apply this context effectively without adding too much complexity to the implementation of your system. This, in fact, is a key theme that we'll address when we dig into SaaS microservices in Chapter 7.

As a SaaS architect, this means that you must be always thinking about how tenant context will be conveyed across your system. You'll also have to be thinking about the specific technology strategies that will be used to package and apply this tenant context in ways that limit complexity and promote agility. This is a continual balancing act for SaaS architects and builders.

Tenant Isolation

Multi-tenancy, by its very nature, focuses squarely on placing our customers and their resources into environments where resources may be shared or at least reside side by side in common infrastructure environments. This reality means that multi-tenant solutions are often required to apply and implement creative measures to ensure that tenant resources are protected against any potential cross-tenant access.

To better understand the fundamentals of this concept, let's look at a simple conceptual view of a solution running in our application plane (shown in Figure 2-8).

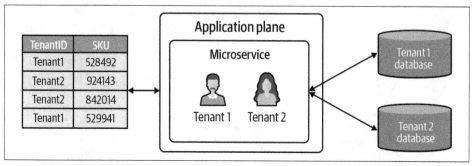

Figure 2-8. Implementing tenant isolation

You'll see we have the simplest of application planes running a single microservice. For this example, our microservice is managing two different sets of data. On the right there is an example where tenant data is stored in two separate databases. On the left, the same microservice has data that commingled in the same table. At the same time, our microservice is sharing its compute with all tenants. This means that our microservice can process requests from Tenants 1 and 2 simultaneously.

While the data for our tenants is stored in separate storage constructs, there is nothing in our solution that ensures that Tenant 1 can't access the data of Tenant 2. This holds true even with my separate databases. Nothing about putting the data in a separate database guarantees that tenants can't cross this boundary. Generally, deploying a resource in a dedicated model doesn't equate to achieving tenant isolation. It can make it easier to implement, though.

To prevent any access to another tenant's resources, our application plane must introduce a construct to prevent this cross-tenant access. The mechanisms to implement this will vary wildly based on a number of different considerations. However, the basic concept of tenant isolation spans all possible solutions. The idea is that every application plane must introduce targeted constructs that strictly enforce the isolation of individual tenant resources—even when they may be running in a shared construct.

We'll dig into this concept in great detail in Chapter 9. It goes without saying that tenant isolation represents one of the most fundamental building blocks of SaaS architecture. As you build out your application plane, you'll need to find the flavor and approach that allows you to enforce isolation at the various levels of your SaaS architecture.

Data Partitioning

The services and capabilities within our application plane often need to store data for tenants. Of course, how and where you choose to store that data can vary significantly based on the multi-tenant profile of your SaaS application. Any number of factors might influence your approach to storing data. The type of data, your compliance requirements, your usage patterns, the size of the data, the technology you're using—these are all pieces of the multi-tenant storage puzzle.

In the world of multi-tenant storage, we refer to the design of these different storage models as data partitioning. The key idea is that you are picking a storage strategy that partitions tenant data based on the multi-tenant profile of that data. This could mean the data is stored in some dedicated construct, or it could mean it lands in some shared construct. These partitioning strategies are influenced by a wide range of variables. The storage technology you're using (object, relational, NoSQL, etc.) obviously has a significant impact on the options you'll have for representing and storing tenant data. The business and use cases of your application can also influence the strategy you select. The list of variables and options here is extensive.

As a SaaS architect, it will be your job to look at the range of different data that's stored by your system and figure out which partitioning strategy best aligns with your needs. You'll also want to consider how these strategies might impact the agility of your solution. How data impacts the deployment of new features, the uptime of your solution, and the complexity of your operational footprint requires careful consideration when selecting a data partitioning strategy. It's also important to note that, when picking a strategy, this is often a fine-grained decision. How you partition data can vary across the different services within your application plane.

This is a much deeper topic that we'll cover more extensively in Chapter 8. By the end of that chapter, you'll have a much better sense of what it means to bring a range of different strategies to life using a variety of different storage technologies.

Tenant Routing

In this simplest of SaaS architecture models, you may find that all tenants are sharing their resources. However, in most cases, your architecture is going to have variations where some or all of your tenant's infrastructure may be dedicated. In fact, it would not be uncommon to have microservices that are deployed on a per tenant basis.

The main point is that SaaS application architectures are often required to support a distributed footprint that has any number of resources running in a combination of shared and dedicated models. Figure 2-9 provides a simplified sample of a SaaS architecture that supports a mix of shared and dedicated tenant resources.

In this example, we have three tenants that will be making requests to invoke operations on our application services. In this particular example, we have some resources that are shared and some that are dedicated. On the left, Tenant 1 has an entirely dedicated set of services. Meanwhile, on the righthand side, you'll see that we have the services that are being used by Tenants 2 and 3. Note that we have the product and rating services that are being shared by both of these tenants. However, these tenants each have dedicated instances of the order service.

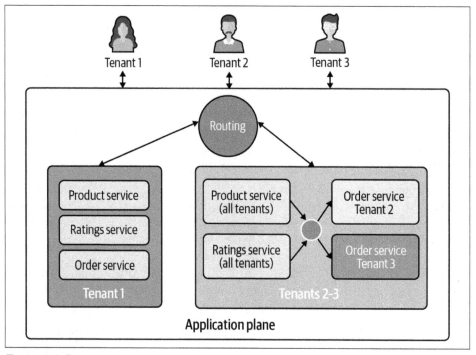

Figure 2-9. Routing on tenant context

Now, as you step back and look at the overall configuration of these services, you can see where our multi-tenant architecture would need to include strategies and constructs that would correctly route tenant requests to the appropriate services. This happens at two levels within this example. Starting at the top, you'll see where our application plane is receiving requests from three separate tenants. It's here that I've introduced a conceptual placeholder for a router. This router must accept requests from all tenants and use the injected tenant context (that we discussed earlier) to determine how and where to route each request. Also, within the Tenant 2/3 box on the right, you'll see that there is another placeholder for routing that will determine which instance of the order service will receive requests (based on tenant context).

Let's look at a couple concrete examples to sort this out. Suppose we get a request from Tenant 1 to look up a product. When the router receives this request, it will examine the tenant context and route the traffic to the product service on the left (for Tenant 1). Now, let's say we get a request from Tenant 2 to update a product that must also update an order. In this scenario, the top-level router would send the request to the shared product service on the right (based on the Tenant 2 context). Then, the product service would send a request to the order service via the service-to-service router. This router would look at the tenant context, resolve it to Tenant 2, and send a request to the order service that's dedicated to Tenant 2.

This example is meant to highlight the need for multi-tenant-aware routing constructs that can handle the various deployments we might have in a SaaS environment. Naturally, the technology and strategy that you apply here will vary based on a number of parameters. There's also a rich collection of routing tools and technologies, each of which might approach this differently. Often, this comes down to finding a tool that provides flexible and efficient ways to acquire and dynamically route traffic based on tenant context.

We'll see these routing constructs applied in specific solutions later in this book. At this stage, it's just important to understand that routing in multi-tenant environments often adds a new wrinkle to our infrastructure routing model.

Multi-Tenant Application Deployment

Deployment is a pretty well understood topic. Every application you build will require some DevOps technology and tooling that can deploy the initial version of your application and any subsequent updates. While these same concepts apply to the application plane of our multi-tenant environment, you'll also discover that different flavors of tenant application models will add new considerations to your application deployment model.

We've already noted that tenants may have a mix of dedicated and shared resources. Some may have fully dedicated resources, some may have fully shared, and others may have some mix of dedicated and shared. Knowing this, we have to now consider how this will influence the DevOps implementation of our application deployment.

Imagine deploying an application with two dedicated microservices and three shared microservices. In this model, our deployment automation code will have to have some visibility into the multi-tenant configuration of our SaaS application. It won't just deploy updated services like you would in a classic environment. It will need to consult the tenant deployment profile and determine which tenants might need a separate deployment of a microservice for each dedicated microservice. So, microservices within our application plane might be deployed multiple times. Our infrastructure automation code may also need to apply tenant context to the configuration and security profile of each of these microservices.

Technically, this is not directly part of the application plane. However, it has a tight connection to the design and strategies we apply within the application plane. In general, you'll find that the application plane and the provisioning of tenant environments will end up being very interconnected.

The Gray Area

While the control and application planes cover most of the fundamental multi-tenant architecture constructs, there are still some concepts that don't fit cleanly into either of these planes. At the same time, these areas still belong in the discussion of foundational SaaS topics. While there are arguments that could be made for landing these in specific planes, to steer clear of the debate, I'm going to handle these few items separately and address the factors that might push them into one plane or the other.

Tiering

Tiering is a strategy most architects have encountered as part of consuming various third-party offerings. The basic idea here is that SaaS companies use tiers to create different variations of an offering with separate price points. As an example, a SaaS provider could offer their customers basic, advanced, and premium tiers where each tier progressively adds additional value. Basic tier tenants might have constraints on performance, number of users, features, and so on. Premium tier tenants might have better service-level agreements (SLAs), a higher number of users, and access to additional features.

The mistake some SaaS architects and builders make is that they assume that these tiers are mostly pricing and packaging strategies. In reality, tiering can have a significant impact on many of the dimensions of your multi-tenant architecture. Tiering is enabled by building a more pliable SaaS architecture that offers the business more opportunities to create value boundaries that they may not have otherwise been able to offer.

Tiering naturally layers onto our discussion of tenant context, since the context that gets shared across our architecture often includes a reference to a given tenant's tier. This tier is applied across the architecture and can influence routing, security, and a host of other aspects of the underlying implementation of your system.

In some implementations of tiering, we'll see teams place this within their control plane as a first-class concept. It's true that onboarding often includes some need to map a tenant's profile to a given tier. Tiers are also often correlated to a billing plan, which would seem natural to maintain within the scope of the control plane. At the same time, tiers are also used heavily within the application plane. They can be used to configure routing strategies or they could also be referenced as part of the configuration of throttling policies. The real answer is that tiering has a home in both planes. However, I would probably lean toward placing it in the control plane since the tier can be managed and returned by interactions with the control plane (authentication, for example). The returned tier can be attached to the tenant context and applied through that mechanism within the application plane.

Tenant, Tenant Admin, and System Admin Users

The term "user" can easily get overloaded when we're talking about SaaS architecture. In a multi-tenant environment, we have multiple notions of what it means to be a user—each of which plays a distinct role. Figure 2-10 provides a conceptual view of the different flavors of users that you will need to support in your multi-tenant solution.

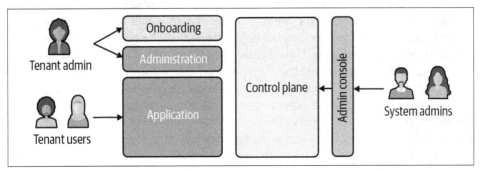

Figure 2-10. Multi-tenant user roles

On the lefthand side of the diagram, you'll see that we have the typical tenant-related roles. There are two distinct types of roles here: tenant administrators and tenant users. A tenant administrator represents the initial user from your tenant that is onboarded to the system. This user is typically given admin privileges. This allows them to access the unique application administration functionality that is used to configure, manage, and maintain application-level constructs. This includes being able to create new tenant users. A tenant user represents users that are utilizing the application without any administrative capabilities. These users may also be assigned different application-based roles that influence their application experience.

On the righthand side of the diagram, you'll see that we also have system administrators. These users are connected to the SaaS provider and have access to the control plane of your environment to manage, operate, and analyze the health and activity of a SaaS environment. These admins may also have varying roles that are used to characterize their administrative privileges. Some may have full access, while others may have limits on their ability to access or configure different views and settings.

You'll notice that I've also shown an administration console as part of the control plane. This represents an often overlooked part of the system admin role. It's here to highlight the need for a targeted SaaS administration console that is used to manage, configure, and operate your tenants. It is typically something your team needs to build to support the unique needs of your SaaS environment (separate from other tooling that might be used to manage the health of your system). Your system admin users will need an authentication experience to be able to access this SaaS admin console.

SaaS architects need to consider each of these roles when building out a multi-tenant environment. While the tenant roles are typically better understood, many teams invest less energy in the system admin roles. The process for introducing and managing the lifecycle of these users should be addressed as part of your overall design and implementation. You'll want to have a repeatable, secure mechanism for managing these users.

The control plane versus application plane debate is particularly sticky when it comes to managing users. There's little doubt that the system admin users should be managed via the control plane. In fact, the initial diagram of the two planes shown at the outset of this chapter (Figure 2-4) actually includes an admin user management service as part of its control plane. It's when you start discussing the placement of tenant users that things can get fuzzier. Some would argue that the application should own the tenant user management experience and, therefore, management of these users should happen within the scope of the application plane. At the same time, our tenant onboarding process needs to be able to create the identities for these users during the onboarding process, which suggests this should remain in the control plane. You can see how this can get circular in a hurry.

My general preference here, with caveats, is that identity belongs in the control plane—especially since this is where tenant context gets connected to user identities. This aspect of the identity would never be managed in the scope of the application plane.

You could make a compromise in this scenario, having the control plane manage the identity and authentication experience while still allowing the application to manage the non-identity attributes of the tenant outside of the identity experience. The other option would be to have a tenant user management service in your control plane that supports any additional user management functionality that may be needed by your application. You could also have instances where you have separate identities for your admin and tenant experiences. That would add another wrinkle.

The key takeaway is that you'll need to give careful consideration to determining how and where identity fits into your environment.

Tenant Provisioning

So far, we've highlighted the role of onboarding within the control plane. We also looked at how the onboarding process may need to provision and configure application infrastructure as part of the onboarding experience. This raises an important question: should tenant provisioning live within the control plane or the application plane?

Figure 2-11 provides a conceptual view of the two options. On the left, you'll see the model where tenant provisioning runs within the application plane. In this scenario, all the elements of onboarding (tenant creation, billing configuration, and identity setup) still happen within the scope of the control plane. The provisioning step is triggered and orchestrated by the onboarding service but runs within the application plane.

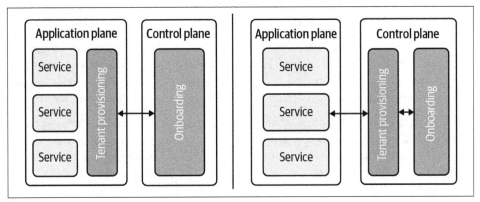

Figure 2-11. Placing the tenant provisioning process

The alternate approach is shown on the right side of this diagram. Here, tenant provisioning is executed from within the control plane. This means that the tenant provisioning would execute infrastructure configuration scripts that are applied within the application plane. This puts all the moving parts of onboarding within the control plane.

The trade-offs center around the encapsulation and abstraction of the application plane. If you believe the structure and footprint of application infrastructure should be unknown to the control plane, then you'll favor the model on the left. If you feel strongly that onboarding is already owned by the control plane, you could argue that it's natural for it to also own the application provisioning and configuration process.

My bias leans toward keeping provisioning closest to the resources that are being described and configured. I'd prefer not to make updates to the control plane based on changes in the architecture of the application plane. The trade-off is that the control plane must support a more distributed onboarding experience and rely on messaging between the control and application planes to track the provisioning status. Both models have their merits. The key is that provisioning should be a standalone part of the onboarding experience. So, if at some point you choose to move it, it would be somewhat encapsulated and could move without significant rethink.

Integrating the Control and Application Planes

Some organizations will create very specific boundaries between the control and application planes. This might be a network boundary or some other architectural construct that separates these two planes. This has advantages for some organizations in that it allows these planes to be configured, managed, and operated based on the unique needs of each plane. It also introduces opportunities to design more secure interactions between these planes.

With this in mind, we can then start to consider different approaches to integrating the control and application planes. The integration strategy you choose here will be heavily influenced by the nature of the interactions between the planes, the geographic footprint of your solution, and the security profile of your environment.

Some teams may opt for a more loosely coupled model that is more event or message driven while others may require a more native integration that enables more direct control of the application plane resources. There are few absolutes here, and there are a wide range of technologies that bring different possibilities to this discussion. The key is to be thoughtful in picking an integration model that enables the level of control that fits the needs of your particular domain, application, and environment.

 Much of the discussion here leans toward a model where the application and control planes are deployed and managed in separate infrastructures. While the merits of separating these planes are compelling, it's important to note that there is no rule that suggests that these planes must be divided along some hard boundary. There are valid scenarios where a SaaS provider may choose to deploy the control and application planes into a shared environment. The needs of your environment, the nature of your technology, and a range of other considerations will determine how you deploy these planes with more concrete architectural boundaries. The key is to ensure that you divide your system into these distinct planes—regardless of how and where they are deployed.

As we dig into the specifics of the control plane, we can look at the common touch points between these two planes and get into the specific integration use cases and their potential solutions. For now, though, just know that integration is a key piece of the overall control plane and application plane model.

Picking Technologies for Your Planes

SaaS teams pick the technologies for implementing their SaaS solutions based on any number of different variables. Skill sets, cloud providers, domain needs, legacy considerations—these are just a few of the many parameters that go into selecting a technology for your multi-tenant SaaS offering.

Now, as we look at SaaS through the lens of our control and application planes, it's also natural to think about how the needs of these two planes might influence your choice of technologies. If you choose an entirely container-based model for your application plane, should that mean your control plane must also be implemented with containers? The reality is that the planes will support different needs and different consumption profiles. There is nothing that suggests that the technologies they use must somehow match.

Consider, for example, the cost and consumption profile of your control plane. Many of these services may be consumed on a more limited basis than services running in our application plane. We might favor choosing a different technology for our control plane that yields a more cost-efficient model. Some teams might choose to use serverless technologies to implement their control plane.

The decisions can also be much more granular. I might choose one technology for some types of services and different technologies for other services. The key is that you should not assume that the profile, consumption, and performance profile of your control and application planes will be the same. As part of architecting your SaaS environment, you want to consider the technology needs of these two planes independently.

Avoiding the Absolutes

This discussion of SaaS architecture concepts devoted lots of attention to defining SaaS architecture through the lens of the control and application planes. The planes equip us with a natural way to think about the different components of a multi-tenant architecture and they give us a good mental model for thinking about how the different features of a multi-tenant architecture should land in your SaaS environment.

While these constructs are useful, I would also be careful about attaching absolutes to this model. Yes, it's a good way to think about SaaS and it provides us with a framework for talking about how we can approach building multi-tenant solutions. It's certainly provided me with a powerful construct for engaging teams that are trying to design and architect their SaaS systems. It has also put emphasis on the need for a set of shared services that are outside the scope of the multi-tenant architecture of your application.

The key here, though, is to use these concepts to shape how you approach your SaaS architecture, allowing for the fact that there may be nuances of your environment that may require variations in your approach. It's less about being absolute about what's in each plane and more about creating an architecture that creates a clear division of responsibility and aligns with the security, management, and operational profile of your SaaS offering.

Conclusion

This chapter was all about building a foundation of SaaS architecture concepts. We looked at the core elements of SaaS architecture with the goal of framing multi-tenant architecture patterns and strategies without getting into the specifics of any particular technology or domain. The concepts covered here should apply to any SaaS environment and provide any team with any technology a mental model for approaching SaaS architecture.

We've really only touched the surface of multi-tenant architecture here. As we move forward, we'll start mapping these concepts to concrete examples that tease out all the underlying details and add another layer of design considerations to the mental model that we've created. This added layer of detail will start to illustrate the web of possibilities you'll need to navigate as you consider how best to connect the needs of your SaaS business with the realities that come with realizing these principles with languages, technology stacks, and tools that bring their own set of variables to your multi-tenant equation.

Our next step is to start looking at SaaS deployment models. This will shift us from thinking about concepts, to mapping these concepts, to seeing those concepts landed in different patterns of deployment. The goal is to start thinking about and bringing more clarity to the strategies that are used to support the various SaaS models that you'll need to consider as you shape your SaaS architecture.

## CHAPTER 3

Multi-Tenant Deployment Models

Selecting your multi-tenant deployment model is one of the first things you'll do as a SaaS architect. It's here that you step back from the details of the multi-tenant implementation and ask yourself broader questions about the fundamental footprint of your SaaS environment. The choices you make around the deployment model of your application will have a profound influence on the cost, operations, tiering, and a host of other attributes that will have a direct impact on the success of your SaaS business.

In this chapter, I'll be walking through a range of different multi-tenant deployment models, exploring how each of these models can be used to address a variety of different technology and business requirements. Along the way, I'll highlight the pros and cons of the various models and give you a good sense of how the model you select can shape the complexity, scalability, performance, and agility of your SaaS offering. Understanding these models and their core values and trade-offs is essential to arriving at an architecture strategy that balances the realities of your business, customers, time pressures, and long-term SaaS objectives. While there are themes in these models that are common to many SaaS teams, there is no one blueprint that everyone will follow. Instead, it will be your job to navigate these deployment models, weigh the options, and select a model or combination of models that address your current and emerging needs.

We'll also use this chapter to continue to expand our SaaS vocabulary, attaching terminology to these models and their supporting constructs that will be referenced throughout the remainder of this book. These new terms will give you more precise ways to describe the nature of SaaS environments and enable you to be crisper and more granular about how you describe the moving parts of a multi-tenant architecture. These terms and concepts allow you to describe and classify SaaS architectures in a way that better accommodates the range of multi-tenant permutations that you will find in the wild.

As we begin to deploy models, you'll start to see hints of specific technology finding its way into our exploration of these patterns. While the deployment models patterns have no direct mapping to a specific technology, you'll begin to see how they take shape as I start connecting them to more concrete constructs. This is where you'll start to see more native Amazon Web Services (AWS) services and mechanisms surfacing. Generally, though, you are likely to find equivalents to these AWS constructs in whatever tools and technologies you're using.

The broader goal is to get you exposed to the language and mindset that surround selecting a deployment model. By the end of this chapter, you should have a better sense of the options and the forces that might shape the deployment model you choose for your application.

What's a Deployment Model?

Part of the challenge of describing SaaS architectures is that there is no single architecture strategy that somehow applies to all SaaS solutions. Instead, we find that SaaS architectures come in a range of shapes, sizes, and footprints, each of which has its own unique set of values and principles. It's your job to figure out which permutations of these strategies best fits the needs of your solution. Will some tenants require entirely dedicated infrastructure? Will others need to share their infrastructure? Or will you need a mix of these options? It's these higher-level, fundamental questions that you'll need to ask yourself as you begin defining the deployment footprint of your SaaS architecture.

The first hurdle I faced in this space was the absence of any precise terminology that accurately categorized the different patterns of multi-tenant deployments. The domain needed a better way to characterize how resources could be landed in your environment to support the varying requirements of tenants. This is where the notion of deployment models originated. The goal with defining deployment models was to give builders a way to describe the higher-level architecture strategies that are used to describe the deployment signatures of different tenant environments. A deployment model indicates how you'll be deploying resources and infrastructure within the application plane of your multi-tenant solution.

Let's look at a couple of conceptual deployment models to help clarify this concept. Figure 3-1 provides examples of two sample deployment models.

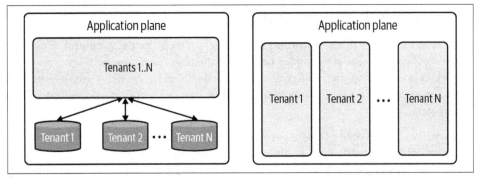

Figure 3-1. Conceptual deployment models

On the left, you'll see a deployment model that has all of its tenant resources being shared across the compute layers of our multi-tenant environment. However, the storage resources are dedicated to individual tenants. In contrast, the righthand side of the diagram provides another variation of a deployment model where all of a tenant's infrastructure (compute, storage, etc.) is deployed in a dedicated model. These are just a small sample of two deployment models, but they give you a more concrete view of what we're talking about when we're describing the fundamental aspects of a SaaS deployment model. The key takeaway here is that your deployment model represents the strategy that you're using to determine how tenant workloads will be mapped to their corresponding infrastructure resources. It expresses which resources will be shared and which will be dedicated.

At this level, a deployment model is a relatively straightforward concept. As you move forward and start to look at how these deployment models come to life, you'll get a better sense of the nuances that come with defining a deployment model. This becomes especially relevant as you start thinking about the workloads, compliance, isolation, and tiering needs of your multi-tenant solution. These factors end up playing a big role in shaping the overall footprint of your deployment model. The deployment model you choose can reach across your architecture, influencing the routing, authorization, cost efficiency, and operational profile of your environment. The choices you make when selecting a deployment model will have a profound influence on nearly every dimension of our SaaS offering.

Picking a Deployment Model

Understanding the value proposition of each deployment model is helpful. However, selecting a deployment model goes beyond evaluating the characteristics of any one model. When you sit down to figure out which deployment model is going to be best for your application and business, you'll often have to weigh a wide spectrum of parameters.

In some cases, the state of your current solution might have a huge impact on the deployment model you choose. A SaaS migration, for example, can often be more about finding a target deployment model that lets you get to SaaS without rebuilding your entire solution. Time to market, competitive pressures, legacy technology considerations, and team makeup are also factors that could represent significant variables in a SaaS migration story. Each of these factors would likely shape the selection of a deployment model.

Obviously, teams that are building a new SaaS solution have more of a blank canvas to work with. Here, the deployment model that you choose is probably more driven by the target personas and experience that you're hoping to achieve with your multi-tenant offering. The challenge is selecting a deployment model that balances the near- and long-term goals of the business. Selecting a model that is too narrowly focused on a near-term experience could limit growth as your business hits critical mass. At the same time, over-rotating to a deployment model that reaches too far beyond the needs of current customers may represent pre-optimization. Finding the right blend of flexibility and focus can be challenging.

No matter where you start your path to SaaS, there are certainly some broader global factors that will influence your deployment model selection. Packaging, tiering, and pricing goals, for example, often play a key role in determining which deployment model(s) might best fit with your business goals. Cost and operational efficiency are also part of the deployment model puzzle. While every solution would like to be as cost and operationally efficient as possible, your domain or business realities may require you to make compromises that will influence how you approach selecting a deployment model. If your business has very tight margins, you might lean more toward deployment models that squeeze every last bit of cost efficiency out of your deployment model. Others may be facing challenging compliance or performance considerations that might lead to deployment models that strike a balance between cost and customer demands.

These are just some simple examples that are part of the fundamental thought process you'll go through as part of figuring out which deployment model will address the core needs of your business. As I get deeper into the details of multi-tenant architecture patterns, you'll see more and more places where the nuances of multi-tenant architecture strategies will end up adding more dimensions to the deployment model picture. This will also give you a better sense of how the differences in these models might influence the complexity of your underlying solution. The nature of each deployment model can move the complexity from one area of our system to another.

The key here is that you should not be looking for a one-size-fits-all deployment model for your application. Instead, you should start with the needs of your domain, customers, and business and work backward to the combination of requirements that will point you toward the deployment model that fits with your current and aspirational goals.

It's also important to note that the deployment model of your SaaS environment is expected to evolve over time. Yes, you'll likely have some core aspects of your architecture that will remain fairly constant. However, you should also expect and be looking for ways to refine your deployment model based on the changing/emerging needs of customers, shifts in the market, and new business strategies. Worry less about getting it right on day one and just expect that you'll be using data from your environment to find opportunities to refactor your deployment model. A resource that started out as a dedicated resource might end up switched to a shared resource based on consumption, scaling, and cost considerations. A new tier might have you offering some parts of your system in a dedicated model. Being data driven and adaptable are all part of the multi-tenant technical experience.

Introducing the Silo and Pool Models

As we look at deployment models, we're going to discover that these models will require the introduction of new terminology that can add precision to how we characterize SaaS architecture constructs. This relates to our earlier exploration of how the term "multi-tenant" had to take on a broader meaning to fit the realities of SaaS businesses. Now, as we start to look at deployment models, you'll notice that we still need terminology that can better capture and accurately convey how the resources in our multi-tenant architecture are consumed by tenants.

There are two terms that I'm going to introduce here to give us a more granular way to think about classifying dedicated and shared resources. Across the rest of this book, you'll see that I will use the term "silo" to refer to any model where a resource is dedicated to a given tenant. I'll use the term "pool" to reference any model where a tenant resource is shared by one or more tenants.

This may seem like a subtle nuance in language. In reality, it has significant implications on how we describe multi-tenant architecture. It allows us to describe the behavior and scope of our SaaS architecture resources without the ambiguity and legacy baggage that comes with labeling resources as multi-tenant. As we look more at deployment models and the full range of SaaS architecture concepts that span this book, I will be using silo and pool as the foundational terms that characterize the usage, deployment, and consumption of the resources in our multi-tenant architecture.

To help crystallize this concept, let's look at a conceptual architecture that includes resources that are being consumed in a combination of dedicated and shared models. Figure 3-2 provides a view of a series of microservices that have been deployed into a SaaS architecture. In this image, I've created a hypothetical environment where we have a series of microservices that are using different strategies for dedicating and sharing tenant resources.

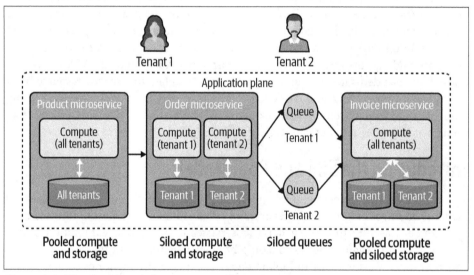

Figure 3-2. Siloed and pooled resource models

At the top of Figure 3-2, you'll see that I've put two tenants to illustrate how the tenants in our environment are landing in and consuming resources. These tenants are running an ecommerce application that is implemented via Product, Order, and Invoice microservices. Now, if we follow a path through these microservices from left to right, you'll see how we've applied different deployment strategies for each of these microservices.

Let's start with the Product microservice. With this service, I've chosen a strategy where the compute and storage for all of our tenants will be deployed in a pooled model. For this scenario, I have decided that the isolation and performance profile of this service fits best with the values of a pooled approach. As we move to the Order microservice, you'll see that I've chosen a very different model. In this case, the service has siloed compute and storage for every tenant. Again, this was done based on the specific needs of my environment. This could have been driven by some SLA requirement or, perhaps, a compliance need.

From the Order service, you'll then see that our system sends a message to a queue that prepares these orders for billing. This scenario is included to highlight the fact that our siloed and pooled concepts are extended beyond our microservices and applied to any resource that might be part of our environment. For this solution, I've opted to have siloed queues for each tenant. Finally, I have an Invoice service on the righthand side that pulls messages from these queues and generates invoices. To meet the requirements of our solution, I've used a mix of siloed and pooled models in this microservice. Here, the compute is pooled and the storage is siloed.

The key takeaway is that the terms "silo" and "pool" are used to generally characterize the architecture footprint of one or more resources. These terms can be applied in a very granular fashion, highlighting how tenancy is mapped to very specific elements of your architecture. These same terms can also be used more broadly to describe how a collection of resources are deployed for a tenant, so don't try to map silo and pool to specific constructs. Instead, think of them as describing the tenancy of a single resource or a group of resources.

This caveat will be especially important as we look at deployment models throughout this chapter, allowing us to apply silo and pool concepts at varying scopes across our multi-tenant architecture.

Full Stack Silo Deployment

Now that you have a high-level sense of the scope and role of deployment models, it's time to dig in a bit more and start looking at defining specific types of deployment models. Let's start by looking at what I'll label as a full stack silo deployment model.

As its name suggests, the full stack silo model places each tenant into an environment where all of their resources are completely siloed. Figure 3-3 provides an example of a full stack silo environment. Here you'll see that we have an environment where our application plane is running workloads for two tenants. These two tenants are running in silos where the compute, storage, and every resource that's needed for the tenant is deployed into some logical construct that creates a clear boundary between our tenants.

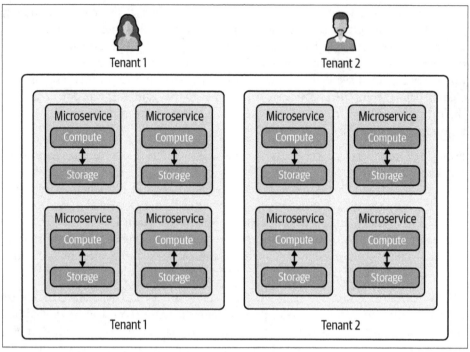

Figure 3-3. Full stack silo deployment model

In this particular example, I simplified the contents of the silo, showing a range of microservices that are running in each tenant environment. In reality, what's in the silo could be represented by any number of different technologies and design strategies. This could have been an n-tier environment with separate web, application, and storage tiers. I could have included any number of different compute models and other services as well (queues, object storage, messaging, and so on). The emphasis, at this stage, is less on what's in each of these tenant environments and more on the nature of how they are deployed.

Where Full Stack Silo Fits

The full stack silo model can feel like a bit of a SaaS antipattern. After all, so much of our discussion of SaaS is centered around agility and efficiency. Here, where we have fully siloed tenant resources, it can appear as though we've compromised on some of the fundamental goals of SaaS. However, if you think back to the definition of SaaS in Chapter 1, you'll recall that SaaS isn't exclusively about sharing infrastructure for economies of scale. SaaS is about operating in a model where all of our tenants are operated, managed, and deployed collectively. This is the key thing to keep in mind when you're looking at the full stack silo model. Yes, it has efficiency challenges. We'll get into those. At the same time, as long as every one of these environments is the same and as long as these are running the same version of our application, then we can still realize much of the value proposition of SaaS.

So, knowing that full stack silo meets our criteria for SaaS, the real question is more about when it might make sense for you to employ this model. Which factors typically steer organizations toward a full stack silo experience? When might it be a fit for the business and technology realities of your environment? While there are no absolutes here, there are common themes and environmental factors that have teams selecting the full stack silo model. Compliance and legacy considerations are two of the typical reasons teams will end up opting for a full stack silo footprint. In some heavily regulated domains, teams may choose a full stack silo model to simplify their architecture and make it easier for them to address specific compliance criteria. Customers in these domains might also have some influence on the adoption of a full stack silo, insisting on having siloed resources as part of selecting a SaaS solution.

The full stack silo model can also represent a good fit for organizations that are migrating a legacy solution to SaaS. The fully siloed nature of this model allows these organizations to move their existing code into a SaaS model without major refactoring. This gets them to SaaS faster and reduces their need to more immediately take on adding tenancy to all the moving parts of their architecture. Migrating teams will still be required to retrofit your legacy environment to align with the SaaS control plane, its identity model, and a host of other multi-tenant considerations. However, the scope and reach of these impacts can be less pronounced if your solution is moving into a full stack silo environment that doesn't need to consider scenarios where any of a tenant's resources are pooled.

Full stack silo can also be a tiering strategy. For example, some organizations may offer a premium version of their solution that, for the right price, will offer tenants a fully dedicated experience. It's important to note that this dedicated experience is not created as a one-off environment for these tenants. It's still running the same version of the application and is centrally managed alongside all the other tiers of the system.

In some cases, the full stack model simply represents a lower barrier of entry for teams—especially those that may not be targeting a large number of tenants. For these organizations, full stack silo allows them to get to SaaS without tackling some of the added complexities that come with building, isolating, and operating a pooled environment. Of course, these teams also have to consider how adoption of a full stack silo model might impact their ability to rapidly scale the business. In this case, the advantages of starting with a full stack could be offset by the inefficiencies and margin impacts of being in a full stack silo model.

Full Stack Silo Considerations

Teams that opt for a full stack silo model will need to consider some of the nuances that come with this model. There are definitely pros and cons to this approach that you'll want to add to your mental model when selecting this type of deployment. The sections that follow provide a breakdown of some of the key design, build, and deployment considerations that are associated with the full stack silo deployment model.

Control plane complexity

As you may recall, I have described all SaaS architectures as having control and application planes where our tenant environments live in the application plane and are centrally managed by the control plane. Now, with the full stack silo model, you have to consider how the distributed nature of the full stack model will influence the complexity of your control plane.

In Figure 3-4, you can see an example of a full stack silo deployment that highlights some of the elements that come with building and managing this model. Since our solution is running in a silo per tenant model, the application plane must support completely separate environments for each tenant. Instead of interacting with a single, shared resource, our control plane must have some awareness of each of these tenant silos. This inherently adds complexity to our control plane, which now must be able to operate each of these separate environments.

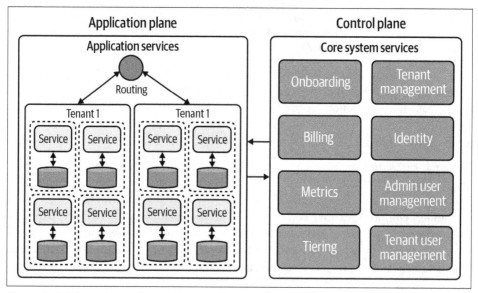

Figure 3-4. Managing and operating a full stack silo

Imagine implementing tenant onboarding in this example. The addition of each new tenant to this environment must fully provision and configure each siloed tenant environment. This also complicates any tooling that may need to monitor and manage the health of tenant environments. Your control plane code must know where each tenant environment can be found and be authorized to access each tenant silo. Any operational tooling that you have that is used to manage infrastructure resources will also need to deal with the larger, more distributed footprint of these tenant environments, which could make troubleshooting and managing infrastructure resources unwieldy. Any tooling you've created to centralized metrics, logs, and analytics for your tenants will also need to be able to aggregate the data from these separate tenant environments. Deployment of application updates is also more complicated in this model. Your DevOps code will have to roll out updates to each tenant silo.

There are likely more complexities to cover here. However, the theme is that the distributed nature of the full stack silo model touches many of the moving parts of your control plane experience, adding complexity that may not be as pronounced in other deployment models. While the challenges here are all manageable, it definitely will take extra effort to create a fully unified view of management and operations for any full stack silo environment.

Scaling impacts

Scale is another important consideration for the full stack silo deployment model. Whenever you're provisioning separate infrastructure for each tenant, you need to think about how this model will scale as you add more tenants. While the full stack silo model can be appealing when you have 10 tenants, its value can begin to erode as you consider supporting hundreds or thousands of tenants. The full stack silo model would not be practical for any B2C environment where the scale and number of tenants would be massive. Naturally, the nature of your architecture would also have some influence on this. If you're running Kubernetes, for example, it might come down to how effectively the silo constructs of Kubernetes would scale here (clusters, namespaces, etc.). If you're using separate cloud networking or account constructs for each siloed tenant, you'll have to consider any limits and constraints that might be applied by your cloud provider.

The broader theme is that full stack siloed deployments are not for everyone. As I get into specific full stack silo architectures, you'll see how this model can run into important scaling limits. More importantly, even if your environment can scale in a full stack silo model, you may find that there's a point at which the full stack silo can become difficult to manage. This could undermine your broader agility and innovation goals.

Cost considerations

Costs are also a key area to explore if you're looking at using a full stack silo model. While there are measures you can take to limit overprovisioning of siloed environments, this model does put limits on your ability to maximize the economies of scale of your SaaS environment. Typically, these environments will require lots of dedicated infrastructure to support each tenant and, in some cases, this infrastructure may not have an idle state where it's not incurring costs. For each tenant, then, you will have some baseline set of costs for tenants that you'll incur—even if there is no load on the system. Also, because these environments aren't shared, we don't get the efficiencies that would come with distributing the load of many tenants across shared infrastructure that scales based on the load of all tenants. Compute, for example, can scale dynamically in a silo, but it will only do so based on the load and activity of a single tenant. This may lead to some overprovisioning within each silo to prepare for the spikes that may come from individual tenants.

Generally, organizations offering full stack silo models are required to create cost models that help overcome the added infrastructure costs that come with this model. That can be a mix of consumption and some additional fixed fees. It could just be a higher subscription price. The key here is that, while the full stack silo may be the right fit for some tiers or business scenarios, you'll still need to consider how the siloed nature of this model will influence the pricing model of your SaaS environment.

As part of the cost formulas, we must also consider how the full stack silo model impacts the operational efficiency of your organization. If you've built a robust control plane and you've automated all the bits of your onboarding, deployment, and so on, you can still surround your full stack silo model with a rich operational experience. However, there is some inherent complexity that comes with this model that will likely add some overhead to your operational experience. This might mean that you will be required to invest more in the staff and tooling that's needed to support this model, which will add additional costs to your SaaS business.

Routing considerations

In Figure 3-4, I also included a conceptual placeholder for the routing of traffic within our application plane. With a full stack silo, you'll need to consider how the traffic will be routed to each silo based on tenant context. While there are any number of different networking constructs that we can use to route this load, you'll still need to consider how this will be configured. Are you using subdomains for each tenant? Will you have a shared domain with the tenant context embedded in each request? Each strategy you choose will require some way for your system to extract that context and route your tenants to the appropriate silo.

The configuration of this routing construct must be entirely dynamic. As each new tenant is onboarded to your system, you'll need to update the routing configuration to support routing this new tenant to its corresponding silo. None of this is wildly hard, but this is an area that will need careful consideration as you design your full stack siloed environment. Each technology stack will bring its own set of considerations to the routing problem.

Availability and blast radius

The full stack silo model does offer some advantages when it comes to the overall availability and durability of your solution. Here, with each tenant in its own environment, there is potential to limit the blast radius of any potential operational issue. The dedicated nature of the silo model gives you the opportunity to contain some issues to individual tenant environments. This can certainly have an overall positive effect on the availability profiles of your service.

Rolling out new releases also behaves a bit differently in siloed environments. Instead of having your release pushed to all customers at the same time, the full stack silo model may release to customers in waves. This can allow you to detect and recover from issues related to a deployment before it is released to the entire population. It, of course, also complicates the availability profile. Having to deploy to each silo separately requires you to have a more complicated rollout process that can, in some cases, undermine the availability of your solution.

Simpler cost attribution

One significant upside to the full stack silo model is its ability to attribute costs to individual tenants. Calculating cost per tenant for multi-tenant environments, as you'll see in Chapter 14, can be tricky in SaaS environments where some or all of a tenant's resources may be shared. Knowing just how much of a shared database or compute resource was consumed by a given tenant is not so easy to infer in pooled environments. However, in a full stack silo model, you won't face these complexities. Since each tenant has its own dedicated infrastructure, it becomes relatively easy to aggregate and map costs to individual tenants. Cloud providers and third-party tools are generally good at mapping costs to individual infrastructure resources and calculating a cost for each tenant.

Full Stack Silo in Action

Now that we have a good sense of the full stack silo model, let's look at some working examples of how this model is brought to life in real-world architectures. As you can imagine, there are any number of ways to implement this model across the various cloud providers, technology stacks, and so on. The nuances of each technology stack adds their own set of considerations to your design and implementation.

The technology and strategy you use to implement your full stack silo model will likely be influenced by some of the factors that were outlined above. They might also be shaped by attributes of your technology stack and your domain realities.

The examples are pulled from my experience building SaaS solutions at AWS. While specific to AWS, these patterns have corresponding constructs that have mappings to other cloud providers. And, in some instances, these full stack silo models could also be built in an on-premises model.

The account-per-tenant model

If you're running in a cloud environment—which is where many SaaS applications often land—you'll find that these cloud providers have some notion of an account. These accounts represent a binding between an entity (an organization or individual) and the infrastructure that they are consuming. And while there's a billing and security dimension to these accounts, our focus is on how these accounts are used to group infrastructure resources.

In this model, accounts are often viewed as the strictest of boundaries that can be created between tenants. This, for some, makes an account a natural home for each tenant in your full stack silo model. The account allows each silo of your tenant environments to be surrounded and protected by all the isolation mechanisms that cloud providers use to isolate their customer accounts. This limits the effort and energy you'll have to expend to implement tenant isolation in your SaaS environment. Here, it's almost a natural side effect of using an account per tenant in your full stack silo model.

Attributing infrastructure costs to individual tenants also becomes a much simpler process in an account-per-tenant model. Generally, your cloud provider already has all the built-in mechanisms needed to track costs at the account level, so with an account-per-tenant model, you can just rely on these ready-made solutions to attribute infrastructure costs to each of your tenants. You might have to do a bit of extra work to aggregate these costs into a unified experience, but the effort to assemble this cost data should be relatively straightforward.

In Figure 3-5, I've provided a view of an account-per-tenant architecture. You'll see that I've shown two full stack siloed tenant environments. These environments are mirror images, configured as clones that are running the exact same infrastructure and application services. When any updates are applied, they are applied universally to all tenant accounts.

Within each account, you'll see examples of the infrastructure and services that might be deployed to support the needs of your SaaS application. There are placeholders to represent the services that support the functionality of your solution. To the right of these services, I also included some additional infrastructure resources that are used within our tenant environments. Specifically, I put an object store (Amazon Simple Storage Service) and a managed queue service (Amazon Simple Queue Service). The object store might hold some global assets, and the queue is here to support asynchronous messaging between our services. I included these to drive home the point that our account-per-tenant silo model will typically encapsulate all of the infrastructure that is needed to support the needs of a given tenant.

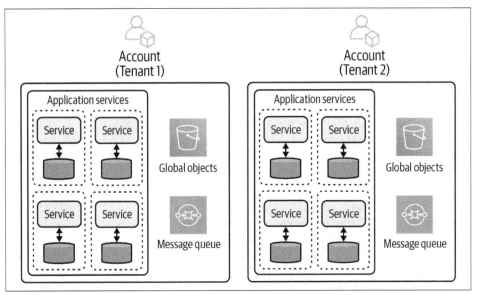

Figure 3-5. The account-per-tenant full stack silo model

Now, the question is: does this model mean that infrastructure resources cannot be shared between our tenant accounts? For example, could these two tenants be running all of their microservices in separate accounts and share access to a centralized identity provider? This wouldn't be unnatural. The choices you make here are driven by a combination of business/tenant requirements as well as the complexities associated with accessing resources that are outside the scope of a given account.

Let's be clear—the application functionality of your solution is running completely in its own account. The only area here where we might allow something to be outside of the account is when it plays some more global role in our system. Let's imagine the object store represents a globally managed construct that holds information that is centrally managed for all tenants. In some cases, you may find one-off reasons to have some bits of your infrastructure running in some shared model. However, anything that is shared cannot have an impact on the performance, compliance, and isolation requirements of our full stack silo experience. Essentially, if you create some centralized, shared resource that impacts the rationale for adopting a full stack silo model, then you've probably violated the spirit of using this model.

The choices you make here should start with assessing the intent of your full stack silo model. Did you choose this model based on an expectation that customers would want *all* of their infrastructure to be completely separated from other tenants, or was it more based on a desire to avoid noisy neighbor and data isolation requirements? Your answers to these questions will have a significant influence on how you choose to share parts of your infrastructure in this model.

If your code needs to access any resources that are outside of your account, this can introduce new challenges. Any externally accessed resource would need to be running within the scope of some other account, and as a rule of thumb, accounts have very intentional and hard boundaries to secure the resources in each account. So, then, you'd have to delve into authorizing cross-account access to enable your system to interact with any resource that lives outside of a tenant account.

Generally, I would stick with the assumption that, in a full stack silo model, your goal is to have all of a tenant's resources in the same account. Only when there's a compelling reason that still meets the spirit of your full stack silo should you consider how you might support any centralized resources.

Onboarding automation. The account-per-tenant silo model adds some additional twists to the onboarding of new tenants. As each new tenant is onboarded (as we'll see in Chapter 4), you will have to consider how you'll automate all the provisioning and configuration that comes with introducing a new tenant. For the account-per-tenant model, our provisioning goes beyond the creation of tenant infrastructure—it also includes the creation of new accounts.

While there are definitely ways to automate the creation of accounts, there are aspects that can't always be fully automated. In cloud environments, there are some intentional constraints that may restrict your ability to automate the configuration or provisioning of resources that may exceed the default limits for those resources. For example, your system may rely on a certain number of load balancers for each new tenant account, but the number you require for each tenant may exceed the default limits of your cloud provider. Now, you'll need to go through the processes, some of which may not be automated, to increase the limits to meet the requirements of each new tenant account. This is where your onboarding process may not be able to fully automate every step in a tenant onboarding. Instead, you may need to absorb some of the friction that comes with using the processes that are supported by your cloud provider. In general, the default limits for many resources could be well below what you'll need to effectively scale your environment.

While teams do their best to create clear mechanisms for creating each new tenant account, you may just need to allow for the fact that, as part of adopting an account-per-tenant model, you'll need to consider how these potential limit issues might influence your onboarding experience. This might mean creating different expectations around onboarding SLAs and better managing tenant expectations around this process.

Scaling considerations. I've already highlighted some of the scaling challenges that are typically associated with the full stack silo model. However, with the account-per-tenant model, there's another layer to the full stack silo scaling story.

Generally speaking, mapping accounts to tenants could be viewed as a bit of an anti-pattern. Accounts, for many cloud providers, were not necessarily intended to be used as the home for tenants in multi-tenant SaaS environments. Instead, SaaS providers just gravitated toward them because they seemed to align well with their goals. And, to a degree, this makes perfect sense.

Now, if you have an environment with tens of tenants, you may not feel much of the pain as part of your account-per-tenant model. However, if you have plans to scale to a large number of tenants, you may begin to hit a wall with this model. The most basic issue you can face here is that you may exceed the maximum number of accounts supported by your cloud provider. The more subtle challenge shows up over time. The proliferation of accounts can end up undermining the agility and efficiency of your SaaS business. Imagine having hundreds or thousands of tenants running in this model. This will translate into a massive footprint of infrastructure that you'll need to manage. While you can take measures to try to streamline and automate the management and operation of all these accounts, there could be points at which this may no longer be practical.

So, where is the point of no return? I can't say there's an absolute data point at which the diminishing returns kick in. So much depends on the nature of your tenant infrastructure footprint. I mention this mostly to ensure that you're factoring this into your thinking when you take on an account-per-tenant model.

The VPC-per-tenant model

The account-per-tenant model relies on a pretty coarse-grained boundary. Let's shift our focus to constructs that realize a full stack silo within the scope of a single account. This will allow us to overcome some of the challenges of creating accounts for individual tenants. The model we'll look at now, the Virtual Private Cloud (VPC)-per-tenant model, is one that relies more on networking constructs to house the infrastructure that belongs to each of our siloed tenants.

Within most cloud environments you're given access to a rich collection of virtualized networking constructs that can be used to build, control, and secure the footprint of your application environments. These networking constructs provide natural mechanisms for implementing a full stack siloed implementation. The very nature of networks and their ability to describe and control access to their resources provides SaaS builders with a powerful collection of tools that can be used to silo tenant resources.

Let's look at an example of how a sample networking construct can be used to realize a full stack silo model. Figure 3-6 provides a look at a sample network environment that uses Amazon's VPC to silo tenant environments.

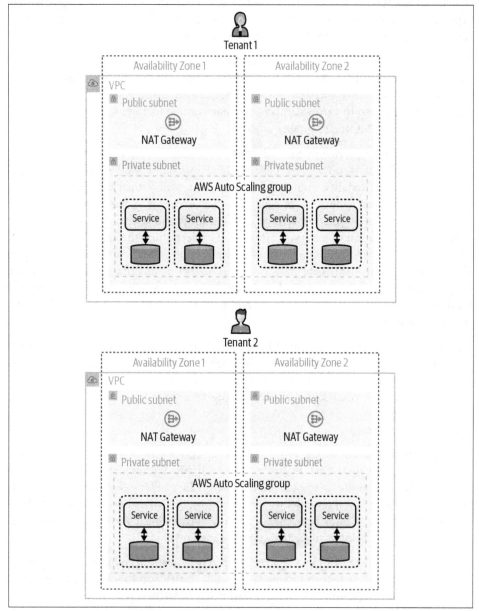

Figure 3-6. The VPC-per-tenant full stack silo model

At first glance, there are many moving parts in this diagram. While it's a tad busy, I wanted to bring in enough of the networking infrastructure to give you a better sense of the elements that are part of this model.

In Figure 3-6, we have two tenants who are accessing siloed application services that are running in separate VPCs. The VPC is the box that is at the outer edge of our tenant environments. I also wanted to illustrate the high availability footprint of our VPC by having it include two separate Availability Zones (AZs). We won't get into AZs, but just know that AZs represent distinct locations within an AWS Region that are engineered to be isolated from failures in other AZs. We also have separate subnets to separate the public and private subnets of our solution. Finally, you'll see the application services of our solution deployed into private subnets within our two AZs. These are surrounded by what AWS labels an Auto Scaling group, which allows services to dynamically scale based on tenant load.

I've included all these network details to highlight the idea that we're running our tenants in network silos that offer each of them an isolated and resilient networking environment that leans on all the virtualized networking goodness that comes with building and deploying your solution in a VPC-per-tenant siloed model.

While this model may seem less rigid than the account-per-tenant model, it actually provides you with a solid set of constructs for preventing any cross-tenant access. As part of their very nature, these networking tools allow you to create very carefully controlled ingress and egress for your tenant environments. We won't get into the specifics, but the list of access and flow control mechanisms that are available is extensive. More details can be found online (*https://oreil.ly/NKNBW*).

Another model that shows up occasionally is the subnet-per-tenant model. While I rarely see this model, there are some instances where teams will put each tenant silo in a given subnet. This, of course, can also become unwieldy and difficult to manage as you scale.

It's worth noting that the VPC-per-tenant model doesn't map to every AWS technology stack. A serverless environment, for example, doesn't use VPCs to group its compute services. In fact, in general, the full stack silo model for serverless would simply deploy a completely standalone set of functions. You'll see more on this approach when we look at serverless SaaS architecture patterns in Chapter 11.

Onboarding automation. With the account-per-tenant model, I dug into some of the challenges it could create as part of automating your onboarding experience. With the VPC-per-tenant model, the onboarding experience changes some. The good news is that since you're not provisioning individual accounts, you won't run into the same account limits automation issues. Instead, the assumption is that the single account that is running our VPCs will be sized to handle the addition of new tenants. This may still require some specialized processes, but they can be applied outside the scope of onboarding.

In the VPC-per-tenant model, the focus is more on provisioning your VPC constructs and deploying your application services. That will likely still be a heavy process, but most of what you need to create and configure can be achieved through a fully automated process.

Scaling considerations. As with accounts, VPCs also face some scaling considerations. Just as there are limits on the number of accounts you can have, there can be limits on the number of VPCs that you can have. The management and operation of VPCs can also get complicated as you begin to scale this model. Having tenant infrastructure sprawling across hundreds of VPCs may impact the agility and efficiency of your SaaS experience. So, while VPC has some upsides, you'll want to think about how many tenants you'll be supporting and whether the VPC-per-tenant model is practical for your environment.

Remaining Aligned on a Full Stack Silo Mindset

Before I move on to any new deployment models, it's essential that we align on some key principles in the full stack silo. For some, the full stack silo model can be appealing because it can feel like it opens (or reopens) the door for SaaS providers to offer one-off customization to their tenants. While it's true that the full stack silo model offers dedicated resources, this should never be viewed as an opportunity to fall back into per-tenant customization. The full stack silo only exists to accommodate domain, compliance, tiering, and any other business realities that might warrant the use of a full stack silo model.

In all respects, a full stack silo environment is treated the same as a pooled environment. Whenever new features are released, they are deployed to *all* customers. If your infrastructure configuration needs to be changed, that change should be applied to *all* of your siloed environments. If you have policies for scaling or other runtime behaviors, they are applied based on tenant tiers. You should never have a policy that applies to an individual tenant. The whole point of SaaS is that we are trying to achieve agility, innovation, scale, and efficiency through our ability to manage and operate our tenants collectively. Any drift toward a one-off model will take you away from those SaaS goals. In some cases, organizations that move to SaaS to maximize efficiency will end up regressing through one-off customizations that undermine much of the value they hoped to get out of a true SaaS model.

The guidance I always offer to drive this point home centers around how you arrive at a full stack silo model. I tell teams that even if you're targeting a full stack silo as your starting point, you should build your solution as if it were going to be a full stack pool model. Then, treat each full stack silo as an instance of your pooled environment that happens to have a single tenant. This serves as a forcing function that allows full stack siloed environments to inherit the same values that are applied to a full stack pool (which we're covering next).

The Full Stack Pool Model

The full stack pool model, as its name suggests, represents a complete shift from the full stack silo mindset and mechanisms we've been exploring. With the full stack pool model, we'll now look at SaaS environments where all of the application plane resources for our tenants are running in a shared infrastructure model.

For many, the profile of a fully pooled environment maps to their classic notion of multi-tenancy. It's here where the focus is squarely on achieving economies of scale, operational efficiencies, cost benefits, and a simpler management profile that are the natural byproducts of a shared infrastructure model. The more we can share infrastructure resources, the more opportunities we have to align the consumption of those resources with the activity of our tenants. At the same time, these added efficiencies also introduce a range of new challenges.

Figure 3-7 provides a conceptual view of the full stack silo model. You'll see that I've still included the control plane to make it clear that it is a constant across any SaaS model. On the left of the diagram is the application plane, which now has a collection of application services that are shared by all tenants. The tenants shown at the top of the application plane are all accessing and invoking operations on the application microservices and infrastructure.

Now, within this pool model, tenant context plays a much bigger role. In the full stack silo model, tenant context was primarily used to route tenants to their dedicated stack. Once a tenant lands in a silo, that silo knows that all operations within that silo are associated with a single tenant. With our full stack pool, however, this context is essential to every operation that is performed. Accessing data, logging messages, recording metrics—all of these operations will need to resolve the current tenant context at runtime to successfully complete their task.

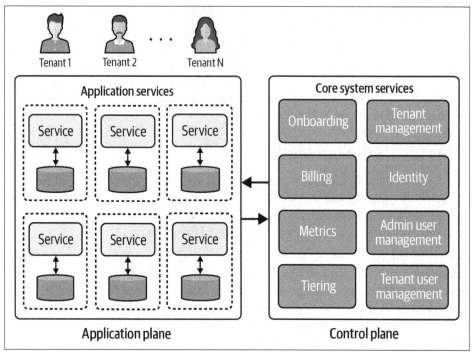

Figure 3-7. A full stack pool model

Figure 3-8 gives you a better sense of how tenant context touches every dimension of our infrastructure, operations, and implementation in a pooled model. This conceptual diagram highlights how each microservice must acquire tenant context and apply it as part of its interactions with data, the control plane, and other microservices. You'll see tenant context being acquired and applied as we send billing events and metrics data to the control plane. You'll see it injected in your call to downstream microservices. It also shows up in our interaction with data.

The fundamental idea is that when we have a pooled resource, that resource belongs to multiple tenants. As a result, tenant context is needed to apply scope and context to each operation at runtime.

Now, to be fair, tenant context is valid across all SaaS deployment models. A silo still needs tenant context as well. What's different here is that the silo model knows its binding to the tenant at the moment it's provisioned and deployed. So, for example, I could associate an environment variable as the tenant context for a siloed resource (since its relationship to the tenant does not change at runtime). However, a pooled resource is provisioned and deployed for all tenants and must resolve its tenant context based on the nature of each request it processes.

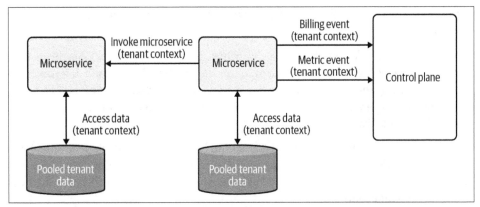

Figure 3-8. Tenant context in the full stack pooled environment

As we dig deeper into more multi-tenant implementation details, we'll discover that these differences between silo and pool models can have a profound impact on how we architect, deploy, manage, and build the elements of our SaaS environment.

Full Stack Pool Considerations

The full stack pool model also comes with a set of considerations that might influence whether you choose to adopt this model. In many respects, the considerations for the full stack pool model are the natural inverse of the full stack silo model. The full stack pool model certainly has strengths that are appealing to many SaaS providers. It also presents a set of challenges that come with having shared infrastructure. The sections that follow highlight these considerations.

Scale

Our goal in multi-tenant environments is to do everything we can to align infrastructure consumption with tenant activity. In an ideal scenario, your system would, at a given moment in time, only have enough resources allocated to accommodate the current load being imposed by tenants. There would be zero overprovisioned resources, which would let the business optimize margins and ensure that the addition of new tenants would not drive a spike in costs that could undermine the bottom line of the business.

This is the dream of the full stack pool model. If your design is somehow able to fully optimize the scaling policies of your underlying infrastructure in a full stack pool, you have achieved multi-tenant nirvana. This is not practical or realistic, but it is the mindset that often surrounds the full stack pool model. The reality is that creating a solid scaling strategy for a full stack pool environment is very challenging. The loads of tenants are often constantly changing, and new tenants may be arriving every day, so the scaling strategy that worked yesterday may not work today. What typically happens here is teams will accept some degree of overprovisioning to account for this continually shifting target.

The technology stack you choose can also have a significant impact on the scaling dynamics of your full stack pool environment. In Chapter 11 we'll look at a serverless SaaS architecture and get a closer look at how using serverless technologies can simplify your scale story and achieve better alignment between infrastructure consumption and tenant activity.

While there are significant scaling advantages to be had in a full stack pool model, the effort to make this scaling a reality can be challenging to fully realize. You'll need to work hard to craft a scaling strategy that can optimize resource utilization without impacting tenant experience.

Isolation

In a full stack silo model, isolation is a very straightforward process. When resources run in a dedicated model, you have a natural set of constructs that allow you to ensure that one tenant cannot access the resources of another tenant. However, when you start using pooled resources, your isolation story tends to get more complicated. How do you isolate a resource that is shared by multiple tenants? How is isolation realized and applied across all the different resource types and infrastructure services that are part of your multi-tenant architecture? In Chapter 9, we'll dig into the strategies that are used to address these isolation nuances. However, it's important to note that as part of adopting a full stack pool model, you will be faced with a range of new isolation considerations that may influence your design and architecture. The assumption is that the economies of scale and efficiencies of the pooled model offset any of the added overhead and complexity associated with isolating pooled resources.

Availability and blast radius

In many respects, a full stack pool model represents an all-in commitment to a model that places all the tenants of your business into a shared experience. Any outage or issue that shows up in a full stack pool environment is likely to impact *all* of your customers and could potentially damage the reputation of your SaaS business. There are examples across the industry of SaaS service outages that created a flurry of social media outcry and negative press that had a lasting impact on these businesses.

As you consider adopting a full stack pool model, you need to understand that you're committing to a higher DevOps, testing, and availability bar that makes every effort to ensure that your system can prevent, detect, and rapidly recover from any potential outage. It's true that every team should have a high bar for availability. However, the risk and impact of any outage in a full stack pool environment demands a greater focus on ensuring that your team can deliver a zero downtime experience. This includes adopting best-of-breed continuous integration/continuous deployment

(CI/CD) strategies that allow you to release and roll back new features on a regular basis without impacting the stability of your solution.

Generally, you'll see full stack pool teams leaning into fault-tolerant strategies that allow their microservices and components to limit the blast radius of localized issues. Here, you'll see greater application of asynchronous interactions between services, fallback strategies, and bulkhead patterns being used to localize and manage potential microservice outages. Operational tooling that can proactively identify and apply policies is also essential in a full stack pool environment.

It's worth noting that these strategies apply to any and all SaaS deployment models. However, the impact of getting this wrong in a full stack pool environment can be much more significant for a SaaS business.

Noisy neighbor

Full stack pool environments rely on carefully orchestrated scaling policies that ensure that your system will effectively add and remove capacity based on the consumption activity of your tenants. The shifting needs of tenants along with the potential influx of new tenants means that the scaling policies you have today may not apply tomorrow. While teams can take measures to try and anticipate these tenant activity trends, many teams find themselves overprovisioning resources to create the cushion needed to handle the spikes that may not be effectively addressed through scaling strategies.

Every multi-tenant system must employ strategies that will allow them to anticipate spikes and address what is referred to as noisy neighbor conditions. However, noisy neighbor takes on added weight in full stack pool environments. When everything is shared, the potential for noisy neighbor conditions is much higher. You must be especially careful with the sizing and scaling profile of your resources since everything must be able to react successfully to shifts in tenant consumption activity. This means accounting for and using defensive tactics to ensure that one tenant isn't saturating your system and impacting the experience of other tenants.

Cost attribution

Associating and tracking costs at the tenant level is a much more challenging proposition in a full stack pool environment. While many environments give you tools to map tenants to specific infrastructure resources, they don't typically support mechanisms that allow you to attribute consumption to the individual tenants that are consuming a shared resource. For example, if three tenants are consuming a compute resource in a multi-tenant setting, I won't typically have access to tools or mechanisms that would let me determine what percentage of that resource was consumed by each tenant at a given moment in time. We'll get into this challenge in more detail in Chapter 14. The efficiency of a full stack pool model also comes with new challenges around understanding the cost footprint of individual tenants.

Operational simplification

I've talked about this need for a single pane of glass that provides a unified operational and management view of your multi-tenant environment. Building this operational experience requires teams to ingest metrics, logs, and other data that can be surfaced in this centralized experience. Creating these operational experiences in a full stack pool environment tends to be a simpler experience. Here, where all tenants are running in shared infrastructure, I can more easily assemble an aggregate view of my multi-tenant environment. There's no need to connect with one-off tenant infrastructure and create paths for each of those tenant-specific resources to publish data to some aggregation mechanism.

Deployment is also simpler in the full stack pool environment. Releasing a new version of a microservice simply means deploying one instance of that service to the pooled environment. Once it's deployed, all tenants are now running on the new version.

A Sample Architecture

The architecture of a full stack pool environment is pretty straightforward. In fact, on the surface, it doesn't look all that unlike any classic application architecture. Figure 3-9 provides an example of a fully pooled architecture deployed in an AWS architecture.

I've included many of the same constructs that were part of our full stack silo environment. There's a VPC for the network of our environment, and it includes two Availability Zones for high availability. Within the VPC there are separate private and public subnets that separate the external and internal view of our resources. And finally, within the private subnet you'll see placeholders for the various microservices that deliver the server-side functionality of our application. These services have storage that is deployed in a pooled model and their compute is scaled horizontally using an Auto Scaling group. At the top, of course, we also illustrate that this environment is being consumed by multiple tenants.

Now, in looking at this at this level of detail, you'd be hard-pressed to find anything distinctly multi-tenant about this architecture. In reality, this could be the architecture of almost any flavor of application. Multi-tenancy doesn't really show up in a full stack pool model as some concrete construct; it is only seen if you look inside the runtime activity that's happening within this environment. Every request that is being sent through this architecture is accompanied by tenant context. The infrastructure and the services must acquire and apply this context as part of every request that is sent through this experience.

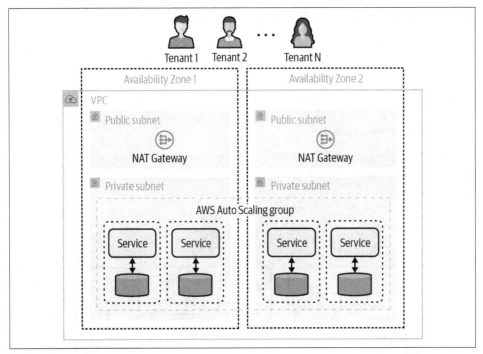

Figure 3-9. A full stack pool architecture

Imagine, for example, a scenario where Tenant 1 makes a request to fetch an item from storage. To process that request, your multi-tenant services will need to extract the tenant context and use it to determine which items within the pooled storage are associated with Tenant 1. As I move through the upcoming chapters, you'll see how this context ends up having a profound influence on the implementation and deployment of these services. For now, though, the key is to understand that a full stack pool model relies more on its runtime ability to share resources and apply tenant context where needed.

This architecture represents just one flavor of a full stack pool model. Each technology stack (containers, serverless, relational storage, NoSQL storage, queues) can influence the footprint of the full stack pool environment. The spirit of full stack pool remains the same across most of these experiences. Whether you're in a Kubernetes cluster or a VPC, the resources in that environment will be pooled and will need to scale based on the collective load of all tenants.

A Hybrid Full Stack Deployment Model

So far, I've mostly presented full stack silo and full stack pool deployment models as two separate approaches to the full stack problem. It's fair to think of these two models as addressing a somewhat opposing set of needs and almost view them as being mutually exclusive. However, if you step back and overlay market and business realities on the problem, you'll see how some organizations might see value in supporting both of these models.

Figure 3-10 provides a view of a sample hybrid full stack deployment model. Here we have the same concepts we covered with full stack silo and pool deployment models sitting side by side.

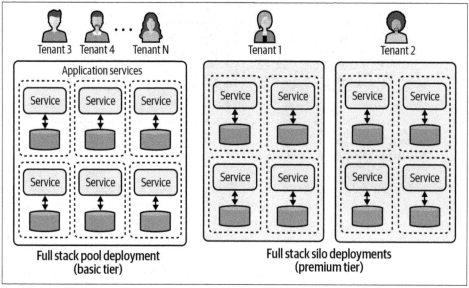

Figure 3-10. A hybrid deployment model

So, why both models? What would motivate adopting this approach? Well, imagine you've built your SaaS business and started out offering all customers a full stack pool model (shown on the left). Then, somewhere along the way, you ran into a customer that was uncomfortable running in a pooled model. They may have noisy neighbor concerns or be worried about compliance issues. Now, you're not necessarily going to cave to every customer that has this pushback. That would undermine much of what you're trying to achieve as a SaaS business. Instead, you're going to make efforts to help customers understand the security, isolation, and strategies you've adopted to address their needs. This is always part of the job of selling a SaaS solution. At the same time, there may be rare conditions when you might be open to offering a customer their own full stack siloed environment. This could be driven by a strategic opportunity or it may be that some customer is willing to write a large check that could justify offering a full stack silo option.

In Figure 3-10, you can see how the hybrid full stack deployment model lets you create a blended approach to this problem. On the lefthand side of this diagram is an instance of a full stack pool environment. This environment supports the bulk of your customers, and we label these tenants, in this example, as belonging to the basic tier experience.

Now, for the tenants that demanded a more siloed experience, I have created a new premium tier that allows tenants to have a full stack silo environment. Here we have two full stack siloed tenants that are running their own stacks. The assumption (for this example) is that these tenants are connected to a premium tier strategy that has a separate pricing model.

For this model to be viable, you must apply constraints to the number of tenants that are allowed to operate in a full stack silo model. If the ratio of siloed tenants becomes too high, this can undermine your entire SaaS experience.

The Mixed Mode Deployment Model

So far, I've focused heavily on the full stack models. While it's tempting to view multi-tenant deployments through these more coarse-grained models, the reality is that many systems rely on a much more fine-grained approach to multi-tenancy, making silo and pool choices across the entire surface of their SaaS environment. This is where we look more at what I refer to as a mixed mode deployment model.

With mixed mode deployments, you're not dealing with the heavy absolutes that come with full stack models. Instead, mixed mode allows us to look at the workloads within our SaaS environment and determine how each of the different services and resources should be deployed to meet the specific requirements of a given use case.

Let's take a simple example. Imagine I have two services in my ecommerce solution. I have an order service that has challenging throughput requirements that are prone to noisy neighbor problems. This same service also stores data that is going to grow significantly and has strict compliance requirements that are hard to support in a pooled model. I also have a ratings service that is used to manage product ratings. It doesn't really face any significant throughput challenges and can easily scale to handle the needs of tenants—even when a single tenant might be putting a disproportionate load on the service. Its storage is also relatively small and contains data that isn't part of the system's compliance profile.

In this scenario, I can step back and consider these specific parameters to arrive at a deployment strategy that best serves the needs of these services. Here, I might choose to make both the compute and the storage of my order service siloed and the compute and storage of my rating service pooled. There might even be cases where the individual layers of a service could have separate silo/pool strategies. This is the basic point I was making when I was first introducing the notion of silo and pool at the outset of this chapter.

Equipped with this more granular approach to silo and pool strategies, you can now imagine how this might yield much more diverse deployment models. Consider a scenario where you might use this strategy in combination with a tiering model to define your multi-tenant deployment footprint.

Figure 3-11 provides a conceptual view of how you might employ a mixed mode deployment model in your SaaS environment. I've shown a variety of different deployment experiences spanning the basic and premium tier tenants.

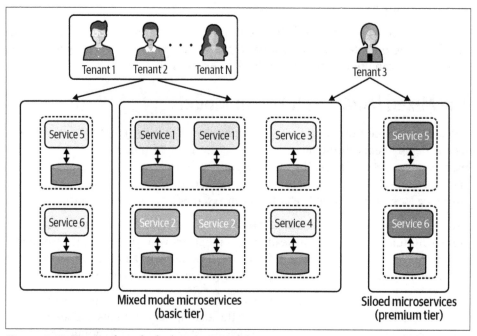

Figure 3-11. A mixed mode deployment model

On the lefthand side of this image, we have our basic tier services. These services cover all the functionality that is needed for our SaaS environment. However, you'll note that they are deployed in different silo/pool configurations. Service 1, for example, has siloed compute and pooled storage. Meanwhile, Service 2 has siloed compute and siloed storage. Services 3 to 6 are all pooled compute and pooled storage. The idea is that I've looked across the needs of my pooled tenants and identified, on a service-by-service basis, which silo/pool strategy will best fit the needs of that service.

The optimizations that have been introduced here were created as baseline strategies that were core to the experience of *any* tenant using the system.

Now, where tiers do come into play is when you look at what I've done with the premium tier tenants. You'll notice that Services 5 and 6 are deployed in the basic tier and they're also deployed separately for a premium tier tenant. The thought was that, for these services, the business determined that offering these services in a dedicated model would represent value that could distinguish the experience of the system's premium tier. So, for each premium tier tenant, we'll create new deployments of Service 5 and 6 to support the tiering requirements of our tenants. In this particular example, Tenant 3 is a premium tier tenant that consumes a mix of the services on the left and these dedicated instances of Services 5 and 6 on the right.

Approaching your deployment model in this more granular fashion provides a much higher degree of flexibility to you as the architect and to the business. By supporting silo and pool models at all layers, you have the option to compose the right blend of experiences to meet tenant, operational, and other needs that might emerge throughout the life of your solution. If you have a pooled microservice with performance issues that are creating noisy neighbor challenges, you could silo the compute and/or storage of the service to address this problem. If your business wants to offer some parts of your system in a dedicated model to enable new tiering strategies, you are better positioned to make this shift.

This mixed mode deployment model often represents a compelling option for many multi-tenant builders. It allows them to move away from having to approach problems purely through the lens of full stack solutions that don't always align with the needs of the business. Yes, there will always be solutions that use the full stack model. For some SaaS providers, this will be the only way to meet the demands of their market and customers. However, there are also cases where you can use the strengths of the mixed mode deployment model to address this need without moving everything into a full stack silo. If you can just move specific services into the silo and keep some lower profile services in the pool, that could still represent a solid win for the business.

The Pod Deployment Model

So far, I've mostly looked at deployment models through the lens of how you can represent the application of siloed and pooled concepts. We've explored coarse- and fine-grained ways to apply the silo and pool models across your SaaS environment. I also need to step out of the silo/pool focus and think about how an application might need to support a deployment variation that is shaped more by where it needs to land, how it deals with environmental constraints, and how it might need to morph to support the scale and reach of your SaaS business. This is where the pod deployment model comes into the picture. It's also worth highlighting the terminology collision that comes with the model. Kubernetes also has its own view of pods, which is entirely separate from this concept.

When I talk about pods here, I'm talking about how you might group a collection of tenants into some unit of deployment. I may have some technical, operational, compliance, scale, or business motivation that pushes me toward a model where I put tenants into individual pods, and these pods become a unit of deployment, management, and operation for my SaaS business. Figure 3-12 provides a conceptual view of a pod deployment.

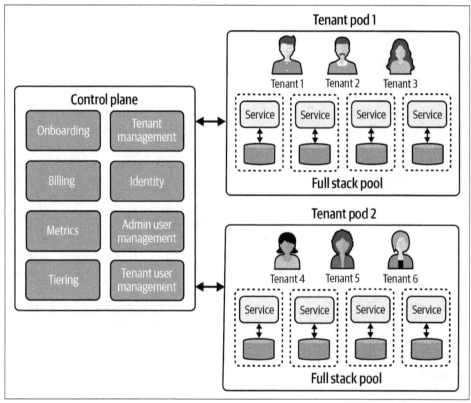

Figure 3-12. A pod deployment model

In this pod deployment model, you'll notice that we have the same centralized control plane on the lefthand side of this experience. On the righthand side, I have included individual pods that are used to represent self-contained environments that support the workload of one or more tenants. In this example, I have Tenants 1–3 in pod 1 and Tenants 4–6 in pod 2.

These separate pods bring a degree of complexity to a SaaS environment, requiring your control to build in the mechanisms to support this distribution model. How tenants are onboarded, for example, must account for which pod a given tenant will land in. Your management and operations must also become pod aware, providing insights into the health and activity of each pod.

There are a number of factors that could drive the adoption of a pod-based delivery model. Imagine, for example, having a full stack pool model running in the cloud that, at a certain number of tenants, begins to exceed the infrastructure limits of specific services. In this scenario, your only option to work around these constraints might be to create separate cloud accounts that host different groups of tenants. This could also be driven by a need to deploy a SaaS product into multiple geographies; geography requirements or performance considerations could tip you toward a pod-based deployment model, where different geographies might be running different pods.

Some teams may also use pods as an isolation strategy to reduce cross-tenant impacts. This can be motivated by a need for greater protections from noisy neighbor conditions, or it might play a role in the security and availability story of a SaaS provider.

If you choose to adopt a pod model, you'll want to consider how this will influence the agility of your business. Adopting a pod model means committing to absorbing the extra complexity and automation that allows you to support and manage pods without having any one-off mechanisms for individual pods. To scale successfully, the configuration and deployment of these pods must all be automated through your control plane. If some change is required, that change is applied universally to all pods. This is the mirror of the mindset I outlined with full stack silo environments. The pod cannot be viewed as an opportunity to enable targeted customization for individual tenants.

One dynamic that comes with pods is this idea of viewing membership within a pod as something that can be shifted during the life of a tenant. Some organizations may have distinct pod configurations optimized around the profile of a tenant, so that if a tenant's profile somehow changes and their sizing or consumption patterns aren't aligned with those of a given pod, they can consider moving that tenant to another pod. However, this would come with some heavy lifting to get the entire footprint of the tenant transferred to another pod. This would not be a daily exercise but is something that some SaaS teams support—especially those that have pods that are tuned to a specific experience.

While pods have a clear place in the deployment model discussion, it's important not to see pods as a shortcut for dealing with multi-tenant challenges. Yes, the pod model can simplify some aspects of scale, deployment, and isolation, but pods also add complexity and inefficiencies that can undermine the broader value proposition of SaaS. You may not, for example, be able to maximize the alignment between tenant consumption and infrastructure resources in this model. Instead, you may end up with more instances of idle or overprovisioned resources distributed across the collection of pods that your system supports, which could have a significant impact on the overall infrastructure cost profile and margins of your SaaS business.

Conclusion

This chapter focused on identifying the range of SaaS deployment models that architects must consider when designing a multi-tenant architecture. While some of these models have very different footprints, they all fit within the definition of what it means to be SaaS. This aligns with the fundamental mindset I outlined in Chapter 1, identifying SaaS as a business model that can be realized through multiple architecture models. You should see that even though I outlined multiple deployment models, they all shared the idea of having a single control plane that enables each environment and its tenant to be deployed, managed, operated, onboarded, and billed through a unified experience. Full stack silo, full stack pool, mixed mode—they all conform with the notion of having all tenants running the same version of a solution and being operated through a single pane of glass.

From looking at these deployment models, it should be clear that there are a number of factors that might push you toward one model or another. Legacy, domain, compliance, scale, cost efficiency, and a host of other business and technical parameters are used to find the deployment model (or combination of deployment models) that best align with the needs of your team and business. It's important to note that the models I covered represent the core themes while still allowing for the fact that you might adopt some variation of one of these models based on the needs of your organization. As you saw with the hybrid full stack model, it's also possible that your tiering or other considerations might have you supporting multiple models based on the profile of your tenants.

Now that you have a better sense of these foundational models, we can start to dig into the more detailed aspects of building a multi-tenant SaaS solution. I'll start covering the under-the-hood moving parts of the application and control planes, highlighting the services and code needed to bring these concepts to life. The first step in that process is to look at multi-tenant identity and onboarding. Identity and onboarding often represent the starting point of any SaaS architecture discussion. They lay the foundation for how we associate tenancy with users and how that tenancy flows through the moving parts of your multi-tenant architecture. As part of looking at identity, I'll also explore tenant onboarding, which is directly connected to this identity concept. As each new tenant is onboarded to a system, you must consider how that tenant will be configured and connected to its corresponding identity. Starting here will allow us to explore the path to a SaaS architecture from the outside in.

CHAPTER 4

Onboarding and Identity

Now that you have a sense of the broader multi-tenant terminology and landscape, let's look at what it means to bring these concepts to life in a working solution. The question is: where do you start? So many teams ask me this question. Fortunately, this is an area where I think there's a pretty uniform answer. Whether you're migrating or greenfield, I'd always point you at onboarding, identity, and the control plane as the starting point for building most multi-tenant architectures. Each of these elements forces important, foundational constructs into your environment, defining how tenants will be introduced and how users will be created and bound to tenants. These first steps will begin to establish the building blocks of our control plane.

By starting here, you'll put tenancy front and center. This means that all the layers of your architecture are now forced to be multi-tenant aware. Each component of your system will now have to consider how tenancy might shape its design and implementation. While this may seem like a subtle nuance, its impact is quite profound. The mere presence of tenancy touches how you isolate tenants, how you represent their data, how you support multiple personas, how you bill tenants, and a host of other aspects of your solution. It also begins to establish the clear boundary between the control and application planes. The goal is to avoid falling into the trap of starting with the application and bolting on tenancy after the fact. This never works well and typically leads to significant refactoring and compromises that undermine the design of your SaaS architecture.

I'll start the chapter by looking at what it takes to get the basics of our control plane up and running. This is where we'll look at the provisioning of the infrastructure and resources that are needed to host the various services that will be used to manage and operate your SaaS architecture. While this control plane will ultimately host many services, I'll keep this chapter mostly focused on the onboarding and identity functionality. Then, later, we can see how we build out more aspects of the control plane.

As we dig into onboarding, you'll get a much better sense of all the moving parts that are part of this process. For some environments, the orchestration of this process can be quite complex. While the nature of onboarding can vary for each SaaS environment, there are still some common themes that span many implementations. I'll dig into some of these themes as I walk you through a sample onboarding flow. This should surface some of the considerations that go into building your own onboarding service. It should also highlight the critical role onboarding plays within your SaaS architecture.

The next area I'll review is identity. I'll look more into the details of how we bind individual users to tenants to arrive at the notion of tenant context that was discussed in Chapter 1. This will include going deeper into the specific identity mechanisms that allow us to shape how tenants are authenticated, injecting tenant context into the requests that flow through all the backend services of your SaaS application. We'll see how this context ends up shaping and influencing how teams build and manage the multi-tenant features of their SaaS architecture.

Looking at all these foundational concepts together should give you a clearer view into just how essential it is to address these concepts up front. The goal is to expose you to the key strategies, patterns, and considerations without getting too close to the specifics of any one technology. Understanding these core concepts will equip you with the insights that will shape how you approach many of the multi-tenant topics we'll be covering in subsequent chapters.

Creating a Baseline Environment

To get started on this journey, I want to approach onboarding and identity as if we are starting from scratch. This should give you a better sense of how you might approach implementing these strategies from the ground up. That means we have to take a step back from the specifics of onboarding and identity and first think about what foundational pieces we have to put in place before we can start onboarding tenants. The services that support onboarding run inside of the control plane, so we need to start by putting in place all the bits that are needed to run all the control plane microservices that support onboarding and identity.

Creation of infrastructure, its dependent resources, and the control plane is what I refer to as creating a baseline environment. We essentially need to create the scripts and the automation that will allow us to spin up all of the constructs that are needed to host our SaaS environment. While our goal is to get onboarding and identity up and running, the scope of the baseline environment includes all the resources that would be one-time provisioned to set up our multi-tenant environment before we start onboarding. This means we'll be setting up some resources that go beyond the scope of tenant onboarding and identity. We won't focus on those other bits right now, but it's important to note that a baseline environment is inclusive of all of these concepts.

The actual creation of our baseline environment is achieved through a classic DevOps model, using infrastructure automation tooling to create, configure, and deploy all the assets that are required by our baseline environment. Figure 4-1 provides a highly conceptualized view of this experience.

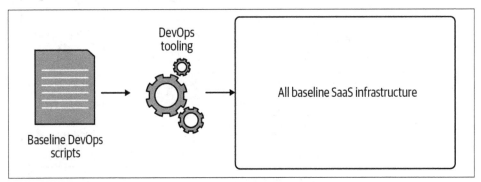

Figure 4-1. Automating creation of a baseline environment

The basic idea is that you'll pick the DevOps tool(s) that fits your environment and create a single, repeatable automation model that can configure everything you need to get your environment moved to a state where it can begin onboarding tenants.

Of course, what's actually in your baseline environment will vary wildly based on the nature of the specific technology stack you're using for your SaaS solution. A Kubernetes stack, for example, could look very different from a serverless stack. The nuances of different cloud providers would also influence the provisioning process. We'll look at more specific examples to see how they land, but for now we want to come up a level and just focus on what needs to get provisioned in this step to prepare our system to begin onboarding tenants.

Creating Your Baseline Environment

To get a better sense of what's in this baseline environment, let's look at a sample of what might get provisioned, configured, and deployed to bring your baseline environment to life. In Figure 4-2 you'll see that I've assembled a conceptual view of the components and infrastructure that might get created in a baseline environment. The goal was to represent some of the core baseline infrastructure concepts without getting too lost in the details of any specific technology.

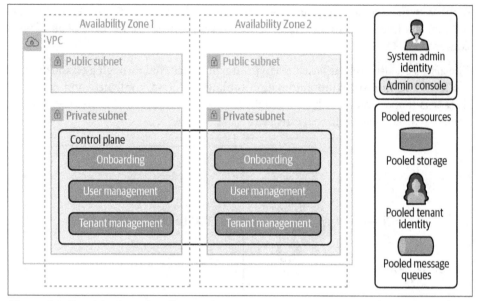

Figure 4-2. Provisioning a baseline environment

In the middle of Figure 4-2, you'll see that I've created the foundational networking infrastructure that's needed to host my multi-tenant SaaS environment. For this example, I've just grabbed some common AWS networking constructs (a VPC, Availability Zones, and some subnets) to represent the high availability network that will host my SaaS environment. These same networking constructs could be mapped to any number of different technologies. The key at this stage is just to focus on the fact that the configuration and setup of this baseline environment will require you to provision and configure all the core networking constructs that will be used by your control plane and, potentially, your tenants.

Within this network, I've also shown the deployment of the control plane. Since the control plane is shared by all tenants, it can be configured and deployed as part of the provisioning of your baseline environment. The control plane must also be in place for us to begin onboarding tenants and establishing their identity. Here, to simplify matters, I included a sampling of a few services. In reality the list of control plane services would include a much broader range. We'll see those services in more detail when we start digging into more concrete solutions.

On the bottom righthand side of Figure 4-2, you'll also see a collection of pooled resources. The items here represent the conceptual placeholders for any resources that might be shared by tenants. Generally, if you have pooled resources that will be shared by all tenants, you can provision them during the setup of your baseline environment (since they won't need to be created during the onboarding process). Storage often provides a good example here. Imagine having a pooled database for some microservice in your solution. If it's pooled, it could be created when the baseline environment is provisioned. You'll also see the setup of a shared identity construct and a pooled message queue. Again, these are just here to highlight the fact that you'll want to consider whether these should be provisioned during the setup of your baseline environment. I'll get into some of the trade-offs when we go deeper into the tenant onboarding experience later in this chapter.

Finally, on the top right, I've shown placeholders for the system admin identity and administration console. This represents the users that are logging into the specific tooling that you've created to support, update, configure, and generally manage the state of your multi-tenant architecture. I refer to this targeted tooling as your system admin console. It's this console that serves as the single plane of glass for your SaaS environment, providing your team with a purpose-built collection of features and capabilities that are essential to operating your multi-tenant environment; it will be used in combination with other off-the-shelf solutions that provide more generalized functionality. Even with these other tools, most SaaS teams require their own custom admin application that can address the specific multi-tenant needs of their environment.

Figure 4-3 provides a snapshot of a simple SaaS administration console application to help make this concept more concrete. It's through this application that you'll have access to all core information about your SaaS solution. You'll be able to monitor the status of onboarding tenants, activate/deactivate tenants, manage tenant policies, view tenant/tier metrics, and any other functionality that's needed to manage and operate your SaaS solution. This application must be configured and deployed as part of the setup of your baseline environment.

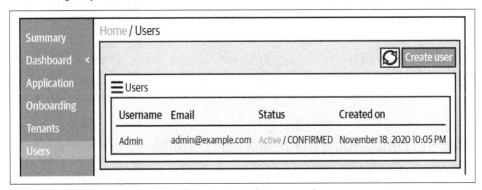

Figure 4-3. Creating and deploying a system admin console

It's worth noting that some teams tend to underinvest in their admin consoles, deferring to ready-made solutions in favor of building something themselves. Generally, this trade-off rarely seems worth it. While you might be able to use third-party solutions to compose a console experience, there are specific operations, insights, and configuration options that can only be addressed effectively through the creation of a targeted experience.

Creating and Managing System Admin Identities

As part of setting up your baseline environment and configuring your administration application, you'll see that your provisioning process must also set up your system admin identity model. Each time you trigger the creation of a baseline environment, you'll be required to provide the profile of the initial administrative user that will be able to log into your admin console. Creation of this identity is entirely separate from the creation of a tenant identity. This also means you'll need to have a completely separate authentication experience to allow these system admin users to access the admin console or any command-line tooling you might be using to manage your multi-tenant environment.

To support this system admin identity, you'll need to have some identity provider that owns and authenticates these users. The identity provider you use here could be the same identity provider that will be used for your tenant identities. Or, it could be a separate identity provider that is used as part of a more global enterprise administration strategy. Regardless of which identity provider you use, the basic mechanics of introducing a system admin identity are going to be very similar.

The key takeaway is that you'll need some steps on your baseline provisioning automation to create and configure your system administration identity model. This automation will include the creation and configuration of the identity provider along with the creation of the initial system admin users. Once that user is set up, you should be able to use this identity to access your system admin console. Once you're made it into the system admin console, you'll be able to manage and create more system admin users.

The example in Figure 4-3 happens to show a view of system admin user management. Here, I've accessed and authenticated into the console after provisioning my environment. I can now use this same page to create and manage other system admin users.

Triggering Onboarding from the Admin Console

Once you've established your system admin user and you have your admin console up and running, you have all the pieces in place to create and onboard tenants. Now, in the final version of your offering, your onboarding could be invoked as part of some self-service experience, or it could be driven by some internal process. Obviously, if this is an internally driven process, then you'll want to use your system admin console to manage onboarding. This would mean having some operation within your console that collects all the data needed for a new tenant before invoking the onboarding operation.

Some teams find lots of value in being able to onboard tenants from within the system admin console. Even if onboarding were to eventually be a self-service model, you could still have the ability to test and validate your onboarding experience from the admin console. This can be especially helpful to teams that are validating and testing the onboarding experience of your application.

Control Plane Provisioning Options

In Figure 4-2, I showed the control plane being deployed into the same baseline infrastructure where your tenants would also land. This is a perfectly valid option. However, it's worth noting that how and where this control plane is placed can vary based on the needs of your environment and the technology stack that's being used for your multi-tenant architecture. In Kubernetes, for example, I could have a separate namespace for the control plane, placing my tenant environments alongside the control plane within the same cluster and networking infrastructure. I could also choose to land the control plane in a completely separate infrastructure that is dedicated to the control plane.

Figure 4-4 provides a conceptual view of these two options. On the left, you'll see the shared control plane model where the control plane is deployed into the same environment with your tenant infrastructure. And, on the right, you'll see an approach where the control plane gets its own dedicated environment. Here the tenants are running in a completely separate network or cluster that draws a harder line between the control and application planes.

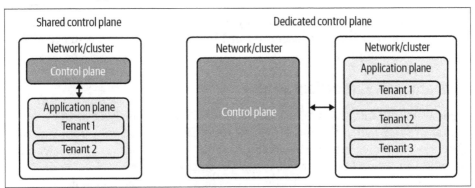

Figure 4-4. Picking a control plane deployment model

The trade-offs of these two choices are pretty straightforward. You might choose to have a dedicated control plane environment if you want to scale, manage, and operate these environments completely independently. Compliance could also factor in here; those requirements or your domain may be better addressed by placing stronger boundaries between your control and application panes. Of course, putting the control plane in the same environment with the application plane does simplify things a bit. It reduces the number of moving parts you have to manage, configure, and provision. It might also reduce your cost footprint. If you do opt for the dedicated model, you'll need to decide how you'll integrate these separate constructs to allow the control plane to interact with your application plane.

Your technology stack choices might also influence how you deploy your control plane. Some teams, for example, might opt for different technology stacks for the control and application planes. I might, for example, choose serverless for the control plane and containers for the application plane. This might steer you more toward a dedicated control plane model.

The Onboarding Experience

Now that our baseline environment is provisioned and configured, we can turn our attention to the onboarding of tenants. It's through onboarding that you'll find that you're establishing and exercising some of the most foundational elements of a multi-tenant architecture. In fact, when working with greenfield or migrating SaaS customers, I always suggest that they focus their initial attention on the onboarding process.

Starting here forces teams to answer many of the hard questions that will influence and shape the rest of their SaaS architecture. Onboarding isn't just about creating a tenant. It's about creating and configuring all the moving parts of your infrastructure that are needed to support that new tenant. In some cases, that might be a lightweight exercise and, in others, it might require a significant amount of code to orchestrate each step in the onboarding process. How your tenants are tiered, how they authenticate, how their policies are managed, how their isolation is configured, how they're routed—these are all areas that are touched by the onboarding experience of your multi-tenant environment.

Onboarding Is Part of Your Service

Many teams fall into the trap of viewing onboarding as something that gets bolted onto their system after it's built. They'll create placeholders and workarounds to simulate the onboarding experience with the idea that they can "make it real" later in the process. This comes back to the discussion of comparing a service to a product. In a SaaS environment, onboarding isn't viewed as some script or automation that's somehow outside of the scope of your offering. Instead, it is one of the most fundamental components of your SaaS experience and getting it right should be key to any team that is building a multi-tenant solution.

Onboarding sits right in the middle of both your business and technical priorities. The experience each customer has with onboarding can have a profound impact on the broader success of the business. How seamless, efficient, and reliable this process is will have a direct impact on the experience and perception of the customers consuming your product. It is your chance to make a positive first impression. The onboarding experience is also directly connected to the notion of time to value, which looks at how long it takes a customer to move from sign-up to actual productivity and value within your SaaS offering. Any added friction that shows up here is going to impact the impression you make as a service and could, potentially, influence your ability to move customers from adopters to promoters.

Onboarding is also where the deployment, identity, routing, and tiering strategies are put into action. How tenants are siloed and pooled, for example, will need to be expressed and realized directly through your onboarding experience. How and where you authenticate tenants will be configured and applied as part of onboarding. How your tenants are contextually routed based on their tier and deployment model will be configured within the scope of onboarding. So many of these key multi-tenant design choices that you make in your SaaS architecture are ultimately expressed and brought to life through the onboarding process of your system. In many respects, your onboarding configuration, automation, and deployment code will be at the epicenter of realizing the multi-tenant strategies that you adopt for your SaaS environment.

The amount of effort and code that goes into automating onboarding may come as a surprise to some teams. It's not uncommon for SaaS teams to underestimate the level of effort and investment that comes with building a robust onboarding experience. In reality, onboarding represents one of the most fundamental elements of a multi-tenant environment. It's through onboarding that you can achieve the operational and agility goals that are essential to a SaaS business.

Self-Service Versus Internal Onboarding

So far, this discussion of onboarding may seem like it's mostly describing mechanisms that are used by organizations that rely on a self-service tenant registration experience. Many of us have signed up for countless B2C SaaS offerings where we filled out some form, submitted our information, and started using some SaaS service. While this classic mode of onboarding is within our scope, we must also consider scenarios where our onboarding process may not support a self-service model. Imagine, for example, some B2B SaaS provider that only onboards after you've reached a deal and agreed to onboard them to your system. These SaaS vendors may only have some internally managed onboarding experience.

My point is that onboarding has no binding to a particular experience. You might have self-service onboarding or you might use internal onboarding. Every SaaS solution, regardless of how it presents its onboarding experience, must still lean into the same set of values. To me, the bar for self-service and internally managed onboarding processes is the same. Both of these approaches should be creating a fully automated, repeatable, low-friction onboarding process that focuses on maximizing a customer's time to value. Yes, someone in operations might run your internal process. This, however, does not mean that you'd expect less automation, scale, or durability from that onboarding process.

For any SaaS system that I build, I want to be sure that I'm treating this onboarding experience as a key part of my system. It is at the center of ensuring that I have a consistent, repeatable, automated onboarding mechanism that ensures that each new tenant will be introduced without requiring any manual processes or one-off configuration.

The Fundamental Parts of Onboarding

Now that you have a better sense of the onboarding importance, let's shift our focus more toward the details of the underlying components of an onboarding experience. While there are lots of details within the implementation of the onboarding process, my goal at this stage is to give you a top-level view of the core components of this process and outline the guiding principles that typically shape this experience.

Figure 4-5 provides a conceptual view of the moving parts of a multi-tenant onboarding experience.

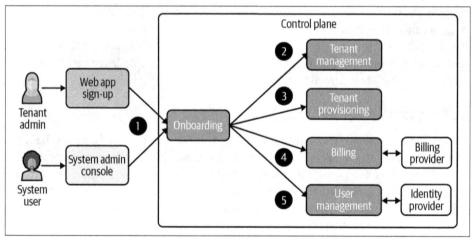

Figure 4-5. The fundamentals of tenant onboarding

On the left you'll see the illustration of the two common patterns that could be used to drive an onboarding process. First, I've shown a tenant administrator that is onboarding through some self-service sign-up process, presumably a web application that allows the tenant to submit their information, select a plan, and provide whatever configuration information is needed to establish themselves as a new tenant in the system. I've also shown a second onboarding flow that, in this example, is initiated by a system administrator. This represents some internal role at the SaaS provider using an administration console (or some other tooling) to enter the onboarding data for a new tenant and triggering the onboarding process. For this example, I included both of these onboarding paths. However, in most instances, a SaaS organization will support one of these two approaches. I only showed both here to drive home the idea that onboarding, regardless of its entry point, is meant to be a fully automated process for either of these two use cases.

For these onboarding paths, you'll see that they both send an onboarding request to the Onboarding service (step 1). For onboarding, I generally prefer to have a single onboarding service that can own all the orchestration of onboarding. This service owns the full lifecycle of the onboarding process, managing and ensuring that all steps in the process are completed successfully. This is especially important since some aspects of onboarding may run asynchronously or have dependencies on third-party integrations that could have availability issues.

The onboarding process then calls a series of distributed services that are used to create and configure the tenant's settings and supporting infrastructure. The sequencing of this onboarding flow can vary based on the nature of your SaaS application. Generally, the goal is to create and configure all of the required tenant assets before making the tenant active and/or notifying the tenant admin user that their account is active.

While there are multiple ways to implement this onboarding flow, you'll need to start with creating a tenant identifier. In our example, this tenant identifier will be created by sending a create tenant request to the Tenant Management service (step 2), passing in all the information about our tenant (company name, identity configuration, tier, and so on). It will also generate the unique identifier that will be associated with our tenant. Teams will often use a globally unique identifier (GUID) as the value for their tenant identifier, avoiding the inclusion of any attributes that might be connected to the name or other identifying information about the tenant. This prevents anyone from being able to connect a tenant with a given identifier. This tenant also is created with some notion of an "active" status that manages the current state of a tenant. In this case, where we're onboarding, the active state will initially be set to false. Once the system creates this tenant, you'll have a tenant identifier that can be used across the rest of the onboarding experience. I'll get into more detail about the Tenant Management service and its role within the control plane in Chapter 5.

The next step in our tenant onboarding example will involve the provisioning of any tenant resources that are required (step 3). This provisioning step can, for some multi-tenant architectures, represent one of the most significant pieces of your onboarding implementation. For a full stack silo deployment, for example, this could mean provisioning a completely new collection of infrastructure and application services. In contrast, a full stack pool environment might require minimal infrastructure provisioning and configuration.

As we dig into more working examples, you may be surprised to find out how much code and automation is devoted to this onboarding experience. In fact, this is often an area where SaaS systems blur the DevOps boundaries. While, in traditional environments, much of the DevOps lifecycle is focused on provisioning and updating your baseline infrastructure, SaaS environments may rely on the execution of DevOps code during the onboarding of each individual tenant. Your system may be provisioning and configuring new infrastructure at runtime to process the creation of a siloed tenant infrastructure. As you can imagine, this brings new considerations and mindsets to how you organize and build the overall DevOps footprint of your multi-tenant solution. For some, this represents a new mindset and new approaches to the tooling used to provision tenant environments.

At this stage, we have a tenant created and our tenant resources are provisioned. Now we can add this new tenant to the billing system (step 4). This is essentially where you'll provide information to the billing system that identifies the new tenant and any information that's needed to characterize the billing model that should be applied to this particular tenant. The assumption here is that, in advance of onboarding a new tenant, you've configured and set up the different tiers or billing plans that determine the overall pricing model of your solution. Then, during onboarding, your Billing service will correlate the tenant's onboarding profile with the appropriate (pre-configured) billing plan.

You'll notice that Figure 4-5 calls out a separate billing provider. The idea is that your Billing service will manage and orchestrate any integration you might have with your billing system. In many instances, this billing provider may be supported by a third-party system. It's in these cases where you may see value in putting a separate Billing service between your onboarding process and the billing provider, allowing you to manage any unique considerations that might be required to support a given billing provider. In other instances, you might directly integrate with the billing provider from your Onboarding service. It's also worth noting that some SaaS companies will use an internal billing system. Even in this scenario, you'd still want your onboarding process to follow a similar pattern of integration. There's lots more about billing to consider (outside the scope of onboarding). I'll get more into those details in Chapter 14.

For the final piece of the onboarding experience, we need to create the tenant admin user (step 5). If you recall, the tenant admin role represents the first user that is created for a given tenant. This tenant will have the ability to create any additional users that will be able to access the system. At this stage, though, our main goal is to create this initial user within our identity provider to enable our tenant to authenticate and access their provisioned environment. Here, you'll need to rely on the features of your identity provider to orchestrate the notification and validation of this new tenant. Most identity providers will support the generation of an email message that includes a URL and temporary password for accessing the system. This process then triggers the authenticating user to enter a new password as part of the login flow. The goal is to push much of the automation of this sign-up process to your identity provider. Rely on these providers to send email invites and temporary passwords and handle password resets.

There is one last bit to this onboarding flow that you'll need to consider. Earlier, when the tenant was created (step 2), I set the active status of the tenant to false. It's the job of your Onboarding service to track the state of all of these different onboarding states. Only after it determines that each process has completed successfully will it set the tenant's active status to true. This may include process retries and other fallback strategies to address any failure that may have happened during the provisioning and configuration of the tenant environment. Assuming the onboarding succeeds, the Onboarding service can now call the Tenant Management service and update the active status to true. This is especially important to the administration console of your SaaS environment, which provides the functionality that is used to view and manage the state of tenants. During this onboarding process, the view of tenants should show the state of any tenant that is being onboarded and highlight the active status of your tenants.

Tracking and Surfacing Onboarding States

From looking at this process, it should be clear that your onboarding process includes lots of moving parts and dependencies. The more complex this process becomes, the more important it is to have useful, detailed operational insights into the various states of your onboarding flow. This is essential to analyzing progress, identifying issues, and profiling the overall behavior and trends of your onboarding automation. It also means identifying the right design and tooling to effectively capture and surface the onboarding profile of your solution.

At a minimum, you could imagine having a distinct set of states mapped to each of the steps in our onboarding flow. So, you might have separate states for TENANT _CREATED, TENANT_PROVISIONED, BILLING_INITIALIZED, USER_CREATED, and TENANT _ACTIVATED. Each of these states could be surfaced through the tenant view in your administration console, allowing you to inspect the onboarding of any tenant at a given moment in time.

The real value of assigning and surfacing onboarding states is to provide richer operational insights into the status of your onboarding progress. This will be essential to troubleshooting any unexpected onboarding issues. Knowing precisely where your onboarding process is failing is of prime importance to your operational teams. This is especially important when your onboarding process includes a significant amount of infrastructure provisioning and configuration. In these cases, you might track more granular states that give you insights into the various stages that are within the moving parts of your provisioning process.

Tier-Based Onboarding

As part of looking at the onboarding flow, I outlined the role of the Provisioning service and its role in creating and configuring tenant environments. This provisioning process gets a bit more interesting when you consider how different tenant tiers could influence how you implement your provisioning lifecycle. If you recall, we use tiers to present different tenant profiles with different experiences. These different experiences often translate into a need for separate infrastructure and configurations based on the tier of your system.

To better understand this, let's look at a conceptual example of a tier-based onboarding example. Figure 4-6 provides a view of an environment that supports two separate tiers (basic and premium).

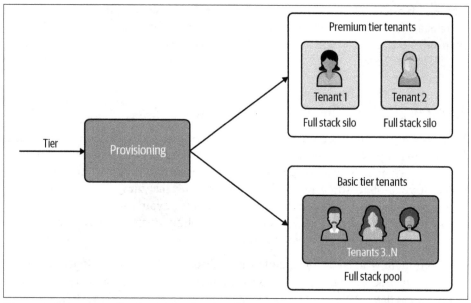

Figure 4-6. An example of tier-based onboarding

I've narrowed the view down to focus exclusively on the Provisioning service within our control plane. Whenever the Onboarding service triggers this Provisioning service, it provides the tenant contextual information that includes the tier that will be associated with the new tenant. When the Provisioning service receives this request, it will evaluate the tier and determine how the selected tier will influence the configuration and infrastructure that will be needed to support your tenant environment. In this example, our SaaS solution offers premium tier tenants a full stack silo deployment mode with fully dedicated resources for each tenant. This means each onboarding event will need to automate the provisioning of these full tenant stacks. Basic tier tenants, however, are onboarded into a full stack pool model where all the infrastructure is shared by tenants. Here, the onboarding will be a lighter weight experience, simply augmenting the configuration to add support for this new tenant.

These full stack deployment models have pretty distinct onboarding experiences that are relatively easy to digest. Where this gets more interesting is when you have a mixed deployment model. With a mixed mode deployment, your resources are siloed and pooled with finer granularity. This means that your onboarding process will need to apply the tier-based onboarding policies to each resource based on its silo or pool configuration. Figure 4-7 provides an example of how mixed mode deployment influences your provisioning process.

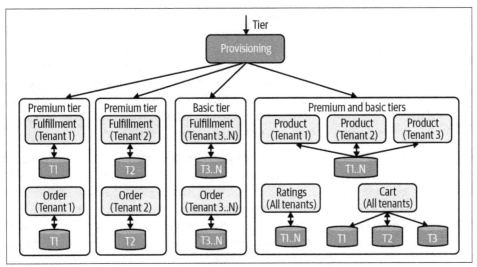

Figure 4-7. Tier-based onboarding with mixed mode deployments

I've intentionally made this architecture a bit busy. Our same Provisioning service is shown here, but now it has much more to consider as each tenant onboards. Let's start on the left of Figure 4-7 where you'll see that I have two services that are deployed separately for Tenant 1 and Tenant 2. So, for every premium tier tenant, your Provisioning service will need to configure and deploy Fulfillment and Order services in a fully siloed model. The storage and compute of these two microservices are fully siloed.

Now, even though these two microservices are deployed separately for premium tier tenants, these same services are also consumed by your Basic tier tenants. This is represented in the middle of the diagram where I've identified pooled versions of the Fulfillment and Order microservices that are shared by all non-premium tier tenants (in this case, Tenants 3..N). This means the Provisioning service must perform a one-time configuration and deployment of these services to support the pooled tenants. Once these services are up and running, the job of the Provisioning service for each new tenant will require fewer moving parts. You may need to configure routing or set up some policies, but most of the heavy lifting will be done after the initial provisioning and deployment of these services.

Finally, on the righthand side of the environment in Figure 4-7, you'll see a range of services that are deployed in varying models to support the needs of both premium and basic tier tenants. The silo and pool choices that you make here are driven more by the universal needs of your multi-tenant architecture (instead of tiers). The idea is that you're selecting silo and pool options based on a set of global needs (noisy neighbor, compliance, and so on).

In this example, I've intentionally created some variation in these services to highlight the use cases you may need to support as part of tenant onboarding. The Product microservice, for example, uses siloed compute for all tenants; that's why you see a separate instance of the service for Tenants 1–3. However, you'll also see that this same service uses pooled storage. This adds a new wrinkle to the onboarding story. Now, your Provisioning service must handle this variation, provisioning the storage a single time for all tenants while still provisioning and deploying separate instances of the Product microservice as each tenant is onboarded.

The other services (Ratings and Cart) are just here to highlight additional patterns you could see when implementing your Provisioning service. Ratings is entirely pooled for compute and storage, while the Cart microservice has pooled compute and siloed storage. Supporting onboarding for these services is about knowing what's siloed and what's pooled and contextually triggering the creation and configuration of these resources. This mirrors the discussion we had (in Chapter 3) around mixed mode deployment. However, here we're looking at how that mixed mode can influence the onboarding experience of your multi-tenant environment.

One key question often comes up around the general timing of provisioning pooled resources during the onboarding process. Since these resources are configured and deployed once, many may prefer to pre-provision these resources as part of the initial setup of your entire multi-tenant environment. So, if you're setting up a brand-new baseline environment, you could choose to provision all the pooled resources at this time. To me, this seems like the more natural approach. This could mean that your Provisioning service would support a separate path that is invoked by your DevOps tooling to perform the one-time creation of these resources. Then, as each new tenant onboards, this shared infrastructure would already be in place.

The other option could be to delay the creation of these pooled resources and trigger their creation during the onboarding of your first tenant (almost like the Lazy loading pattern). While this could slow your onboarding process, the overhead of this process would only be absorbed by your first tenant. My general bias is to pre-provision these resources. However, there could be other factors that steer you toward either one of these strategies.

While it can be interesting and powerful to support these different tier-based deployment models, it's also essential to consider how your onboarding complexity might impact the complexity of our overall SaaS environment. Yes, you want to give the business lots of tools to be able to support different tenant profiles. At the same time, you don't want to over-rotate here. Also, it is important to emphasize that this is still a tier level of customization. You should never view this mechanism as a way to support any notion of one-off customization for individual tenants.

Tracking Onboarded Resources

If your onboarding process needs to provision dedicated tenant resources, then you'll also have to consider how your multi-tenant environment will track and identify these resources. What you'll find here is that other aspects of your system will end up needing to locate and target these tenant-specific resources.

To really understand what I'm getting at, let's consider a more concrete example. Imagine you've onboarded a tenant in the mixed model deployment model in Figure 4-7. This model includes plenty of examples of siloed and pooled resources. Now, imagine you just onboarded a premium tier tenant into this environment and created the individual resources that were needed to support that tenant.

Once onboarding is done and our tenant is up and running, you'll still be deploying updates to this environment. Patches, new features, and other changes will certainly need to get deployed through the lifecycle of your application. This is where things get a bit interesting. With the mixed mode deployment we have here, we can't simply deploy to one static location to update our system. Imagine, for example, rolling out a new version of the Order service. To get the new code deployed, your DevOps experience will need to find the separate deployments of the Order service that span all the different resources that were provisioned by the onboarding experience. Here, that would mean deploying the Order service to the Tenant 1 and Tenant 2 premium tier silos and to the basic tier pooled instance that is shared by the other tenants.

So, that begs the question: how would your deployment process know how to handle this? How would it know which resources are siloed for each tenant? The only way for this to work is to have your onboarding experience capture and record the location and identity of these per-tenant resources. While the need for this tracking information is clear, there's no clear or standard strategy that is commonly applied to address this. Some place the data in a table as new tenants are onboarded and reference this table during their deployment process. Others might use pieces of their DevOps tool chain to address this challenge. The main takeaway is that if your onboarding process provisions dedicated tenant resources, you'll need to capture and record the information about these resources so they can be referenced by other parts of your deployment and operational experience. You'll see more concrete examples of this when we start looking at orchestrating onboarding in EKS (Chapter 10) and ser-verless (Chapter 11) examples.

Handling Onboarding Failures

Any failure in the onboarding process can represent a significant issue for SaaS pro-viders. However, these failures take on added importance in any multi-tenant envi-ronment that has a self-service onboarding experience. Onboarding represents the first impression you're making with a tenant and any failure in this process could translate into lost business.

While some of your reliability here will be extracted from applying solid engineering practices, there are also areas within onboarding where your dependencies on exter-nal systems can impact the durability of your onboarding process. To get a better sense of the options, let's look at a specific example of a potential external dependency that could be part of your onboarding experience. Figure 4-8 provides a conceptual view of the billing integration that could be part of your onboarding flow.

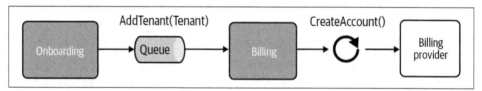

Figure 4-8. Fault-tolerant integration with a billing provider

In this example, let's presume you are reliant on an integration with a third-party bill-ing provider. By including a third-party billing solution in your onboarding (which is common), you've made the reliability of your onboarding experience directly depen-dent on the availability of the billing provider. If the billing system is down, so is your tenant onboarding.

Now, you might just presume that this is just the risk associated with using third-party solutions. However, in this scenario, your system may very likely be able to con-tinue to operate—even when the billing system is down. While it's true that you need to get the billing account created, your system could still finish its onboarding process and complete the billing configuration when the system is back online.

In Figure 4-8, I've highlighted a potential approach to this problem: making the bill-ing integration completely asynchronous. In this model, your onboarding process would request the addition of a new tenant through a queue. The Billing service then picks up the request and attempts to create an account in the billing system using an asynchronous request. If this request fails, the Billing service will capture the failure and schedule a retry. There are lots of different strategies for implementing a fault-tolerant integration. Don't get lost in the details. The key takeaway is that I've created an integration model with the billing provider that enables my onboarding flow to continue without waiting for the creation of the billing account. For some, it may simply be preferable to have this always be an asynchronous integration purely for the benefit of expediting the onboarding experience.

I've focused on billing just because it provides a natural illustration of the importance of having a fault-tolerant onboarding experience. In reality, you should look at all the moving parts of your onboarding automation and look for points of failure or bottlenecks that might require new strategies that can expedite or add durability to your onboarding process. The cost of a failed onboarding is generally high and you want to do whatever you can to make this mechanism as robust as possible.

Testing Your Onboarding Experience

At this point, the role and importance of onboarding should be clear. The potential complexity and the number of moving parts in this process can make it particularly prone to errors. With this in mind, it should also be clear that you'll want to take extra measures to validate the efficiency and repeatability of your onboarding process. Too many teams build an onboarding process and simply rely on the activity of customers to uncover any bottlenecks or design flaws that might be impacting their onboarding experience. To get around this, I always suggest that teams invest in building a rich collection of onboarding tests that can be used to exercise and push on all the dimensions of the onboarding experience.

There's a range of potential test types you might consider here. You might, for example, create load tests for onboarding that simulate different onboarding workloads. Or, you might create tests that validate your ability to recover from failures. Some teams will introduce performance tests that measure the time it takes to onboard tenants. Each of these tests could be executed with a mix of different tenant tiers where a tenant's tier might exercise different paths of your onboarding experience.

The goal is to ensure that the design, architecture, and automation assumptions of your onboarding experience are being fully realized in your working solution. That means pushing scale by simulating a full range of use cases that will push your onboarding design and implementation. It will also allow you to verify that your environment is correctly surfacing any key metrics that are used to measure your ability to meet any SLAs you've defined. The emphasis here is not just on ensuring that the happy path works—it's about ensuring that onboarding meets the scale and availability requirements and delivers the service experience that meets the expectations of your customers.

Creating a SaaS Identity

So far, I've touched briefly on the role of identity as part of the onboarding process. However, there are lots of pieces to the identity puzzle that need exploring. Yes, onboarding sets up identity, but what does that mean? How does identity get configured, and how does multi-tenancy affect the overall experience of our SaaS environment? Here, we'll dig more deeply into how tenancy shapes the authentication, authorization, and general multi-tenant footprint of a SaaS environment.

With multi-tenant identity, you'll have to go beyond thinking about identity purely as a tool for authenticating users. You must broaden your view of identity to include the idea that each authenticated user must always be authenticated in the context of a tenant. It's true that users are connected to this experience, but much of the underlying implementation of your multi-tenant architecture is primarily focused on the tenant associated with that user. So, this means our identity model must be expanded to cover both users and tenants. The basic goal is to create a tighter binding between users and tenants that allows them to be accessed, shared, and managed as a single unit.

In Figure 4-9 you'll see a conceptual view of how a SaaS identity is composed. On the left, I have the classic view of what I've labeled as a user identity. This identity is focused squarely on describing and capturing the attributes of an individual. Names, phone number, email—these are all typical descriptors that would be used to characterize the user of a system. On the righthand side, however, I have also introduced the idea of a tenant identity. A tenant is more of an entity than an individual. A company, for example, subscribes to your SaaS service as a tenant, and that tenant often has many users.

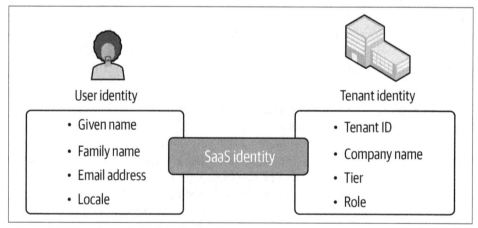

Figure 4-9. Creating a logical SaaS identity

For multi-tenant environments, these two distinct notions of identity are joined together to create what I refer to as a SaaS identity. This SaaS identity must be introduced in a way that allows it to become a first-class identity construct that is passed through all the layers of your system. It becomes the vehicle for conveying your tenant context to all the parts of your system that need access to these user and tenant attributes. This SaaS identity maps directly to the tenant context concept that I described in Chapter 1.

The key is that this SaaS identity needs to be introduced without somehow impacting or complicating the traditional authentication experience. Your SaaS authentication experience must retain the freedom to follow a classic authentication flow while still enabling the merging of the user and tenant identities. Figure 4-10 provides a view of this concept in action.

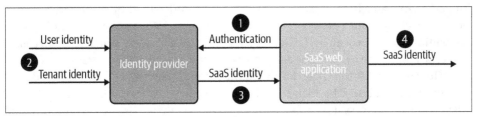

Figure 4-10. SaaS identity authentication flow

In the flow you see here, a tenant user attempts to access a SaaS web application (step 1). The application detects that the user is not authenticated and redirects them to an identity provider that has awareness of both the user and tenant identities (step 2). When the user is authenticated, the identity provider will own responsibility for returning the SaaS identity (step 3). Then, this SaaS identity is passed downstream to all the rest of the moving parts of our system (step 4). This identity includes all of the tenant and user attributes that are needed to support the needs of the remaining elements of your SaaS application.

While this flow might vary based on the nature of your identity technology, the spirit of this experience should remain similar across different identity models. It also might be influenced by how tenants flow into your system and get routed to an identity provider. Subdomains, email addresses, or lookup tables, for example, could shape how you resolve a tenant's path to the corresponding identity provider. In the end, your goal is to resolve and create this SaaS identity at the front of this process and avoid pushing this responsibility further into the details of your design and implementation.

Attaching a Tenant Identity

At this stage, I've talked about joining user and tenant identities. While this may make sense conceptually, we still haven't talked about how you can combine these two concepts into a true, first-class SaaS identity construct. Naturally, how you do this will vary from one identity provider to the next.

For this discussion, I'm going to focus on how the Open Authorization (OAuth) and OpenID Connect (OIDC) specifications can be used to create and configure a SaaS identity. These specifications are used widely by a number of modern identity providers, serving as an open standard for decentralized authentication and authorization. As such, you should find that the techniques I've covered here should have some natural mapping to your application's identity model.

To get tenants attached to users, we first need to understand how the OIDC specification packages and conveys a user's authentication information. Generally, when authenticating against an OIDC-compliant identity provider, you'll find that each authentication returns identity and access tokens. These are represented as JSON Web Tokens (JWTs) that hold all the authentication context to be used for downstream authorization. The identity token is meant to convey information about a user, while the access token is used to authorize that user's access to different resources.

Within these JWTs, you'll find a set of properties and values that provide more detailed information about a user. This data is referred to as claims. There is a default set of claims that are generally included with each token to ensure a standardized representation of common attributes. It's these JWTs that become the universal currency of our multi-tenant identity model.

The good news with JWTs is that they allow for the introduction of custom claims. These custom claims are essentially the equivalent of user-defined fields that can be used to attach your own property/value pairs to JWTs. This creates the opportunity for you to attach tenant contextual data to these tokens. Figure 4-11 provides an illustration of how these custom tenant claims would get added to your JWTs.

On the left is a sample JWT populated with the example claims that are part of the OIDC specification. I won't go through all of these, but it is worth calling out the specific user attributes that show up here. You'll see that `name`, `given_name`, `family_name`, `gender`, `birthdate`, and `email` are all in this list. On the right, however, are the attributes of our tenant that need to be merged into the JWT. These simply get added as property/value pairs to standardized representation.

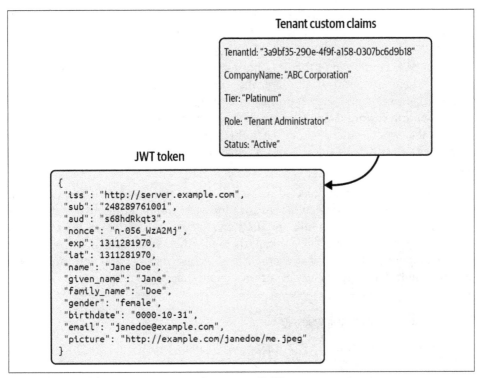

Figure 4-11. Adding tenant custom claims to a JWT

While there's nothing magical or elegant about this model, being able to introduce these custom claims as first-class citizens provides a significant upside. Imagine how having these attributes embedded as claims ends up shaping your multi-tenant authentication and authorization experience. Figure 4-12 highlights how this seemingly simple construct ends up having a cascading impact across your multi-tenant architecture.

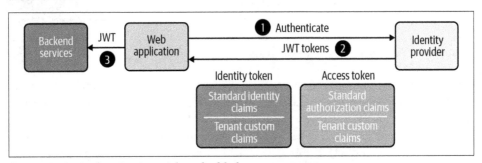

Figure 4-12. Authenticating with embedded tenant context

In this example, the flow starts at the web application. The user hits this page and is not authenticated, which sends them off to the identity provider for authentication (step 1). This represents a very familiar and vanilla flow that you've likely built multiple times. What's different is that the data comes back from this authentication experience. When you authenticate here, the identity provider is going to return its standard tokens (step 2). However, because I've configured the identity provider with tenant-specific custom claims, the tokens that are returned now align with the SaaS identity that was discussed earlier. The tokens participate and behave like any other token, but are enriched with the added tenant context that we need to create a SaaS identity.

Now, these tokens can be injected as bearer tokens and sent downstream to your backend services, inheriting all the security, lifecycle, and other mechanisms that are built into the OIDC and OAuth specifications (step 3). This strategy is particularly powerful when you look at how it impacts the broader experience of your backend services. Figure 4-13 provides an example of how these tokens could flow through the different multi-tenant microservices of your application.

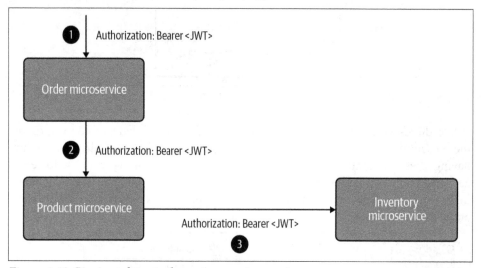

Figure 4-13. Passing tokens to downstream microservices

I have three different microservices, each of which requires access to tenant context. When you authenticate and receive a tenant-aware token, this token is passed into whichever microservice you're initially calling. In this case, the call comes into the Order microservice (step 1). Then, imagine that this service needs to invoke another backend service (Product) to complete its task. It can then pass this same token along to the Product service (step 2). This pattern can then continue to cascade through additional downstream service invocations (step 3). In this example, I've assumed I can insert the JWT into an HTTP request as a bearer token. However, even if you're using another protocol here, there are likely ways you can inject this JWT as part of your context.

You can imagine how this very simple mechanism ends up having a rather profound impact on your overall multi-tenant architecture. This single JWT will touch so many of the moving parts within the implementation of your multi-tenant environment. Microservices will use it for logging, metrics, billing, tenant isolation, data partitioning, and a host of other areas. Your broader SaaS architecture will use it for tiering, throttling, routing, and other global mechanisms that require tenant context. So, yes, it's a simple concept, but the importance of its role within your SaaS architecture cannot be understated.

Populating Custom Claims During Onboarding

We've now seen how custom claims give us a way to connect users to tenants. What may be less clear is how and when these claims are actually introduced. There are two pretty straightforward steps associated with adding and populating these custom claims. First, before you onboard any tenant, you'll typically need to configure your identity provider, identifying each of the custom attributes that you'd like to have added to your authentication experience. Here, you'll define each property and type that you'll want to end up in your custom claims. This prepares your identity provider to accept new tenants that can store and configure their tenants with the additional attributes.

The second half of this process is executed during onboarding. Earlier, I discussed the creation of the tenant administration user as part of the overall onboarding flow. However, what I didn't mention was the population of the custom claims for your newly created tenant. As you're adding the information about your user (name, email, etc.), you'll also populate all the tenant context fields for that user (tenant ID, role, tier). This data must be populated for each user within the identity provider, so even after onboarding has been completed, the introduction of additional users must include the population of these custom attributes.

Using Custom Claims Judiciously

Custom claims are a useful construct for attaching tenant context to your tokens. In some cases, teams will get attached to this mechanism and expand its role, using it to capture and convey application security context. While there are no hard and fast rules here, I generally assume that if something is a custom claim, it's playing an essential role in shaping tenant context and influencing your global authorization story.

Many applications rely on access control constructs to enable or disable access to specific application functionality. These controls should be managed outside the scope of your identity provider. Generally, I'd view it as a mistake to bloat your tokens with custom claims that are part of your traditional application access control strategy. Instead, these kinds of controls should be implemented with any one of the language or technology stack mechanisms built exclusively for this purpose.

There may be times where it's unclear whether an attribute belongs in a custom claim or your application access control model. To me, this is often resolved based on the lifecycle and role of the attribute. If the attribute tends to be evolving with the introduction of application features, functions, and capabilities, then it should be managed more through application access controls. Generally, attributes that land in your custom claims are unlikely to be changing as your application changes. The content of your tokens, for example, should not be shifting on a weekly basis based on the addition of new application features or configuration options.

No Centralized Services for Resolving Tenant Context

Some teams try to draw a harder line between tenant identity and user identity. In these environments, the identity provider is only used to authenticate users. Here, when a user is authenticated, the tokens returned from this process do not include any tenant contextual information. In this model, these systems must rely on some downstream mechanisms to resolve tenancy. Figure 4-14 provides an example of how this might be implemented.

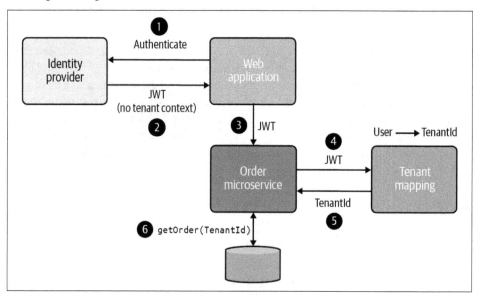

Figure 4-14. Using a separate user/tenant mapping service

In this example, the web application authenticates against an identity provider that has no awareness of tenant context (step 1). A successful authentication here will still return the JWTs we discussed. However, these tokens will not include any of the tenant-specific custom claims that were outlined earlier (step 2). Instead, the only data here is user data. This token is then passed along to the Order microservice (step 3). Now, when this order service needs to access data for a specific tenant, it needs to identify which tenant is associated with the current request. Since the JWT doesn't include this information, your code would need to acquire the context from another service (step 4). In this example, I've introduced a Tenant Mapping service that takes the JWT, extracts the user information, resolves the user to a tenant, and returns the tenant identifier (step 5). This identifier is then used to get an order for this specific tenant (step 6).

On the surface this may seem like a perfectly valid strategy. However, it actually presents real challenges for many SaaS environments. The lesser of the issues here is that it creates a hard separation between the user and the tenant, requiring teams to manage the coupled state of the user and the tenant independently. The bigger issue, though, is that every service in the system must go through this centralized mapping mechanism to resolve tenant context. Imagine this step being performed across hundreds of services and thousands of requests. Many who adopt this approach quickly discover that this Tenant Mapping service ends up creating a significant bottleneck in their system, which then leads teams down a path of trying to optimize a service that is actually providing no business value.

This is another reason why it's so essential that the user and tenant contexts are bound together and shared universally across the entire surface of your multi-tenant architecture. As a rule of thumb, my goal is to never have a service need to invoke some external mechanism to resolve and acquire tenant context. You want to have most everything you need to know about the tenant shared through the JWT that includes your SaaS identity information. Yes, there may be exceptions, but this should be the general mindset you take when thinking about how you're mapping users to tenants.

Federated SaaS Identity

Most of what I've described so far assumes that your SaaS system will be able to run with a single identity provider that is under your control. While this represents the ideal scenario and maximizes your options, it's also not practical to assume that every SaaS solution is built with this model. Some SaaS providers face business, domain, or customer needs that require them to support a customer or third-party hosted identity provider.

One common case I've seen is a scenario where a SaaS customer has some enterprise dependency on an existing, internal identity provider. Some of these customers may, as a condition of their purchase, require a SaaS provider to support authentication from these internal identity providers. These cases often come down to weighing the value of acquiring this customer against adding complexity to your environment that could impact the agility and operational efficiency of your overall SaaS experience. Still, when the right opportunity presents itself, the business parameters can push teams toward strategies that allow them to support this model.

Typically, this is achieved through some added level of tenant configuration where your tenant onboarding will add additional support for configuring this externally hosted identity provider. The goal would be to make this as seamless as possible, limiting the introduction of any invasive or one-off code that would include tenant-centric customization. The other challenge is that, in some cases, you'll need to provide side-by-side support for the external and internal identity providers. The reality is that most of your customers are likely to expect your solution to include built-in identity support. Figure 4-15 provides a view of the moving parts of this identity pattern.

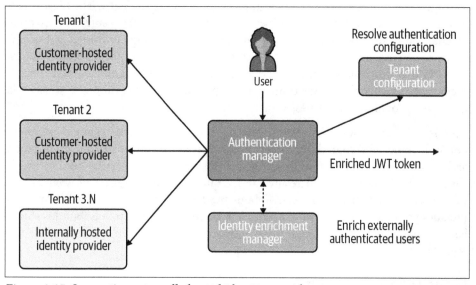

Figure 4-15. Supporting externally hosted identity providers

At the center of this example, you'll see that I have an authentication manager. This is a conceptual placeholder for introducing some service into your authentication flow that can support a more distributed set of identity providers. To make this work, your system will need to always determine how an identity provider is hosted. Each time a user needs to authenticate, you'll need to examine that user and retrieve the identity configuration, which will include data that describes the location and configuration of a given tenant.

On the lefthand side of Figure 4-15, I've included a mix of internally and externally hosted identity providers that need to be supported by a single SaaS experience. Two tenants are using their own identity provider. The remaining tenants are using your internally hosted identity provider.

This model seems pretty straightforward. However, the twist is that your system has no control over these external identity providers. As such, you can't configure the claims of these providers or have your onboarding process add additional tenant context to the identity data that's managed by these providers. This means that the JWTs returned from your authentication requests will not include any of the tenant context that is essential to your multi-tenant environment. To resolve this, your solution will need to introduce new functionality that can enrich the tokens returned from these external identity providers, assuming responsibility for enriching these tokens with tenant context that is managed within your SaaS environment. This allows all downstream services to continue to rely on tenant-aware JWT tokens regardless of which identity provider was used to authenticate your user. How these tokens are enriched will depend on the nature of our solution. There are strategies that will provide hooks that allow you to dynamically inject the added tenant context. In other instances, you may need a more custom solution. Generally, though, the federation models of the identity space often offer you different techniques to deal with this use case.

I've included this model because it represents an inevitable pattern that appears in the wild. It's worth noting that there are clear downsides to this approach. Any time you have to insert yourself into the authentication flow, you are taking on an added role within the security footprint of your multi-tenant architecture. You may also be required to address scale and single point of failure requirements that come with sitting in the authentication flow. So, while this may be necessary, it comes with real baggage that you'll want to consider carefully.

Tenant Grouping/Mapping Constructs

While identity providers often conform to well established specifications (OIDC, OAuth2), the constructs that are used to organize and manage identities can vary from one identity provider to the next. These providers offer a range of different constructs to group and organize users. This is especially important in multi-tenant environments where you may want to group all the users that belong to a tenant together. These group constructs can have implications that will influence how you land tenants within your identity provider. In some cases, you might also be able to use these groups to apply tiering policies to tenants to shape their authentication and authorization experience.

If we look at Amazon Cognito, for example, you'll see that it offers multiple ways to organize tenants. Cognito introduces the idea of a User Pool. These User Pools are used to hold a collection of users, and they can be individually configured, allowing pools to offer separate authentication experiences. This might lead to a User Pool per tenant model where each tenant would be given its own pool. The alternative would be to put all tenants in a single User Pool and use other mechanisms (groups, for example) to associate users with tenants. You'd also want to consider how any limits from your identity provider might factor into choosing a strategy.

There are trade-offs you'll want to consider as you pick between these different identity constructs. The number of tenants you have, for example, might make it impractical to have separate User Pools for every tenant. Or you may not need much variation between tenants and prefer to have all tenants configured and managed collectively. You might also be thinking about how the choices you make here could impact the authentication flow of your SaaS solution. If you have separate User Pools for each tenant, you need to think about how to map tenants to their designated pools during the authentication process. This may add a level of indirection that you may not want to absorb as part of your solution.

Scale, identity requirements, and a host of other considerations are going to shape how you choose to map tenants to whichever constructs are supported by your identity provider. The key is that as you start to lay out your SaaS identity strategy, you'll want to identify the different units of organization that can be used to group your tenants and determine how those will shape the scale, authentication, and configuration of your multi-tenant authentication experience.

With different organizational constructs also come different identity configuration options. Identity providers generally provide a range of options that can be used to configure your authentication experience. Multi-factor authentication (MFA), for example, is offered as an identity feature that can be enabled or disabled. You can also configure password formatting requirements and expiration policies.

The settings for these different configuration options do not have to be globally applied to all of your tenants. You may want to make different identity features available to different tenant tiers. Maybe you'll only make MFA available to your premium tier tenants, or you might decide to surface these configuration options within the tenant administration experience of your SaaS application and allow each tenant to configure these different identity settings. This can be a differentiating feature that can add value for your tenants and allow them to create the identity experience that best fits the needs of their business.

How or if you can offer this identity customization will depend on how your specific identity provider organizes and surfaces these options. Some providers will allow you to configure this separately for individual tenants, and others will only allow this to be configured globally. You'll need to dig into the constructs of your specific identity provider to figure out whether you can associate these identity policies with individual tenants.

Sharing User IDs Across Tenants

Each user of your SaaS system has some user ID that identifies that user to a tenant. This user identifier is often represented by an email address. In many cases, a single user will be associated with a single SaaS tenant. However, there are times when SaaS providers have interest in associating a single email address with many tenants. This, of course, adds a level of indirection to your authentication. Somewhere in your login flow, your SaaS system will need to determine which tenant you're accessing.

While I've seen requests for supporting this mode, I have yet to uncover any out-of-the-box strategy for handling this use case. That being said, there are some patterns that I have seen applied here. The most brute force way I've seen is one that pushes the tenant resolution to the end user; during sign-in, the system will detect that a user belongs to multiple tenants and will prompt the user to select a target tenant. This is anything but elegant and it does create an information leak in that anyone can use an email address to see which tenants you belong to (if and only if you belong to more than one). In the model, you'd have a mapping table that connected users to tenants and you would use this as a lookup in advance of starting the authentication flow.

A cleaner approach to this would be to rely on an authentication experience that supplied context more explicitly. The best example is probably domains and subdomains. If each of your tenants is assigned a subdomain (*tenant1.saasprovider.com*), your authentication process can use this subdomain to acquire the tenant context. Then the system would authenticate you against the specified tenant. This would allow the user to authenticate without any intermediate process to identify the target tenant.

There are other complications in this scenario. Imagine, for example, all of your users are running in a shared identity provider construct. In that mode, the identity provider is going to require each user to be unique. This would make it impossible to support having a single user ID associated with multiple tenants. Instead, you may want to consider relying on a more granular construct to hold each tenant's data (like the User Pool mentioned earlier).

Tenant Authentication Is Not Tenant Isolation

As part of this discussion of authentication and JWTs, I sometimes find that teams will equate authentication to tenant isolation. The assumption here is that authentication is the barrier to entry for tenants and that, once you've made it beyond that challenge, you have met the criteria for tenant isolation in multi-tenant environments.

This is definitely an area of disconnect. Yes, authentication starts the isolation story by issuing a JWT with tenant context. However, the code in your microservices can still include implementation that—even when working on behalf of an authenticated user—can access the resources of another tenant. Tenant isolation builds upon the tenant context that you get from an authenticated user, implementing a completely separate layer of controls and measures to ensure that your code is not allowed to cross a tenant boundary. You'll get a deeper look at these strategies in Chapter 9.

Conclusion

This chapter was all about describing the foundational elements that represent the starting point for creating a multi-tenant architecture. My focus was on introducing the core constructs that are used to inject the notion of tenancy into your architecture. You'll notice that nothing about these first steps includes any effort to define the application experience. Instead, it's putting tenancy front and center in your architecture. Putting these fundamental pieces in place early will require your team to design, build, test, and operate in a multi-tenant context across all the stages of your development process. From day one, your architecture will need to account for all the dynamics that come with supporting multiple tenants. The overall goal is to avoid the trap of viewing multi-tenancy as a bolt-on that can be added after you've built your application. That mode rarely works and usually leads to painful compromises and refactoring.

We started the chapter at the most basic level, exploring the process of creating your baseline environment and deploying the first bits of your control plane. Getting the shell of the control plane in place allows you to carve out the space that will eventually house all the services that will be part of it. It also forces you to begin thinking about the overall deployment, versioning, and general lifecycle of your control plane.

From there, we shifted our attention to the onboarding experience, highlighting the complexity, challenges, and considerations that come with introducing tenants into your environment. We walked through a conceptual view of an onboarding flow to give you a better sense of the moving parts that are part of this experience. A big part of this discussion also surrounded the mindset that comes with automating your onboarding flow. It's here that we saw how automating this onboarding automation brings new DevOps nuances to your environment, stretching how you might think about where and when tenant environments are provisioned and configured. Our look at onboarding also emphasized the broader role it plays in supporting and enabling the scale, agility, and innovation goals of your business.

With onboarding, we talked about how tenants get introduced into your environment. The natural progression was to look at how the setup of these tenants influences the authentication experience of your environment. It's through authentication that we see some of the payoff of the work that was done during onboarding. Our review of authentication shifted our focus to the role identity plays in a SaaS environment. We examined how our identity provider creates a connection between users and tenants, establishing what I referred to as a SaaS identity. This makes SaaS identity a first-class concept in our architecture. We explored how the authentication of tenants yields tokens that include all the context we need to inject into all the downstream bits of our SaaS architecture. This should have highlighted just how essential it is to have this SaaS identity woven into your experience from the outset of building a multi-tenant environment.

While I've only touched on the conceptual elements of onboarding and identity, this should give you a better sense of the moving parts and considerations that come with creating these foundational constructs. As we move forward, we'll see more concrete versions of these mechanisms and see how different deployment models and technology stacks can influence the design and implementation of onboarding and identity. We'll also see this notion of tenant context showing up in our review of other dimensions of your architecture, including data partitioning, tenant isolation, multi-tenant microservices, and so on.

First, though, we're going to look a little deeper inside the control plane and examine the Tenant Management component. This chapter already hinted at how Tenant Management surfaces as part of the onboarding experience. Now, I want to look more exclusively at the role of this service within your control plane. While not exotic or overly complex, it often sits at the middle of our multi-tenant story. I'll look at what it means to create this service and outline some of the key considerations that can influence its implementation.

## CHAPTER 5

Tenant Management

In the previous chapter, we started our foray into the control plane, looking at the broader role that onboarding and identity play in bringing your multi-tenant architecture to life. As part of that process, I touched on how the Tenant Management service is used to introduce new tenants into the system. Now, it's time to dig more into this service, getting a better sense of its inner workings and examining the full scope of its responsibility. This will give you a better sense of the data, operations, and constructs that put tenant management at the center of configuring aspects of your tenant architecture and managing the lifecycle of key tenant events.

We'll start by looking at the fundamentals of what it means to build your Tenant Management service, exploring the elements of its core design and implementation. As part of this, I'll get into some of the common tenant attributes that are managed by this service. You'll see that storing and managing these attributes is mostly straightforward. However, what you choose to store here can have other downstream implications, expanding its role and usage across the overall footprint of your SaaS architecture.

To better understand the broader role and experience of tenant management, we also have to look at how you will enable management of your tenants. We'll look at how this can surface through APIs or a system administration console. It's here that you'll get another view into how your Tenant Management service fits into the control plane experience. We'll look at how you can use the Tenant Management service to create operational views into your environment, enabling you to manage the state of your system's tenants.

The other dimension of tenant management we'll review is tenant lifecycle management. The goal is to look beyond the initial configuration of a tenant and examine the different events that can happen that will impact the state of a tenant. What does it mean for tenants to change from an active to an inactive state? How does your system manage and apply a tenant's move from one tier to another? How does the state of other systems (billing, for example) get conveyed to your Tenant Management service? These are all areas that can have some interaction with tenant management and, potentially, have some cascading impact across different layers of your SaaS architecture.

The focus of this chapter is to highlight all these nuances of tenant management and equip you with a better sense of the considerations that can influence the multi-tenant strategies and patterns that are applied within your solution.

Tenant Management Fundamentals

To get a better understanding of the scope and nature of tenant management, let's start by looking at the core moving parts of the tenant management universe. Figure 5-1 provides a conceptual view of the various elements that are often part of the overall tenant management footprint.

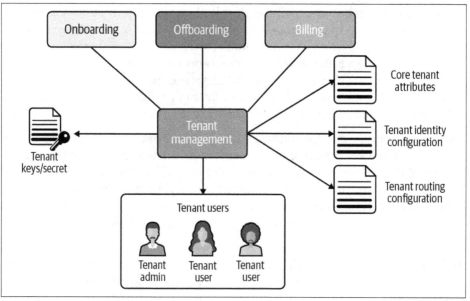

Figure 5-1. Tenant management's influence

You'll see that I have placed tenant management in the center of the diagram and identified the areas that are commonly configured or managed through their connection to a tenant. At the top I've represented a few areas that might commonly interact with the Tenant Management service. A key player here is onboarding (discussed in Chapter 4), which has a significant influence on tenant management. Each time a tenant is created, this will trigger the configuration and setup of a number of different resources that are related to your new tenant. I've shown some specific examples here. You'll also see that I've put offboarding and billing, both of which will have touch points with tenant management as tenants go through different stages of their life-cycle (changing tiers, being decommissioned, and so on).

On the righthand side of Figure 5-1, you'll see two different flavors of data are managed and configured through the Tenant Management service. In this grouping, you'll see what I've labeled as core tenant attributes. This represents the core, baseline data that is needed for most tenants: tenant identifier, status (enabled/disabled), tier, company name, onboarding status, date last active, and so on. I've also shown a separate placeholder for Identity settings. These settings hold the different tenant authentication properties that could be configured through the Tenant Management service. Here's where MFA, password policies, identity provider mappings, and other identity related settings live. Routing policy configuration is also here. The configuration data stored here captures any tenant-specific settings that are used to determine how tenants might be routed to different parts of your infrastructure. URLs, for example, might appear here.

On the left of Figure 5-1, I've shown the configuration of keys and secrets. These settings are used to configure different security aspects of your environment. You might, for example, have per-tenant secrets or encryption keys that are managed by this experience. For some environments, management of these settings can play a bigger role in the overall isolation and security profile of your SaaS solution.

Finally, at the bottom of Figure 5-1 is a representation of the different users that can be associated with a tenant. I've shown a tenant administrator and a few tenant users to illustrate the relationship between a tenant and the various users that may be associated with that tenant. The tenant administrator is created when the tenant is first introduced. However, after onboarding, the tenant can also create additional users for their system, including other tenant administrators. These users are all logically connected to a tenant. Any change in tenant configuration will be applied to all of these users.

 There is a tendency for some to want to equate tenants to users. Now, in a B2C setting, it's true that tenants are likely to have a one-to-one mapping to users. However, even in this case, you still have a tenant, and there are still attributes and policies that may need to be configured for that tenant. I still want to draw a line between managing users and managing tenants, and I would generally keep a user's role and its other application-related settings separate from its tenant settings. This isn't a hard-and-fast rule, but I see teams folding these two into one construct when, in many cases, they should be separately managed.

As I get into the details of specific multi-tenant architectures later in this book, you'll see how tenant management interacts with these different services. You'll also see more examples of how tenant management is used to shape the per-tenant configuration options of your multi-tenant infrastructure and identity experience.

Building a Tenant Management Service

Let's shift from the conceptual view of tenant management and its role and look more at what it actually means to implement a Tenant Management service. The interface of this service is typically broken down into two logical categories. First, you'll have a range of operations that are focused on the basic management of configuration data. These operations are typically exposed via a create, read, update, and delete (CRUD) interface. The other category of operations that land here are centered around broader tenant management operations (tenant deactivation, tenant decommissioning, and so on). These operations tend to contribute the most to the overall complexity of your Tenant Management service.

Figure 5-2 provides a simple view of the moving parts of a sample Tenant Management service. What I've tried to do here is provide a conceptual view into the common interfaces and experience that could be included in this service. On the left, you'll see all the entry points that mirror the summary I provided earlier. The top set of functions manages configuration, and the bottom entry points support the different management-related operations.

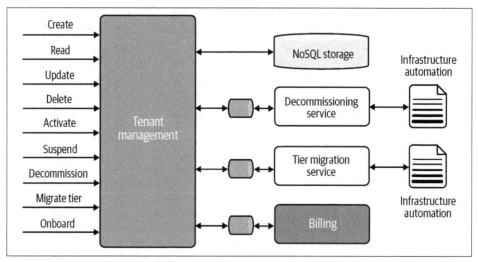

Figure 5-2. A sample tenant management implementation

The righthand side of this diagram highlights the various backend resources and integrations that would be part of your tenant management experience. At the top right, I've shown some storage. For this example, I chose to use NoSQL storage

(DynamoDB) to hold my tenant configuration information. Generally, the size and consumption patterns for this data tends to fit well with a schemaless storage model. This also makes it easy to apply changes to the tenant configuration structure without needing to update schemas or migrate data.

I've also put placeholders here to represent some of the tenant lifecycle components that may be part of your tenant management service. I'll be covering these lifecycle concepts in more detail later, but I wanted to show them here to make it clear that this service may need to support decommissioning of tenants, tier migration, and other tenant lifecycle events. Each of these may require some level of infrastructure configuration, provisioning, or removal depending on the nature of the operation. This often means invoking infrastructure automation scripts or code associated with these operational events. I've shown these concepts as being integrated via a queue only to highlight the idea that the actual work of processing these events might be triggered by an event and executed as part of some asynchronous job.

The last piece that I included was billing. Your service may have multiple integrations with your control plane's billing service (or directly with your billing provider). Your billing system may trigger events that make updates to the state of tenants. Or, your tenant management service might trigger events that end up sending requests to the billing service.

You can see that the Tenant Management service, on its own, doesn't introduce a significant amount of complexity into your control plane. At the same time, it sits at the center of managing key elements of your tenant state that directly influence the implementation and behavior of your multi-tenant architecture. It also provides a centralized home for processing tenant lifecycle events.

Generating a Tenant Identifier

Within the implementation of your Tenant Management service, you'll be responsible for generating the tenant identifier that represents the universal unique identity of any tenant in your system. The most common mechanism that is used for tenant identifiers is a GUID. It provides a natural way to have a globally unique value that has no dependency on other attributes of the tenant. The goals here are twofold. First, you just need to have some separate immutable value that can universally represent your tenant across your multi-tenant environment. Second, you want to ensure that any other consumer of this identity cannot map it back to a specific tenant or entity in your system. This identifier provides a way to represent tenants without surfacing anything specific about the tenant.

It's important to note that some multi-tenant environments may include alternate, more friendly ways to identify a tenant. For example, If the system uses a subdomain or vanity domain for individual tenants, then you'll need some way to map from that entity name to the tenant identifier. In this case, I might have *mycompany.saasprovider.com* where the "mycompany" subdomain represents an externally facing name that would then get mapped to an internal tenant identifier. Even when you have some other name you're using as part of the entry into your system, these entity names or references should not be viewed as your tenant identifier. There are good reasons to keep these separate. The most obvious of these is the need to ensure that you can change these friendly names without having any impact on the rest of the system. This goes back to the basics of data management that led to the use of GUIDs to identify the different items in a database.

Storing Infrastructure Configuration

In addition to storing basic tenant attributes, tenant management can also be used to store tenant-specific infrastructure configuration information. Depending on the deployment model of your multi-tenant application, you might have identity configuration, routing patterns, and other infrastructure options stored and managed by your tenant management service. This data is not typically managed directly by your administration experience. Instead, it's stored here during the configuration of your multi-tenant infrastructure then referenced by different parts of your experience that need this information to configure or resolve tenant mappings that are part of your environment.

The data that you end up putting here is shaped by the specifics of your SaaS architecture. If, for example, you have separate identity constructs for each of your tenants, you may need to use tenant management to store a tenant's mapping to its identity construct. If you have siloed tenant environments and you have mapping to tenant specific entry points or URLs, those could be stored by the tenant management service. These are just a few examples. The key is that tenant management may manage data that goes beyond the scope of basic tenant attributes.

While the tenant management service makes a good, centralized home for tenant state and configuration, you always need to ensure that this service does not become a bottleneck of your system. If the data that's stored here is being frequently accessed by all the moving parts of your system, you'll need to consider alternate strategies for managing and accessing this data. Ideally, the state that's here will not be used heavily by the application services of your application. This is part of why we put the critical tenant attributes into the JWT, limiting your need to continually return to any single, centralized service to continually acquire this context.

Managing Tenant Configuration

Much of the initial focus of tenant management is on its role in creating and configuring tenants as part of the onboarding experience. It's important to note that tenant management has a life beyond onboarding. This service is also used to support different operations and use cases throughout the lifetime of a tenant. To better understand this, let's return to the system admin console that we discussed in Chapter 4. This console provides an administrative view into your multi-tenant environment, allowing you to inspect, configure, and manage your tenants (see Figure 5-3).

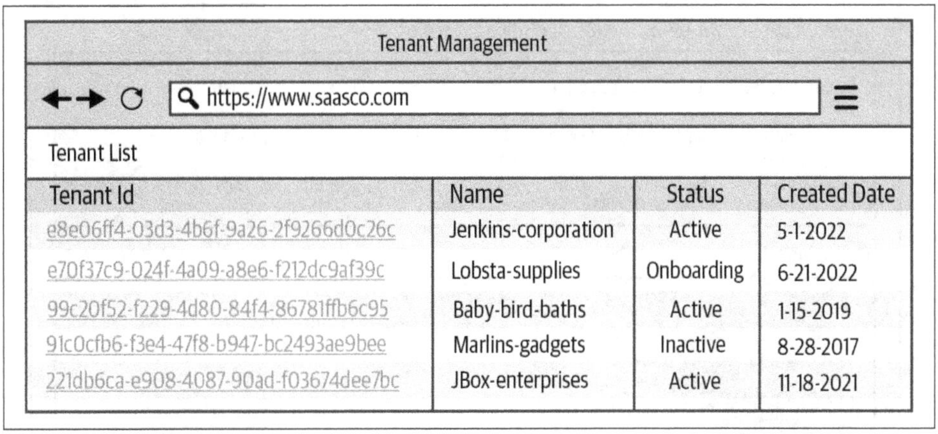
Tenant Management
https://www.saasco.com
Tenant List
Tenant Id
Name
Status
Created Date
e8e06ff4-03d3-4b6f-9a26-2f9266d0c26c
Jenkins-corporation
Active
5-1-2022
e70f37c9-024f-4a09-a8e6-f212dc9af39c
Lobsta-supplies
Onboarding
6-21-2022
99c20f52-f229-4d80-84f4-86781ffb6c95
Baby-bird-baths
Active
1-15-2019
91c0cfb6-f3e4-47f8-b947-bc2493ae9bee
Marlins-gadgets
Inactive
8-28-2017
221db6ca-e908-4087-90ad-f03674dee7bc
JBox-enterprises
Active
11-18-2021

Figure 5-3. Managing tenants from the admin console

This is a very straightforward experience that essentially grabs a list of tenants and lists them on the screen. This list, of course, is acquired from your Tenant Management service, which fetches all the tenants that are stored by your service and lists them on this page. With each tenant, you'll see its identifier, name, status, and any other attributes that you might deem worthy of including in this view.

At a minimum, this view would be used to look up and resolve the status of tenants. It's also commonly used to locate the unique identifier when you're searching logs or doing any other troubleshooting that might rely on the tenant information.

In addition to surfacing information about the tenant, the console is also where you would edit and manage any policies for a given tenant. Perhaps the most common functionality that's configured here is the tier or status of the tenant. In this particular example, you can see additional configuration details by selecting the link to the tenant identifier. Figure 5-4 provides an example of a detailed view of a specific tenant.

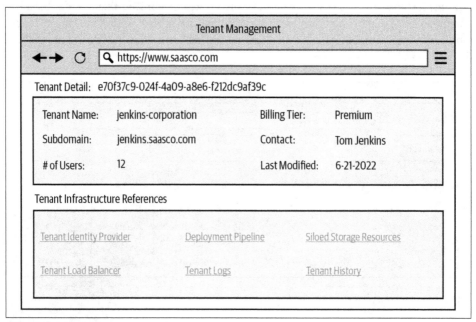

Figure 5-4. Managing tenant details from the console

Again, this is just an example, but it highlights some of the additional options you might attach to your tenant management view. Here you see the next level of detail associated with your tenants, including subdomain, onboarding status, and so on. You can imagine how this screen would be filled with more detail based on the presence of any additional tenant configuration options that are part of your multi-tenant environment.

There are two key things to note here as conceptual placeholders. First, in the top portion of Figure 5-4, you'll see additional details that provide more data on the state of a single tenant. Then, at the bottom of the image, you'll see a section that includes hyperlinks that take you to key infrastructure resources that are associated with the current tenant. These links take you directly to the admin or cloud provider infrastructure page for each resource, allowing you to rapidly access resources in the context of a specific tenant. This can streamline your operational experience, allowing you to rapidly navigate (with tenant context) to any specific tenant infrastructure resources.

It's important to note that you may or may not choose to include these links. They are especially valuable if you are running full stack silo environments. However, the more pooled your environment is, the less likely that you'll get lots of value out of providing this tenant contextual access to infrastructure resources.

Finally, you'll also see that there's an Actions pulldown button in the top right of Figure 5-4. This is where you'll perform specific operations on your tenant. At a minimum, your system will likely include functionality to update the active status of a tenant. To perform this operation, an operator would access the administrator console and temporarily deactivate a tenant. There may be additional options here to decommission a tenant or move them between tiers (these options are explored more in the section that follows).

This particular example focuses more on managing tenants through a console. However, all functionality enabled here typically is enabled through operations that are performed on the API of the Tenant Management service. In reality, you could create an experience where these operations and insights were performed directly through the API. How you approach this will vary based on the nature of the tenant management experience you need to support. You can do everything through a console, everything through an API, or a mix of the two.

In our discussion of onboarding in Chapter 4, I talked about the different models for triggering the onboarding of a tenant. I emphasized the point that onboarding of new tenants could be executed by tenants as part of a self-service experience or through some internal onboarding tooling developed by your team. In fact, the internal mechanism could be surfaced as part of the admin console.

The self-service flavor of onboarding is pretty straightforward. You land on the sign-up page, fill in the data, and submit your request. The question is, though, where should you surface an internally managed onboarding experience? There is no one answer to this. You might have your own command-line interface (CLI) or other tools that allow you to onboard tenants. However, one common approach would be to manage this onboarding through your tenant management console experience.

You could achieve this by adding an "Onboarding Tenant" action to your console. Triggering that action would open a form where you would fill in all the data needed to onboard a new tenant. Figure 5-5 provides an example of what this form might look like.

Figure 5-5. Internally onboarding a tenant

This is a basic form that just collects and submits your data. Every multi-tenant onboarding process will likely include a tenant entity name, an email address for the tenant admin user, and the plan or tier they're signing up for. From there, the rest would depend on the configuration options and nature of your multi-tenant environment. You might need to collect a subdomain here, for example. Or, you might have a more elaborate process that allows you to bring in a full vanity domain for a tenant. The key at this point is just to highlight the fact that the tenant management experience may provide a good home for surfacing your internal process via the admin console.

Managing Tenant Lifecycle

Up to this point, the focus of tenant management has largely been on the mechanics of the front of the tenant management process where you're onboarding and configuring tenants. Now, I want to shift gears and look at the role tenant management plays beyond this initial phase. The focus now transitions to thinking about the various states that a tenant might go through during its time within your system.

Teams often overlook the entire notion of managing a tenant's lifecycle. They focus squarely on what it means to get a tenant introduced or configured and view that as the one and only role of their Tenant Management service. It's true that, for some tenants, you'll create them once and that will be it for them. However, there will also be tenants in your system that will need to go through changes in state that are more involved than just changing the value of some attribute in your tenant database.

When you set out to build your multi-tenant environment, you have to consider all the phases that a tenant could go through within your system. How will these state changes be conveyed to you? Will they be in response to some external event or driven directly from your Tenant Management service? What are the policies associated with these state changes? These are amongst the questions you'll want to ask yourself as you assemble the tenant management elements of your SaaS solution.

While there are any number of phases that could be part of your tenant lifecycle, there are a few common states that you'll want to consider when building any multi-tenant SaaS environment. The sections that follow will enumerate these lifecycle changes.

Activating and Deactivating a Tenant

The first and most obvious state you'll want to focus on is activation/deactivation. In general, your SaaS environment should include some ability to enable and disable tenants. Generally, this setting is used to manage a tenant's ability to access your system. In this mindset, we're *not* removing tenants from the system. We're only flipping a switch to turn their access on or off. When a tenant is deactivated, your Tenant Management service will need to own responsibility for figuring out what actions may need to be orchestrated to ensure that a tenant is blocked from accessing the system. This could be as simple as making a call to the User Management service to disable authentication for all users for that tenant or it could be more involved.

Managing a tenant's active state can also be connected to the billing experience of your application. It's the billing system that can, in some cases, be at the front line of managing your tenant's active state. Imagine a scenario where a tenant has stopped making payments. In this case, this information might surface first within your billing system, which identifies delinquent tenants. When this event is triggered by the billing system, you have to determine how your system will respond to these events. You might have policies that send messages during some grace period that allow tenants to continue using the system while the billing issues are being resolved. At some point, though, you can reach a point where you've determined that a tenant needs to be deactivated. In this case, if the billing system originates this event, you'll need some way for this to be conveyed to your Tenant Management service.

Figure 5-6 provides a view of how billing might be connected with other services within the control plane of your SaaS environment.

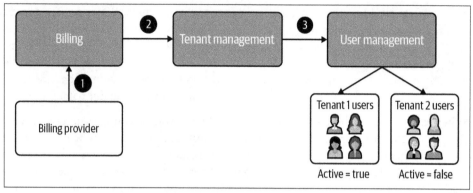

Figure 5-6. Deactivation triggered by the Billing service

In this example, I've pulled in the various services that could be used to deactivate a tenant based on an event that originates from your billing provider. I also have a third-party billing system that's being used to manage the billing state of my tenants. For this scenario let's assume that a customer success manager or some automation policies within the billing provider has deactivated a tenant. Now, the Billing service within your control plane needs some way to acquire and react to this event. How this is achieved will depend largely on the nature of the billing provider's API and integration model. Ideally, the billing provider will generate an event when a tenant is deactivated. If not, your Billing service may need to have some process that periodically looks for these changes in state. In this scenario, I've presumed the billing provider is sending a message to my Billing service (step 1).

Once the billing system detects this event, it will call your Tenant Management service with a deactivate tenant request (step 2). The service will update the state of the tenant to inactive and convey this new state change to any part of your system that might be impacted by this change in status. In this diagram, I've presumed that deactivation is achieved by preventing tenants from authenticating. This is represented by a call to your control plane's User Management service, which updates the active status of all users associated with your tenant (step 3). Ideally, if your identity provider supports a group construct for your tenants, you may be able to apply this change at the group level. This would certainly be much simpler than toggling the states of individual users.

As part of deactivation, you also have to determine how this impacts the state of any users currently logged into the system. Do you allow them to continue or do you immediately terminate their active session? Many SaaS providers tend to lean toward a model that is more passive, allowing tenant users to finish any active sessions.

Of course, whatever can be deactivated may also be reactivated, so you'll want to consider that path as well. This is likely just a matter of reversing whatever was done to deactivate a tenant. In our example, this would just update the status of the tenant to active and re-enable authentication for your tenant.

In some cases, deactivation may be initiated by your own services (instead of via a billing system). This would mean that your admin console would provide a specific operation that would be used to trigger tenant deactivation. Here, your Tenant Management service would originate the deactivation event and update any downstream services that would be impacted by this deactivation event.

The key takeaway is that tenant status must be centrally managed by your Tenant Management service. It should be viewed as the single source of truth for managing the state of tenants, ensuring that any impacts of changes in status are synchronized with dependent parts of your system.

Decommissioning a Tenant

Now let's look at what it means to decommission a tenant. You might be wondering where the line is between deactivation and decommissioning. Deactivation is only meant to suspend a tenant's account. It does not impact the existing footprint of the tenant's environment. Essentially, it's just disabling access, allowing for the fact that the tenant may be reactivated at some point.

Decommissioning would typically come after deactivation. Imagine a scenario where a tenant decides not to renew its subscription. When they reach the last day of the subscription period, your system might choose to deactivate the tenant and leave them in a deactivated state for some window of time. This strategy allows a tenant to return, reactivate, and continue to resume using their system with no impact. It's as if they never left the system. This certainly creates a better customer experience. However, after a certain amount of time, the unused resources of this tenant may be contributing to costs and complexity that are not adding any value for the business. Now, you have to consider how you move from a deactivated state to decommissioning the tenant's resources.

There is no one-size-fits-all approach to choosing your system's decommissioning policies. The strategy you choose will be influenced by a variety of factors. How much overhead is a deactivated tenant adding to your system? How frequently are tenants deactivating? How are these deactivated tenants impacting the complexity of your management and operations experience? There are a wide range of factors you'll need to consider to determine how, when, and if you choose to decommission tenants.

Now, let's assume you've reached a point where you've decided tenants do need to be decommissioned. You have a few choices when it comes to picking a decommissioning strategy. You could choose to simply delete any resources that are associated with the tenant, essentially removing them completely from the system, or you could choose to archive the tenant's state before decommissioning its resources. As part of this, you'll want to reconsider what it means to rehydrate a tenant that has been decommissioned. You might, for example, leave elements of the tenant in place that have minimal impact on your system (the tenant, its users, and so on). This could make bringing the tenant back to life a somewhat simpler process without adding much cost or complexity to your environment. Ultimately, this is all part of the balancing act that comes with creating your decommissioning strategy.

Figure 5-7 provides a conceptual view of some of the moving parts that might be included in your decommissioning model.

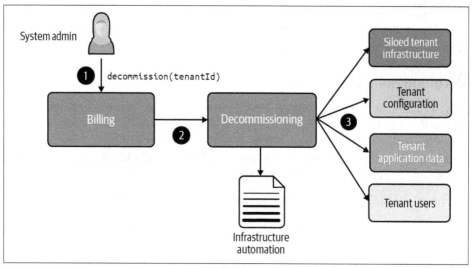

Figure 5-7. Decommissioning tenant resources

In this example, I've shown a scenario where a system administrator starts the decommissioning process, which sends a decommission request to the Tenant Management service (step 1). At this point, you could have decommissioning implemented within the scope of the Tenant Management service. Instead, I've shown decommissioning as a completely separate service that owns orchestration of all the steps needed to remove a tenant from your system. This service is then called by the Tenant Management service to begin the decommissioning process (step 3).

To me, it feels more natural to carve this out and allow decommissioning to exist as its own process that would be deployed, managed, and executed outside the context of the Tenant Management service. The Decommissioning service has the job of iterating over all the different tenant constructs and removing each one. This will be achieved through a combination of infrastructure automation tooling and scripts as well as API calls. The nature of each tenant resource may require a different decommissioning strategy.

While each SaaS solution will have its own unique blend of tenant resources, I did include a few examples in the diagram to highlight the kinds of resources that might be touched by your Decommissioning service. Naturally, if we have any siloed tenant infrastructure here, those siloed resources will be removed from your system. This may be about removing all the pieces of a full stack silo deployment or just the individual resources that might be deployed in a siloed model. Tenant configuration and tenant users are also listed here as examples of resources that would get touched as part of this process.

Tenant data can certainly be one of the more challenging areas to address when you're decommissioning a tenant. Imagine all the places where you might have pooled storage in your system. When you have pooled data, that means that your decommissioning process will need to be able to locate and selectively remove the data that sits alongside the data of other tenants. Figure 5-8 provides a conceptual view of the nature of this decommissioning challenge.

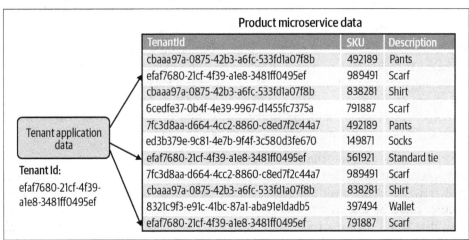

Figure 5-8. Decommissioning tenant data

I've provided an example of the data that might be associated with our product service. Within this table, I have a TenantId column that includes the GUIDs that associate each product with a tenant. Now, let's assume we want to decommission the tenant with the ID efaf7680-21cf-4f39-a1e8-3481ff0495ef. Our decommissioning process must locate and remove all the items in this table that are associated with this tenant.

On the surface, this may not seem all that challenging. However, consider that this table is one of many in our system that may hold data in a pooled model. Each microservice in our system could manage pooled tenant data and each of these services may rely on different storage technologies. This means that your decommissioning process may need separate code to remove data from each of these sources.

In some instances, decommissioning can be more involved than your onboarding process. The nuances of identifying and gracefully removing these tenant resources can be quite involved. Automating this process can be daunting, requiring teams to be hypervigilant about ensuring that their decommissioning strategy doesn't impact existing tenants. This includes ensuring that the load of your decommissioning process avoids creating bottlenecks or performance issues for your existing tenants. Generally, if you can run this as an asynchronous process that has a very conservative consumption profile, you'll be better positioned to limit tenant impacts. This falls very much into the old school batch mentality, where we try to run processes of this nature after hours to limit impacts. For some SaaS providers, that will work; others may not have this luxury.

The last piece around decommissioning focuses on archiving tenant state and data. For some SaaS providers, this can allow them to continue to preserve existing tenant state without retaining all the other moving parts of a tenant's environment. This is especially valuable when you have high-profile tenants or tenants with a significant investment in their data.

While the concept of archiving decommissioned tenant state and data is not all that complex, the variations in multi-tenant architecture models make it difficult to prescribe any one approach for this problem. There is no standard "take a snapshot" of my tenant environment model—especially if you rely on pooled resources. Instead, this is usually more about taking on the heavy lifting of building your own tools and strategies that can navigate the nuances of your tenant environment.

Ultimately, how or if you choose to decommission data will vary based on the nature of your SaaS offering. This is often about weighing the business, cost, and complexity trade-offs. For some businesses, the value of being able to reactivate with minimal friction could be essential to reacquiring key customers. For others, the nature of their data and the tendencies of their customers may suggest that there's not enough upside in investing in the build out of this capability.

Changing Tenant Tiers

The last piece of our tenant lifecycle management story looks at what it means to move from a tenant from one tier to another. For many, this change represents one of the more challenging dimensions of managing tenant state.

For simple use cases, the move from one tier to another may not be all that exotic. Let's consider a scenario where you have basic and premium tier tenants where the primary difference between these tiers is throughput and features. Essentially, the premium tier tenants have better overall throughput and are granted access to additional features based on their move from the basic tier. Figure 5-9 provides a view of how these concepts might land in a multi-tenant architecture.

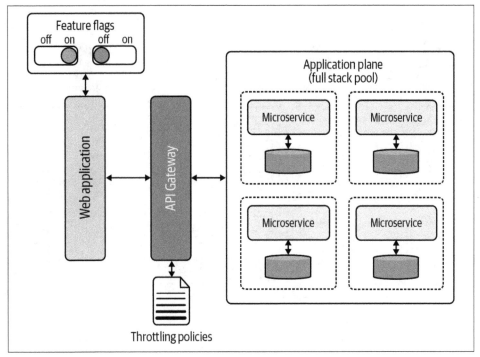

Figure 5-9. Switching tiers in a full stack pool model

Moving between basic and premium tiers in this example is limited to a few very isolated areas of this multi-tenant environment. Here, feature flags are used within our application to enable paths, features, and workflows that are available to the premium tier tenant. Also, the tier-based throttling policies that are configured as part of our API gateway will simply apply the throttling policies of the premium tier tenant to our requests (instead of the basic tier policies). This will prevent the tenant from being throttled based on the more restrictive constraints of the basic tier and, generally, ensure this tenant will have better SLAs.

You can see how moving between tiers is a pretty straightforward model. With all of your tenant resources running in a pooled model, your system will simply update the tenant configuration to reflect the new tier. From there, the system will just use the existing feature flag and throttling policies to apply the new tier to your tenant's experience. This is the upside of having a pooled experience. You can apply changes of this nature with minimal complexity and overhead.

Now, let's consider what it would mean to move between tiers in an environment that has a more complex footprint. Figure 5-10 looks at what it would mean to migrate between tiers that are using the full stack pool and full stack silo deployment models that we talked about in Chapter 3.

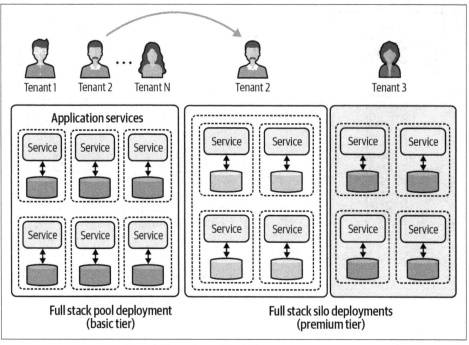

Figure 5-10. Migrating from full stack pool to full stack silo

In this example, Tenant 2 is migrating from the basic tier where it is running in a full stack pool model sharing all of its resources with other tenants. Now, when this tenant migrates to the premium tier, they are essentially moving into the full stack silo deployment model on the right. This migration starts by provisioning a full stack of resources for Tenant 2 and configuring any routing that's needed to send traffic to this silo. If you think about it, parts of this migration will very much simulate your onboarding experience of any premium tier tenant. In fact, it would not be unheard of to leverage parts of your onboarding code to facilitate this migration.

Where this gets a bit trickier is when you have to move the existing state of the tenant to the full stack silo environment. Now you must think about whether this will be a zero-downtime migration or whether you'll require tenants to deactivate to move to the new tier. You'll also have to write the new code that moves all the data and state from the pooled environment to your new full stack silo. This is where lifting gets heavy. In many respects, you're taking on lots of the classic challenges that come with any environment migration. Many of the principles and strategies that are commonly used to migrate any software environment apply here—they're just being scoped at the tenant level.

While this migration to a full stack silo model has lots of moving parts, the logic and path forward is relatively straightforward. The data movement is the biggest piece of this effort. Now, let's add another wrinkle here. Let's look at what it would mean to change tiers in an environment that uses a mixed mode deployment model where each microservice in our environment may have more granular implementations of silo and pool based on the tier of a given tenant.

Consider what it might mean to migrate from a basic to premium tier in an environment that might look something like the model shown in Figure 5-11.

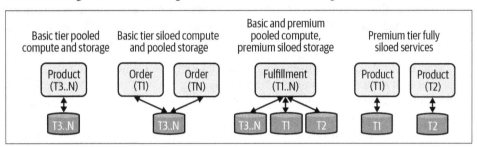

Figure 5-11. Mixed mode tier migration

I've made this a bit more convoluted to highlight some of the complexities that come into the picture when you're migrating in a mixed mode deployment environment. If you look across these microservices, you'll see that they have much more granular mappings to tiers. On the left, you'll see services that are for our basic tier tenants. One interesting twist here is that the Order microservice is siloed for all tiers. In the middle, fulfillment supports pooled compute for both basic and premium tiers. However, it has pooled storage for the basic tier and siloed storage for premium tiers. Then, the premium tier tenant gets fully siloed compute and storage for the Product microservice.

This very much mimics the patterns we looked at when we were examining the basics of the mixed mode deployment model. Now, though, we need to consider the impact of a tenant migrating from the basic to the premium tier. Let's say, for example, Tenant 3 (T3) is moving to the premium tier. The steps here are less obvious. You must now think about how each service is applying the tiering model and figure out which new resources might be needed to make this transition.

There would be no changes to the Order microservice to achieve this migration. For fulfillment, you'd need to migrate the storage from the shared model to the siloed storage model. And, finally, for the Product microservice, you'd need to provision new compute and storage for Tenant 3 and migrate the data from the pooled database to this new siloed Product footprint.

Lots of the same challenges that we saw with the migration to a full stack silo deployment follow us to this mixed mode deployment environment. Movement of the data remains a challenge. However, you will have a more interesting web of changes that are influenced based on how you've mapped tiering to the various layers of your environment. The good news is that, like the full stack silo deployment migration, this migration can also lean on some of the tooling and mechanics that are connected to your onboarding experience. The complexities associated with migration often overlap with the nuances of your onboarding experience.

For any flavor of tier migration that you consider, you'll also have to consider how this migration could impact tenants that are currently using your system. You'll want to be sure that the extraction of tenant data and state doesn't have any adverse impact on existing workloads. If this migration is at all disruptive to your environment, it can undermine the overall stability and availability of your environment.

While all the focus here has been migrating to a higher-level tier, your environment must also support a model where tenants can downgrade to a lower-level tier. In this mode, we're essentially looking at a model that is basically the inverse of what was done for upgrading tiers. It might just be about updating configuration to reflect your new tier or it could be more about migrating your infrastructure and data to the new tier.

If you're moving from premium to the basic tier and this move has some parts of your system moving from siloed to pooled infrastructure, then your migration now will look at how to move compute and data into their pooled constructs.

Conclusion

For this chapter, I looked at the core parts of managing all the moving parts of a tenant. This included looking at the overall role that tenant management plays as a microservice within the control plane of your SaaS architecture, examining the data and state that is typically managed by this service. The goal was to highlight the role this service plays in your broader multi-tenant environment, providing the single home and source of truth for key tenant information that is used across all the moving parts of your SaaS architecture.

As part of this topic, I also looked at how tenants are surfaced and managed through your admin console experience. The emphasis here was on outlining how this console connects to your Tenant Management service and is used by the administrators to manage, configure, and update your tenant information. Creating this centralized console for managing tenants often represents an essential component of your overall administration experience.

The last bits of this chapter looked at managing your tenant's lifecycle. This had us exploring the different events that can happen across the entire lifetime of your tenants, reviewing how your Tenant Management service would support key events that alter the state of a tenant. Some of these events are as simple as activating and deactivating tenants. Other events (like tier migration) often require a much more intensive effort to orchestrate these transitions.

Now that we've looked at how tenants are introduced and managed, we have all the elements in place for representing and managing tenants. The next logical area to explore is tenant authentication and routing. Chapter 6 will look at how tenants enter through the front door of our application and leverage the bits we've put in place in your control plane to authenticate users. The authentication and routing story will consider all the steps that are needed for a tenant to access your application, route to the appropriate resources, and inject tenant context into that experience. This will set up our ability to continue to push deeper into the underlying implementation of your SaaS application services.

## CHAPTER 6

Tenant Authentication and Routing

At this stage, our focus on the control plane has been squarely on building a foundation that allows us to introduce multi-tenancy into our architecture. Onboarding, user management, and tenant management all allow us to configure, capture, and prepare our tenant for entry into a SaaS environment. Now it's time to start thinking about how a tenant uses these constructs (and others) to enter the front door of our multi-tenant environment.

It's at this point where you authenticate a user that all the pieces of your onboarding and tenant management come together. Here you'll see how the configuration information that was stored in tenant management can play a role in the flow and implementation of your authentication experience. We'll also see how the work that was done to connect our users to tenants will yield the tenant context that becomes essential to the downstream services that are part of your multi-tenant architecture.

For this chapter, I'll begin by looking at the fundamentals of how you expose the entry point to your multi-tenant solution. There are multiple strategies that can be used to access a SaaS environment, some of which explicitly identify the tenant that is entering the system and others that rely on internal mechanisms to determine which tenant is accessing the system. Each of these have implications on how your tenant is authenticated and connected with the appropriate identity provider.

We'll also look at how your path through the front door influences the authentication model of your multi-tenant environment. As part of this, I'll also examine how you might use different identity provider constructs to support various tenant authentication experiences. You'll see how the identity strategies we discussed in Chapter 4 will come into play as you begin to authenticate individual tenants.

The last bit of the chapter will look at how this authentication experience projects into the downstream elements of your multi-tenant architecture. This includes examining how JWTs are injected into your application's services and how the context of authentication can be used to route your tenant requests to specific elements of your multi-tenant environment. This routing context often ends up tightly connected to how you access your SaaS application.

The basic goal is to go to the next level of bringing your SaaS environment to life, building on the foundation established in Chapters 1 through 5. It's here that we see how an actual tenant enters a SaaS environment and how the constructs we put in place allow us to authenticate tenants and acquire the context that's needed to shape the rest of the downstream multi-tenant footprint of your SaaS architecture.

Entering the Front Door

Now that we have a sense of the scope of this authentication topic, let's start our discovery at its most natural point—the front door. The core elements of your authentication always begin with determining how tenants will access your application. While these access patterns seem trivial, you'll begin to see how the strategy you choose here goes beyond the URL that's used to expose your application to tenants.

There are multiple options available to you when thinking about how you might have tenants access your system. You may want the domain of your system, for example, to include a tenant name and rely on this domain as part of your tenant-mapping and routing strategy. Or you might just allow tenants to have their own unique domains based on branding or other considerations. In either case, the domain still typically ends up playing some role in identifying the tenant that is accessing your system. Some SaaS solutions, however, have no dependency on the domain, using a single domain for all tenants. In this approach, you'll need the authentication flow of your environment to inject the tenant context into the system.

The key is that—even as you're selecting a path into your application—you're making choices that can have a cascading impact across other dimensions of your SaaS architecture. This access strategy may even have impacts on the technologies and services that are used to implement specific elements of your solution.

In the sections that follow, we'll look at some of the common patterns that are used when selecting an access model for your SaaS environment. With each of these patterns, we'll review some of the considerations that are associated with each approach.

Access via a Tenant Domain

One of the common ways that tenants enter the front door of your application is through a domain. More specifically, tenants can enter with a domain that includes information used to identify a tenant. Figure 6-1 provides a conceptual view of how the context of this domain influences the downstream footprint of your multi-tenant architecture.

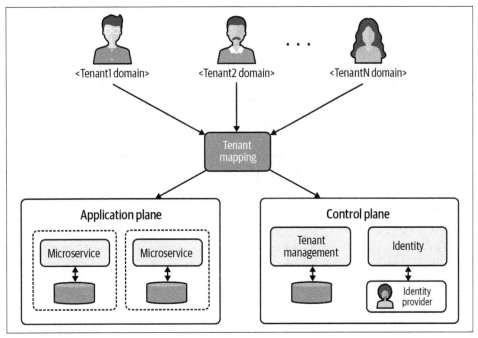

Figure 6-1. A domain-driven access model

Figure 6-1 shows a range of different tenants that are accessing a SaaS environment using a domain. In this model, each tenant's domain is configured during the onboarding process. Once the domain is configured, the URL is shared with the tenant as their entry point into your SaaS service.

With this approach, all inbound tenant requests from these different domains are routed through what I've labeled as tenant mapping. This box represents a conceptual placeholder for the different technologies, infrastructure, and services that would be used to map a tenant's domain to the appropriate backend services. This mapping service is usually needed to extract the incoming tenant context from the domain and use that context to resolve any mappings to dedicated tenant resources.

There are at least two common places this mapping may be applied. The first of these is authentication. When the system is authenticating a tenant user, it may need to map an incoming authentication request to its corresponding identity construct. This applies primarily to tenant environments that don't have a single, shared identity provider. In these cases, a separate identity provider may support your authentication or there may be distinct identity constructs within a single identity provider (groups, user pools, etc.) that are bound to individual tenants to provide specific features or experiences.

In Figure 6-1 you can see how this authentication mapping unfolds. In this example, the tenant accesses your system with a tenant-specific domain, then that domain goes through the Tenant Mapping service, which extracts the tenant information from the origin of the incoming request. This information is used to look up the tenant identity setting in tenant management, which is then used to authenticate the tenant user against the target identity provider or construct.

The other area where tenant mapping is applied is related to the routing of application requests. In instances where your architecture is using one or more siloed tenant resources, your incoming tenant requests will need to be routed to each of these specific resources. Here, the mapping service must use the tenant context to identify that route that will be taken for a given request. We'll cover this use case later in this chapter.

While the technologies used to support the unique tenant domains can vary, the fundamentals are typically not all that different. How, where, and when it is applied will vary based on what you need to do with the context of this domain. It might be used to look up a tenant identifier, map your tenant user to an identity provider, configure routing, or perform any other operation that may need tenant context to process a request.

It's also worth noting that the domain name (or subdomain) represents a friendly, publicly visible name that you've exposed as the URL entry of a tenant. This name may change over the life of the tenant and, as such, is maintained entirely separate from the internal notion of a tenant identifier, which will not change over the life of the tenant.

The subdomain-per-tenant model

At this point, the fundamentals of the domain-per-tenant model should be clear. Of course, even though I've talked about domains generically, the reality is there are multiple ways to associate domains with tenants. In many SaaS environments, there's a desire to use domains to identify tenants without requiring each tenant to have a completely unique domain. In this scenario, you might have a SaaS company (ABC Software, for example) that owns the *abc-software.com* domain, and they want to use that domain as part of the presence and branding of their SaaS experience. Their customers, in this example, also don't see value in having their own domains.

In this scenario, it's very natural to use subdomains as a way to identify tenants without creating an entirely new domain for each tenant. So, with our *abc-software.com* example, you would prepend a friendly tenant name to the existing domain. The end result would yield domains like *tenant1.abc-software.com* and *tenant2.abc-software.com*. You've likely seen this pattern implemented across existing SaaS solutions that you consume today.

This approach is often very appealing to SaaS providers, enabling them to provide a unique access point for each tenant without absorbing the complexity and overhead of creating a unique domain for each tenant.

The vanity domain-per-tenant model

The other option here is to use a vanity domain for each tenant. This approach is often used in scenarios where a tenant is presenting a branded experience to its customers. In fact, in these scenarios, the tenant's users may have no awareness of the underlying SaaS system that they are running.

To better understand this model, consider an example where a SaaS provider offers an ecommerce solution. With this offering, tenants use the SaaS environment to configure and host their own, privately branded stores. In this scenario, tenants would have their own unique domains that are used to access your multi-tenant environment.

In most respects, this vanity domain model looks very much like the subdomain model that we outlined. It still uses the origin to extract the tenant name and then map it to tenant context for downstream consumption. It's worth noting that this same model could be used as part of a white-labeling strategy where tenants are allowed to apply their own branding. For example, imagine an ecommerce SaaS platform where each store on the platform uses a vanity domain and applies its own brand to the entire experience.

Onboarding with tenant domains

When you use a domain to identify tenants, you have to consider how this will influence the design of your tenant onboarding model. Now, as each new tenant is created, you'll need to configure the setup of these domains and create any mappings that will be needed to support a tenant's entry into your environment.

The subdomain-per-tenant model has a lighter weight impact on your onboarding flow. Here, your effort is primarily focused on setting up the various DNS configuration options that are part of your environment. Figure 6-2 provides an example of some of the elements that could be configured as part of onboarding a new tenant in a subdomain-per-tenant model.

I've outlined a specific AWS example that shows how you'll need to configure the moving parts of your network routing to support the subdomain-per-tenant model. At the top of the diagram I have shown the configuration of the content delivery network (CDN) that will be processing our tenant requests. It uses Amazon's CloudFront service. The table shown here illustrates how you'll configure the CDN to support tenant subdomains. The first row in this CDN table includes the settings that are configured when you initially provision your baseline SaaS environment. In this example, the general domain was assigned the alternate name of *app.sassco.com*, where "saasco" represents the branded domain name of our fictitious SaaS company. Now, when a new tenant is onboarded to the system, you must add a new row to this CDN table. In this case, I've added one new tenant that gets configured as *tenant1.sassco.com*.

 Amazon CloudFront

Origin	Domain Name	Alternate Names
App-Bucket	https://abc123.cloudfront.net	app.saasco.com
		tenant1.saasco.com

 Amazon Route 53

Record Name	Type	Route To
app.saasco.com	A	https://abc123.cloudfront.net
tenant1.saasco.com	A	https://abc123.cloudfront.net

Figure 6-2. Configuring tenant subdomains during onboarding

In addition to configuring the CDN, we must also set up the DNS routing for this new tenant subdomain. The table at the bottom of Figure 6-2 provides an example of how you might configure your DNS service. For this example, we're looking at how this is achieved with the Amazon Route 53 service. The table shows two entries. The first row contains the baseline set of values that are populated when you first set up your environment. The second row gets populated when you onboard tenant1. This creates the A record that points the *tenant1.saasco.com* subdomain to the general domain of your SaaS environment.

While many of the steps to make this work are mirrored in the vanity domain model, there is one key difference you'll need to factor into your domain onboarding story. When a tenant requires a vanity domain, your onboarding process will need to support a way to bring that domain to life within your multi-tenant environment. If the domain exists and is being migrated to your environment, your onboarding flow will need to include the steps required to make this migration happen. However, there may also be instances where the tenant creates their domain as part of their onboarding process. As you can imagine, this would be a much more involved process. The complexity is often centered around the various steps required to validate and register a new domain. Choosing to support automation of this entire experience can represent a significant investment for some teams.

While I used AWS services to illustrate the onboarding experience, the fundamentals of configuring this experience would likely be similar with other tools and services. The key is that you'll need to consider how you will automate the configuration of these domain settings as part of onboarding new tenants.

Access via a Single Domain

So far, I've focused mostly on strategies that rely on domains to identify tenants that are entering the front door of your application. However, some SaaS providers—especially those using a B2C model—will use a single domain for all tenants. In these instances, all tenants will use the same domain to access your SaaS environment. Figure 6-3 provides a conceptual view of an environment with a single domain.

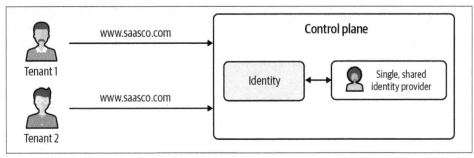

Figure 6-3. Single domain with a shared identity provider

In this example, I have two tenants that are accessing my system via a single, shared domain (*www.saasco.com*). Now, as these tenants attempt to authenticate an existing tenant user, they are directed to the identity provider hosted within our control plane. Since this model uses a global identity construct to house all of our tenant users, it can authenticate all tenants against this single endpoint without any real challenges. Of course, having all of your users in a single identity provider construct will also mean that each user of your system can be associated with one and only one tenant.

Where this gets more interesting is when your architecture supports more flavors of your authentication experience. If you recall, in Chapter 4 I talked about how identity providers may offer different grouping constructs for users that allow you to have separate authentication policies for each tenant. If your identity provider supports these grouping constructs, this can enable you to offer authentication options for the different tiers of your solution.

Figure 6-4 provides an updated view of the single domain strategy that employs separate identity constructs for your tenant.

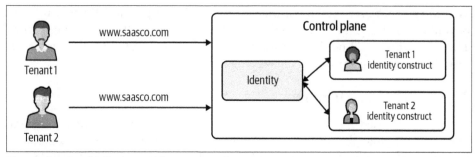

Figure 6-4. Single domain with separate identity constructs

This is mostly a mirror of the diagram in Figure 6-3. However, the one change is that we now have separate identity constructs for each of our two tenants. This is where things get a bit more complicated with the single domain model. Without a domain to identify tenants as they enter the environment, you have no context that will allow you to determine which identity construct should be used to authenticate your users. Each tenant request looks the same to your environment regardless of which tenant initiated the request.

There are a few ways you might approach resolving tenant context for your authentication flow. One strategy is to use the domain of your user email address to associate the user with a given tenant. In this model, you'd presume that tenants coming from a specific domain/customer would be mapped to the tenant for that customer. This can work if you can presume that all tenants from a domain belong to a specific tenant. However, this does impose limits on your ability to support a broader range of users with various email domains. Another possibility here is to consider mapping individual user identifiers to specific tenants. The diagram in Figure 6-5 provides a conceptual view of this approach.

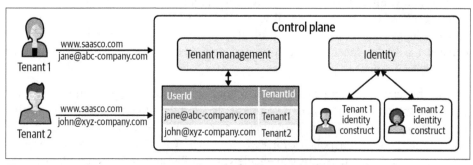

Figure 6-5. Authentication mapping based on tenant identifiers

In this example, we inherit the same single domain model I've used throughout this section, using *www.saasco.com* as the single entry point for all tenants. I've also added two sample user identifiers that represent the different values used during the authentication experience. To be able to authenticate in this model, you'll need to first resolve the user identifier to its corresponding tenant. This is represented with the table associated with the Tenant Management service, mapping individual users to tenants. In reality, this mapping is likely a mapping from the user to a tenant's identity construct. Once you have that identity construct, you can authenticate the user against the target identity construct. This model still relies on having a one-to-one relationship between a user ID and a tenant. However, it does let you have separately configured identity policies for tenant tiers.

The Man in the Middle Challenge

In looking at the solution in Figure 6-5, you'll notice that this strategy relies on a level of indirection to successfully map tenants to their identity providers. This does present some challenges if you're trying to precisely conform to standard authentication models. To better understand this, let's step back and consider a more traditional web application authentication implementation.

Figure 6-6 provides a conceptual view of a classic authentication experience that you may have implemented multiple times. This flow starts with a tenant user attempting to access your web application (step 1) is redirected to an identity provider to be authenticated (step 2). When the user successfully authenticates, the identity provider returns tokens that will provide identity and authorization information (step 3). The identity provider then directs you back to the web application as an authenticated user (step 4) before calling one or more downstream microservices with this authentication context (step 5).

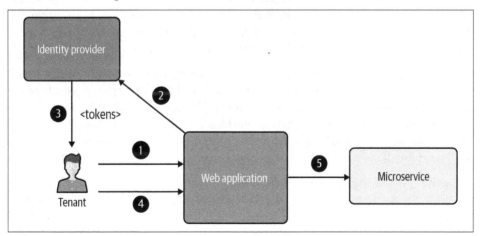

Figure 6-6. A classic web application authentication flow

The beauty of this flow is that it is orchestrated entirely by the identity constructs of your environment. The path to the identity provider and back into your web application is mostly outside of the control of your code and conforms to the standard authentication flows that are supported by identity providers.

Ideally, you'd be able to implement your SaaS solution without straying too far from this flow. At the same time, I've also talked about how different identity configurations and access patterns may rely on code that can map a tenant to its corresponding identity construct. These strategies often require the injection of additional mapping constructs that reside within the flow of your authentication experience.

In Figure 6-5, for example, you saw an instance where the tenant management service was used to look up and map a user to an identity construct. This approach means that your authentication flow cannot go directly to the identity provider to process your authentication. Instead, it must first determine the target identity construct and then drive the redirection to the appropriate identity model.

Any time you add this layer of indirection to your authentication flow, you're essentially adding a point of scale and failure to the authentication model of your environment. While this may be exactly what you need to do, you want to be sure you consider the trade-offs associated with injecting yourself into the authentication flow.

The Multi-Tenant Authentication Flow

It should be clear at this point that there's a strong connection between how you enter the front door of your application and how that influences the overall authentication experience of your multi-tenant architecture. Now, let's assume you have a path into your environment that enables you to direct authentication requests to the appropriate identity provider construct. Assuming those bits are lined up, we can look more closely at the remaining steps in the authentication process.

It's important to note that this process is squarely focused on authenticating a tenant user and returning the SaaS identity that was described in Chapter 4. Much of the onboarding experience that was covered in that chapter was setting the stage for this moment of authentication, configuring our identity model with all the pieces needed to authenticate a user and return the tokens that will represent the tenant context that we'll need for all the downstream elements of our multi-tenant implementation.

Generally, the moving parts of this experience align with the OAuth and OIDC specifications that are implemented by most identity providers. Still, it's helpful to see the end-to-end flow of this experience to give you a better sense of what's happening. It also connects key dots in illustrating the injection of tenant context that's been referenced across several dimensions of our multi-tenant architecture discussion.

A Sample Authentication Flow

While we've poked around elements of authentication concepts, let's look at a sample flow to see all the moving parts in one end-to-end flow (shown in Figure 6-7).

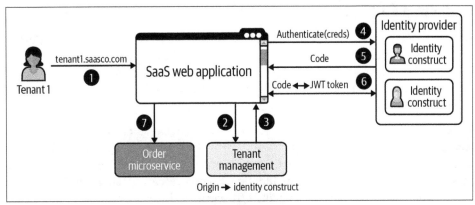

Figure 6-7. A sample multi-tenant authentication flow

In this example, I have used a subdomain-per-tenant model as part of this authentication flow. Tenants that are authenticating into this environment enter via their assigned subdomain, in this case *tenant1.saasco.com*. The tenant user hits our web application (step 1) and our application determines that the user is not authenticated. Since the user is not authenticated, your web application will redirect your user to the application login experience where the user will enter their credentials. This is a bit different from the classic authentication flow in that we'll rely on the web application to detect and direct the user to the login form.

Now, before you can authenticate the user, you'll need to determine the specific identity provider construct that is associated with this tenant. This is achieved by calling the Tenant Management service (step 2) and requesting the information for the target identity constructs that will be used to authenticate the user. The Tenant Management service will inspect the origin (subdomain) of the tenant, look up its mapping to the identity provider, and return this information to the web application (step 3). Now, you have everything you need to authenticate the tenant user. The next steps in this process follow the classic bits of an OAuth flow. First, we call the identity provider, passing along the tenant user credentials (step 4). The identity provider will then return a code (step 5) before exchanging this code for a JWT (step 6). Finally, now that you have the JWT with our tenant context, this token can be injected into the calls to our microservices (step 7).

The tokens that come out of this process, as discussed in Chapter 4, are injected into the downstream services as bearer tokens where the authorization header of your HTTP request is set to be a "bearer" token and assigned the value of the access token that comes back from your authentication flow. Then, your downstream services can use this token to implement the authorization of your microservices and provide access to a request's tenant context.

Federated Authentication

Where the federated authentication story gets more complicated is when we start to consider scenarios where your identity footprint might be more distributed. If your solution, for example, needs to authenticate against some externally hosted identity provider that's outside of your control, this can add a layer of complexity to your overall multi-tenant authentication model.

When you control all aspects of the identity experience, you can control the custom claims and policies through your identity provider. However, when a third party is authenticating your user in some federated model, it's less clear how these essential moving parts of the multi-tenant identity experience can be supported. You can't really require that third party to include the custom claims that provide tenant context. At the same time, our multi-tenant design relies heavily on its ability to issue JWTs that include this tenant context.

The good news is that there are federated identity solutions that can fill in bits of the multi-tenant experience. With Amazon Cognito, for example, you can have custom claims configured within Cognito for users that will be authenticated from a third-party provider. In this model, when you authenticate against the federated provider, Cognito can seamlessly stitch its custom claims into the JWTs that are returned from this authentication. This gives you the ability to support a third-party provider while still retaining the ability to manage custom claims for each user.

There are any number of different federated identity models that you may need to support in your SaaS environment. Each identity provider also tends to have its own unique approach to federating these users. Some may allow you to inject the custom claims and others may not. The key here is that if you're federating to a third-party provider, you'll have to determine which strategy you'll be using to acquire tenant context. In some cases, this may require you to manipulate or inject JWTs to achieve the desired experience.

No One-Size-Fits-All Authentication

As you can see, there are many approaches to authenticating a user in a multi-tenant environment. This is part of the general challenge for SaaS solutions. The path into your application, the identity constructs you're using, and other factors may require you to consider a variety of different approaches to connect the dots of your identity flow.

The key is that this is rarely as simple as hitting an identity provider and following any one of the typical authentication flows that are outlined by various identity providers. Instead, you have to wrap your multi-tenant requirements around these identity flows to align them with the multi-tenant patterns that are implemented in your environment. In the end, you're definitely conforming to the OAuth and OIDC specifications that are supported by identity providers, but your path into those flows is shaped by how tenants are mapped into the overall identity scheme of your multi-tenant environment.

Routing Authenticated Tenants

After you've made it through the front door of your application and you're ready to invoke backend services, you still need to consider how tenant context can influence the routing of these requests. Now, you could argue that this is not part of authentication and, technically, you'd be correct. However, the context that comes out of the authentication process has a direct impact on the downstream routing story of your application. So, it seems natural to make routing part of this discussion. You'll also see that, in some cases, your routing strategy might also influence the authentication model that you select.

When I talk about routing here, I'm generally referring to how tenants are mapped to their corresponding resources on a request-by-request basis. Figure 6-8 provides a conceptual view of the routing mental model.

You'll see that I have a tenant entering the front door of our SaaS environment and authenticating with any one of the models discussed earlier. Once you've authenticated, your application will begin consuming the microservices and functionality of your SaaS application. Now, if all of your application services are running in a pooled model, you can just make these calls directly. However, it would not be uncommon for you to have a more diverse architecture footprint for your application services, some of which are running in a siloed model and some of which are running in a pooled model.

When you have a mix of tenant deployment models, you'll now have to consider how you'll route requests to the appropriate tenant resources. In Figure 6-8, I've shown a simple conceptual model where we have Tenants 1 and 2 running with siloed resources and the remaining tenants running with pooled resources. With this split of siloed and pooled resources, you'll be required to introduce some notion of routing in your multi-tenant architecture to determine how this routing will be achieved.

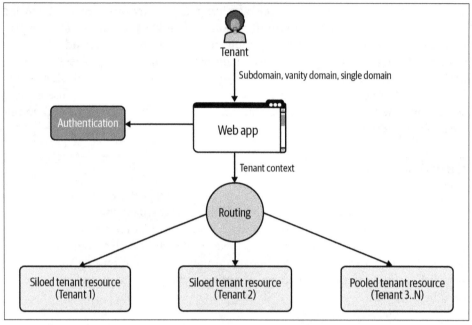

Figure 6-8. Tenant routing basics

As you can imagine, the approach you take will vary based on the technology stack you're using, the front door entry point of your application, and the deployment model of your application. Certainly, though, the approach you choose for users to enter and authenticate will have a significant impact on the options you'll have available when you're looking at routing strategies. A tenant-specific domain, for example, might be able to be combined with other networking tools/services to implement your routing strategy. As you're thinking about the entry into your application, you should also be thinking about how it will align with the routing requirements of your SaaS environment.

The routing model of your application also has implications for the onboarding experience of your SaaS solution. As each new tenant is onboarded to your system, you may need to update the configuration of your routing infrastructure to provision and configure the constructs that will be needed to route the workloads of this new tenant.

Routing with Different Technology Stacks

I mentioned that the technology stack you're using can have an influence on the routing model of your environment. While there's far too many permutations to cover all the possibilities, I thought I'd review a few examples of different multi-tenant technology stacks and look at how you might implement routing in these different models.

For this discussion, I'm going to look at two of the more common SaaS technology models: serverless and containers. The sections that follow will examine some of the nuances associated with routing for each of these stacks to give you a better sense of some of the variables that come into play as part of developing a tenant-aware routing model.

To get into the details of any routing strategy, I'll have to discuss specific technologies. The tools and mechanisms available for serverless on AWS for example might look somewhat different when realized on Azure or GCP. The routing models for Kubernetes, however, are likely to be more similar (with caveats).

Serverless Tenant Routing

Let's start by looking at how you might implement a routing strategy that uses serverless technology to implement its multi-tenant application. In a serverless environment, you will have a set of functions that are composed to create the various microservices that represent the functionality of your application.

With AWS Lambda, these functions are typically accessed through an API Gateway. This gateway describes and exposes the HTTP entry points into your services, mapping requests to their corresponding functions. In this respect, you can view the API Gateway as an essential path through which all activity flows to your application services. In fact, as we look more at a detailed serverless SaaS implementation in Chapter 11, you'll see how this gateway plays multiple roles in your overall multi-tenant architecture. For now, though, let's just focus on how the gateway(s) are provisioned and configured to support the basic routing needs of your SaaS environment.

Figure 6-9 provides a conceptual view of a basic serverless SaaS environment constructed with AWS Lambda. Here, we have a web application that's hosted in an Amazon S3 bucket. This application makes requests through the Amazon API Gateway that are then routed to the Lambda functions that are composed as part of the various microservices that are part of your application.

Now, if the functions of our serverless application are all pooled, then the role of the gateway is pretty straightforward. All requests are simply directed to their target function without regard for tenant context. However, imagine a scenario where some or all of your microservices (and functions) are running in a siloed model. This is where you'll need to evaluate the tenant context and route requests to the correct tenant functions. Figure 6-10 provides an example of a scenario where we have a mix of siloed and pooled compute resources that require targeted routing.

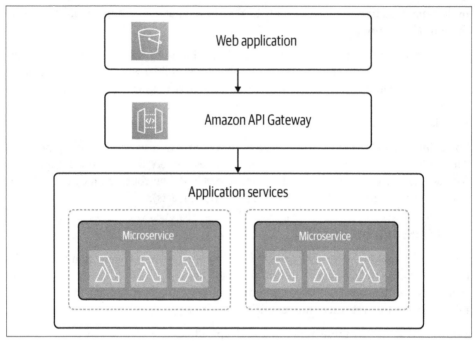

Figure 6-9. API Gateway routing in serverless environments

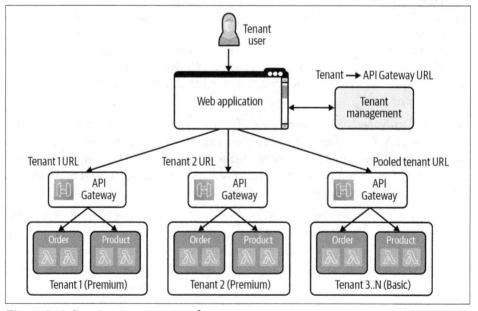

Figure 6-10. Routing to tenant-specific gateways

In Figure 6-10, I've opted for an API Gateway-per-tenant model where I provision and configure separate gateways for the different tiers of my application. I have two premium tier tenants (Tenants 1 and 2) that have siloed Lambda functions that implement their microservices. I also have basic tier tenants running in a pooled model where their functions are shared by all tenants. If you have a mixed mode deployment (some silo and some pool), then your routing will be a bit more contextual. Based on the nature of the request, you could be sending some traffic to a dedicated API Gateway URL and some traffic to a shared API Gateway URL.

As each request is processed in this model, I need to use tenant context to identify the tenant and route these requests to the appropriate gateway URL. There are multiple ways you might achieve this mapping. If, for example, your tenants used a subdomain to access your system, you could use the origin of the HTTP request header to map the tenant to a specific gateway URL. In Figure 6-10, I presumed that I had a single domain for all tenants, which required the use of the Tenant Management service (in the top right of the diagram) to look up the API Gateway URL for each tenant.

The downside of this particular model is that it requires the client to play a role in this mapping exercise. The client must acquire the URL from the Tenant Management service and apply that URL as part of making requests.

There are certainly downsides that you'll need to consider with this mapping model. Performing these mappings on every request may add overhead and latency that impacts the performance of your solution. Some address this by resolving this mapping on the client side, but it feels unnatural to distribute this problem to the client. The more typical approach here is to introduce a caching strategy at the mapping or gateway levels to hold recently mapped tenants. The key is to be sure that you're factoring the performance impacts of this mapping into the overall strategy.

Scale is also an area that deserves attention here. Having a gateway-per-tenant may not scale well in environments with a large number of tenants. This is where limiting the number of siloed tenant resources becomes an important piece of the puzzle. If you have a few premium tier tenants and the rest are basic, you'll likely be fine. However, if the number of premium tier tenants is expected to grow substantially, you'll want to reevaluate your options.

Container Tenant Routing

While the serverless routing example was more focused on mapping tenants to specific API Gateway entry points, this next strategy is more driven by the fundamental nature of how serverless applications are built and deployed with AWS Lambda. For contrast, let's look at how you might implement tenant-aware routing in an environment where your application plane is primarily built with Kubernetes.

Within a Kubernetes multi-tenant architecture, you have lots of native constructs that can be used to shape the routing footprint of your SaaS application. The list of options is pretty extensive, but, for now, I want to illustrate how you might use a service mesh to build out this routing experience. If you're new to the idea of a service mesh, you can think of it as a Kubernetes platform mechanism that lets you configure/implement different security and observability aspects of your system (outside of your application). There are multiple service mesh implementations. For this solution, I've chosen to use Istio to implement our routing model.

Figure 6-11 provides a conceptual view of a multi-tenant Kubernetes environment that uses a service mesh to control the flow of both your authentication and routing to tenant environments.

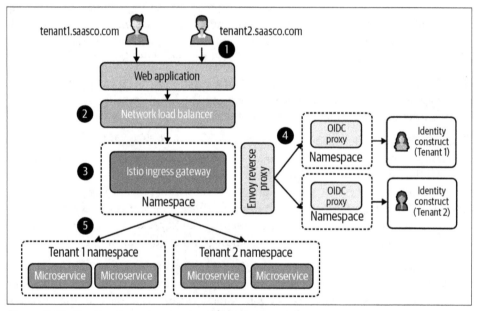

Figure 6-11. Routing tenant requests with a service mesh

You'll see that our tenants enter through the front door using the subdomain-per-tenant model described earlier in this chapter (step 1). Requests from your web application are, for this example, sent through a network load balancer that provides a durable endpoint that can be easily referenced from the web application (step 2). The request then passes through the network load balancer and arrives at the Istio ingress gateway that runs in its own namespace within your Kubernetes cluster. It's this gateway that orchestrates and applies all the policies that are required to route to our identity providers as well as our application microservices.

Let's presume that, in this example, the tenant is not authenticated. In this scenario, the gateway will send the requisition off through an Envoy reverse proxy (step 4), which will use the incoming origin subdomain to route authentication requests to the tenant-specific OIDC proxy that is also running in a separate Kubernetes namespace. Each of these OIDC proxies forwards authentication requests along to the corresponding tenant identity construct. This could be separate identity providers. It could be separate grouping constructs within a provider.

Once your tenant user has been authenticated, the gateway can send your request to the services of your application (step 5). In this example, you'll see that I have two tenants running in separate Kubernetes namespaces. This means our gateway must examine the origin and route each request to the appropriate tenant namespace.

While there are a lot of moving parts to this solution, to me it still feels a bit more graceful than those strategies that rely on your service's lookup and map tenants. Here, we're able to lean on the natural routing and proxy mechanisms of the gateway to redirect requests, moving much of the heavy lifting out of the code of our microservices. Generally, if you can offload these routing responsibilities to other bits of infrastructure that already manage routing, this often represents a cleaner, more manageable routing experience.

Considering Scale

The nuances of the authentication and routing mechanisms that I've covered here are clearly influenced by how/if you have siloed resources in your multi-tenant architecture. I discussed scenarios where you might have separate identity constructs for tenants. I also talked about how the siloed resources in your application plane can impact your routing model. While these are entirely valid strategies, you must also consider how the scale of your environment will shape your approach to authentication and routing. The more you introduce separate tenant constructs to support tenant-specific identity models or siloed deployment patterns, the more you must think about how effectively these will scale based on the number of tenants you have in your system. If you're dealing with large numbers of tenants, some of the concepts may not align well with your cost, scale, or operational goals.

Conclusion

In this chapter, we continued our path into bringing up the foundational bits of our SaaS architecture, looking into how onboarded tenants enter the front door of a multi-tenant application. The goal was to examine the different considerations that are associated with getting a tenant authenticated, acquiring their tenant context, and injecting that tenant context into the downstream services of our environment.

We explored some of the key elements that go into designing and shaping the authentication experience. This included looking at how something as simple as how the path into your SaaS environment influences the broader architectural footprint of your multi-tenant architecture. The use of subdomains, vanity domains, and a single shared domain all have implications on how you will identify tenants during your authentication flow. As we got further into the elements of authentication, we also saw how supporting different per-tenant identity constructs shaped the overall authentication flow of your environment.

Once we got beyond the front door, we moved more into examining how the authentication context could be used as part of routing tenant requests. More specifically, we looked into how this routing was applied in different technology stacks. It was here that we got a better sense of the connection between authentication and the different deployment models and technology stacks employed by your system.

Now that we have the foundational bits in place and we're authenticated tenants, we can start to look into the landscape of multi-tenant microservices and see how this tenant context influences how we decompose and construct the services of our application. In the next chapter, we'll look at how multi-tenancy influences your approach to designing and building microservices, getting more into the details of how you can realize the benefits of multi-tenancy while still limiting complexity for developers.

## CHAPTER 7

Building Multi-Tenant Services

Much of our focus up to this point has been centered around building out all the foundational elements of our multi-tenant architecture. This meant digging into the control plane and figuring out how to put a core set of services in place that would allow us to introduce the notion of tenants into a SaaS environment. We looked at how tenants are onboarded, how their identity is established, how they are authenticated, and—most importantly—how all of this ends up injecting tenant context into the services of our application. This should have given you a healthy respect for the role that the control plane plays in a SaaS environment and illustrated just how critical it is to invest in creating a seamless strategy for introducing foundational tenant constructs into your multi-tenant architecture.

Now, we can start to shift our attention to the application plane. It is here where we can start to think about how we will apply multi-tenancy to the design and implementation of the services that will bring our application to life. In this chapter, we will begin to look at how the nuances of multi-tenant workloads will influence the way we approach the design and decomposition of services. Isolation, noisy neighbor, data partitioning—these all represent new parameters that you'll need to factor into the design of your services. You'll see that multi-tenancy adds new wrinkles to the classic services design discussion, forcing you to take new approaches to the size, deployment, and footprint of your services.

The introduction of tenancy also has a direct impact on how you implement your services. We'll look closely at how and where multi-tenancy will weave its way into the code of your services, highlighting different strategies that can be used to prevent tenancy from adding complexity and/or bloat to the overall footprint of your services. I'll explore a few sample service implementations and outline tools and strategies that can be used to push multi-tenant constructs into helpers and libraries that simplify the overall developer experience.

The broader goal is to give you a better sense of the landscape of considerations that should be on your list when you're starting to build out the multi-tenant services. Making this a priority from the outset can have a significant impact on the efficiency, complexity, and maintainability of your SaaS solution.

 Throughout this chapter, you'll find that I have used the more generic term "services" when describing the components of your SaaS application. I intentionally avoided mapping these examples to any specific service implementation strategy. Yes, you could presume that this concept correlates to microservices. However, I didn't want to presume that your solution used microservices.

Designing Multi-Tenant Services

Before we can talk about how we build multi-tenant services, we need to come up a level and look at the size, shape, and general decomposition strategies that you need to think about as you identify the different services that will be part of your system. The boundaries of your services and how you distribute load/responsibilities to those services adds a dimension of complexity and forethought in a multi-tenant model.

Services in Classic Software Environments

To better understand this dynamic, let's start by looking at a classic application where the entire footprint of an application is installed, deployed, and managed separately. Figure 7-1 provides a simplified example of how services land in one of these classic, installed software environments.

You'll see that services are entirely dedicated to individual customers. When you're designing services for these environments, your focus is mostly on finding a good collection of services that can meet the scaling, performance, and fault tolerance needs of a single customer. Yes, there may be some variation in how customers use your system, but the general focus is often on creating an experience that is limited to the behaviors and profile of a single customer.

This narrower focus makes it somewhat simpler to find the boundaries of your services. Much of the focus is often more on the single responsibility design principle where you attempt to ensure that you have decomposed the services in a way that ensures that each service has a clear, well-defined scope and functional role. The idea is that these services have one well-defined job.

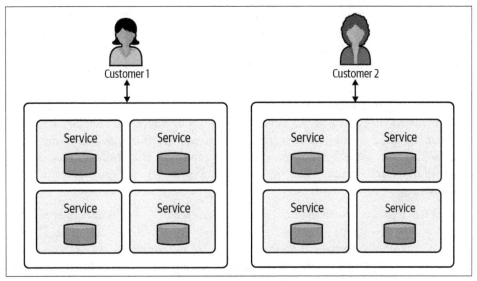

Figure 7-1. Services in a classic software environment

Services in Pooled Multi-Tenant Environments

Now, let's look at a full stack pooled multi-tenant environment. Figure 7-2 provides an example of a SaaS architecture that is supporting the needs of multiple tenants that are sharing their infrastructure resources in a pooled model.

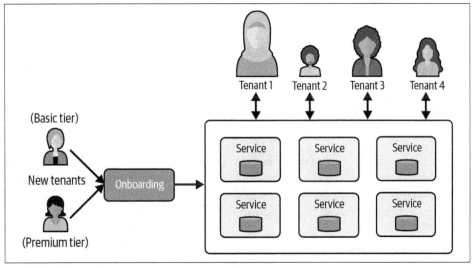

Figure 7-2. Services in a pooled multi-tenant environment

On the surface, it may seem like all that has changed here is the number of tenants that are consuming these services. However, the fact that these tenants are all exercising these services at the same time as shared resources has significant implications for how you approach the size, decomposition, and footprint of each of these services.

The first thing you'll see is that, at the top of Figure 7-2, I've intentionally introduced tenants of varying sizes. This was done to illustrate the fact that there can be huge variation in how tenants put load on your system. One tenant may saturate part of your system. Another tenant may consume the entire surface of your solution but place minimal load on the environment. The permutations can be all over the map.

On the left, I've also shown the onboarding of new tenants. This is here to convey the idea that new tenants may be introduced into your environment at any time. There is little you can do to anticipate the workload and profiles of these new tenants. I've also highlighted the fact these new, incoming tenants may belong to different tiers with different experience and performance expectations.

Now step back and think about what we really have here. The services in this environment, which are shared by all of the tenants, must somehow anticipate all the scaling, performance, and consumption needs of each of the tenant personas. You'll need to be hyper-focused on ensuring that these tenants are not creating noisy neighbor conditions where one tenant is impacting the experience of another tenant. These services will also need to dynamically scale based on what could be a fairly elusive set of parameters. The scaling strategy you use today may not align with how your services need to scale tomorrow (or in the next hour). SLAs, tiering profiles, compliance, and other considerations may also be in this equation.

This is essentially where the benefits of shared infrastructure collide with the realities of supporting a constantly shifting landscape of customer consumption profiles. For some, this leads to overprovisioning of resources to account for shifting needs and load profiles, which is exactly counter to the efficiency and economies of scale goals that are associated with the SaaS business model.

In some respects, this is all part of having a multi-tenant pooled architecture. Even if your services are overprovisioned, the collective value of sharing these resources is likely much higher than having dedicated, per-tenant infrastructure. The design of your services, however, can play a big role in giving you more tools and strategies for addressing the shifting needs of tenant workloads and profiles. Generally, our approach to designing services is focused on giving yourself more knobs and dials to address the diverse range of dynamics that your tenants are imposing on your environment.

Extending Existing Best Practices

The process of arriving at your multi-tenant services will still mirror many of the accepted methodologies and strategies that are typically used to identify candidate services. The theme is that, as part of applying those concepts, you'll also want to add additional multi-tenant design considerations to the list of factors that shape your service design, blending foundational best practices with a collection of multi-tenant considerations (as shown in Figure 7-3).

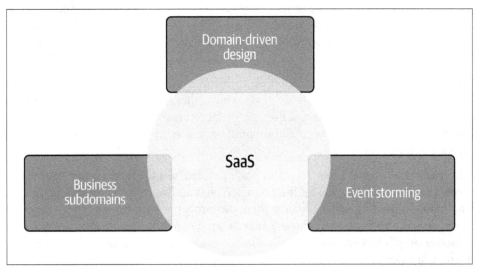

Figure 7-3. Blending service design methodologies

Figure 7-3 provides a clearer mental model of the approach that I'm advocating. Here you'll see examples of some of the common service design methodologies that teams often use to identify the different candidate services. While these methodologies have clear value, they don't always include discussion of the multi-tenant realities that must be factored into the design of multi-tenant services. Yes, I know I will end up with services that map to many of the logical entities and operations that are part of my domain. The challenge, though, is that the multi-tenant profile of my environment might end up leading me to introduce services and deployment patterns that wouldn't naturally be uncovered if you're just looking at domain objects, operations, and spheres of interaction.

To acknowledge this, I've put SaaS as a placeholder at the center of Figure 7-3. The idea was that you'd take all the design considerations that come with multi-tenancy and overlay them with other methodologies, ensuring that these concepts are front and center as you are beginning to model your application's services.

To drive this point home, let's dig into some of the common areas where multi-tenancy could have an influence on the design of your services.

Addressing Noisy Neighbor

Noisy neighbor is a concept that is not unique to multi-tenancy. Builders generally have to consider how and where users might impose load on your system that could saturate your system or degrade performance. While this is a general area of concern, you can imagine how the nature of multi-tenancy and shared infrastructure put more focus, weight, and complexity on the noisy neighbor problem. A noisy neighbor in a SaaS environment has the potential to bring your whole system down or, minimally, degrade the experience of the other tenants in your multi-tenant environment. So, as you sit down to design the services of your multi-tenant environment, you'll want to be sure that you're testing assumptions about how/if your services address potential noisy neighbor conditions.

Noisy neighbor can show up in multiple forms in a multi-tenant environment. There may be specific operations in your environment that have high latency or consume resources in patterns that have a high potential to create bottlenecks. You may have areas where certain tenant personas are prone to saturating a particular set of services that are part of your system.

The basic challenge is often all about scaling. Certainly, if a service can scale effectively enough to address the multitude of personas and workloads without overprovisioning or impacting other tenants, then you probably have a reasonable scope for your service. Our focus is on those scenarios where horizontal scale alone may not be effective or efficient enough to deal with the multi-tenant realities of your environment. Consider the sample service shown in Figure 7-4.

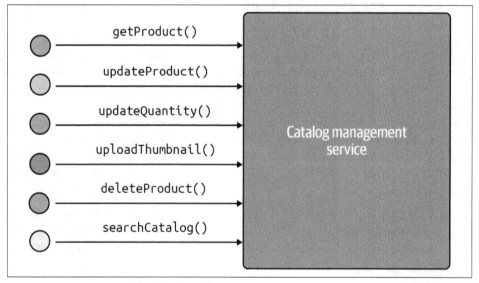

Figure 7-4. A noisy neighbor bottleneck

You'll see that I've created a catalog management service that manages all the products in my ecommerce SaaS solution. This service exposes an API that includes a pretty basic set of operations that might be used to manage catalog data. However, if you look at the far left, I've also highlighted the operational profile of each of the service's API entry points, using colors to convey their current status. You'll notice most of the operations are healthy or healthy enough. However, the `uploadThumbnail()` operation appears to be suffering from some kind of performance issue that, in this case, is yielding a noisy neighbor condition.

It turns out that this particular function happens to do some heavy lifting that is creating bottlenecks for this service. Callers are uploading images and triggering an image scaling mechanism to generate different sized thumbnails that are used in multiple contexts across the application. Left as is, your primary approach to solving for this might be to simply scale the service out, potentially overprovisioning, and hoping that this will limit any cascading impacts on your tenants. Essentially, you may be scaling this entire service when only one operation of the service needs better throughput. The better option might be to think about whether this operation could be extracted and moved to a separate service where it can scale more proportionately to tenant activity without absorbing the inefficiencies of scaling out the entire catalog management service to address your performance issues.

The general mindset is that you'll want to think differently about the scope of your service's responsibility and consider how these services will scale to meet the varying loads of a multi-tenant environment. As you're identifying your services, look for those areas that stand out as potential noisy neighbor candidates. Figure 7-5 provides a conceptual view of the overall theme here.

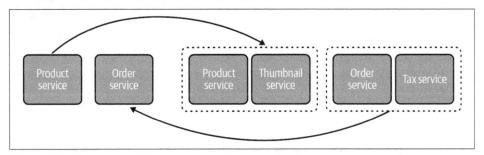

Figure 7-5. The noisy neighbor decomposition mindset

I've just illustrated how a given service could be further decomposed into smaller services that give you more targeted scaling options that, ideally, would limit noisy neighbor conditions and limit overprovisioning. The Product service separates out a Thumbnail service to better distribute the load and the Order service breaks out a standalone Tax service. The core idea is that we must incorporate these noisy neighbor and scaling efficiency considerations into our service design, using this information to identify areas where a more granular decomposition strategy might yield a better result.

It's fair to ask if this approach is really unique to SaaS. The answer is no. As a rule of thumb, any environment should be looking at ways to better address performance and scale through more granular services. What's different, though, is the diversity of tenant personas and workloads that end up requiring SaaS architects to be much more diligent about addressing these kinds of challenges. An inefficiently scaled, bottlenecked, or overprovisioned service is likely to show up more in a multi-tenant environment, which can have profound impacts on your tenants and the operational profile of your SaaS environment. So, while this is a good general approach, it deserves much greater focus and attention when you're designing services for a multi-tenant environment.

It's worth noting that it's fully expected that your noisy neighbor strategy is going to evolve over time. The services you pick on day one should be expected to morph as your system evolves and you have richer insights into how and where you're observing noisy neighbor conditions. Start with the services that make sense, and then use the strategies outlined here based on the operational profile of your environment.

Identifying Siloed Services

In Chapter 3, we talked about different deployment models and how these models might require you to have some or all of a tenant's resources deployed in a siloed (dedicated) model. On the surface, it may seem as though there's no real connection between siloing resources and the design of your services. However, there can actually be a strong correlation here between the services you choose and how/when/if those services get deployed in a siloed experience.

Whenever you choose to silo a service, you're often doing so to support a specific system or tenant need. You might, for example, need to silo some service to support a compliance requirement that's part of your domain. Tiering, performance, and isolation may also have some influence on which services that you opt to deploy in a siloed model.

Of course, any time you're siloing a resource, you're making a compromise that can impact the operational, cost, deployment, and management complexity of your environment. So, if you are going to have siloed resources, it's ideal to limit the number of services that need to be deployed in silos. Figure 7-6 provides an example of how the isolation requirements of your environment might influence the footprint of your services.

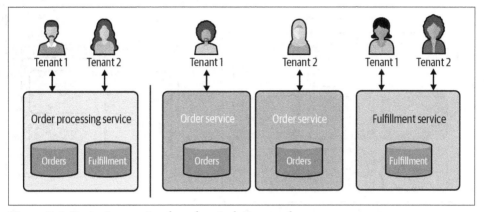

Figure 7-6. Designing services based on isolation needs

This diagram includes two different approaches to designing an Order Management service that address all the order processing and fulfillment needs of your solution. On the left, you'll see this service deployed in a pooled model that shares compute and storage for all tenants. Now, let's presume that our tenants have expressed a concern about having this service running in a pooled model. Your first instinct might be to move this service to a fully siloed deployment model to ensure that each tenant would run a dedicated copy of this service. However, after probing further, you find that your tenants are actually only concerned about having dedicated compute and storage for the order processing portion of the service.

Instead of fully siloing this service as is, you may be able to break the service down into one or more services to address the isolation needs of your customer. This is precisely what I've done in this example, breaking the original service into two separate services. Here, our new Order Processing service is deployed in a siloed model where each tenant gets access to a dedicated service, directly addressing our tenant's isolation requirement. As part of this move, I also introduced a new Order Fulfillment service that continues to run in a pooled configuration.

You can imagine how this same approach could be applied to any number of scenarios where a customer may require siloed resources. You might, for example, apply some variation of this same mindset for compliance, noisy neighbor, or general performance reasons, breaking up larger services to give yourself more granular control over what is siloed and what is not.

This approach of picking what's pooled and what's siloed doesn't have to be about breaking services into more services. It might just be about grouping services based on their need to be siloed. Figure 7-7 provides a conceptual view of how you might align the boundaries of your services based on their silo versus pool requirements.

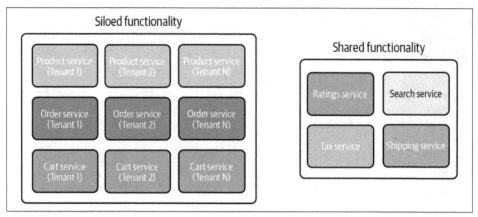

Figure 7-7. Aligning services with silo/pool requirements

For this scenario, my tenants have indicated that they need specific functionality to be deployed in a siloed model. In Figure 7-7, you'll see that the Product, Order, and Cart services are all deployed in a siloed model where each tenant has a dedicated instance of these services. Then, on the righthand side, I have a set of services that are running in a pooled model.

You could just view this purely through the lens of deployment and say some services are siloed and some are pooled, and that would be accurate. However, the idea is that you want to be as thoughtful as possible about which services land in the siloed side of this experience. So, if you're designing services that you know are going to have to support this mix of silo and pool, you should be thinking about how you can decompose these services in a way that will allow you to land as much as you can in the pooled model.

This siloing strategy is something you should make a core part of your service design mindset, identifying the use cases and requirements that might justify deploying a service in a siloed model. This list typically includes compliance, isolation, security, tiering, and performance. It's also important to note that you may silo services entirely based on your own internal operational needs. For example, you may have some services that simply can't meet the demands of tenants in a pooled model. In this case, you might opt to carve that piece of functionality out and deploy it in a siloed model purely based on the operational realities of your environment.

In some instances, the siloed boundaries of your services may stand out early in your design process. In other instances, however, you may need to collect data and iterate some to arrive at a set of services that balance this siloed/pooled universe. For me, the main thing I'm trying to avoid is just moving services into a silo without challenging myself to see if there are more creative ways to decompose my service. Again, as I mentioned earlier, you may not discover these boundaries until after you've collected more operational insights from the working system.

It's important to note that this silo strategy should be adopted with caution. It's not exactly operationally or cost efficient. So, you'll want to be selective about how and when you consider this approach. For systems with a smaller population of tenants, this could be a good strategy. However, for systems with a larger pool of tenants, this would become challenging to scale and support.

The Influence of Compute Technologies

While it may be less obvious, there are also scenarios where the compute technology you're using can have some influence on the footprint of your services. Containers, serverless, and other compute constructs can introduce their own set of considerations to your multi-tenant design. Suppose, for example, you are considering having some services that run in a serverless compute model and others that run in a container compute model. It turns out that the nature of these different compute models can play a direct role in defining the size, scope, and boundaries of your services. To better understand this, let's look at Figure 7-8.

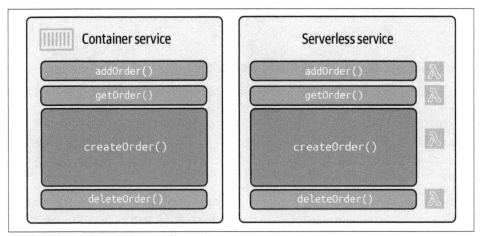

Figure 7-8. Compute and service design

In this example, I have included two mostly identical instances of an Order service. On the left, the service is running in a container compute model. Meanwhile, on the righthand side, this same service is running in a serverless model (in this case using AWS Lambda). I've highlighted the different operations that are part of this service and sized the box of each operation based on the load associated with these operations. In this case, it should be clear that the createOrder() operation is receiving the bulk of the requests. So much so that you might ask whether this service will be able to scale efficiently or whether it's essentially going to scale based on this one operation —even though the other operations are not really being pushed.

Now, when we look at the container-based deployment, we might consider how to refactor this service to improve the overall scaling efficiency of our environment. With containers, all of this functionality is packaged, scaled, and deployed collectively so that the container becomes our unit of scale.

With the serverless model on the right, though, each of the operations that are deployed as part of our service represents a separate function that can be deployed, managed, and scaled independently. So, if `createOrder()` or any other operation is receiving a disproportionate level of load, that function will scale on its own. This represents one of the significant advantages of the serverless model where the scaling is more granular and becomes someone else's problem to manage. The better news is that if the load profile shifts tomorrow and another operation starts taking all the load, there's nothing I need to do to adjust the scaling policies or profile of my service. This makes it much easier to accommodate and optimize for the continually shifting workloads of multi-tenant environments.

The key takeaway is that the compute model you're using may have some influence on your service decomposition model. It's not the primary factor, but it does add another wrinkle to your design mindset.

The Influence of Storage Considerations

When we're designing services, we're also often thinking about the scope and the nature of the data that will be accessed and managed by these services. Since each service is expected to encapsulate the data that it manages, you must consider how this data will be consumed. Splitting a service along the wrong data boundary could end up leading to extremely chatty services that are constantly in need of data that lives in the scope of some other service.

These are all general considerations that are associated with designing any service. Now, as we look at multi-tenant services, we have some new factors to add to our design considerations. Our multi-tenant data can be stored in a siloed model where each tenant has its own dedicated storage structure, or it could be stored in a pooled model where tenants data is commingled within a shared storage construct. You may also need to think about how the different operations on your data will scale effectively when customers are competing for a shared storage resource. Imagine thousands of tenants all querying some relational database that has stored all of its tenant data in a shared table. Will these tenants saturate the compute of the storage technology? Will you end up creating another flavor of a noisy neighbor condition? These are all just examples of how the footprint of your storage might influence the scope and granularity of your services. In some cases, a more coarse-grained service might be your preferred model. In others, there may be compelling reasons to break your services into smaller bits to support different data profiles.

In many respects, the storage needs of your service must also look at many of the factors that shaped the noisy neighbor and siloing discussion outlined earlier. With storage, we're going inside the service and thinking about how multi-tenant requirements, tenant personas, and workloads might shape the footprint of your service. This is essentially a mirror of the compute considerations that we discussed earlier. Storage has its own compute and data footprint that must also address noisy neighbor, compliance, tiering, and isolation considerations.

The key takeaway is that storage can and often does play a significant role in the decomposition of your services, so as you're sitting down to identify your services and their scope and granularity, you'll want to be sure to give storage the attention it deserves. In some instances, this will be straightforward, and in others the storage profile of your services may be the driving force that shapes a service's design.

Using Metrics to Analyze Your Design

The design of your services will be continually evolving. New features, new tenants, new tiers, and new workloads will have your team continually evaluating the performance, scale, and efficiency of your multi-tenant architecture. Of course, in a multi-tenant environment, it can be more challenging to get a handle on whether the design of your services is delivering the experience you intend. You might be able to use some basic monitoring data to draw some high-level conclusions about how your system is behaving, but this data won't typically allow you to evaluate the consumption and activity patterns of individual tenants and tiers. This makes it difficult to perform any kind of deeper analysis of the factors that are shaping the operational profile of your SaaS environment. Is the consumption profile of a particular tenant or tier impacting the scaling profile of a given service? Are basic tier tenants pushing your services in ways that are impacting your premium tier tenants? These are just examples of insights you really need to assess the efficacy of your service design.

It's only when you have these richer insights that you can really begin to evaluate whether the design of your services is successfully addressing the various factors that we've been exploring (noisy neighbor, tiering, performance, and so on). Getting these metrics means adding instrumentation to your services that will surface the data you need to analyze the operational profile of your services. Figure 7-9 provides a conceptual illustration of this instrumentation model.

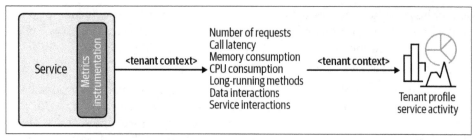

Figure 7-9. Surfacing tenant-aware service metrics

On the left is a sample service that includes instrumentation that publishes the data that is used to assess the performance, scale, and operational profile of your service. In the middle there are some examples of data that you might capture for a service. What you choose to instrument here will depend on the nature of the services and the nature of the data that would best characterize its activity. All the data that's recorded will minimally include tenant context and tenant tier (if you're using tiers).

Finally, on the right is a placeholder for the aggregation and analysis of this data. It's here that you'll use the tool of your choice to analyze this metric data and evaluate the runtime profile of your services. We'll dig into the whole area of multi-tenant operations and metrics in Chapter 12. The key is that in a multi-tenant environment, you really need to invest in capturing the metrics and analytics that can tell you how your design is performing. Without this data, you'll have limited ability to examine how the variations in tenant workload and activity are exercising your architecture.

One Theme, Many Lenses

Across this entire discussion of services design, I focused on finding the granularity and deployment model that best addresses the compliance, isolation, storage model, noisy neighbor, tiering, and performance requirements of your environment. While each of these factors brings its own nuances to the services design discussion, you can also see that the strategies used to address these needs definitely overlap.

There were two basic themes that were sprinkled throughout our design discussion. In some cases, your design strategies will focus on creating more granular services that can better respond to your multi-tenant scaling and performance needs. In other situations, you may look at using siloed deployments to create a profile that addresses your system's requirements. The key is to add these possibilities to your design mindset and look for opportunities to support the realities of your multi-tenant workloads.

Inside Multi-Tenant Services

With this backdrop of multi-tenant service design in place, we can now start looking at what it actually means to build a multi-tenant service. As a rule of thumb, I tell

---

teams that they should make every effort to limit a developer's awareness of multi-tenancy when they are coding the business capabilities of their SaaS application. Our focus, then, is on the strategies and techniques you can introduce that will limit the overhead builders will absorb when they're implementing multi-tenant services.

To get a better sense of how multi-tenancy lands in your services, let's start with a basic service that has no support for any notion of tenancy. The following code provides a snippet of an Order service that is responsible for fetching all orders matching a given status:

```
def query_orders(self, status):
  # get database client (DynamoDB)
  ddb = boto3.client('dynamodb')


  # query for orders with a specific status
  logger.info("Querying orders with the status of %s", status)
  try:
    response = ddb.query(
                TableName = "order_table",
                KeyConditionExpression = Key('status').eq(status))
  except ClientError as err:
    logger.error(
        "Find order error, status: %s. Info: %s: %s",
        status,
        err.response['Error']['Code'],
        err.response['Error']['Message'])
      raise
  else:
    return response['Items']
```

For this service, I happened to choose an AWS NoSQL storage service (Amazon DynamoDB) to store my orders. I've coded this example in Python and Boto3, a library that's used to integrate with AWS services. The order data will land in DynamoDB with a "status" key that will be used to access the orders in our system.

Overall, the code represents a relatively vanilla service that essentially takes an incoming status as a parameter and queries a database for orders that match that status. You've likely seen or written some variation of this function at some point along the way.

For our purposes, we're more interested in what's not here. Since this code is not running in a multi-tenant environment, there's nothing in the code that has to concern itself with multi-tenancy. The logging data it emits, the data it's accessing—none of it has to consider which tenant is actually invoking these operations.

As a multi-tenant architect, it should be your goal to have this code remain as straightforward and familiar as it is here. You must find a way to introduce tenant context and support for multi-tenant constructs without adding bloat and overhead to the builder experience. The more you can move tenant context outside the view of builders, the more opportunities you will give yourself to centralize these strategies and policies for all of your services.

Extracting Tenant Context

Now we can start to look at how our service code will begin to morph as tenancy is injected into our code. Before we can even think about applying tenant context, we have to think about how that tenant context lands in our services. This starts by first looking back at the identity and authentication topics that were discussed in Chapters 4 and 6, respectively. In these chapters, we looked at how tenant context was bound to an individual tenant user and injected as a JWT that flowed into the services of our solution. We can now get into what we do to leverage this token as it arrives in the context of our services.

If you recall, the JWT gets embedded as a header within each HTTP request that is sent to your services. This token is passed as what is known as a "bearer token." The term "bearer" maps to the idea that you are granting access to the bearer of this token. For your service, it indicates that you're authorizing the system to perform an operation on behalf of the tenant associated with that bearer token.

If you were to crack open one of these HTTP requests, you'd see the bearer token represented as part of the request's authorization header. The request would resemble the following format:

```
GET /api/orders HTTP/1.1
Authorization: Bearer <JWT>
```

You can see this is a basic GET request to the */api/orders* URL with an authorization header that has the value of "Bearer" followed by the contents of your JWT. Let's look at the code we need to add to our service to access the tenant context that's embedded in this token. It's important to note that this token is encoded and signed, so we'll need to unpack it to get access to the claims that we're interested in. The following example adds code to the prior example, introducing the steps needed to extract the tenant context from the incoming JWT:

```
def query_orders(self, status):
  # get tenant context
  auth_header = request.headers.get('Authorization')
  token = auth_header.split(" ")
  if (token[0] != "Bearer")
    raise Exception('No bearer token in request')
  bearer_token = token[1]
  decoded_jwt = jwt.decode(bearer_token, "secret",
                  algorithms=["HS256"])
  tenant_id = decoded_jwt['tenantId']
  tenant_tier = decoded_jwt['tenantTier']
```

```
# query for orders with a specific status
logger.info("Finding orders with the status of %s", status)
...
```

I've trimmed out the actual query execution code since it is, at the moment, unchanged. The code we want to focus is the snippet where I'm accessing and extracting the tenant context from the incoming request. This block of code first pulls the authorization header out of the overall HTTP request, setting the auth_header equal to "Bearer <JWT>" where the JWT represents your encoded token. The next bit of code performs the basic string operations needed to get the contents of the JWT copied into a separate string. This string is then decoded using a JWT library. The end result is that the decoded JWT ends up in the decoded_jwt variable. The last step is to acquire the tenant ID from the JWT's custom claims. You might also be accessing other claims here (role, tier, etc.) based on the nature of your solution.

In this particular example, I'm assuming that your service would own responsibility for decoding each token. However, there are other options. You could, for example, have an API gateway that would sit in front of all your services, processing each inbound request. This gateway could crack open these JWTs, access the tenant context, and inject that into each service. This could allow you to implement more interesting strategies to deal with the latency that comes with accessing tenant context on each request. This is just one of the alternate strategies you might consider. The key is that somewhere at the front of these requests, you'll need code that can go through the motions of acquiring this tenant context for every request (whether it's cached or extracted from the JWT each time).

Once this code is executed—wherever it resides—your service will now have access to the tenant context it needs for other downstream operations. This processing of tenant context illustrates the payoff of the onboarding and authentication flows we discussed in earlier chapters, illustrating how services can begin to address multitenancy without calling other services or mechanisms to get their tenant context.

Logging and Metrics with Tenant Context

At this stage, our code now has access to tenant context. However, it's not doing anything with that context. Let's start by looking at one of the areas where you can apply context in your multi-tenant services: logging. Logging represents one of those foundational mechanisms every service is going to use, emitting messages that create an informational and debugging audit trail that is essential to troubleshooting and analyzing the activity in your system.

Now, imagine using these logs in a SaaS environment where multiple tenants are exercising your service at the same time. By default, if you did nothing to your logs, they would contain a mixed collection of insights that had no correlation to any specific tenant. This would make it nearly impossible to piece together a view of the activity of any one tenant. If you're on the operations team and you're told that Tenant 1 is having issues that nobody else is reporting, you would have a very difficult time using your logs to identify the log messages and events that were contributing to that tenant's specific problem. Even if you found an error message, it's unlikely you'd be able to explicitly associate that error with a specific tenant.

The good news is that now that we have tenant context at our fingertips, we can inject this context to our log messages. This will introduce the tenant context that will allow your operations team to analyze logs through the lens of individual tenants, tiers, and so on. Let's look at what our code would look like with the addition of this tenant-aware logging:

```
def query_orders(self, status):
    # get tenant context
    auth_header = request.headers.get('Authorization')
    token = auth_header.split(" ")
    if (token[0] != "Bearer")
        raise Exception('No bearer token in request')
    bearer_token = token[1]
    decoded_jwt = jwt.decode(bearer_token, "secret",
                    algorithms=["HS256"])
    tenant_id = decoded_jwt['tenantId']
    tenant_tier = decoded_jwt['tenantTier']

    # query for orders with a specific status
    logger.info("Tenant: %s, Tier: %s, Find orders with status %s",
                tenant_id, tenant_tier, status);
    ...
```

I've just changed one of the logging messages that is part of the Order service. Our message simply prepends the tenant context to the front of our logging message. This context would be added to all of the logging messages within your services, introducing the data that equips teams with much richer insights into the specific behavior of their tenants. If you're querying logs, you can now filter by a specific tenant's context and assemble a more complete view of how individual tenants are interacting with your system. There's no magic to this, but it's one of those small changes that can have a huge impact on the operational profile of your environment.

The same logging mindset should also be applied to the metrics instrumentation of your multi-tenant architecture. Yes, we want logs to build a forensic view of tenant activity, but we also need data used by the business to profile the consumption and activity of tenants that doesn't quite fit into the operational profile of log messages.

The mental model is that the metrics emitted from our services represent insights that are focused on providing the data that can be used to analyze and answer questions that shape your business, operational, and architecture strategy. Here you're profiling how your service is influencing the tenant experience and tracking your ability to measure a range of key metrics that business and technical teams can use to evaluate the system's efficacy, agility, efficiency, and so on. We'll cover the use of these metrics more in Chapter 12. For now, though, we need to consider how the publishing of these metrics fits into the footprint of our multi-tenant services.

Let go back to the Order service and add a metrics call just to provide a more concrete example of publishing a metric event:

```
def query_orders(self, status):
  # get tenant context
  ...
  tenant_id = decoded_jwt['tenantId']
  tenant_tier = decoded_jwt['tenantTier']

  # query for orders with a specific status
  logger.info("Tenant: %s, Role: %s, Finding orders with status: %s",
              tenant_id, tenant_role, status);
  try:
    start_time = time.time()
    response = ddb.query(
                TableName = "order_table",
                KeyConditionExpression = Key(status).eq(status))
    duration = (time.time() - start_time)
    message = {
                "tenantId": tenant_id,
                "tier": tenant_tier,
                "service": "order",
                "operation": "query_orders",
                "duration": duration
              }
    firehose = boto3.client('firehose')
    firehose.put_record(
      DeliveryStreamName = "saas_metrics",
      Record = message
    )
  except ClientError as err:
    logger.error(
      "Tenant: %s, Find order error, status: %s. Info: %s: %s",
      tenant_id, status,
      err.response['Error']['Code'],
      err.response['Error']['Message'])
    raise
  else:
    return response['Items']
```

For this example, I've added the recording of a metric to the Order service query. To keep it simple, I just added something to track the duration of the query. Then, I created a JSON object that included all the data about the tenant context and the operation being performed. Now I need to publish this metric to some service that can ingest and aggregate these metric events. For this example, I used an AWS streaming data pipeline (Amazon Kinesis Data Firehose) to ingest my metrics data, constructing the Firehose client and calling the put_record() method to send the metrics event into the service.

Again, you can see that the instrumentation of metrics, on its own, doesn't really represent a particularly complex process. The majority of the effort will go into determining what you want to capture and how you'll introduce the code that publishes your metric data. The investment is small if it's adopted widely by your teams, but the return can be substantial.

The challenge of telling the metrics story is that there is no single, universal metrics approach that everyone should apply to their services. The value is clear, but the specifics are hard to nail down. This often needs to be driven by your own desire to identify the metrics that will add the most value for your business. At the same time, I will also say that some of the most effective SaaS companies are those that prioritize metrics and work to identify the insights that will best inform their ability to assess the internal and external experience of their systems.

Accessing Data with Tenant Context

Logging and metrics are relatively straightforward and are more focused on capturing insights about the activity of your services. Let's shift to looking at how tenant context will influence how data is accessed for individual tenants.

At the moment, the data returned by our Order service hasn't really done anything to account for tenant context. In fact, without any further modification, this service would return the same data for every tenant that requested orders. This, of course, is not the intended behavior of our system. To address this, we need to apply the incoming tenant context to our query, limiting the view of orders to those that are associated with the calling tenant.

The natural and simplest way to apply tenant context is to add the tenant to the parameters that are part of your search. We already have our tenant identifier and simply need to decide how to use this tenant identifier to access our data. You have multiple options here. Let's presume, for the moment, that you have a pooled database model where your tenant data is commingled in the same table. When the data is pooled, we can simply add a TenantId key to our order table that will associate each order with a specific tenant. This tenant identifier will become the key of our table. This means that the status we were using will now become a secondary search parameter that returns all orders for a tenant that match the supplied status.

The code to apply this tenant context to your query is pretty straightforward. In the following example, I've augmented the query portion of the service, using the tenant identifier as the key and the status as a filter:

```
response = ddb.query(
            TableName = "order_table",
```

```
KeyConditionExpression = Key('TenantId').eq(tenant_id),
FilterExpression=Attr('status').eq(status))
```

This slight tweak to your database search is all that's needed to ensure that the orders that are returned here are limited to just those that are associated with the current tenant.

In this scenario, I started with the simplest of use cases. Where data access discussion gets more interesting is when we start thinking about the various combinations of storage strategies your service might need to support. Suppose, for example, your system offered different storage for different tiers as shown in Figure 7-10.

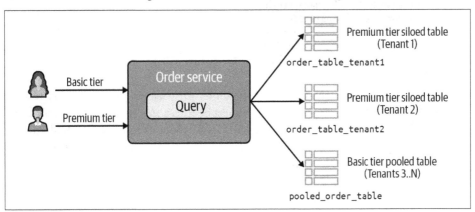

Figure 7-10. Supporting tiered storage models

In this scenario, our Order service is processing requests from basic and premium tier tenants. The compute is completely shared by these tenants. However, on the righthand side of Figure 7-10, you'll see that the service employs different storage strategies for each of these tiers. The basic tier tenants are all stored in a single table that's indexed by tenant ID (as was the case in our prior example). However, the premium tier tenants store their data in a siloed model where each tenant has its own dedicated storage. In this example, each of these dedicated tables are assigned a name that conveys their binding to a specific tenant.

Now, with this new wrinkle in the mix, let's think about what this means for the implementation of your service. Somewhere within the code of our service, you must have logic that examines the tier of each tenant to determine which table will be used to process their requests. And, depending on how their data is stored, you may need multiple paths of execution within your service to support identifying and interacting with the tenant's order data.

Let's start with a brute force approach to this, knowing that we'll need to refine to make this simpler. To make this work, we'll essentially need to add some mapping operation to our query to resolve the name of the table that will be used (based on a tenant's tier). I've revisited the query we had within our service above, adding a new getTenantOrderTable() function that examines a tenant's tier and returns the name that will be used for a given tenant request. Here's the snippets of code that add this functionality:

```
response = ddb.query(
            TableName = getTenantOrderTable(tenant_id, tenant_tier),
            KeyConditionExpression = Key('TenantId').eq(tenant_id),
            FilterExpression=Attr('status').eq(status))

# helper function to get generate tier-based table name
def getTenantOrderTableName(tenant_id, tenant_tier):
  if tenant_tier == BASIC_TIER:
      table_name = "pooled_order_table"
  elif tenant_tier == PREMIUM_TIER:
      table_name = "order_table_" + tenantId
  return table_name
```

This approach, however, presumes that the tables for basic and premium tier tenants will be identical. For the most part, they would be the same; however, our pooled tenants rely on a TenantId key that is used to access the orders for individual tenants. This key has no value or meaning in the siloed tables. Many teams will keep this key in their siloed tables simply to avoid having to support additional one-off behavior. If you choose to remove this key from the siloed resources, you'll need to have more specialized code to compose your interaction with the data to account for the presence or absence of this key.

Naturally, the type of data that your service stores and the technologies it uses are going to vary significantly. The example we covered here represents just one of many ways that multi-tenant data might shape how you implement your service.

Supporting Tenant Isolation

The data access example we just covered relies on inserting tenant context into our query to scope the data to a given tenant. It's easy to assume that, if we're filtering these queries by tenant, then you've put all the measures in place to ensure that one tenant can't access the data of another tenant. And, in theory, it's not an unreasonable expectation. However, in multi-tenant environments—where tenant isolation is essential to the trust of your tenants—filtering data access by tenant isn't really enough.

It's critical that we draw a clear line between the strategies that are used to partition and access data and the strategies that are used to enforce tenant isolation. How data is stored and accessed is what we would consider your "data partitioning" strategy, which is covered in depth in Chapter 8. How we protect resources (including data) from cross-tenant access is referred to as "tenant isolation," which is covered in detail in Chapter 9. When we're talking about isolating tenant resources, we're talking about the measures that we use to surround the code within our services to ensure that developers don't intentionally or unintentionally cross tenant boundaries. So, regardless of what tenant parameter might be in your query, for example, the tenant isolation policies that surround that query will prevent that code from accessing the resources of another tenant.

This, of course, means that we need to introduce new constructs and mechanisms into the implementation of our services to apply tenant isolation strategies. The goal is to have your code somehow acquire an isolation context before it accesses any resource and use that context to scope your resource access to the current tenant. With this context applied, any attempt to interact with a resource will be constrained to just those resources that belong to the current tenant.

Now, let's look at how we can take this theory and turn it into something more concrete to give you a better idea of how this might land in your multi-tenant services. For this particular example where we're accessing DynamoDB, we can achieve our isolation goals by configuring our session with a set of credentials that will scope data access based on tenant context. If you look back to the starting point for our Order service, you'll see where the Boto3 client was initialized as the client library that would be used to access our order data. The initialization code is as follows:

```
def query_orders(self, status):
  # get database client (DynamoDB)
  ddb = boto3.client('dynamodb')
    ...
```

This initialization of the Boto3 library used a broader, default set of credentials to initialize the client. In this state, your client is initialized with a much wider scope, allowing it to access any item in your order table. That means any query here could access data for any tenant, regardless of what tenant context was passed into our service.

Our goal, then, is to scope down the access of this client for each request that is attempting to get orders, initializing the client with a scope that includes the context of the calling tenant. To achieve this, we'd need to change the way our client is initialized. The code that would apply this scope would resemble the following:

```
def query_orders(self, status):
  # get database client (DynamoDB) with tenant scoped credentials
  sts = boto3.client('sts')

  # get credentials based on tenant scope policy
  tenant_credentials = sts.assume_role(
    RoleArn = os.environ.get('IDENTITY_ROLE'),
    RoleSessionName = tenant_id,
    Policy = scoped_policy,
    DurationSeconds = 1000
  )
```

```
# get a scoped session using assumed role credentials
tenant_scoped_session = boto3.Session(
  aws_access_key_id =
    tenant_credentials['Credentials']['AccessKeyId'],
  aws_secret_access_key =
    tenant_credentials['Credentials']['SecretAccessKey'],
  aws_session_token =
    tenant_credentials['Credentials']['SessionToken']
)
# get database client with tenant scoped credentials
ddb = tenant_scoped_session.client('dynamodb')
  ...
```

There are a few moving parts to this solution. First, note that our first block of code focuses on getting a narrower set of credentials that are scoped based on the current tenant identifier. In this particular example, we're staying within the family of AWS services, relying on the AWS Security Token Service (STS) to facilitate this scoping exercise. With STS, I can define a policy that restricts access to my order table. We won't dig into the details of this policy here, but just know that it essentially restricts access to just those items in the database that match a given tenant ID. So, when I call the `assume_role()` function and supply my policy and tenant identifier (extracted from the JWT), this service will return a set of credentials that will limit access to just those items that belong to the current tenant. These credentials are stored in the `tenant_credentials` variable.

Once we have these credentials, we can declare and initialize a session with the specific credential values that were returned from our `assume_role()` call. Here you'll see the typical credential values that are used by AWS services when accessing resources.

All that remains now is to declare our DynamoDB client (as we did before). However, the client is now created using the `tenant_scoped_session` variable. This essentially tells Boto3 to initialize the client with the credential values that we set up in the prior steps. Now, when we invoke the query command using this client, it will inherit the scoping policies and apply these to any call made with this client.

This mechanism creates a true tenant isolation experience, providing a tenant-scoped context for any call to the database. Now, no matter what value or configuration a developer puts into their query, the system will prevent the service from accessing data that's not valid for the current tenant.

This example should give you a better sense of how tenant isolation can influence the footprint of your multi-tenant services. Getting this right is essential to building a robust isolation story for your solution. The challenge, though, is that there are a number of factors that make it difficult to have a one-size-fits-all approach to isolation. The technology you're using, the cloud you're on, the services you're consuming, the silo or pool footprint of your resources—each of these elements may all require a different strategy to describe and enforce tenant isolation within your service. The spirit and mindset of what we've done here is still valid for any service. It's really in the implementation and realization of these concepts where you'll run into significant variation.

It's also important to note that your services are likely to interact with a range of different types of resources. The isolation policies and approach we've covered are meant to be applied across any resource that might be managing or touching tenant-specific constructs. If you have queues, for example, those queues may require some form of isolation.

 As you look at these tenant isolation mechanisms, you must consider whether these constructs will undermine the scale and performance of our solution. Will this added overhead create bottlenecks in your experience? Is there something more you can do to make application of these policies more efficient (caching, etc.)? These are the kinds of questions you'll want to ask yourself as you're introducing these constructs.

Hiding Away and Centralizing Multi-Tenant Details

When I kicked off our discussion of building multi-tenant services, I put great emphasis on being able to introduce these constructs without bloating or adding complexity to your developer experience. My goal was to hide away and centralize many of the multi-tenant constructs and keep your service code focused squarely on implementing the business logic of your application.

Up to this point, I really haven't achieved this goal. In fact, if I were to put all the concepts we discussed into one final version of my Order service, it would likely have tripled in size and complexity. You can also imagine how having this code in each service would be inefficient, distributing common concepts and constructs to every service in my system. At a minimum, this would represent a bad bit of programming. It would also limit my ability to centrally manage my multi-tenant strategies and policies.

This is where we put our basic builder skills to work and look for the natural opportunities to move these concepts out of our services and into libraries that can hide away much of the detail that we have been covering. There's nothing uniquely multi-tenant to this approach. It's more that, as a multi-tenant architect, I want to be sure I'm doing what I can to streamline the service developer's experience.

If you look back to our example, you can see where there is code that could easily be moved into helper libraries. Consider, for example, how the code that we added to acquire tenant context from the JWT could be moved into a separate function. The code would simply be lifted out of our service and turned into a function that resembled the following:

```
def get_tenant_context(request):
  auth_header = request.headers.get('Authorization')
  token = auth_header.split(" ")
  if (token[0] != "Bearer")
    raise Exception('No bearer token in request')
  bearer_token = token[1]
  decoded_jwt = jwt.decode(bearer_token, "secret",
                    algorithms=["HS256"])
  tenant_context = {
                "TenantId": decoded_jwt['tenantId'],
                "Tier": decoded_jwt['tenantTier']
              }
  return tenant_context
```

This new `get_tenant_context()` function takes an HTTP request and does all the work we described earlier to extract the JWT, decode it, and pull out the custom claims that have our tenant context. I tweaked the function some, putting all the custom claims into a JSON object. How and what you chose to return here will depend on what's in your custom claims. You might have separate functions to get specific custom claims (`get_tenant_id()`, for example). This is more a matter of style and what works best for your particular environment.

The key, though, is that this library now means that any service needed to extract tenant context can make a single call to this library and shrink the amount of code that lands in your services. It also allows you to alter JWT policies without having these changes cascade across your solution. Imagine choosing a different approach to encoding or signing your JWT. With this in a centralized function, you can now make these alterations outside the view of service developers.

This same theme can also be applied to the logging, metrics, data access, and tenant isolation code that we covered earlier. Each one of these areas can be addressed through the introduction of libraries that standardize the handling of these multi-tenant concepts.

With logging and metrics, the key is really just removing the added overhead of injecting tenant context every time you log a message or record a metric. Now you can simply share the request context with each of these calls and let some external function determine how to acquire tenant context and inject it into your message and events.

Data access is one area that may be a bit less generic and may require helpers that are local to a specific service. If you recall, we discussed a use case in which our Order service might need to support a tier-based storage model where each tier might need to route its requests to a different order table. In this scenario, you might lean on the traditional data access library (DAL) or repository pattern to create a targeted construct that abstracts away the details of interacting with our service's storage. Here, this DAL could encapsulate all the multi-tenant requirements, including applying isolation within that layer (completely outside the view of service developers).

Now, let's assume we moved all of this multi-tenant code into a library. The code of our service would be streamlined substantially, returning it to the version that resembles the copy that we had before multi-tenancy was introduced. The following code introduces a new function to get tenant context, introduces a logging wrapper that injects tenant context, adds a function to get a tenant-scoped database client, and employs an order DAL to hide away the details of mapping tiers to specific tables:

```
def query_orders(request, status):
  # get tenant context from request
  tenant_context = get_tenant_context(request)

  # get scoped database client
  ddb = get_scoped_client(tenant_context, policy)

  # query for orders with a specific status
  log_helper.info(request, "Find order with the status of %s", status)
  Try:
    response = get_orders(ddb, tenant_context, status)
  except ClientError as err:
    log_helper.error(
        request,
        "Find order error, status: %s. Info: %s: %s",
        status,
        err.response['Error']['Code'],
        err.response['Error']['Message'])
      raise
  else:
    return response['Items']
```

While there are lots of nuances in how this concept could end up getting applied in your services, this example gives you a sense of just how this approach can influence the implementation of your services. In many respects, this comes down to following fundamental programming best practices. The elegance here is less in the detail of what's in these libraries and more about the value they bring to service builders.

Interception Tools and Strategies

At this point, you can see how simply moving these shared multi-tenant concepts into libraries makes sense. However, in addition to moving this code outside of your services, you should also consider the different technology and language constructs you can use to streamline your developer experience and centralize your multi-tenant strategies.

The basic idea is that we want to look at how we might leverage the built-in capabilities of a given technology construct to support these horizontal multi-tenant needs, allowing you to introduce and configure multi-tenant operations and policies with minimal cooperation of your service builders.

Consider, for example, our approach to tenant isolation. If my language and tools provide me with a mechanism that allows me to insert processing between my service and the resources I am accessing, this might enable me to enforce aspects of my isolation model completely outside the view of my services.

The hard part of providing guidance here is that the list of possible strategies that enable this approach is quite long. Each language and its supporting frameworks, for example, will bring its own unique blend of options to this discussion. Also, the different technology stacks and cloud services that are part of your architecture may include their own constructs that can be applied in this scenario. How and where these constructs are applied will vary significantly based on the specifics of each of these different options. While it would be counterproductive to review the spectrum of possibilities, I do want to highlight a few sample strategies to give you a better sense of the different types of mechanisms that could fit with this mindset.

Aspects

Aspects are generally introduced as a language or framework construct. They allow you to weave cross-cutting mechanisms into your code that enable you to inject pre- and post-processing logic into the footprint of your services. This allows you to introduce global policies and strategies into your services that may align well with some of the multi-tenant mechanisms that are part of your environment. Figure 7-11 provides a conceptual view of the aspects model.

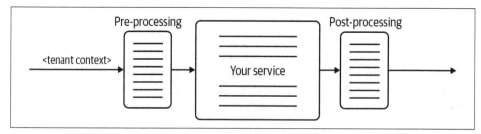

Figure 7-11. Using aspects to apply tenant context

At the center of this diagram is the code of your service. Much of the development of your services has no awareness of the policies that surround it. With aspect-oriented programming, I can bolt extra handling logic into my service that will be executed as tenant requests enter and exit. This code is woven into my services with whatever aspect tooling or technology I've chosen.

You can imagine how this could represent a great fit for handling, processing, and applying tenant contextual operations. For example, you could use an aspect to intercept each request that comes into your service, adding pre-processing that would extract the JWT from the HTTP header, decode it, and initialize the tenant context for the rest of your request. You could also consider implementing elements of your tenant isolation model, acquiring and injecting the tenant-scoped credentials that are needed to enforce your isolation policies.

The key is that this becomes a standard mechanism for all of your services that is woven into them as part of a global strategy (instead of relying on developers to call the appropriate helper functions in their code).

Sidecars

If your multi-tenant architecture is built with Kubernetes, you may want to consider whether sidecars could be used to apply multi-tenant strategies to your services. A sidecar runs in a separate container within your Kubernetes environment and has the ability to sit between your service and other resources and services. The nice part of these sidecars is that they are entirely outside the view of your service. This allows you to apply any global multi-tenant policies in a way that may not require the cooperation of your service. Figure 7-12 provides a conceptual view of the sidecar model.

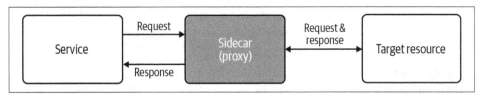

Figure 7-12. Using sidecars for horizontal concepts

On the left of Figure 7-12, you'll see my application service that has my business logic. And on the far right is some resource that my service will interact with. This could be another service, a database, or any number of different constructs. The key here is that the sidecar sits between me and that resource. This allows the sidecar to intercept and apply tenant context outside the view of my service, extracting context and applying any policies that are associated with my service and the resource it's consuming. Being able to separately deploy and configure this sidecar allows me to create a much more robust multi-tenant enforcement story, allowing me to have greater control over my service's interactions with other resources.

Middleware

Some development frameworks support the notion of middleware. The idea is that you can introduce code that sits between your inbound request and your target operation. This allows you to intercept and apply any global policies that would be applied across your service.

This middleware mechanism is commonly used in the Node.js Express framework. The framework provides all the built-in constructs that are needed to implement many of the multi-tenant service strategies that we've covered here (tenant context, isolation, etc.).

AWS Lambda Layers/Extensions

I mentioned that different cloud providers and their services may include constructs that could be a good fit for realizing some of these cross-cutting multi-tenant strategies. I thought it would be worth highlighting one example here. If you're building a serverless SaaS environment on AWS, you have the opportunity to use Lambda Layers or Lambda Extensions to move your shared libraries into a standalone mechanism.

With Lambda Layers, you can essentially move all of your helpers into a shared library that is then deployed independently. Each of the Lambda functions that are part of your service can reference the code in this shared library, allowing them to access the different helper functions you have without having that code being part of each service. This allows you to manage, version, and deploy these globally shared constructs entirely separately. Now, when you want to update your isolation mechanism, for example, you could update the code in your Lambda Layer, deploy it, and have each of your services get updated with this new capability.

Lambda Extensions, on the other hand, fit more into the aspect pattern that we discussed earlier, allowing you to associate custom code with the lifecycle of a Lambda function. For example, you could use a Lambda Extension to pre-process a request upon entry to a function of your service. The code for a Lambda Extension can also live within a Lambda Layer.

Conclusion

At this point, you should have a much better sense of what it means to design and build a multi-tenant service. In this chapter, we started by looking at how the needs of multi-tenant environments directly influences the shape, size, and footprint of the services that support the core functionality of your SaaS offering. This required us to examine the various factors that must be added to your mental model when identifying the boundaries of your services.

Much of our design discussion was focused on the continually shifting workloads and consumption profiles of your tenants and how this influences your approach to picking the combinations of services that will allow you to best address these realities—especially in environments that have pooled resources. This led to a much deeper dive into the different ways that noisy neighbor possibilities might impact the design of your services, potentially driving new service decomposition strategies that can better address the tendencies of a given service or workload. We also looked at how you might apply siloing strategies across your system's services to address targeted performance, experience, and tiering requirements.

As part of looking at design, I also highlighted the importance and value of investing in metrics that can continually inform the design of your services. The key was to acknowledge that you should expect your design to evolve based on the operational insights that will come once it's alive and running under real workloads. It's only with solid multi-tenant metrics and insights that you can understand how your service design is meeting the current and emerging needs of your tenants.

Once we had a grasp of the design considerations, we shifted our attention to looking inside our services to better understand how multi-tenant shapes the actual implementation of these services. The focus here was first on determining how and where multi-tenancy needs to land within the implementation of your service. I highlighted how your service would acquire tenant context and then apply it across logging, metrics, data access, and tenant isolation. A key point of emphasis here was on making every effort to ensure that the introduction of these multi-tenant strategies/policies would not come at the cost of adding complexity or bloat to your services. We looked at specific ways to address this goal, outlining different ways to move these multi-tenant constructs outside the view of developers and to a more centrally developed and managed model.

Overall, the broader theme is that multi-tenancy can have a significant impact on both the design and implementation of your services. At the design level, it's all about anticipating the dynamic, shifting, and elusive profile of your tenant consumption tendencies and multi-tenant requirements. Within the services, it's more about focusing on thinking about how you can ensure that your services are implementing the core best practices without undermining the experience or productivity of your builders.

Now that we have a sense of how multi-tenant is implemented in our services, we can start digging into the various strategies that are used to represent the data used by these services. While I've provided glimpses of how you might store data in multi-tenant environments, we mostly looked at this through the lens of other concepts. Now, in the next chapter, we'll focus exclusively on the different approaches and considerations that are associated with representing, operating, and managing multi-tenant data. This will give you a more complete view of the different factors you should consider when working with multi-tenant data and highlight key points of inflection that will influence how/where you store the data that's part of your multi-tenant environment.

## CHAPTER 8

Data Partitioning

As we wander deeper into the multi-tenant services of a SaaS environment, we must also begin to look at how these services represent, access, and manage data in a multi-tenant model. While the fundamentals of multi-tenant data are relatively easy to wrap your mind around, there are lots of nuances that come with selecting a multi-tenant storage strategy that aligns with the requirements of your environment.

There are multiple factors that can have a direct influence on how you store data for a given workload in your SaaS environment. Compliance, noisy neighbor, isolation, performance, cost—any of these might have a significant influence on how you choose to represent your data in a multi-tenant setting. Technology also plays a big part in this story. Each storage technology has its own set of constraints, constructs, and mechanisms that will need to be considered as part of your data partitioning strategy.

In this chapter, we'll cover the full range of data partitioning considerations, highlighting the different factors that are typically going to shape your data partitioning model. We'll start by looking at some of the fundamentals of data partitioning, reviewing the common themes and considerations that apply regardless of the storage technology you may be using. We'll also look at the natural connections between data partitioning and tenant isolation to help you understand how isolation might play a larger role in determining the data partitioning model you ultimately select.

Once we have a sense of the core concepts, the emphasis will shift to looking at the specifics of how data partitioning is realized across a range of different storage technologies and services. Here, the goal will be to dig into each of these technologies and understand how the nature of each storage service influences your data partitioning design. This will also give you a clearer view into how different storage technologies are able to address key multi-tenant storage challenges (noisy neighbor, tenant isolation, compliance, and so on). We'll also look at the trade-offs associated with multi-tenant data models, identifying key areas you'll want to focus on when storing different types of data (object, relational, NoSQL, and so on).

Data Partitioning Fundamentals

Before we can start looking at concrete multi-tenant storage constructs, we need to first review some of the foundational data partitioning concepts. Let's start by being clear about what I mean when I refer to data partitioning. To me, when I think about storing data in a multi-tenant environment, I'm always thinking about how an individual tenant's data will be partitioned based on the type of data being stored, the technology that I'll be using to store and manage it, how the tenant will consume it, and so on.

The partitioning of data does not presume that each tenant's data must somehow land in a complete standalone storage construct. This, in fact, is where the silo and pool concepts end up playing a key role again. The terms come forward with us as we look at how we describe the representation of tenant data. To help clarify this point, let's look at how siloed and pooled models are applied to storage. Figure 8-1 provides a basic conceptual view of how siloed and pooled strategies are mapped to the realm of multi-tenant data partitioning.

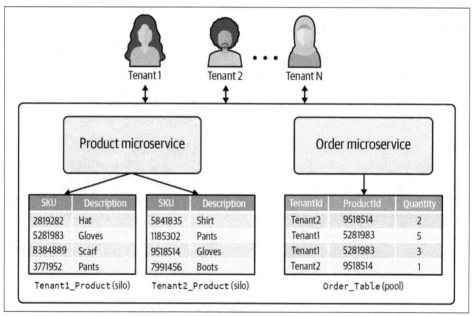

Figure 8-1. Siloed and pooled data partitioning models

In this example, I have shown Product and Order services that are both running with pooled compute that is shared by all tenants. However, you'll also notice that each of these services employs different data partitioning models. On the left, the Product service uses a separate, dedicated storage construct for each tenant. Given this footprint, we would refer to this storage as being siloed.

On the righthand side, you'll see that I have an Order service that uses a different data partitioning model. Here there's only one shared storage construct that is used to store and manage all tenant orders. This is what we would refer to as a pooled storage model.

You'll also see that how I mapped tenants to their data is different for each of these data partitioning schemes. For silo, the tenants are generally associated with their siloed storage construct based on some naming model. In this instance, I prepended a tenant identifier to the name of each storage construct. You'll also note that there's nothing in the actual product data that references or connects each item to a tenant. It's not needed. The order table, on the other hand, has data for all tenants and, as such, it needs some way to associate individual items with each tenant. For this example, I introduced a TenantId column to identify the items that belong to each tenant.

The key is that regardless of which technology you're using to store your data, you still would use these silo and pool terms to characterize how the data is represented. While these concepts are universal, how they are actually brought to life across different technologies can vary significantly. These variations can play a key role in influencing whether your data ends up being stored in a silo or pool model.

It's also worth noting that both of these strategies have different scaling considerations. A siloed strategy, for example, can introduce scaling and management challenges as you attempt to add separate storage constructs for each tenant. Meanwhile, depending on the size of your data, commingling all of your tenant data in a single construct can also introduce scaling limits if you store excessive or poorly distributed data.

 Throughout this chapter, I'll be talking about siloed and pooled data partitioning strategies. It is essential to understand the tradeoffs, design considerations, and operational impact of adopting each of the models across different storage technologies. It's also important to understand that these two models should not be viewed as mutually exclusive. You may, for example, choose a pool model for your basic tier tenants and a siloed model for your premium tier tenants. This approach allows you to offer two experiences to your tenants, enabling a broader range of pricing and packaging options for your service.

Before we get into how these storage models land on specific storage technologies, let's consider some of the cross-cutting concerns that you should be thinking about as you design your multi-tenant storage strategy.

Workloads, SLAs, and Experience

Every multi-tenant storage strategy must be hyper-focused on scale and performance. The nature of multi-tenant data consumption can vary significantly across the services of your solution, requiring creative approaches to supporting the shifting workloads and consumption patterns of your tenants. Finding a storage strategy that effectively addresses these needs can be challenging. The workloads and patterns you see today may not be the same tomorrow. New tenants may also be onboarding, adding all-new wrinkles to the storage profile of your system.

As you sit down to design your data partitioning strategy, you'll want to be sure you are thinking about how each storage experience is going to perform in a multi-tenant model. How will you meet any SLAs that may be required for a given tenant tier? How will you detect and handle scenarios where a tenant saturates your storage? How will you efficiently size the compute that is running your storage service? These are just a few examples of performance and scale questions you'll need to consider when you're picking a data partitioning model.

Part of this exercise is also about estimating the footprint of your data. Having some sense of the amount of data your tenants will be storing across the different services of your system will allow you to project how your system might be able to scale to meet the SLAs of your tenants. This will also be essential to understanding how your data might be pushing the limits of the storage technologies you're using. For some services, you might find that the tenants with disproportionately large data could end up undermining your data partitioning strategy and degrading the performance key areas of your system. Knowing this might tip you toward a different partitioning approach that will allow you to effectively scale your multi-tenant data.

Noisy neighbor is another area you'll want to focus on as you're building out your multi-tenant storage strategy. We've already discussed this as a more global concern, but noisy neighbor brings its own unique set of nuances to the multi-tenant storage puzzle. It's here that you'll have to develop workload profiles and understand how tenants will consume your system's multi-tenant data, identifying areas where you may need to introduce partitioning, siloing, or throttling mechanisms that can prevent tenants from imposing loads that might impact the experience of other tenants. These same policies will also be essential to managing the availability of your environment—especially if you're encountering noisy neighbor conditions with your pooled storage.

Sizing the compute of your storage is also part of this story. It can be challenging to determine what level of compute resources is needed to support the workloads and SLAs of your solutions. It's often challenging to find a balance that doesn't end up requiring an overprovisioning of storage resources to meet your throughput requirements.

Blast Radius

While the goal of any architecture is to ensure that we've done all that we can to prevent outages, there are still scenarios where teams take additional measures to ensure that one tenant can't impact the experience of another tenant. This is, of course, especially significant in a multi-tenant environment where an outage could impact every customer in your system.

Now, as you're picking a storage model, some teams may factor blast radius into their overall strategy, leaning toward siloing data to reduce the scope of potential outages. This might translate into siloing a particularly critical family of data. In this approach, if a siloed database, for example, were to suffer from some fatal condition, the impact of that failure could be limited to a single tenant. This would also allow the operations team to work on this issue in isolation.

This can be especially powerful when you look at the deployment footprint of your SaaS environment. As new versions and capabilities are rolled out, the siloed data for each tenant could be updated separately, creating opportunities to gracefully deploy and update the data constructs without impacting all of your tenants.

While there are merits to siloing your data to limit blast radius issues, this is still something I would consider carefully. This may fit for some environments, but it also can be a crutch that impacts the overall agility, cost efficiency, and operational profile of your environment.

The Influence of Isolation

Isolation touches every dimension of multi-tenant architecture, and it certainly plays a role in shaping the data partitioning model you select. In fact, this is often where the lines between data partitioning and isolation can get blurry. For example, I might choose a partitioning strategy based, at least partly, on its isolation requirements.

Where this gets a bit confusing, though, is that teams will sometimes equate their data partitioning strategy with tenant isolation. So, if they've chosen to use a siloed model for a particular family of data, they will describe that data as being "isolated." While you may have chosen a silo model to enable isolation, siloing the data alone does not mean the data is isolated. Isolation, as we'll see in Chapter 9, represents a layer of enforcement that goes beyond how the data is stored. It enforces and scopes access to data regardless of whether it is siloed or pooled.

I prefer to view isolation as influencing the data partitioning model I select while acknowledging that implementing that isolation will still be achieved separately. This influence of isolation on data partitioning is especially important as you look at different storage technologies. If you're at least partially selecting a data partitioning strategy based on its potential to support a level of isolation, then you must also consider how the storage technology you're selecting will support enforcement of isolation at the level you require. For example, I might silo tenant data in a separate database to enable isolation, only to find out that the database doesn't allow me to define per-tenant isolation policies at the database level. That might persuade me to consider another option.

This is even more pronounced when you're thinking about pooled data partitioning strategies and isolation. Here, as you can imagine, strategies that let you enforce your isolation are even less frequently supported.

Management and Operations

As architects and builders, it's natural to focus on performance and isolation when picking a data partitioning strategy. However, it's equally important to consider how your data partitioning strategy will influence the management and operational footprint of the SaaS environment. When you're weighing your silo or pool partitioning options, for example, you should be thinking about how the footprint of your data might impact the experience and agility of your operations team (backup, deployment, migration, telemetry, and so on).

The pooled data partitioning model, for obvious reasons, typically offers the greatest level of operational efficiency. When you have data represented in a pooled model, you have a much cleaner management and operations story. Any updates to data, for example, would be applied to all tenants with a single operation in a pooled model. Also, the effort required to assemble operational views into the performance and health of your storage services is made simpler when all of your tenants are using shared constructs.

With siloed data partitioning, you have a more distributed model that adds a degree of complexity to your management and operations experience. Here, your DevOps tooling must take on the challenge of applying any data changes or migrations to each tenant individually. Synchronizing these changes across a large collection of siloed data constructs certainly adds a level of complexity and timing to this process. Your operational tooling will also take on an added burden in a siloed data partitioning scheme. Your tooling will now be required to assemble a collective view of health and activity from the various siloed tenant databases that are part of your environment.

Backup and restore should also be part of the discussion. How will your partitioning model influence your ability to back up and restore tenant data? With siloed data, this is simpler. However, with pooled data you need to think about how you'd take a snapshot of a tenant's data from a shared storage service (and consider how you'd restore tenant data without impacting other tenants). There are lots of variables that would shape your approach here. The key is that you have this on your radar as you're selecting a data partitioning strategy.

Ultimately, this often comes down to balancing efficiency and manageability. Just know that where you land could have a significant impact on your ability to meet the scale and agility goals of the business.

The Right Tool for the Job

Some teams look at data partitioning as an all-or-nothing moment where they're picking a technology that meets the requirements of their solution. For example, teams will do their analysis and then go all-in with the one database technology that seems to best suit the needs of their solution. This may even be driven by developer experience, where teams will pick a storage strategy based on their general familiarity with the technology.

It's likely already clear why this is a less than ideal approach to selecting a multi-tenant storage approach. The reality is, there are so many variables that can influence your selection of a storage technology, and—more importantly—these variables may be different for each part of your system.

If you look at your system as a composed collection of services that encapsulate their underlying storage, then you should be evaluating your storage technology options on a service-by-service basis. The storage technology that fits well with the requirements of one service may not fit well with the requirements of another service. The goal is to consider each service in isolation, allowing the service to deliver the best experience it can based on the workload it supports, its isolation needs, its compliance considerations, its management profile, and all the other factors that might shape its footprint. This includes picking siloed and pooled data partitioning strategies on a service-by-service basis. Yes, you'll likely find storage patterns that apply universally to many services. However, you still want to ask these questions for each service you build.

Defaulting to a Pooled Model

In some cases, it may not be entirely clear which data partitioning model—silo or pool—fits best for a given workload. You may need to wait until you've been able to observe and profile the scale, performance, and operational behavior of tenant workload to have a better sense of the preferred approach.

Generally, in these cases, my recommendation is to default to a pooled model for all the storage in your system. The cost, operational, and agility advantages of pooled storage are often so compelling that teams will cling to the model as long as they can. In this mode, you're essentially forcing any siloed data to earn its way out based on a set of clear requirements that justify taking on the trade-offs that come with managing, operating, and deploying data in a siloed model.

It's true that some workloads and data types will be clear candidates for being siloed on day one of your system. The trap you want to avoid, though, is over-rotating to a siloed model for elements of your system that may not demand a siloed experience. Each time you choose to silo any resource in a SaaS environment, you should be challenging your assumptions and ensuring that you have scoped the silo at the appropriate boundary.

Supporting Multiple Environments

As we dig into the specifics of data partitioning with different technologies and services, you'll see scenarios within the siloed model where we create per-tenant constructs (tables, databases, clusters, etc.). Each time we create one of these tenant-specific constructs, we have to assign them a name that associates the construct with a tenant.

Solving for this usually means coming up with some naming convention that ensures that the resource is uniquely identified. Where this gets more interesting is when you start thinking about supporting multiple environments (QA, staging, production). Now, you have to figure out whether your naming convention may need to include a reference to the environment that is hosting your siloed storage resource.

For some services and strategies, you may have a siloing construct that doesn't create a conflict between names. For example, for some cloud storage services, you might have separate accounts for each environment. In this mode, your resource names may be scoped at the account level, ensuring that they are only accessed from within that account. However, there are also instances where names can be global to all accounts. In this scenario, you'd still need a naming convention that would include support for your different environments.

This isn't generally a significant issue. However, it is worth considering as you're defining your data partitioning model.

The Rightsizing Challenge

One theme that you'll find spanning this book is the notion of aligning infrastructure consumption with the activity of tenants. This is all part of the quest for efficiency that's fundamental to every SaaS business. One dimension of this scaling challenge that can get overlooked is the efficiency of your storage compute consumption. It's here that teams have difficulty finding a data partitioning and storage strategy that allows them to optimize their compute consumption footprint.

The sizing of storage compute is trickier in a multi-tenant environment. With our services, we can scale our compute horizontally based on load, which makes it easier to expand and contract their compute footprint based on tenant workloads. However, with storage, you typically don't have this option. Instead, a storage service will often require you to select a particular compute profile when you are initially configuring your environment. This means your storage compute remains fixed for all tenant workloads.

This presents a particularly challenging problem for multi-tenant environments. Figure 8-2 provides a clearer view of the storage sizing issues that come with multi-tenant environments.

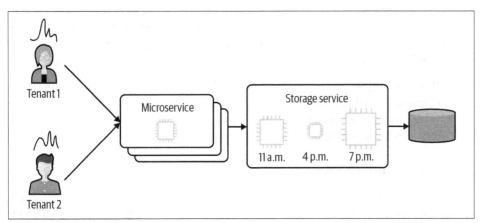

Figure 8-2. Sizing the compute of your storage

In this example, I have two tenants that are consuming a service in a pooled model. This service scales out horizontally based on the workloads of the tenants. All of the instances of this service are pointed at some pooled storage service that manages its data. In this example, let's say that my storage service is some relational database service running in the cloud and that this service, as part of its setup, required us to select a compute size.

The question is: what size should you choose for the compute of this storage service? In the diagram, you'll see that I've highlighted the dilemma, illustrating how the compute sizing changes throughout the day. At 4 p.m., for example, the compute needs are minimal while at 7 p.m. load increases substantially. To top it off, you have new tenants and new workloads coming into your multi-tenant environment that are continually changing these consumption patterns.

Tackling this problem looks a bit different for siloed and pooled data partitioning models. In the pooled model, it's very difficult to rightsize the compute of your storage service. Generally, to accommodate the shifting workloads and spikes of multiple tenants consuming your pooled storage, you'll need to overprovision the compute and just accept that this will negatively impact the cost efficiency strategies of your overall environment.

If you're using a siloed model for your data, there are fewer variables to consider, which should make sizing somewhat easier. The nature of individual tenant loads is likely to be somewhat more predictable and, as such, you may be able to select a compute size that better fits the needs of your siloed tenants. Even in this model, though, you'll accept some degree of overprovisioning. There will likely be times during the day where a siloed tenant's storage is idle or very lightly consumed.

Certainly, profiling your storage consumption will give you more data to better size the compute for your siloed and pooled models. In some cases, teams will use this data to continually size the compute of their storage in an attempt to limit overprovisioning. This constant juggling, however, can also add significant operational complexity and inefficiency.

Overall, there's no magic solution to this challenge. If your storage service requires you to bind to a fixed compute profile, you'll have to accept the challenges that come with it. Ideally, the costs associated with the overprovisioning of your resources will not have a significant impact on the overall margins of your SaaS business.

Throughput and Throttling

One way to deal with rightsizing issues is the use of storage throughput and throttling strategies. These mechanisms allow you to introduce policies that can better manage the consumption of your storage resources, including supporting separate experiences based on tenant tiers and personas. The idea is that you would use the built-in performance configuration options of your storage technology to find the mix of settings that best support the general performance and sizing challenges of your storage workloads.

The key is that, as part of your data partitioning model, you'll want to consider how you will apply these policies. This includes thinking about how these policies might differ for pooled and siloed storage models. These two partitioning schemes may require different approaches to configuring the throughput and throttling profile of each storage experience.

Serverless Storage

As we look at this sizing problem, it's entirely concentrated on those storage technologies that rely on pre-sizing their compute footprint. The good news is, though, there are more and more storage technologies that are embracing a serverless model that removes any binding to a specific compute profile. With serverless storage, these services hide away the details of the storage compute profile, sizing the underlying compute based on the current level of tenant activity. The compute is essentially auto-sized based on the load of your system, which fits perfectly with the needs of a multi-tenant environment.

The serverless storage model has surfaced across a range of different storage technologies. At AWS, for example, you'll find Amazon Aurora Serverless, which is a serverless relational database storage service that employs this serverless model. Amazon DynamoDB is also serverless, providing a managed NoSQL storage service that requires no compute sizing. I suspect that the majority of cloud-based storage technologies will eventually offer some degree of support for the serverless model.

As we look at the different storage technologies in the remainder of this chapter, you'll want to keep this serverless model on your radar. Anywhere you're using the pooled data partitioning model, for example, you'll find that a serverless model could represent a compelling option. The key is that, given the unpredictable nature of multi-tenant storage consumption, you'll likely find yourself leaning toward serverless as the preferred approach to aligning your storage consumption and costs with your tenant's activity. This serverless model also simplifies the operation and management of your storage services, eliminating the need to constantly chase shifting compute sizing requirements.

With these foundational data partitioning concepts in place, we can now start looking at how these principles are realized through different storage technologies. In the sections that follow, I'll map the general concepts we reviewed here to more concrete implementation strategies, highlighting the different nuances that come with each storage technology. There are far too many storage options available to cover them all, but I've selected a sampling of common storage technologies that should give a good sense of how variations within these individual technologies influence your data partitioning strategies.

Relational Database Partitioning

Now that we have a sense of the data partitioning fundamentals, let's start by looking at how these concepts would land in a relational database. When we look at how you can implement data partitioning in a relational database, much of the discussion focuses on the sizing, scale, and operational efficiency.

Relational databases generally support a range of different constructs that can be used to partition our data. One constant is the dependency on a schema. This means, regardless of which data partitioning model we chose, our data is going to be represented in an environment that has a binding to schema. This can present challenges in multi-tenant environments where we may need to gracefully migrate tenants from one schema representation to the next. This can add complexity to the overall agility story of your storage model.

This doesn't mean that relational databases and SaaS are not a fit. In fact, there are compelling use cases where a relational model might better align with a given workload in your environment. At the same time, you should be sure to weigh the migration and agility impacts of a relational model when selecting a storage strategy.

Pooled Relational Data Partitioning

Let's start by looking at what it would take to implement a pooled model with a relational database. The mechanics of storing data in a pooled model with a relational database are pretty straightforward. Here, you're simply taking your existing database design and introducing a tenant identifier to associate the items in a table with a specific tenant. The end result, shown in Figure 8-3, is exactly what you would expect.

	TenantId	CustomerId	FirstName	LastName
Tenant1	5d4402a6-e759-432c-9e27-c9e1c8d1f970	84829349	Jane	Smith
Tenant2	24150732-cba3-49ad-a39e-a955e01d3ba7	64829451	Mike	Jones
Tenant1	5d4402a6-e759-432c-9e27-c9e1c8d1f970	28192826	Sue	Henderson
Tenant3	702257a5-fbdf-4890-932f-f1a4faabae3b	95185144	Joe	Michaels
Tenant4	de1115e1-cf6b-4bf2-b22b-616b247ead0e	84965872	Lisa	Lewis
Tenant2	24150732-cba3-49ad-a39e-a955e01d3ba7	20594091	Rob	Hanson

Figure 8-3. Pooled relational database

I've shown a customer table that stores multi-tenant data in a pooled model. A new TenantId column has been introduced as the foreign key of this table, serving as the primary index for accessing data. The tenant identifier GUIDs in this column represent the ID of each tenant that is associated with a given row.

The basic idea of any pooled storage model is that we are commingling the data of all tenants within some shared construct. Then, the data that would have previously been the foreign key for this table becomes a secondary index or a filter. In this case, our CustomerId column has become the secondary key for this table. This means that our interactions with this table must now introduce this tenant identifier into the queries that are accessing data from this table.

For this example, I wanted to include a table with rows that were associated with separate tenants. Rows 1 and 3 are associated with Tenant 1 (as shown on the lefthand side of the diagram). Rows 2 and 6 are associated with Tenant 2. This pattern would be repeated across all the pooled tables in your system that are holding tenant data.

Introducing a TenantId column also gives us a way to potentially apply policies that will be part of our tenant isolation story. These policies (described in Chapter 9) will illustrate how we can filter the view of a table and prevent cross-tenant access to data. Each database technology may have its own unique approach to defining these policies. The key is that, in some instances, the partitioning model of your pooled data may influence the isolation strategies that can be applied to your data.

Siloed Relational Data Partitioning

While the pooled relational model is straightforward, there are often more options to consider when you silo data in a relational database. A relational database technology may offer you multiple constructs to define the siloed boundaries of your data. Figure 8-4 provides a conceptual view of some of the different constructs that can be used when siloing data in a relational database.

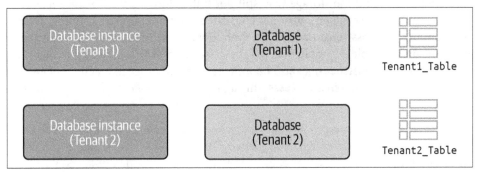

Figure 8-4. Picking a relational siloed storage construct

On the left of this diagram, I've shown a database instance per tenant model. With the Amazon Relational Database Service (RDS), for example, this would essentially equate to spinning up entirely separate infrastructure for every tenant. The compute and all the infrastructure resources of the instance would be dedicated to a single tenant.

In the middle, I've shown the concept of a database. Here, you have a dedicated database for each tenant running within a database instance. While each database is entirely separate, they all share the underlying compute of their parent database instance. Finally, on the righthand side, you'll see a model where separate tables are used to silo each tenant's data. These tables would all be created within a shared database.

With any of these models, it would become the responsibility of your environment to associate names or tags with these siloed relational storage constructs. Then, at runtime, your code would need to map a given tenant request to its corresponding database instance, database, or table.

For each of these different silo constructs, you'll need to consider whether the construct can scale to meet your needs. Within RDS, for example, there are limits that will shape the options you have here. You can only have so many databases within a database instance. The same applies to tables. The technology you choose to use may impose other flavors of constraints that should be part of your scaling math. The general guidance is to be sure you're giving careful consideration to the range of limits that come with your relational technology. Doing some basic modeling of your potential growth will give a better sense of whether you're safely within the scaling constraints of your relational database environment.

Your choice to silo might also be driven by a need to achieve isolation based on the security and compliance considerations of your domain. Certainly, the more coarse-grained nature of siloed relational constructs often represents an appealing way to address these needs. However, as you examine different relational technologies, you may find that siloing the storage may still not fully address your isolation needs. In some instances, these siloed relational constructs may not support defining policies that can prevent cross-tenant access. So, even though your data is siloed, there are no mechanisms available to implement a robust isolation policy. The key is that your choice of siloing construct may also be influenced by whether that construct enables you to prevent cross-tenant access through isolation policies (more on this in Chapter 9).

With Amazon RDS, you also have a wide array of database engines to choose from: MySQL, PostgreSQL, MariaDB, SQL Server, Oracle, and so on. There are nuances within each of these engines that could add new dimensions to your siloed partitioning model. While each cloud and/or relational database vendor may add their own twist to this story, the mindset and approach generally maps well to the patterns and considerations that I outlined here.

NoSQL Data Partitioning

The next area we'll look at is NoSQL storage. There are a number of different NoSQL options to choose from, each of which may introduce new constructs that could alter your approach to implementing pooled and siloed data partitioning strategies. To make this a bit more concrete, I'm going to focus on Amazon DynamoDB, which provides builders with a managed NoSQL storage service.

The schemaless nature of NoSQL storage presents multi-tenant builders with some significant advantages. Imagine running a large pooled environment and deploying a change that includes new data structures. With a relational setup, you might need to orchestrate a series of complex migration steps to update your schema as part of rolling out a new feature. That same change is generally much easier to apply in a NoSQL environment. The absence of a schema often removes the need to navigate a series of complex migration scripts, allowing teams to introduce features at a faster pace with fewer deployments. This fits well with the broader SaaS value proposition, promoting operational agility, innovation, and efficiency.

With DynamoDB, you'll also see that we have a pretty limited collection of storage constructs that can be used to partition our data. There's no notion of databases or instances as part of the DynamoDB landscape. DynamoDB also has the advantage of not inheriting all the baggage that comes with supporting different, existing relational database engines. This also means that DynamoDB offers tighter integration with other AWS cloud constructs, providing more granular integration with the identity and access management (IAM) mechanisms that can be used to define isolation policies (covered in Chapter 9).

I do get lots of questions about how teams might choose between NoSQL and relational databases for a SaaS solution. This, to me, is driven mostly by a combination of application and consumption use cases—isolation requirements, agility impacts, and performance considerations. Generally, I tend to tell teams to start with NoSQL and let real-world business drivers steer you toward relational where it makes sense.

Pooled NoSQL Data Partitioning

Pooling data in NoSQL looks very much like it does in a relational database. With DynamoDB, all of our data is stored in tables. The data in these tables will include information for all of the tenants in our system. They are commingled based on a tenant identifier that associates each item in the table with its corresponding tenant. Figure 8-5 provides a simple view of a NoSQL table that is indexed by tenant identifiers.

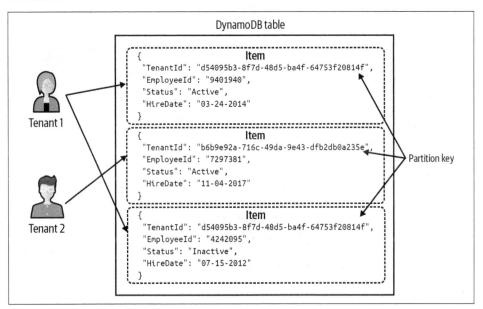

Figure 8-5. Pooled NoSQL data partitioning

This is a mirror image of the pooled relational storage example we looked at earlier. We have a DynamoDB table that is populated with items, each of which has a JSON document that holds the data for a given item.

The items listed in this example happen to represent employees. I've inserted the TenantId attribute into each of these items to associate it with a tenant. I have two tenants that have data in this table. Tenant 1 is associated with the first and third items and Tenant 2 is associated with the second item.

I've denoted that each of the tenant identifiers in my table are what DynamoDB refers to as partition keys. This essentially identifies the attribute as the primary key of the table, improving performance when accessing data for individual tenants. The EmployeeId was the primary key before we introduced tenancy into these tables. It would now be treated as a sort key within DynamoDB.

Siloed NoSQL Data Partitioning

With many siloed models, we tend to look for some logical mapping to a database instance that will hold our siloed data. However, with DynamoDB (and other managed storage services), these constructs don't really exist. Instead, our only silo option here is to use a table-per-tenant model to silo our data. Figure 8-6 provides a conceptual view of this siloed DynamoDB model.

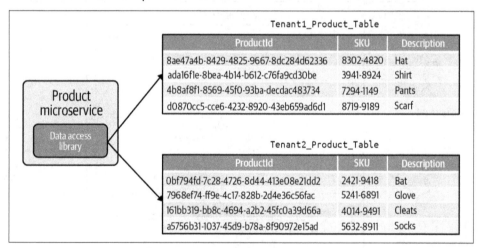

Figure 8-6. NoSQL siloed data partitioning

There's nothing exotic about the siloed approach with DynamoDB. We've essentially created a separate table for each tenant. Then, within the implementation of our service we map each incoming request to the appropriate table.

In this example, I prepended a tenant identifier to the table name to associate the table to a specific tenant. The naming strategy you adopt must be chosen carefully. Table names in DynamoDB are managed globally which means you'll need to identify a naming scheme that ensures that your table is assigned a unique name. Some teams opt for a mix of a generated identifier and a "friendly" name.

Whenever we consider a siloed storage model, we must also consider whether our siloing strategy will support the scaling requirements of our solution. Just as we did with relational databases, we must also consider the limits of DynamoDB (or whichever NoSQL solution you're using). You'll also want to think about how the table-per-tenant model will affect the deployment and operational profile of your environment.

NoSQL Tuning Options

In general, the data partitioning options for DynamoDB are pretty straightforward. There are, however, some additional factors that can come into play when storing multi-tenant data with DynamoDB. For example, DynamoDB offers you options to configure the capacity modes for a table. For each table, you can choose between on-demand or provisioned capacity modes. With on-demand, you're essentially able to have DynamoDB scale based on the actual load of your tenants. This, as you can imagine, fits very well with the unpredictability of tenant consumption that comes with multi-tenant workloads. This would be especially valuable for instances where you're running in a pooled partitioning model.

The provisioned model is a much better fit for environments where you have a better sense of the levels of activity you'll need to support. Here, you configure the minimum capacity, maximum capacity, and target utilization based on the profile of your workload. Now, the system will have a steady, target level it will maintain while still limiting a tenant's ability to exceed a maximum. You might be able to apply this strategy to tables that are in key bottlenecks of the system to ensure that you're maximizing throughput (at the cost of potentially being somewhat overprovisioned). You can also see how, in some cases, this might be aligned with a siloed table where the consumption profile is more predictable.

Obviously, as you look at other NoSQL solutions, you may have other partitioning and configuration options available. Fundamentally, though, this basically comes down to figuring out which constructs you might be able to use to represent your siloed experience. The pooled model will likely employ a similar implementation across different NoSQL offerings.

Object Data Partitioning

Data partitioning with relational and NoSQL storage services is an area that builders easily relate to. For these storage technologies, you have relatively natural mappings to the pooled and siloed models. However, as we move into other storage technology, the mappings are not quite as straightforward. To make this clearer, let's look at how we land these multi-tenant data partitioning models in an object storage service.

With object storage, we're not looking at data through the lens of databases and tables. Instead, we view the assets we're managing as a series of objects that essentially equate to files that are stored and retrieved across a number of different contexts.

For the purposes of our discussion, I'll focus on Amazon's Simple Storage Service (S3), exploring the different mechanisms that S3 provides to partition multi-tenant data. The techniques we'll look at here are specific to S3 and may or may not have good mappings to the other object storage services that are part of other cloud environments. Still, the hope is that this review of S3 strategies will give you a better sense of how your data partitioning approach changes as you move into different storage technologies. The principles stay the same, but the mechanics of implementing these principles often require you to consider a more diverse menu of possibilities.

Pooled Object Data Partitioning

With object storage, we're mostly looking at using a classic hierarchical folder structure to organize and access our objects. For example, in S3 all objects are stored in buckets as a top-level construct. These buckets can also use prefix keys to group and access objects. The net effect is something that looks like a traditional file/folder structure.

With the pooled model, we must start by deciding where our tenant objects will land within S3. Since our tenant objects will all be commingled, we don't necessarily have to worry about creating separate buckets or prefix keys for each tenant. At the same time, it's likely that your application services may want to operate on tenant objects in groups. This suggests that we likely want to use the prefix keys to determine where we place each tenant's objects.

Let's look at an example of how you might represent a pooled data partitioning model within S3. Figure 8-7 provides a conceptual view of a series of buckets that are using prefix keys to store tenant objects in a pooled model.

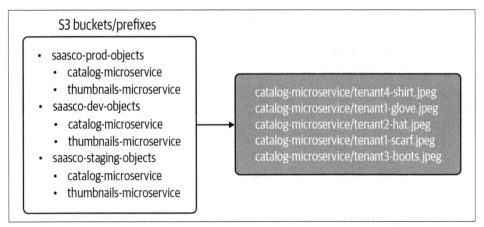

S3 buckets/prefixes

- saasco-prod-objects
  - catalog-microservice
  - thumbnails-microservice
- saasco-dev-objects
  - catalog-microservice
  - thumbnails-microservice
- saasco-staging-objects
  - catalog-microservice
  - thumbnails-microservice

catalog-microservice/tenant4-shirt.jpeg
catalog-microservice/tenant1-glove.jpeg
catalog-microservice/tenant2-hat.jpeg
catalog-microservice/tenant1-scarf.jpeg
catalog-microservice/tenant3-boots.jpeg

Figure 8-7. S3 pooled data partitioning

On the left you'll see the simple bucket hierarchy that I've created. At the top level of the tree, I have buckets for each of my environments (prod, dev, and staging). Then, within each bucket, I've included prefix keys. For this example, I presumed that my prefix keys corresponded to individual services that are managing their own S3 objects.

On the right of the diagram, we have a pooled storage representation of a series of objects from the `saasco-dev-objects` bucket that are associated with the `catalog-service prefix` key. Since this is a pooled model, we named our objects with a prepended tenant identifier that associates each object with its corresponding tenants. Accessing one of these objects would require a caller to prepend the tenant identifier to the name of each object to successfully retrieve a specific tenant object.

While this approach represents a more purist view of the pooled model and S3, it does seem to add unnecessary complexity. The prepending of tenant identifiers seems difficult to manage and adds friction to any calling client. As we shift now to silo, you'll see how the advantages of silo provide builders with a slight variation of the pooled model that eliminates some of the naming overhead and mapping that comes with this pooled model.

Siloed Object Data Partitioning

There are two approaches that you can take with siloing objects with S3. The simplest path to choose is a bucket-per-tenant model. This model would essentially require a new bucket to be created for each new tenant and store all of their objects within that bucket.

Now, if your total number of tenants is less than the upper bucket limit of the S3 service (currently 1,000 buckets), then you could consider this option. It does mean that your onboarding will need to dynamically create new buckets that conform to the naming conventions and uniqueness requirements of S3. You'd also need some part of your system to include a mechanism that maps tenants to their designated buckets.

If these limits are a problem or you'd like to worry less about naming collisions, you could just add a slight twist to the pooled strategy (discussed earlier) and rely on a prefix key as a way to implement your siloed model. Figure 8-8 provides an example of how you'd alter your prefix key structure to silo your tenant objects.

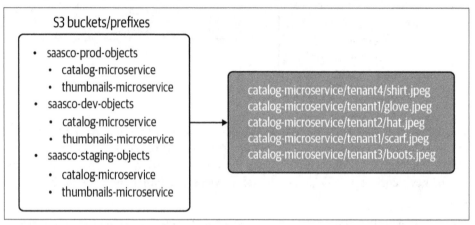

Figure 8-8. S3 siloed data partitioning

You'll notice that there's a subtle difference between this and the pooled model. I've essentially used the prefix key as the boundary of my silo, placing all tenant data under the heading of a single key.

In most of our prior discussions of siloed versus pooled storage, we talked a lot about the added complexity and overhead that comes with siloing data. With the S3 model, you're not really absorbing a great deal of added friction. In the pool setup, if I truly commingle the objects, I have to somehow augment object names to achieve my tenant binding. Here, by simply refining the key, I get a model that is easier to use, consume, and manage without really taking on any significant downside.

There are instances where the siloed story might create better opportunities for implementing isolation via IAM. However, that has little influence on this S3 siloed story. I can configure IAM policies at the bucket or down to the prefix level, enabling me to prevent cross-tenant access across any of these strategies.

Database Managed Access

While S3 does provide APIs for accessing your objects, some use cases demand a more dynamic approach to locating your tenant objects. There are instances where you may need to support more exotic, metadata-driven ways to locate a tenant's S3 object. Imagine, for example, wanting to find all the objects that match a user-specified set of criteria. Here, the metadata you want to search would likely live somewhere outside of your object storage.

It's here that you may want to introduce a layer between your objects and the database that holds all the metadata and attributes that you want to query on. Figure 8-9 provides a conceptual view of this use case.

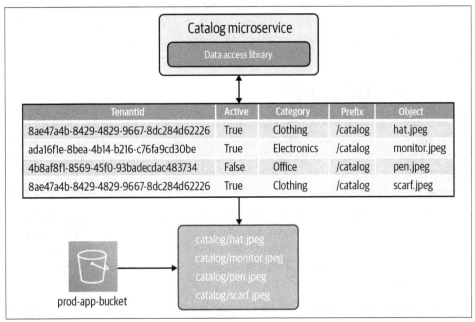

Figure 8-9. Using a database to manage access to objects

At the top of Figure 8-9, I have a catalog service. This service manages a range of attributes (Active, Category, and so on) for the products that are in a catalog. One of the attributes managed by our catalog is the image associated with each catalog item. The actual objects for these images are stored in S3.

Now, suppose your service needs to request a collection of objects that have a specific set of product attributes. To support this experience, you'll see that I have introduced a table that is indexed by tenant identifiers and has other metadata about the items in the catalog. In a complete version of this table, we'd have more attributes. However, for this example, I constrained this to a few attributes that seemed like they might make good search criteria (Active and Category). I've also added columns to reference the prefix key and the object filename that maps to the object as it's stored in S3.

At the bottom Figure 8-9 is the bucket that holds our catalog image objects (and potentially other service data). With all the pieces in place, my catalog service can now query the table to find a tenant's objects that match a set of specified criteria. In fact, you'll notice that the first and last rows of this table are associated with the same tenant. My query could ask for all active catalog items in the clothing category for a tenant and the results would return the prefix and object names that could be used to reference each of the items stored in S3.

I confess that this represents a bit of a corner case. At the same time, it's an especially useful way to provide an alternate way to think about how you might partition objects. Here, the partitioning is all done in the table, removing any tenant mapping from the object database. I can use this table to introduce metadata for my objects that can be applied as part of filtering access to the objects I need for a given use case.

OpenSearch Data Partitioning

As you can see by now, the multi-tenant data partitioning story can look quite different as we move between different storage services. To round things out, I thought it would be helpful to look at how data partitioning is applied in the search and analytics domain. For this example, we'll look at Amazon's OpenSearch service, which is derived from ElasticSearch.

With OpenSearch, we are now working with new flavors of storage constructs and mechanisms to partition our tenant data. How data lands in OpenSearch, how we maximize cost and operational efficiency, and how we isolate data all look a bit different when we're mapping siloed and pooled models to the moving parts of an OpenSearch cluster.

To better understand our OpenSearch data partitioning options, let's start by looking at the different mechanisms that would be used to store and manage our tenant data in an OpenSearch environment (shown in Figure 8-10).

Figure 8-10 provides a high-level view of the core moving parts of the OpenSearch service. At the outermost edge, we have the domains that represent the most coarse-grained units of data partitioning. These are essentially the clusters that are part of our search and analytics experience. This is where you'll configure the size and footprint of the nodes that will shape the scaling profile of your experience. Then, on the right, are a series of indexes that are associated with a given domain. These indexes store the documents that will be indexed for our search and analytics experience.

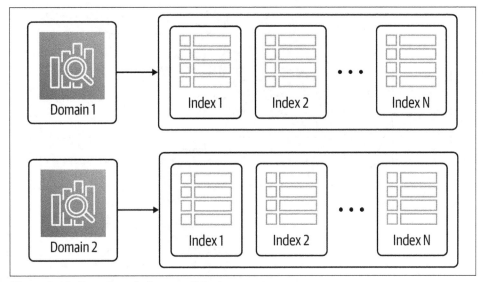

Figure 8-10. OpenSearch data partitioning constructs

Pooled OpenSearch Data Partitioning

If we look at how we land data in a pooled model in OpenSearch, we'll need to adopt a model where our tenant documents are commingled within a single index. This approach, in many respects, follows the pattern we've observed across all the pooled constructs. Any time we have commingled data, we need to have some way to identify the data that is associated with a given tenant.

If we look inside the various documents that are stored in an index, we'll see that we must insert a tenant identifier into each tenant document. This identifier will be included in any search that we perform to scope access to a specific tenant's data. Figure 8-11 provides an example of an OpenSearch pooled model.

In this example, our pooled storage is running all tenants in a single domain and, for this product sample data, all tenant documents are stored in a shared index. Each of the documents in this index includes a `TenantId` attribute that, in this example, is represented by a GUID. The individual products in each of these documents are also assigned a `ProductId` that uniquely identifies individual products. I've essentially taken the document that would normally represent a product and added a `TenantId` attribute.

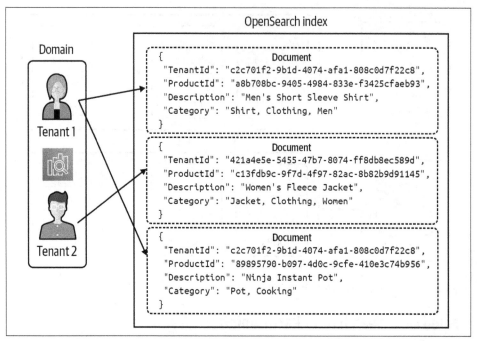

Figure 8-11. Pooled OpenSearch data partitioning

With this experience, you get all the upside and downside that comes with a pooled data partitioning model. The economies of scale and operational profile both benefit from the use of shared infrastructure. However, the sizing of the domain can be difficult and may lead to overprovisioning. This represents yet another scenario where leaning on serverless technologies can bring real value and steer you more toward the OpenSearch Serverless service, which can simplify the sizing and scaling profile of your solution.

You'll also want to think about how data is being sharded by OpenSearch and determine whether the footprint and distribution of your tenant data is impacting the performance of your environment.

Siloed OpenSearch Data Partitioning

You have two options when it comes to implementing a siloed OpenSearch data partitioning model. The first option we'll look at is the domain-per-tenant model. With this approach you'll need to create a completely separate cluster for every tenant. An example of this model is shown in Figure 8-12.

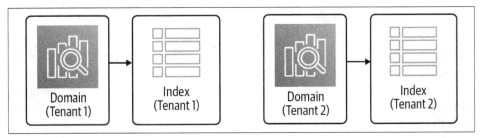

Figure 8-12. Domain-per-tenant OpenSearch siloed data partitioning

This is a very straightforward model that relies on the most coarse-grained Open-Search construct to store each tenant's data. This will appease those tenants that have concerns about compliance, isolation, noisy neighbor, and so on. At the same time, it will also add operational complexity and impact the cost efficiency of your environment.

The other way to implement siloed data partitioning with OpenSearch is through an index-per-tenant model. This is illustrated in Figure 8-13.

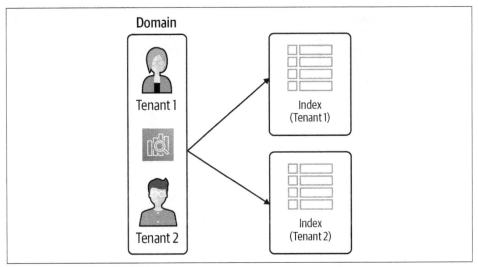

Figure 8-13. Index-per-tenant siloed OpenSearch data partitioning

With this approach, we now have a single domain that is shared by all of our siloed tenants. However, each tenant is given its own index. This allows you to achieve isolation without provisioning an entire cluster for every new tenant. It also means that you're agreeing to share the compute of the domain across these tenant requests. For some, this represents a good compromise in that you're getting some economies of scale for your compute while still offering tenants a unit of isolation that ensures that their data is not commingled and may benefit from more concrete boundaries of isolation.

This siloed model does come with its downsides, though. While this model is more manageable, we now face a rightsizing problem. The shared compute of the domain must now be sized based on the workloads and activity profiles of multiple tenants. This can lead to noisy neighbor conditions or other performance issues that come with the sharing of your storage compute. Also, as is the case for any siloed resources, you'll want to consider the scalability of the model. There may be limits on how many siloed indexes your service will allow.

A Mixed Mode Partitioning Model

In addition to the siloed and pooled models shown above, you may also consider implementing a mixed mode model that offers another approach to balancing the requirements of your tenants. With this mixed mode, you're essentially looking at supporting both siloed and pooled models within a shared domain (shown in Figure 8-14).

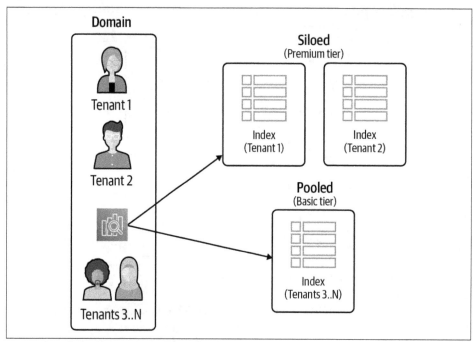

Figure 8-14. Mixed mode OpenSearch data partitioning

On the left, we are still using a shared domain and eliminating the need to provision a separate cluster for our tenants. What's different here is that we're supporting siloed and pooled indexes with this domain. At the top, I have shown two premium tier tenants that have dedicated indexes. Then, at the bottom, I have a pooled index that commingles all the basic tier data in a single construct.

This approach certainly allows us to limit the complexity and footprint of our Open-Search infrastructure while still supporting siloed and pooled models. At the same time, this strategy can present real challenges when it comes to sizing and configuring your domain. You could also consider a model where a separate domain would be used for all your basic tier tenants. This would eliminate scenarios where basic tier tenants impact the scale of your premium tier tenants.

Sharding Tenant Data

So far, I've mostly concentrated on siloed and pooled data partitioning strategies that rely on the different storage constructs that are part of your environment. In general, it tends to make things simpler if you can stay within the built-in capabilities of your storage service. However, there are times when the scale and performance of your storage model cannot meet the needs of your solution. In these instances, you may have to consider introducing your own mechanisms to shard tenant storage. Sharding generally refers to the idea of splitting a resource into multiple parts to address scale, size, and so on.

One pattern that I've seen applied is the idea of custom partitioning where your code owns responsibility for mapping tenants to different storage constructs. Imagine, for example, a scenario where you have a relational database that is using a pooled model. However, you're finding that the scaling and performance of your tenants are exceeding your ability to adequately address their workload. You prefer to keep your tenants pooled, but it's impractical to have them all in one storage database.

In these cases, some teams will consider implementing their own sharding strategy where they distribute pools of tenants to separate constructs. Figure 8-15 provides a conceptual view of the sharding model.

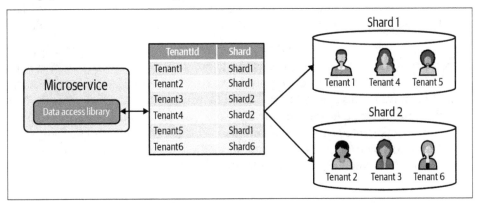

Figure 8-15. Sharding groups of tenants

In this example, I have two separate shards of tenants running in a pooled model on the righthand side of the diagram. You'll all notice that I've distributed these tenants across separate databases. So, I basically have two sets of pooled tenants. Now, if the service on the lefthand side wants to make a request to a database, its data access library would have to look up the shard that is associated with a given tenant request.

This is very much like the pod deployment model we discussed in Chapter 3 where we deployed groups of tenants together in pods. Here we have a similar concept, but it's being applied exclusively at the storage layer of our environment. This allows you to limit the blast radius of tenants and potentially overcome pooled noisy neighbor issues by distributing the workload of these tenants to separate shards. As new tenants are onboarded, you may add new shards to continue distributing the load.

This is a far from ideal model and certainly adds complexity and friction to your SaaS environment. However, I include it here because some workloads or business requirements may view this as a reasonable trade-off.

Data Lifecycle Considerations

As part of looking at how data is partitioned and represented, we also have to consider the broader lifecycle of this data. There are different changes in state that your tenant may go through that could impact how their data is represented.

To better understand the implications, let's look at a specific scenario where you have a tiered environment that uses different storage strategies for your tenant tiers. Your basic tier tenants are using entirely pooled data, while your premium tier tenants have some storage constructs that are siloed. Now, imagine what it will mean if we have a tenant that needs to upgrade from the basic to the premium tier. In this instance, we'd have to have automation in place that could gracefully migrate the data from the pooled environment to a siloed model. The automation would also need to consider how moving this data could impact the overall load on the system. If this adds excess load, it could also impact the availability of your environment. This is a hard problem for which there are few elegant solutions. Still, you need to have this on your radar.

Decommissioning is another area that can impact your data partitioning strategy. The biggest part of decommissioning a tenant usually centers around what you plan to do with a tenant's data. Will you traverse the entire system and remove the tenant data? Will you archive the data, allowing the tenant to restore data when they return? These are all factors that you'll need to consider when you're thinking about how tenant data will be represented in your environment. This is yet another area where you'll have to carefully construct the automation tooling that can execute your decommissioning policies, applying them without degrading the performance of your environment.

Backup and restore is also part of this tenant lifecycle discussion. This can be particularly tricky if you have pooled data. Also, you're likely to have tenant data spread across multiple storage constructs in your environment, potentially using a variety of siloed and pooled models. This, as you can imagine, requires a carefully orchestrated mechanism that can successfully acquire and back up tenant data. For some, there is no concept of per-tenant backup and restore. Instead, the state of data is seen as a global construct. Which mode will work best for your environment will depend on the nature of your domain, tenants, and a host of other factors.

Multi-Tenant Data Security

Protection of tenant data is a given for any SaaS environment and your architecture should already take strong measures to ensure that one tenant can't access the resources of another tenant. In fact, Chapter 9 will dig squarely into this topic, exploring a range of strategies that can be used to ensure that your resources (including data) are protected from cross-tenant access.

There are, however, domains that may impose additional security requirements on the storage of their data. For some, this may be more about encrypting the data to be certain it is protected at rest and in transit. Your ability to encrypt data is very much driven by the encryption capabilities of the storage services you're consuming. Generally, though, many of the AWS storage services offer support for different encryption strategies.

The encryption of data, for some, may still not be enough. You may have tenants that will require encryption and ownership of the keys that are used to manage access to their data. In these scenarios, you'll need to introduce constructs to create and deliver these keys to individual tenants. These keys may also have a lifecycle that will need to be managed as part of the operational footprint of your SaaS environment.

This per-tenant key strategy will also have clear impacts on your siloed versus pooled model considerations. If the tenants want their own keys, you're most likely to be storing their data in a siloed model.

Conclusion

After going through this chapter, you should have a better sense of the different patterns, strategies, and influencing factors that shape your approach to storing data in a multi-tenant environment. We started the chapter by looking at a range of fundamental multi-tenant storage concepts. These models and partitioning terms apply to any technology that might be used to store tenant data.

We started by revisiting the notion of siloed and pooled resources, reviewing how these multi-tenant models are mapped to data partitioning. As part of this, I highlighted some of the general pros and cons of these two models. I emphasized the fact that these two options weren't mutually exclusive and could be combined to address the compliance, performance, and isolation needs of your SaaS environment.

This core concepts section also identified specific factors that should be weighed across any storage strategy. For example, I talked about scaling and noisy neighbor considerations and how the nature of multi-tenant workloads can impact your tenant's impact on storage services. I also looked at how blast radius, isolation models, sizing, and operational experience can influence your data partitioning choices. The key is to look beyond the technical profile of your storage and consider how business and operational factors can influence how you choose to represent tenant data. The choices you make here can have a significant impact on the agility and operational and cost efficiency of your SaaS business.

Once the foundation was established, I shifted to looking at how these concepts land in specific storage services. The goal was to give you a better sense of how the siloed and pooled models are expressed when they are being delivered in the context of a specific storage service. I covered relational, NoSQL, object, and search storage models, highlighting the nuances that come with partitioning data with each of these services. Here, you saw how the different storage constructs of these services could influence the design of your data partitioning model. Each service adds its own twist to the story.

It would be impractical to look at every type of storage technology. However, my hope is that the concepts and examples we reviewed will give you a mental model that you can use as you consider how to implement data partitioning with the various storage technologies that are part of your architecture. The chapter should have also highlighted the idea that data partitioning is not an all-or-nothing decision. The partitioning choices you make and the technologies you choose should be driven by the specific needs of your application's services.

While the design of your storage might be related to your isolation strategy, it's important to note that siloing storage does not isolate that resource. In the next chapter, we'll start to dig into the details of isolation and review the constructs and mechanisms that are used to ensure that tenant resources (including storage) are protected from cross-tenant access. The isolation strategies and patterns we'll cover are foundational to SaaS and critical to providing a multi-tenant experience that secures each tenant's environment—regardless of how it's deployed, designed, and realized.

## CHAPTER 9

Tenant Isolation

I've referred to the concept of tenant isolation throughout my coverage of the different multi-tenant architecture constructs, patterns, and strategies. Our prior glimpses of this topic stayed mostly high level and conceptual, highlighting how isolation is used to ensure that one tenant can't access the resources of another tenant. Now, however, it's time to dig squarely into the details of tenant isolation and look at concrete mechanisms that are used to apply isolation across the different layers of your SaaS architecture.

In this chapter, my goal is to distill the nuances of tenant isolation into a set of terms, patterns, and practices that will provide you with a better framework for thinking about how and when you should be introducing tenant isolation mechanisms into your architecture. I'll start out by establishing a clear view of the role of tenant isolation and the foundational concepts that shape your approach to building a tenant isolation strategy.

From there, we can then start to look at the layered nature of tenant isolation, identifying the different areas within your architecture where you would consider introducing mechanisms that will prevent cross-tenant access. This will give you a better sense of the nuances and considerations that come with creating an isolation model for the different technologies and infrastructure constructs that are part of your multi-tenant environment. This will also highlight some of the challenges and advantages that come with different resource deployment models, giving you more data that can shape the choices you make around microservice decomposition, data partitioning, and the other topics we've been exploring.

Our isolation journey will include a deeper look at the role your microservices and application code might play in the enforcement of your isolation policies. We'll look at the different runtime techniques that use the tenant context of individual requests to scope and control tenant access on a request-by-request basis. This will include highlighting some of the design considerations associated with applying isolation policies at runtime.

The overall goal is to ensure that you're making tenant isolation a priority in your SaaS solutions, reviewing the range of different approaches that come with building a robust, non-invasive multi-tenant isolation model.

Core Concepts

Throughout the chapters so far, I devoted a significant amount of time to describing the different patterns and deployment models that could be used to compose a multi-tenant SaaS architecture. For microservices and storage, for example, I talked about all the different ways you might use siloed or pooled models as part of the design and implementation of these concepts.

Each time I touched on siloed and pooled deployment strategies, I highlighted the potential linkage between deployment models and your tenant isolation strategy. At the same time, I also went out of my way to make it clear that there was a clear line between defining how a resource is deployed and how a resource is isolated. It's essential that you don't treat these two concepts as synonymous. Yes, you might choose a deployment model to enable a specific isolation experience, but actual realization and enforcement of that isolation is still achieved through an entirely separate mechanism that examines each attempt to access a tenant resource and prevents any cross-tenant isolation violations.

To better illustrate this point, imagine a scenario where you choose to silo tenant databases as part of your isolation strategy. Figure 9-1 provides a conceptual view of this scenario.

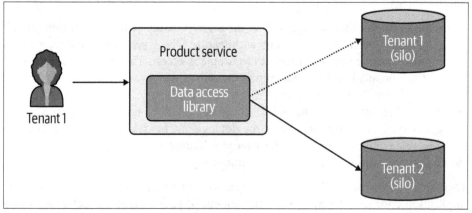

Figure 9-1. Siloed databases with no isolation policies

In this example, we have a Product service that has chosen to silo each tenant's product data. Let's assume that the siloed data model here was chosen based on some customer or domain need that indicated that this data needed to be isolated and could not be commingled with other tenant data. This all fits with the examples of data partitioning and service design that we discussed in earlier chapters.

At first glance, many may look at this diagram and assume that we've already achieved and implemented isolation by putting the tenant data in separate databases. However, being in separate databases just ensured that the data was not commingled. It didn't necessarily do anything to isolate the data.

Consider a scenario where Tenant 1 in this diagram requests a list of products. It will be the job of the Product service to acquire the tenant context and process the request, routing the request to the Tenant 1 siloed database. That all makes sense. At this point, it might feel like you're achieved tenant isolation. However, imagine a scenario where I am processing this same request from Tenant 1, and within the code of my service, I replace Tenant 1 with Tenant 2. What would happen? Well, it turns out that my request from Tenant 1 is still allowed to access the Tenant 2 database. Even though I have separate databases for each tenant, there's nothing here that would prevent our service from crossing a tenant boundary. Merely separating the databases did nothing to ensure the data was actually isolated. This brings us back to the boundary between deployment and isolation.

This is where we need to introduce a separate tenant isolation mechanism that will enforce isolation—regardless of how our resources are deployed. The idea is that we need to add some construct that sits between code and the resources being accessed by that code. This construct becomes the gatekeeper, using tenant context to limit the scope of access of any resource. Figure 9-2 provides a slightly modified version of the prior example that illustrates the addition of a tenant isolation layer.

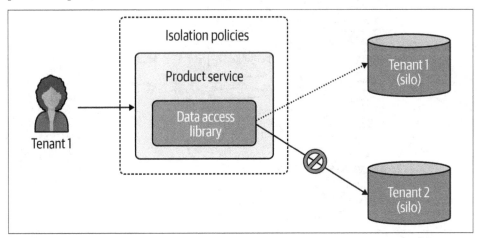

Figure 9-2. Siloed databases with tenant isolation

The only change is the wrapper around my Product service that represents a conceptual view of tenant isolation. In this mode, whenever the code of the Product service attempts to access data, the isolation layer will ensure that the resources you're accessing are valid based on the current tenant context. So, no matter what a developer does in their code, the isolation mechanism will prevent any effort to access another tenant's resources.

When I outline this to other teams, I often get pushback. Developers will often want to view their code as "trusted" and assume that their teams would never write code that would violate a tenant boundary. It's not a good policy to presume your code won't break your isolation rules. Even the most careful and well-intended developers can unintentionally introduce changes that could end up crossing a tenant boundary. The industry is littered with examples of solutions that somehow exposed one tenant's data to another tenant. Even a single instance of cross-tenant access could represent a significant setback for a SaaS business.

The key point is that your multi-tenant environment will be required to isolate tenant resources regardless of their deployment model or technology. From a tenant's perspective, there really shouldn't be any notion of siloed and pooled resources. Tenants should expect that every resource in their system is isolated and protected from any cross-tenant access. Figure 9-3 provides a visual view of this model in action.

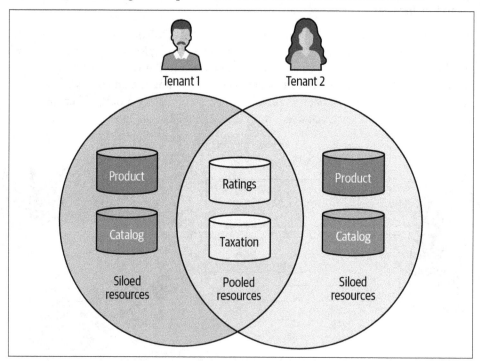

Figure 9-3. The tenant view of isolation

We have two tenants that are using a combination of siloed and pooled resources. To keep it simple, I just showed these as databases, but imagine this projected across every type of resource in your system. Under the hood of this solution, our implementation is owning responsibility for ensuring that its isolation policies are protecting each tenant's resources. The basic message here is that from the tenant's point of view, none of their resources are shared—even when they are running on pooled infrastructure.

For some, this reality often represents a key point of tension within their multi-tenant architecture. You want to design the preferred footprint of your environment that best matches your operational, scale, cost, performance, and tiering profile. At the same time, you have to consider how that solution is also going to be able to meet its isolation requirements. Finding the right balance can be challenging for some solutions and domains.

It should also be clear that isolation is created as a very intentional part of your architecture. It is explicitly implemented as a core element of your design that expects to capture any intentional or unintentional attempt to cross tenant boundaries.

Categorizing Isolation Models

Before we get into the specifics of different isolation strategies, I wanted to first take a step back and define some isolation concepts that will be used to characterize the different flavors of isolation that can be implemented in a SaaS environment. For each of these categories, you'll see how they generally map to different patterns for realizing and applying isolation policies. Figure 9-4 provides a view of the three primary types of isolation I typically see (allowing for the fact that others may exist).

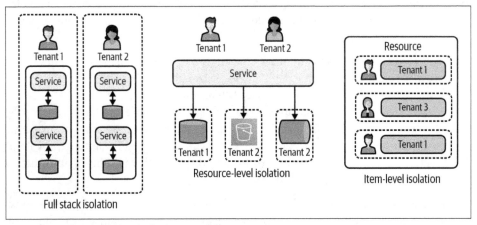

Figure 9-4. Categorizing isolation models

If we work this diagram from left to right, it starts with more coarse-grained isolation and progressively becomes narrower. For each type of isolation, I've drawn a dashed line that represents the boundary of isolation for each model.

The first flavor on the left is what I've labeled full stack isolation. This correlates directly to multi-tenant environments that leverage a full stack deployment model where every tenant is given a dedicated stack of resources. Here, isolating resources is generally a pretty straightforward process that has access to a well-defined set of mechanisms that can isolate your tenant resources.

As we move to the middle, you'll notice that we now have what I've labeled resource-level isolation. In this example, we have a shared compute layer for the service that is consuming resources for multiple tenants. In this model, the unit of isolation is an entire "resource." For example, Tenant 1 has a dedicated database and Tenant 2 has a dedicated bucket (Amazon S3) and a dedicated queue. The fundamental idea is that the boundary of isolation is an entire resource where the definition of resource could vary based on the services in your environment. With this flavor of isolation, you're still likely to have some isolation construct that can control access to a resource. There are scenarios where that mapping may be more challenging, but those are less common.

Finally, on the right is the item-level isolation model. With this model, you'll see that we've gone inside a resource where we have items from different tenants that are commingled within the resource. The simplest example of this is a database (the resource) that has a shared table that commingles the data from multiple tenants (a pooled model). While a database represents a simple way to think about this, the same idea can be mapped to other resources. For example, you could have messages in a queue resource that are associated with multiple tenants. The fundamental, defining trait is that tenant data sits alongside other tenant data within some shared infrastructure resource.

Item-level isolation is clearly the most challenging of all the isolation schemes. Once you move within a resource, the list of available isolation constructs starts to get quite small. Some technologies will give you tools to enforce isolation at this level and others will not. With AWS, for example, there are instances where its identity and access management (IAM) construct can be used to implement item-level isolation. However, there are services where IAM won't allow you to be granular enough for item-level isolation. This is where you have to get creative with building or introducing one-off tools to apply isolation at the item level.

So, now, as you design your multi-tenant architecture, you'll likely find yourself looking at one of these three types of tenant isolation. As you're figuring out how you want to represent tenant resources in your environment, you'll have to determine which of these three models you'll be adopting. You'll also need to consider whether your technology stack gives you the tools you need to apply isolation at the level you're targeting.

Application-Enforced Isolation

In an ideal world, the technology you're using would have clear mappings to security constructs that could be used to enforce your isolation strategy. For example, most cloud environments provide some built-in notion of IAM controls to configure the policies that builders use to control access to the various resources that are part of their environment. Leaning on these mechanisms to implement your tenant isolation represents a natural fit. These security mechanisms sit directly between you and your resources and allow you to define policies that can limit the scope of your access to infrastructure resources, which fits naturally with the spirit of the isolation models you're introducing into your architecture.

The challenge, however, is that these tools don't always offer you the level of control that you need to express your isolation policies. There are a number of factors that shape the IAM profile of each technology or service. Native services that are built from the ground up by a cloud provider, for example, typically have more granular isolation controls than services that are built around pre-existing technologies.

At some point, you're likely to face a scenario where the multi-tenant model you prefer for a resource does not support the level of isolation control you require. This is where you may need to consider introducing your own application-enforced isolation mechanisms to prevent cross-tenant access. I won't go into too much detail, since the range of possibilities and nuances here is quite long. Generally, though, you'll need to look at the different policy and access control frameworks, libraries, or tools that allow you to introduce your own layer of controls for these instances where built-in mechanisms don't support your needs. This is where you might see mechanisms like attribute-based access control (ABAC) or Open Policy Agent (OPA) as part of your isolation model. Which tool fits is highly dependent on what you're isolating, what tool chain you're using, and what flavor of isolation you're implementing. The key takeaway is that your solution should isolate all resources—even if you need to build the isolation tooling yourself.

RBAC, Authorization, and Isolation

There are lots of security mechanisms that can be applied across an application's architecture. Teams, for example, will often use role-based access control (RBAC) and authorization constructs to scope and control access to functionality within their applications. In some instances, I will see teams using these same RBAC tools to implement their tenant isolation policies.

Let's look at an example to better understand how this blurs the lines between application access controls and tenant isolation. Suppose we had a scenario where a tenant authenticates into a SaaS application with a tenant administrator role. Now, within your application, let's say you're using an RBAC framework to enable or disable this user's access to specific application features or capabilities. RBAC might also be used across other contexts where it authorizes access to infrastructure.

For some, it's natural to want to map RBAC to isolation in this example. However, with RBAC, we're generally controlling access based on some notion of an individual user's role within the environment. In fact, I could have many users within a single tenant that would have different roles. RBAC would then offer different experiences to these users based on their role.

With isolation, the scoping is not associated with individual user roles—it is based exclusively on the tenant context of a user. So, with a multi-tenant environment, we may have multiple users with multiple roles within a tenant, and our isolation story would be the same for all of these users. Isolation's only job is to ensure that, for the current tenant, you are restricting access to those resources to that tenant. Any other restrictions that may need to be applied based on a role or some other application construct would be addressed outside of the isolation model.

The main point is that we want to have clear separation between the strategies that are used to isolate tenant resources and the strategies that are used to control access to specific application features and functions. Now, it could be that you have some shared tooling that can cover both of these patterns. That's fine. However, even if the tool you use is universal, the mindset of isolation and controlling application access are very different beasts.

Application Isolation Versus Infrastructure Isolation

There's lots of baggage that comes with the term "tenant isolation." When I work with security-focused teams and I mention tenant isolation, they typically gravitate to a more infrastructure-centric notion of isolation (which makes sense). In their universe, they're often inside the inner workings of some infrastructure technology or service that needs to prevent users or accounts from crossing some foundational boundary of your security model. This is an entirely valid notion of tenant isolation.

However, with multi-tenant isolation, the boundaries and nature of the isolation is really an application-defined construct. When you build your SaaS application, it's up to you to define where these boundaries live and introduce the mechanisms at the application level that will ensure that tenant resources are protected. I view this as another flavor of a shared responsibility model. At the core infrastructure level, I want the technology or service I'm consuming to enforce its notion of tenant isolation. Then, on top of that foundational security model, I am building an application where only my application knows where tenant boundaries exist. Yes, some of these boundaries might correlate to infrastructure boundaries. However, in a multi-tenant setting, your application may also be defining its own set of isolation boundaries on top of that infrastructure.

The key is that, for the scope of our discussion, I view tenant isolation as something that is defined and enforced by my application's design and architecture. In some cases, I may be able to leverage existing isolation constructs to implement isolation and, in others, I may have to design and implement my own mechanisms to enforce my application's isolation policies. It's also important to note that these application-defined boundaries can and will count on code and application libraries as part of their tenant isolation story. This is a foundational reality of building systems where applications will share resources in ways that can't be protected through classic, native security constructs.

The Layers of the Isolation Model

With the core isolation concepts behind us, we can turn our attention to more concrete isolation constructs. Let's start by looking at how isolation is implemented across the various layers of your multi-tenant architecture. Figure 9-5 provides a conceptual view of how layering fits into the isolation story.

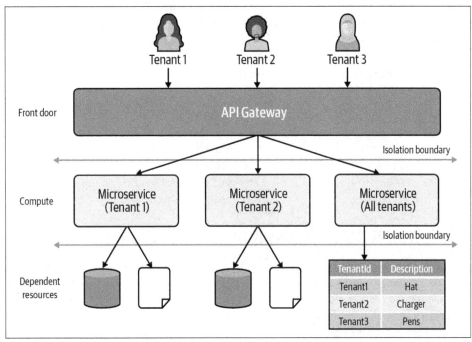

Figure 9-5. A layered view of isolation

In Figure 9-5, you'll see an example of the various isolation layers that could exist within a multi-tenant architecture. At the top is the entry or the "front door" of the application services that will need to be isolated. Each request that comes through this API will include the tenant context that the system will use to apply tenant isolation. Here, at the API layer of this experience, you can begin applying the first bits of isolation. Your API could extract the tenant context on each request and determine which downstream paths are valid for the current tenant, and in some cases, the tenant's role. This can prevent tenants from invoking requests to resources that are not valid for a given tenant context. For this example, an API request that's accessing the siloed microservice for Tenant 1 should not be able to send requests to the other siloed microservice associated with Tenant 2. At this layer, we're not really preventing access to a tenant's data, but we are isolating access to a tenant's compute resources. This is all part of the layered isolation model where we apply isolation at the outermost layer, which introduces an added level of protection before any microservice attempts to access tenant data or some other downstream tenant resources.

Once you're into the compute layer, our next level of isolation is applied as the microservice attempts to access other dependent resources (databases, queues, file systems, etc.). Now, we'll need isolation policies at this level to ensure that each microservice can only access the resources that are dedicated to that tenant. For the two siloed resources, these policies will be relatively straightforward. However, you'll notice our pooled microservice will need to implement item-level isolation to control access to the tenant rows within its share table. Your isolation policies will need to ensure that each request from your pooled microservice is constrained to just those items associated with the current tenant context.

This layered model gives you a better sense of how isolation is applied across multiple dimensions of your multi-tenant architecture. In many respects, this is borrowing from the traditional notion of security at every layer. Here, though, we're building on top of that concept by adding isolation protections as you move between the different layers of your environment. While the layers of your architecture might vary from the model presented here, the notion of layered isolation should still apply universally.

Deployment-Time Versus Runtime Isolation

In addition to layering your isolation model, you also have to consider when isolation will be applied to your environment. For some scenarios, you'll find that you can apply your isolation policies when your resources are deployed and configured. In other instances, your isolation will need to be configured and applied at runtime. The choice between these options is very much driven by a combination of the silo or pool footprint of a resource and the isolation mechanisms that are available for those resources.

Let's start by taking a conceptual look at the differences between the deployment-time and runtime isolation models. We'll start with the key elements of the deployment-time model (shown in Figure 9-6).

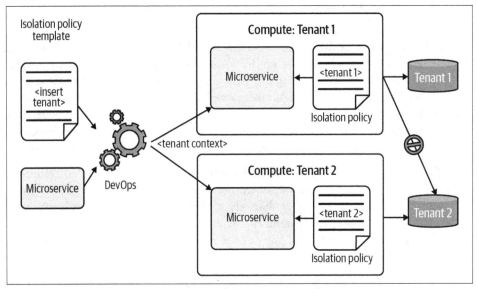

Figure 9-6. Deployment-time isolation model

Figure 9-6 illustrates the use of a microservice deployed in a siloed model for two tenants. Each of these microservices is represented on the righthand side of the diagram. These microservices both have siloed databases associated with them that are also deployed in a siloed model.

You'll notice that the solution's microservices are also running in a siloed mode. This means that for the lifetime of these deployed microservices, they will be bound to a specific tenant. This binding creates an opportunity to simplify our isolation story for these microservices, allowing us to attach a tenant-scoped policy to the compute of each microservice that prevents that microservice from accessing any resources that belong to other tenants.

This is where the notion of deployment-time isolation comes in. On the left of the diagram, I have a microservice and a templatized isolation policy that will be used to scope access for our microservices. Now, when my DevOps process provisions the compute resources for each microservice, it can insert the tenant context into the isolation policy template and attach that policy to the compute infrastructure. This is repeated for each microservice, injecting the tenant context into the policy for each tenant microservice deployment.

The side effect of this is shown on the far right of Figure 9-6. As our microservices attempt to access their associated siloed databases, their access will be limited to those databases that are appropriate for the current tenant context. As an example, an attempt by Tenant 1 to access Tenant 2's database is blocked by these deployment-time attached policies.

There's lots of power in this deployment-time model. Since the policy is attached at deployment time, the isolation has no dependency on any code in your microservice to comply with the isolation strategy. If your code attempts to cross a tenant boundary, it will be stopped. This, in fact, takes compliance out of the view of your microservice developers and makes it more a part of your DevOps and provisioning process. While this makes for a great isolation story, it also relies on a siloed model to work, and we certainly don't want to silo every resource simply to realize this benefit.

So, let's shift our focus now to those environments where we have pooled resources. This is typically where the runtime isolation model is used. With runtime isolation, we now start looking at strategies that rely on the cooperation of your application code or other constructs to dynamically acquire and apply your isolation policies. Figure 9-7 provides a conceptual view of the moving parts of the runtime isolation model.

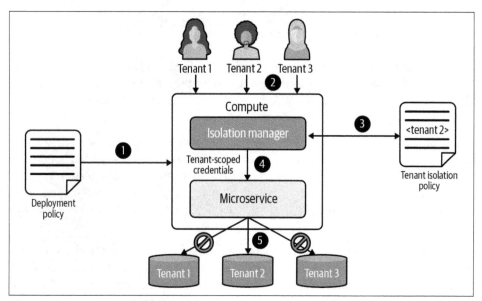

Figure 9-7. Runtime isolation model

With this example, we have compute that is shared amongst all of our tenants. Since this compute must be able to process requests from all tenants, it must be deployed with a policy that covers all tenants (step 1). This means that, at runtime, my microservice must be able to access any of the tenant databases associated with this service (shown at the bottom). In this mode, it becomes the job of our microservice code to use the current tenant context to dynamically scope and control access to these tenant resources.

The flow of this process starts at the top where my tenants are accessing the microservice, passing in their tenant context (step 2). Now, somewhere in my microservices compute environment, I'll need to use the tenant context to populate a policy and acquire the tenant-scoped credentials that will be used to access downstream resources. For this conceptual view I included an isolation manager that performs this process (step 3). In reality, how these tenant-scoped credentials are acquired could vary significantly for each technology and language stack. You might put a wrapper around your microservice, you might use a sidecar, you could use aspects—the list of options here is quite long. However, the key is that some mechanism acquires these tenant-scoped credentials from your dynamically populated policy and provides those credentials to your microservice (step 4).

Once your microservice has these tenant-scoped credentials, it will use them to access its associated tenant resources. In this case, I've stuck with a separate database for each tenant and used the credentials to contextually access each database (step 5). In this scenario, I've assumed that Tenant 2 made a request and that request inserted Tenant 2 into the policy. Then, with this scope, my access to resources was constrained to the Tenant 2 database. Even if my code attempted to insert another tenant identifier into its database access request, that request would not return another tenant's data.

You can see that this approach relies heavily on the code and libraries of my solution. This does leave room for microservices to make choices that go around your isolation mechanisms. However, the more work you put into injecting this isolation context into your code outside the view of developers, the better chances you have of enforcing compliance with your overall isolation strategy.

It's also worth noting that there are alternate strategies that you can apply here that move the runtime resolution outside the scope of your microservice. Figure 9-8 provides an example of a scenario where credentials are injected from outside of your microservice.

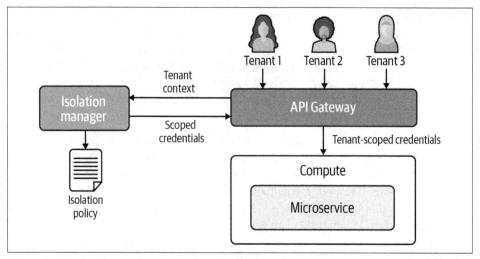

Figure 9-8. Injecting runtime scoped credentials

In the example, you'll see that I've put an API Gateway in front of my microservice. This gateway will pre-process requests, sending tenant context to the isolation manager code that will use the context with an isolation policy to acquire tenant-scoped credentials. This is very similar to the process described in our prior example. I've just moved the resolution of the scoped credentials out to the API Gateway. Once the gateway has the credentials, it passes them into your microservice where they are used to scope access to tenant resources.

This model has some advantages in that it moves resolution of the credentials outside the view of microservice developers. It also creates more natural opportunities to cache scoped credentials to address potential latency issues. The downside of this model, though, is that the isolation policies move outside the microservice. Generally, the scoping of policies is seen as part of the microservice and is closely connected to its implementation. This strategy breaks that mental model (at least somewhat). This is especially true if the gateway is used by multiple microservices.

Isolation Through Interception

One of our goals with runtime isolation is to remove developers from the isolation equation as much as possible. The more you need to rely on developers as part of the isolation story, the more cumbersome and fragile your isolation becomes. This is where teams will often look for opportunities to introduce interception mechanisms that can enforce isolation without relying heavily on developers applying specific conventions and constructs within the body of their microservice code.

There are a number of different technology and language constructs available that could be used as part of your runtime isolation interception policy. The challenge is that there are simply too many permutations of options to cover them all. That being said, there are some themes that are worth noting. Figure 9-9 provides a conceptual view of two general interception strategies.

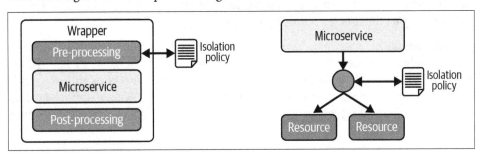

Figure 9-9. Isolation through interception strategies

On the left, you'll see a more language- or framework-based approach to interception. The tools you apply here tend to insert themselves into the execution path of your code, intercepting and pre-processing requests outside the view of your microservice code. Aspects, middleware, and wrapper libraries are amongst a list of possible options that you could use. With this approach, you're essentially intercepting inbound requests and using the tenant context to acquire scoped credentials to access tenant resources. This still fits the same runtime applied model I described earlier, but it relies less on the cooperation of developers to apply your isolation conventions.

The other model, shown on the right, takes a slightly different approach. Here, you put a mechanism between your resource and your microservice that intercepts each attempt to access a tenant resource (like a proxy). This mechanism resolves the tenant context and applies it as each resource is being accessed, which is where you'll see systems using concepts like sidecars to implement this interception scheme.

This is an evolving area where new constructs and mechanisms are showing up regularly. The broader value proposition is that these strategies—even in a runtime enforced model—yield a more robust and more centrally managed isolation scheme. Whether they fit your particular needs, though, will depend on the isolation requirements of your solution, the technology stack you're using, and, in some cases, the languages or frameworks that are part of your environment.

Scaling Considerations

Runtime-applied isolation, while effective, can introduce scaling issues within your environment. If you have a pooled service that is processing a high volume of requests and each request is acquiring tenant-scoped credentials, there is a chance that this may introduce an unreasonable level of latency within your environment. This can impact the broader scale of your system.

In these instances, you may have to consider refining or altering your runtime-applied isolation model to meet the needs of your system. There are caching strategies that you can introduce to hold your scoped credentials. With this approach, some will employ a time-to-live (TTL) setting to manage the lifecycle of these credentials. Figure 9-10 provides an example of how you might introduce this caching scheme.

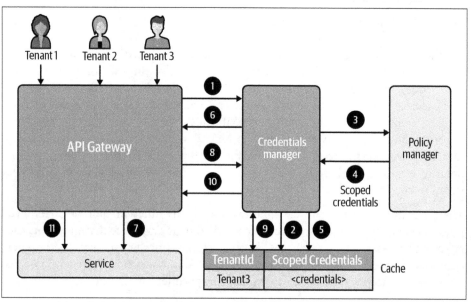

Figure 9-10. Caching isolation credentials

In Figure 9-10, we see the full lifecycle acquiring and applying cached isolation credentials. On the top left, I have a series of tenants that are entering the SaaS application services through an API Gateway. In this particular scenario, let's say that Tenant 3 is making its first request to a service. When that request comes in, the gateway invokes a credentials manager to get the scoped credentials for Tenant 3 (step 1). This credentials manager would attempt to look up the credential in the cache (step 2). In this case, let's presume Tenant 3 is not found. Now, the credentials manager acquires the tenant-scoped credentials from the policy manager (steps 3 and 4). The scoped credentials are then put into the cache (step 5), returned to the API Gateway (step 6), and injected into our downstream interactions with our services (step 7). At this time, it would also be assigned a TTL when it is placed in the cache. On our next call from Tenant 3, the system calls the credentials manager (step 8) and finds the credentials we stored in the cache (step 9). The cached credentials are returned to the API Gateway (step 10) and injected into our downstream service interactions (step 11).

In this model, the credentials manager and helpers are not separate services. They are all running within the same process. Some teams will attempt to centralize all of these isolation mechanisms in standalone services. Generally, the overhead of crossing a boundary to another service can add yet another layer of latency to your experience that creates additional performance problems. You can still move these concepts to libraries and other shared constructs, but I lean toward trying to keep the handling of these isolation management requests within the same process.

Finally, you'll also need to consider the scaling limits of the services you might be using. If, for example, you're using IAM policies to implement isolation on AWS, you'll need to consider whether the number of policies you need could exceed the service limits. This is why you'll see heavy use of policy templates in my examples where a single policy can be used across multiple tenant contexts.

Real-World Examples

At this point, you should have a good handle on the core principles that shape the design of your isolation strategy. Let's shift now to concrete examples that illustrate how isolation can be applied to environments with isolation constructs. The sections that follow will provide a sampling of implementation strategies that span the different flavors of isolation we covered in the preceding sections, connecting concepts to working solutions.

Full Stack Isolation

Let's start by looking at the more coarse-grained constructs used to isolate your tenant resource. Figure 9-11 provides a few examples of different isolation constructs utilized to implement a full stack silo deployment model in the AWS cloud.

In the figure, I have represented a series of full stack silo environments. The basic idea is that each tenant shown here has fully dedicated infrastructure resources. This model, as you might expect, has a natural mapping to the tools and technologies that are already used to place boundaries between resources. For these same reasons, it's also an area where builders see an easy and clear path to building out their isolation story.

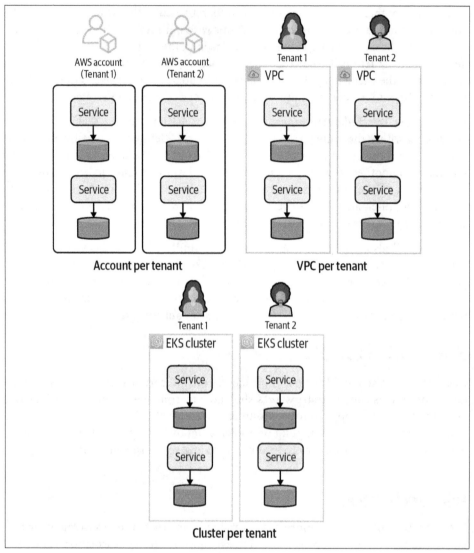

Figure 9-11. Coarse-grained isolation constructs

For this particular example, I showed three distinct isolation constructs. At the top left, you'll see an account-per-tenant isolation model where each account in my cloud provider (AWS) is used to define the isolation boundary. Since accounts prevent cross-account access by default, this represents one of the simplest constructs for achieving isolation in a full stack silo setting.

At the top right, I have shown how a networking construct can be used to isolate my tenant silos. In this case, I used an Amazon Virtual Private Cloud (VPC) to isolate my tenant resources. The VPC, like most networking constructs, gives me lots of built-in options to configure the flow of traffic in and out of my network. So, again, we have a relatively basic unit of isolation for each tenant's resources.

Finally, at the bottom of the diagram, I've shown an example that uses Amazon Elastic Kubernetes Service (EKS) to implement a full stack isolation model. Generally, as we move into container environments, you'll see that you have lots of options when it comes to implementing isolation strategies (we'll dig into those more in Chapter 10). For this scenario, though, I've opted to go to the extreme of having a separate cluster for each tenant. This means that you're essentially provisioning an entirely separate EKS environment for each tenant and relying on the natural cluster boundaries to enforce your isolation.

Resource-Level Isolation

Resource-level isolation tends to have good constructs that map well to isolation mechanisms. When we're working with dedicated resources, our isolation only needs to find a mechanism that can control access to that resource. Figure 9-12 provides an example of a resource-level implementation.

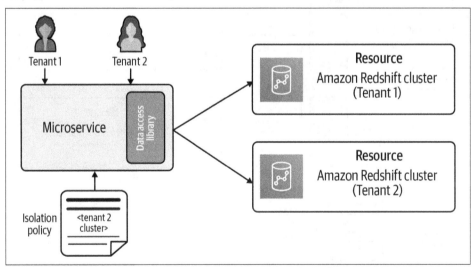

Figure 9-12. Resource-level isolation with Amazon Redshift

This example outlines a scenario where I'm using Amazon Redshift (a columnar database) in a siloed model where each tenant is assigned its own cluster (shown on the righthand side of the diagram). Within these clusters, I have data that is managed and accessed separately for each tenant. While we have a cluster as our unit of isolation, this cluster still maps conceptually to a resource. The boundaries of a resource in this model could take on multiple forms. A database, a queue, an analytics cluster

—these are amongst the different constructs that I would classify as a resource in this scenario.

On the left of the diagram, you'll see a microservice that is accessing my tenant resources. The microservice uses a data access library (DAL) to manage its interactions with its associated Redshift clusters. The DAL will, as part of processing each request, use the current tenant context and its isolation policy to acquire tenant-scoped credentials that will limit your access to a specific tenant's cluster.

This example of resource-level isolation happens to use pooled compute for its microservice and, as such, it relies on a runtime-applied isolation strategy. For contrast, you can see how this shifts when the solution has siloed compute resources (shown in Figure 9-13).

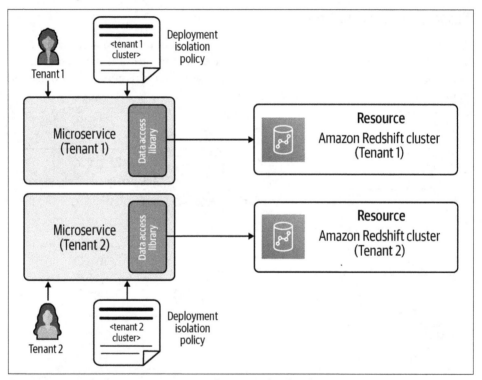

Figure 9-13. A deployment-time view of resource-level isolation

In Figure 9-13, we have most of the same moving parts as in the prior example. What's different now is that we have separate siloed microservices that are dedicated to each tenant. The siloed nature of this model allows me to alter my isolation approach. Instead of acquiring and resolving the isolation scope at runtime, this solution can attach a specific isolation strategy during the provisioning and configuration of the compute that's running our microservices. Now, there's no need for the DAL to absorb any extra overhead or complexity to apply our isolation policies—they are already applied by the policy attached to the compute during deployment.

Item-Level Isolation

Item-level isolation represents one of the most challenging isolation models mostly because it requires a level of granularity that is not often supported by many technologies. At the same time, in multi-tenant environments where there's a significant push for pooled infrastructure, you'll find lots of scenarios where you'll need to improvise strategies that will let you implement policies that can isolate individual items running in shared infrastructure.

The good news is that there are scenarios—especially in the cloud—where some services include built-in support for item-level isolation. To give you a better sense of what this might look like in a working solution, let's look at the item-level isolation model shown in Figure 9-14.

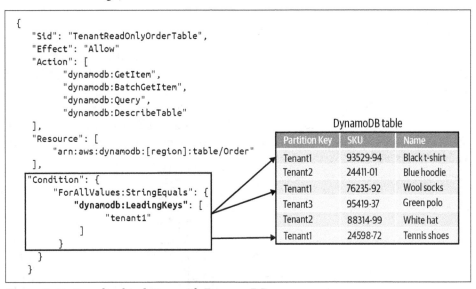

Figure 9-14. Item-level isolation with DynamoDB

On the righthand side of this diagram, you'll see I have a DynamoDB table that's populated with a few items. It also has a partition key that holds the tenant identifiers that associate each item in the table with a specific tenant (to simplify things, I showed these as Tenant1, Tenant2, etc.). Now, to apply isolation to this table, I need to restrict requests to just those items that are associated with a given tenant.

The policy that enforces this isolation is shown on the left. This uses AWS's IAM mechanism to define the scope of access for a DynamoDB table. I've highlighted the "Condition" portion of this policy because it declares the scope of access that will be granted for anyone using this policy. I bolded `"dynamodb:LeadingKeys"`, which, for this scenario, is being used to scope access to Tenant1.

If we put all the pieces together, the flow would go as follows: (1) your microservice populates the policy based on the current tenant context (Tenant1 in this case); (2) your code assumes an IAM role using this policy and gets back a set of credentials; and (3) the credentials are used by your code to access the table, limiting its access to only items that are associated with Tenant1. If another request came through for Tenant2, we'd plug that into the policy, assume the role, and get a set of credentials for Tenant2.

This is the basic theme you'd need to apply across any item-level isolation. You may, however, not have something as straightforward as this IAM policy to implement your isolation. The tools you use here might introduce some new wrinkles into your item-level isolation strategy. Mainly, we're trying to avoid having a model that is entirely dependent on assuming our code simply won't cross any tenant boundaries.

Managing Isolation Policies

Once you have settled on an isolation strategy, you still have to think about the lifecycle of the policies that are typically part of this story. Where your policies are stored, who owns and manages them, when and how are they deployed, how they are versioned—these are all questions you'll need to consider as part of creating and building a deployment experience for the infrastructure and microservices of your application. Figure 9-15 provides a view of two potential approaches to managing your isolation policies.

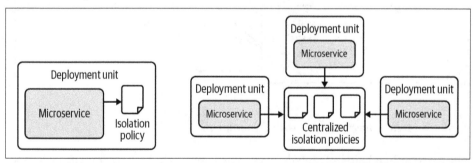

Figure 9-15. The deployment, managing, and versioning of your isolation policies

The model on the left of Figure 9-15 represents an approach that is more centered around the development of individual microservices. Here, developers view their isolation policies as an extension of their microservice, applying strategies that are directly bound to the implementation of their solution. With this mindset, any change to a microservice's implementation or infrastructure will directly shape the scope and nature of the isolation policies associated with that microservice.

This approach most resonates with me. I tend to fall into the camp that views an isolation policy as one of the deliverables that is bound to my microservice. As the owner of a microservice, my team also owns the maintenance and definition of the policies that are needed to ensure that the microservice is complying with its isolation requirements. That means I'll version, manage, and check in my policy configuration somewhere in the scope of the microservice's repository. In this mode, ownership and management of your policies is distributed to the various services of your system.

The other school of thought (shown on the righthand side of the diagram) prefers a model that has all of these policies managed and versioned through a centralized mechanism. With this approach, teams would still own the update of their policies, but they would all be versioned and managed outside the scope of any microservices. They would get deployed to some centralized location that would be referenced by all microservices. This gives a common home and standalone deployment model to policies that makes them easier to manage and provides a uniform scheme for referencing the services from each part of your architecture.

Both models are valid, and you could consider using a mix of these strategies. The key is that you need to look beyond how these isolation policies are being applied and evaluate how and where they fit into your broader build, versioning, and deployment lifecycle.

As you think about operationalizing isolation management and deployment, you also need to think about how you'll introduce tests that will validate that your isolation is actually working. This, surprisingly, has been one of the more challenging aspects of isolation. It turns out that there aren't natural mechanisms that allow you to simulate a tenant crossing a boundary. If you've done everything you can to prevent cross-tenant access, you may find it especially challenging to identify strategies that allow you to effectively mimic real-world, cross-tenant access.

While testing for these conditions can be difficult, not testing this doesn't seem like an option. Having isolation tests in place allows you to potentially detect an unintended leak in your policies or isolation implementation. They also confirm that the principles, when combined, are delivering the desired effect. Generally, given the business impact of any cross-tenant event, it's hard to justify not investing in this area.

The real question is: what can you do to simulate a cross-tenant event within your environment? This really has to happen somewhere within the internals of your application services. There's a point at which your code will be accessing a tenant resource based on a provided tenant context and it's here that you'll need to somehow inject an invalid tenant context. This will likely mean creating special paths or cases in your code to allow for this injection of an invalid tenant. It's also an area where you might consider using classic chaos engineering strategies to generate isolation exceptions.

A simple example might be a scenario where you're fetching a collection of items from a database for Tenant 1. This means that your surrounding isolation constructs are limiting the view of data to resources that belong to Tenant 1. However, in your test, you replace the tenant identifier in your request with the ID that belongs to Tenant 2. This should return no data or an error indicating that you've crossed a boundary. You may also add logs and operational policies that trigger alerts within your operations console, indicating that an attempt was made to cross the tenant boundary.

This may feel a bit artificial, and you may find more creative ways to simulate these cross-tenant conditions. However, even if this feels a bit unnatural, it's still essential to validating the isolation model of your environment.

Conclusion

Isolation is one of the most foundational topics that every multi-tenant developer will need to address. It is essential to creating any environment where tenants will be running their systems and storing their resources alongside other tenants. It becomes your job to ensure that your architecture takes every measure necessary to protect your system's resources from any cross-tenant access.

Implementing these isolation strategies, as you've seen in this chapter, can prove to be challenging. To help navigate the isolation landscape, I introduced a series of patterns and terminology that provided a mental model for the various flavors of isolation you might need to address in a multi-tenant environment. I separated isolation into three distinct categories: full-stack, resource-level, and item-level isolation, highlighting the nuances of each of these models. As part of reviewing these core isolation principles, I also highlighted some of the nuances that come with adopting each of these isolation strategies. This included a review of the misconceptions that are commonly associated with the notion of tenant isolation.

Once the foundation was in place, I looked at different approaches to applying these isolation patterns to your multi-tenant architecture. I started with a general look at how isolation is applied in a solution, illustrating the various layers that could play a role in your isolation model. I also looked at different approaches to introducing isolation policies. This included examining the implications of applying isolation at deployment time and runtime. From there, I started bringing all these concepts together and illustrating how they could be realized with specific technologies or services.

Based on this review, it should be clear that there's no one-size-fits-all approach to isolation. For many environments, you'll need to evaluate the mix of business and technology considerations that will inform the isolation strategies that are applied to the different components of your system. The strategy you apply for one area of the system may not apply to another. It's also important to note that, in some cases, you may not be able to identify a ready-made tool or mechanism that can support your isolation needs. This is where you'll need to be creative and introduce your own mechanisms to implement parts of your isolation model.

At this point, I've carved the multi-tenant landscape up into targeted topics that outline the overall principles and landscape of the multi-tenant SaaS architecture. Now, in the next chapter, I want to start looking at how these principles are realized with specific technology stacks. This will give you a better sense of how the realities and constructs of a given stack will directly impact how you design and build a SaaS environment. The first stack we're going to look at is the container-based model of Amazon Elastic Kubernetes Service (EKS). I'll review the key areas where EKS can influence the deployment, isolation, routing, and other dimensions of your multi-tenant environment.

EKS (Kubernetes) SaaS: Architecture Patterns and Strategies

Up to this point, most of the topics we've covered have been focused on building a foundation of core concepts that would apply to any multi-tenant SaaS architecture. This information should have equipped you with a clear view of the multi-tenant landscape. Now it's time to shift gears a bit and move from best practices strategies to looking more at how these concepts are influenced by the realities of different technology stacks. More specifically, in this chapter I'll be focusing on how multi-tenant principles are landed within a Kubernetes environment. For our scope, I'll actually be looking at Kubernetes through the lens of the Amazon Elastic Kubernetes Service (EKS). Much of what's here will be applicable to any Kubernetes environment. However, there are areas where the managed nature of EKS influences our options.

I'll start this chapter off by reviewing some of the key areas where I see good alignment between the EKS stack and SaaS architecture principles. The goal is to better illuminate some of the key factors that have teams selecting EKS as their preferred technology for building and developing their SaaS solutions. With that foundation in place, we'll shift to exploring the different EKS deployment patterns that SaaS environments use to address their tiering, noisy neighbor, and isolation needs. We'll look at a range of possibilities here, highlighting the different constructs you can use to define the footprint of the tenant environments that are hosted within an EKS cluster. This will be followed by a look at some of the key tools and mechanisms you can use to add tenant-contextual routing to your architecture, allowing you to support different deployment models, authentication strategies, and so on.

Next, I'll dig into EKS onboarding and deployment automation. This is where we'll see how EKS directly shapes your approach to provisioning, configuring, and updating tenant environments. I'll look at how tools like Helm, Argo Workflows, and Flux can be combined to describe and automate all the moving parts of your provisioning and deployment lifecycle. This sampling of the DevOps toolchain will give you a taste of some of the possibilities that come with creating a single automation experience that can address the unique tiering and deployment models that you may need to support your SaaS environment.

I'll then shift to looking at how tenant isolation is realized in EKS architecture. I'll start by looking at how the different EKS deployment strategies can influence your approach to preventing cross-tenant access. As part of this, we'll explore the different EKS constructs that are used to implement deployment- and runtime isolation strategies. Finally, I'll wrap the chapter with a look at how you can optimize the different compute nodes that are running in your underlying EKS cluster, introducing new techniques you can use to align the profile of your compute instance types with the demands of your multi-tenant workloads.

This look at multi-tenancy and EKS should give you a better sense of just how your technology choices can directly shape the design of your overall architecture. It should also highlight the range of possibilities that come with building SaaS solutions with EKS. The current and emerging list of tools, strategies, and patterns can be daunting. At the same time, these tools also introduce you to new and creative ways to address multi-tenant architecture problems.

The EKS–SaaS Fit

It's probably fair to start by asking ourselves why EKS and SaaS represent such a good pairing. I think there are a broad range of factors that, collectively, make EKS a compelling model for teams that are migrating or building SaaS solutions. For some, the appeal starts with the programming model. While EKS brings in a diverse range of new concepts and constructs, how you write and build the services of your application remains mostly unchanged. In most cases, the languages, tools, and libraries you use can come with you. This may seem like an awfully basic advantage, but it can represent a significant upside for many teams. This is especially valuable to organizations that are migrating solutions to a SaaS delivery model. It allows them to lift bits of their system directly into EKS, focusing more of their energy on how to get the core elements of multi-tenancy put into place.

The scaling model of EKS also represents another area where we see solid alignment between SaaS and EKS. Throughout this book I've highlighted some of the complexities that come with supporting the unpredictable needs of tenants and how, for some environments, this can lead to overprovisioning of compute resources. In some cases, this overprovisioning is needed to offset the possibility of rapid spikes in tenant activity. With EKS, new compute resources can be scaled up rapidly to support spiky workloads. It can also scale down efficiently. This can enable some teams to get closer to their goal of achieving greater alignment between tenant activity and compute consumption. Beyond the basics of EKS scale, you'll also discover a rich and evolving set of mechanisms and tools that will allow you to optimize how tenant workloads are mapped to different instance types within your cluster. The number of knobs and dials open up a broad range of possibilities. It's worth noting that there are some legitimate overprovisioning realities that can still surface in an EKS environment since an EKS cluster still needs to add and remove compute nodes to meet the demands of your multi-tenant workloads. Still, overall, I do see EKS offering scaling advantages that might not be found with other compute stacks.

With SaaS architectures, we've also seen how important it is to support a variety of deployment models, enabling resources to be run in siloed and pooled models. This represents another area where EKS fits well with the profile of SaaS environments. As you'll see in the sections that follow, EKS includes grouping constructs that let you determine how the compute resources of your solution are managed, deployed, and landed in your SaaS environment. These grouping constructs fit nicely with our need to selectively group the different compute resources in a multi-tenant architecture.

The EKS deployment tooling is also very appealing to SaaS builders, with a vibrant and continually growing list of tools that address the often complex deployment automation requirements of SaaS environments. These tools, many of which are community driven, enable powerful and highly configurable mechanisms that fit nicely with much of the heavy lifting associated with provisioning and updating a multi-tenant setting. These tools and libraries are able to more naturally support the sometimes complex combinations of tier-based onboarding and deployment, limiting the need to create custom, one-off solutions. This represents a huge advantage to many SaaS teams and enables them to connect their SaaS deployment automation needs with a set of tools that are better suited to the challenges imposed by provisioning and deploying the elements of SaaS environments.

Isolation is another area where EKS introduces another layer of mechanisms that enable you to define your isolation policies. This equips builders with a new set of tools and strategies that are used to prevent cross-tenant access. Sidecars, service meshes, and other EKS constructs give builders a range of new options when thinking about how and where they want to inject and enforce their isolation policies. It's also here that we often see greater opportunities to push isolation to more centralized mechanisms. This can simplify the lives of service developers, removing much of the isolation detail from their view. It can also lead to a stronger isolation profile for your overall system.

Much of the SaaS goodness of EKS (and Kubernetes in general) is rooted in the strength and depth of its community. So many of the mechanisms you'll find to support multi-tenancy are byproducts of community-driven solutions that are continually enriching the multi-tenant possibilities within EKS. AWS is also adding new wrinkles that add new dimensions to the EKS story. This means you'll want to pay close attention to the community to figure out which new options are emerging. Every time I talk about SaaS and EKS, some new tool or mechanism has been added to my multi-tenant toolbag. In some respects, this could be considered both the blessing and the curse of adopting EKS; the architecture strategy you picked might be superseded by the introduction of some Kubernetes tool or construct that didn't exist when you started.

 For the scope of this chapter, the line between EKS and Kubernetes will be blurry. In many cases, the architecture strategies and mechanisms that I've outlined here are part of the native capabilities of Kubernetes. There are, however, some areas where EKS adds a set of considerations and tools to the menu of options. To simplify matters, I'll be referencing everything as EKS in this chapter knowing that significant parts of what I'm covering would apply to any Kubernetes setting.

Deployment Patterns

Whenever I look at a technology stack, the first area I tend to focus on is deployment patterns. For me, once the business has defined a target deployment model, I can start figuring out how this model will be realized within my architecture. It also directly shapes the different strategies and constructs that I'll use to bring this deployment model to life with my chosen technology stack. In this case, where we're focused on EKS, we want to understand what options we have to implement the different siloed and pooled deployments of our SaaS application's compute resources. Typically, this list of options is pretty limited. However, with EKS, we have a slightly more diverse set of strategies that enable you to determine how our compute resources are deployed.

Before we start exploring these models, though, let's start by labeling some of the core EKS constructs to get a better sense of the moving parts of the puzzle. Figure 10-1 provides a conceptual view of some of the key EKS concepts that will be part of our broader deployment patterns discussion.

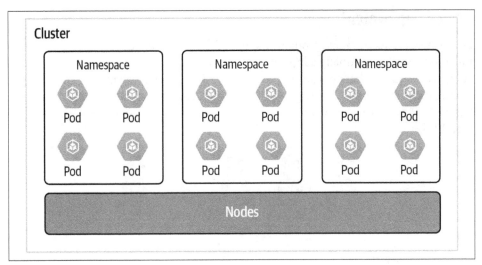

Figure 10-1. Core deployment pattern concepts

At the outer edge of Figure 10-1, you'll notice that I have a cluster that groups and scales all the underlying compute resources of our EKS environment. At the bottom of the diagram, I've also included a reference to the nodes that will be running within this cluster. Each node corresponds to an EC2 instance. These nodes will scale elastically within our cluster based on the load that's being placed on our EKS environment.

The pods that you see here are the EKS units of compute that will be running the services of our solution. EKS will do all the heavy lifting of scheduling how these pods get mapped onto the nodes that are in the cluster. These pods represent the smallest unit of execution within an EKS environment.

Finally, you'll also see that I've created sets of these pods using namespaces. A namespace enables EKS to isolate and group the resources that are in a cluster. Some might think of a namespace as a sub-cluster within an EKS cluster. For our purposes, we'll focus on how this namespace grouping construct is used to support the deployment needs of our SaaS environment.

This is a *very* high-level view of some basic EKS constructs. As you can imagine, there's far more detail here than I can afford to cover in the scope of this book. For our purposes, though, this will give us enough room to start looking at how these concepts can be connected to deployment patterns. The sections that follow will outline how these different EKS mechanisms are used to group, isolate, and scale the compute layer of your multi-tenant environment.

Pooled Deployment

Pooled represents the most straightforward of the EKS SaaS deployment models. In this mode, you're essentially adopting an approach where all tenants will share all the compute resources that are running within your EKS cluster, relying on the collective scaling capabilities of EKS to support the varying compute workloads of your tenants. Figure 10-2 provides a view of a fully pooled multi-tenant compute footprint realized with EKS.

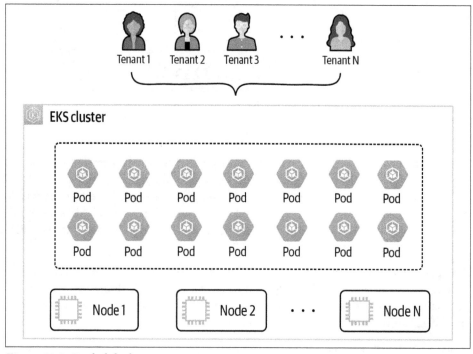

Figure 10-2. Pooled deployment pattern

At the top of Figure 10-2, I've shown a set of tenants that are consuming a single EKS cluster, indicating that all the compute resources are shared by all tenants. The pods in this cluster are also running a single, shared namespace. There are no other grouping constructs that are being applied to separate the workloads that are running in this environment.

At the bottom of the diagram, you'll see where nodes come into play. Our cluster, as noted earlier, is running across a dynamically scaling set of nodes. EKS will be responsible for creating the pods that will execute on these nodes. As more load is placed on the system, more nodes will be added to support these evolving demands. In many respects, the cluster is essentially applying classic cloud elasticity mechanisms to grow and shrink the cluster size to align consumption with tenant activity. It's here that you could see some overprovisioning of the nodes to ensure that you have enough capacity to support spikes in tenant activity. It may take some work to refine your scaling policy to optimize the consumption and sizing of your EKS cluster.

Within EKS you do have lots of knobs and dials that could influence how this pooled environment scales to meet the distinct needs of your system and its services. You might, for example, configure the number of replicas for a pod based on its scale and availability profile. Or you might align the memory settings of a pod to meet the needs of a specific service. My point is that, within the pooled model, it becomes especially important to leverage the different EKS configuration options to ensure that your environment will respond effectively to the realities that come with supporting the continually shifting needs of a fully pooled compute model.

Siloed Deployments

EKS provides builders with a growing list of options when it comes to siloing its compute resources. Many of these strategies can be achieved through the application of EKS grouping constructs, leveraging the natural built-in mechanism of EKS to draw boundaries between your compute resources and enabling them to operate in a per-tenant model. Other silo strategies align more to traditional models where tenants are assigned dedicated infrastructure (cluster per tenant, for example). Let's go through some of the common EKS techniques that are used to implement a siloed deployment model.

As you might suspect, the namespaces grouping model I mentioned earlier represents one of the more commonly used siloing constructs. Figure 10-3 provides a conceptual view of a namespace-per-tenant silo model.

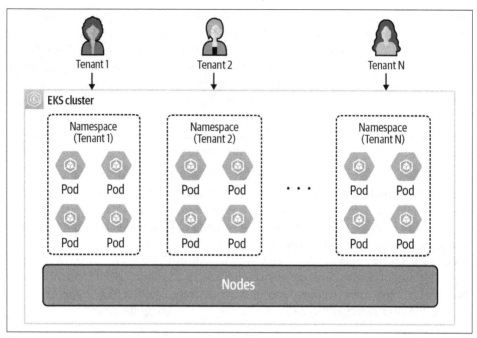

Figure 10-3. Namespace-per-tenant siloed deployments

In this example, I've used the basic grouping capabilities that are provided by namespaces to associate the pods and computing services of my application with specific tenant loads. This means that we'll essentially deploy separate copies of our application's microservices into each tenant namespace. It also means that the pods in these tenant namespaces will only process requests for their assigned tenant. There are multiple advantages to placing our tenant compute resources in a namespace. First, it gives you a mechanism that allows you to collectively manage, configure, and operate an individual tenant's compute environment. It also gives you a construct for attaching policies that can control and limit access between the namespaces. You can imagine how these policies would play a role in defining your overall tenant isolation model.

For this deployment strategy, you'll notice that our cluster's nodes (shown at the bottom of Figure 10-3) are scaled up and down based on the load placed on the namespaces. There's no real correlation between the namespaces and the nodes that are part of our cluster. The nodes will scale collectively to meet the loads that are being placed on the namespaces.

There is an alternate approach that creates more of a binding between the namespace pods and the underlying compute nodes. Figure 10-4 provides a conceptual view of the node-per-tenant model.

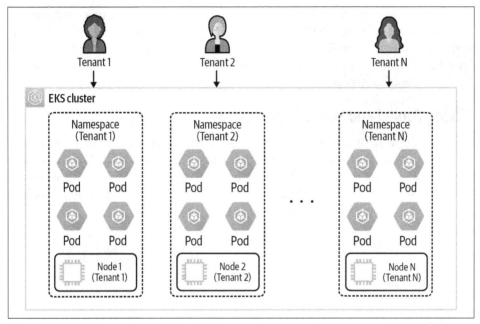

Figure 10-4. Node-per-tenant siloed deployments

In Figure 10-4, we have a series of separate siloed pod collections that are associated with specific tenants. Each of the tenants are also configured to run on a given compute node that's running in the cluster. Now, the silo tenant boundary includes both the namespace, its pods, and the nodes that are running each of these pods. This adds, for some, another layer to your siloed deployment story, ensuring that tenants aren't sharing any compute resources. For some scenarios, this could help address some specific concerns about compliance and the nature of the boundaries between your compute resources.

Now, there is another approach to siloing EKS compute resources that's a bit more heavy-handed. Instead of attempting to silo resources with a common cluster, you could also consider having separate EKS clusters for each tenant. While this might be appealing and applicable for some environments, I generally prefer avoiding this path. To me, the more distributed nature of this approach can introduce operational and cost efficiency challenges. If you're anticipating supporting a large collection of tenants, this approach could also present scaling challenges. Again, it's not invalid, it just feels a bit like overkill given the other options you may have. One variation of this approach would be to employ a pod-based deployment where you distribute groups of tenants across a collection of clusters (the term "pod" gets a bit overloaded here). You might, for example, have a separate cluster for a handful of premium tier tenants and place your remaining basic tier tenants into a shared cluster. You could imagine multiple variations of this theme.

Another variation of siloed that's been on my radar is the notion of virtual clusters. The mental model is one where you get all the isolation that comes with a cluster without needing to actually use physical clusters for each tenant. In this model, you'd have some siloed constructs within the cluster but your workloads would still run on shared nodes. This may represent a compelling option for some teams.

Mixing Pooled and Siloed Deployments

As noted throughout this book, there is no one-size-fits-all to choosing deployment models. So, as we think about how we might map these different deployment models to EKS, we must also consider what it would mean to support a mixture of siloed and pooled models within a single EKS architecture. Figure 10-5 provides an example of how you might implement a mixed mode deployment model.

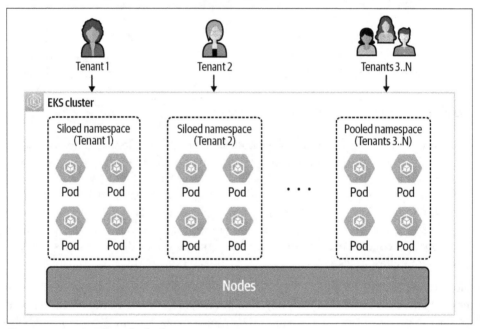

Figure 10-5. Mixed mode deployments

There are no major surprises here. You'll see that I've essentially used the same namespace model to create individual groupings for each flavor of deployment. The siloed tenants (Tenants 1 and 2) are deployed into their own namespaces and our remaining tenants are deployed into a separate "pooled" namespace.

As you can imagine, supporting these models side by side doesn't add a ton of complexity to your overall architecture. Yes, there are other factors (deployment, onboarding, isolation) that will influence the footprint of these namespaces, but, overall, the ability to simply use the namespace construct to create different deployment patterns ends up being relatively straightforward. Much of what is used to describe one namespace can be reused to describe the next (with caveats).

The Control Plane

So far this discussion of multi-tenant EKS deployment patterns has focused primarily on how the various services of your application plane could be grouped and landed in an EKS cluster to support the silo and pool requirements of your workloads. There is one more piece of the puzzle. Somewhere within our EKS environment, we must also place the control plane of our SaaS architecture (assuming our entire environment is EKS-based).

There are few absolutes about how the control plane should be deployed. We do know, however, that its services should be managed, versioned, and deployed separately from the application plane—even if it's running in the same EKS cluster as your application plane. We basically need to select from amongst the different EKS grouping mechanisms, identifying the construct that best aligns with the needs of our SaaS environment. Figure 10-6 provides a view of two different approaches you might use for landing the control plane in your EKS architecture.

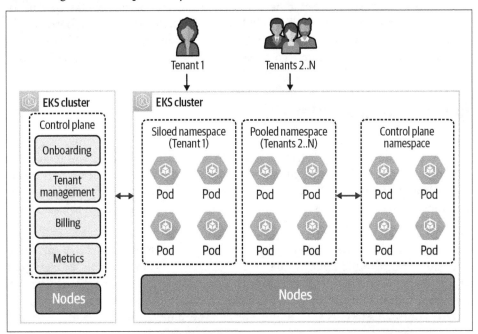

Figure 10-6. Control plane deployment strategies

On the righthand side of Figure 10-6, you'll see a cluster that is meant to host our application plane. The application plane supports both siloed and pooled deployments, using namespaces to group the compute resources that are needed for each of these tenant profiles. Now, the question is: where do we place the control plane?

The first example is shown on the far left where all the services of the control plane are deployed into a completely separate cluster. In this model, the interactions between the control plane and the application plane would need to be allowed to cross cluster boundaries. Some may like having these services deployed entirely on their own. This certainly allows the configuration, deployment, scaling profile, and other attributes of the control plane to be managed and operated exclusively based on the needs of the control plane services.

In contrast, I've also shown (on the far right) an example of a control plane that is hosted within the same cluster as our application plane namespaces. Here I've introduced another namespace that would be used to group all the services that would be associated with the control plane. Placing the control plane within the same cluster would certainly simplify things a bit, reusing many of the mechanisms and automation strategies that are used to deploy and configure the other namespaces that are within the cluster. Some may like that these control plane resources would get scaled within the same cluster, enabling them to use the scale of one shared cluster to maximize operational and cost efficiency. Others might prefer to keep the needs of the control plane more separate. Again, there are no absolutes here. You'll have to sort through the trade-offs and find a good balance that works well with your architecture goals and requirements.

Routing Considerations

As you introduce different per-tenant resources into your deployments, you'll also need to consider how this distribution of tenant compute resources will impact the routing experience of your multi-tenant environment. We explored this concept in some detail in Chapter 6, looking at how different technology stacks might employ different tools and strategies to route tenant-specific traffic to the appropriate compute resources.

This happens to be an area where EKS offers a myriad of mechanisms that can influence how tenant traffic flows within your architecture. There's a long list of vendor and open source tools that are able to proxy your EKS compute services, adding custom handling functionality that can be quite useful in a multi-tenant environment. Ingress controllers (NGINX, Contour, Kong), for example, are used as inbound load balancers that can route activity to your tenant-specific resources. A service mesh (Istio, Linkerd, AWS App Mesh) can also be used to introduce a range of highly configurable routing controls. The key concept is that you're essentially placing some layer of tenant-contextual processing at the front of your environment that can be applied to routing, authentication, and a host of other possibilities.

How you apply these routing technologies will depend heavily on the nature of your solution. This, to me, is one the areas that highlights the multi-tenant strengths of the EKS experience. There are so many existing and emerging tools that you can apply here that it can be difficult to identify which tool best addresses the needs of your environment. Figure 10-7 provides one example of how these different constructs could shape the flow of tenant traffic within your SaaS architecture.

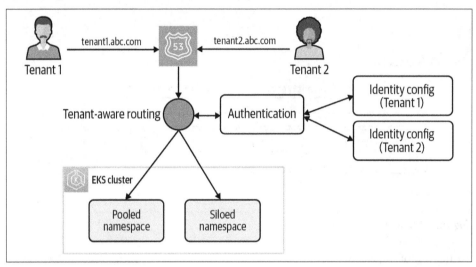

Figure 10-7. Applying EKS routing tools

In this particular example, I've shown two tenants that are interacting with the resources that are in my EKS environment. These tenants both use a subdomain to convey their tenant context as part of the URL that's used to access the environment via Amazon's Route 53 service. Now, as they flow into the environment, this is where you would introduce one of the tenant-aware routing constructs that we've been discussing. These tools would extract and apply the context of individual tenants.

The diagram highlights two specific examples of how you might apply these routing mechanisms. First, I used tenant-contextual routing as part of my authentication model. The idea is that I could extract the subdomain and use it to determine which tenant identity provider would be used to authenticate a given tenant. This is especially powerful when you have a mix of siloed and pooled identity resources. For example, imagine having a dedicated Amazon Cognito User Pool for each siloed, premium tier tenant. Meanwhile, all of our basic tier tenants would share a common User Pool. In this instance, your authentication flow would need to map incoming requests to the appropriate identity provider. Instead of handling this in my application services, I've offloaded these routing policies to one of these proxy tools.

If you move further down the path of our inbound requests, you'll also see that tenant-aware routing is applied here to direct traffic to the appropriate namespace. Figure 10-8 provides an example of how this might be configured using an NGINX ingress controller.

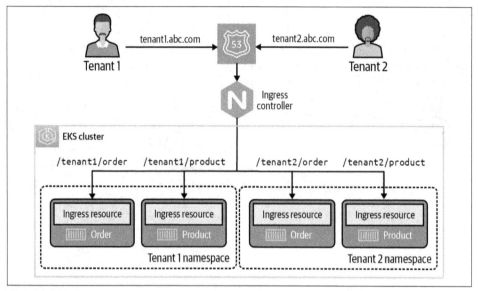

Figure 10-8. Routing tenants to namespaces

At the top of Figure 10-8, you'll see two different tenants coming into our SaaS environment with per-tenant subdomains. As each request flows in from these tenants, they will be routed through the NGINX ingress controller, sending requests to individual tenant microservices based on their ingress resource configuration.

This routing process actually sends requests to the specific tenant microservices that are running in each namespace. For example, on the bottom left, you'll see that I have a namespace that groups the microservices for Tenant 1. Each of these microservices is configured with an ingress resource that includes the paths that connect a given microservice to the appropriate inbound request. For example, you'll see that there is an */tenant1/order* path on the lefthand side of the diagram that illustrates the routing of order requests for the Tenant 1 namespace.

These examples only represent a small sampling of the routing possibilities. Each tool you use brings its own unique set of considerations and mechanisms that can impact the footprint of your architecture. The list of available configuration options and patterns goes well beyond the scope of this chapter. That being said, I do feel like this is an area where, as a SaaS architect, you need to lean into the tooling community and determine which of these technologies best supports the specific needs of your multitenant architecture.

Onboarding and Deployment Automation

The provisioning, configuration, and deployment of your multi-tenant resources can be heavily influenced by the technologies that you're using. Tiering requirements, deployment models, and a host of other factors will directly shape how you build the onboarding and deployment elements of your SaaS solution. This, again, is another area where EKS offers a long list of tools that can address the potentially complex set of automation requirements that are typically associated with multi-tenant environments.

To get a sense of the challenge, let's start by looking at the moving parts that could be part of your onboarding and deployment processes. Figure 10-9 highlights some of the key conceptual elements that could be included in your overall automation strategy.

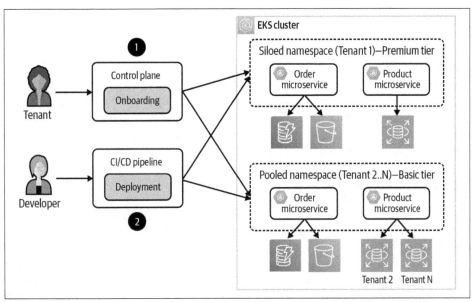

Figure 10-9. The onboarding and deployment challenge

On the righthand side of the diagram you'll see the application plane of a sample multi-tenant environment. It includes two namespaces, one that is for siloed, premium tier tenants and another that is pooled for basic tier tenants. I've added a bit more detail to these tenant configurations, showing the different microservices and their associated storage. The Order service, for example, has dependencies on DynamoDB and Amazon S3. The Product service stores its data in an RDS instance. For the siloed environments, I'm presuming these storage constructs are also siloed (per-tenant) resources—even though they don't have to be. Then, for the pooled namespace, the Order service shares storage for all tenants while the Product service siloes its storage, providing a separate RDS instance for each tenant.

Now, we need to look at how the footprint of the application plane will influence the onboarding and deployment of our environment. At the top left (step 1), I've shown a tenant onboarding via the control plane. While there's no detail included here, you can imagine all the underlying automation and tooling that is needed to contextually provision and configure each new tenant environment. Your tenant onboarding code will need to know which new resources are needed for each tenant based on their tier. For example, the siloed onboarding will need to create a namespace, deploy services, and provision the associated storage. For the pool, we'll mostly be configuring the environment and only creating one-off infrastructure where it's needed. In this case, since the basic tier Product service requires a separate RDS instance for each tenant, your automation will need to create and configure this instance for each newly onboarded tenant.

The other piece of the puzzle is the development CI/CD pipeline, which will need to deploy service updates to the application plane (step 2). Here, the focus is more on the day-to-day developer experience where builders are updating and releasing new versions of services that need to go through their build and deployment pipeline. What's different with this approach is that our CI/CD pipeline must be able to deploy an updated microservice to each tenant namespace. This is where you'll need to assemble a process that can automate deployments across these environments, supporting the various siloed and pooled tenant configurations.

Configuring Onboarding with Helm

With this as our backdrop, we can now turn our attention to figuring out which combination of tools might best support the needs of this particular environment. We certainly have the option of simply using AWS CodePipeline, Terraform, AWS Cloud Development Kit (CDK), and a host of other classic DevOps tooling to automate these processes. This would be entirely valid. At the same time, there's a rich collection of build and deployment tooling that's purpose-built for the EKS and Kubernetes universe that can target these requirements in a way that pushes more of the complexity to the tooling.

To support the various configuration options that are required by our environment, we'll need to start by figuring out how we can best capture and characterize the nuances of the different onboarding configurations. A tool that could be a good fit here is Helm, which enables you to create "charts" that outline all the different attributes of a Kubernetes environment. These charts provide us with a mechanism that naturally addresses our need to define our different tiered configurations. Figure 10-10 provides an example of how these charts could be used to describe the onboarding configuration characteristics of our application plane.

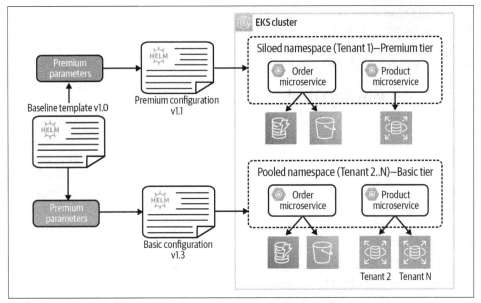

Figure 10-10. Using Helm to describe tenant environments

The design I've settled on here is one where I create a baseline Helm template that describes the core elements that are part of any tenant environment. Here you'll find the bits of configuration that describe all the services and their default settings without any notion of silo or pool being added to the mix. With this baseline template in place, we then generate tier-specific Helm charts that apply the parameters that are associated with each tier. For this example, I've included basic and premium tier parameters that are used to create their corresponding Helm charts.

The beauty of this model is that we're essentially expressing the attributes of our tiering and deployment models through tooling that lets us characterize the attributes of each environment. We're also getting the goodness out of having everything that's common here captured in one baseline template. This lets us maintain, manage, and version all the common settings in one place. The other upside is that we're leaning into tooling that can be woven somewhat seamlessly into our onboarding experience, automating these provisioning and configuration steps through tools that have built-in constructs that allow them to shape and mold the footprint of our multi-tenant EKS environment.

There is one twist you'll need to factor into your approach. While Helm is great at describing our EKS environment, there are typically non-EKS constructs or services that are part of our environment that can't be configured with Helm. For example, the onboarding experience outlined in Figure 10-10 will need to provision and configure S3, DynamoDB, and RDS resources. It's here that you'll likely have to leverage a combination of tools, mixing in CDK, Terraform, or other infrastructure automation tooling to target these non-Kubernetes assets. The net of this is that the full automation and characterization of our environments will end up being packaged as Helm plus whatever other assets are needed to support the other elements of our infrastructure configuration and provisioning model.

Automating with Argo Workflows and Flux

So far, I've mostly talked about how we package and describe the onboarding profiles of our basic and premium tier tenants. Now, we still need to consider what it would mean to automate all the moving parts of the onboarding experience. This is where we can fold in more tools from the DevOps universe, introducing Argo Workflows and Flux into our onboarding flow to orchestrate and reconcile the application of our onboarding configurations. It's the application of these tools that help connect all the dots in this process and deal with the nuances of automating the deployments to these per-tenant environments.

Let's look at a specific example of how you might use Helm, Argo Workflows, and Flux together. Figure 10-11 provides a sample view of how these tools can handle the complexities that come with supporting a tier-based onboarding experience.

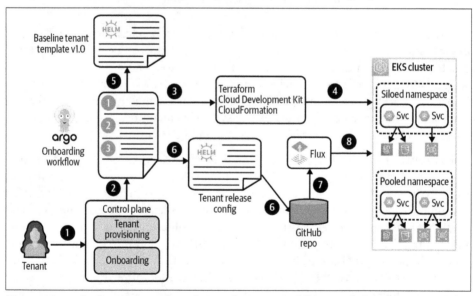

Figure 10-11. Orchestrating onboarding with Argo Workflows and Flux

At the bottom-left corner of the diagram, you'll see the initiation of the onboarding experience (step 1). Here a tenant (or some internal process) triggers the onboarding process, supplying the tier and other attributes of the tenant. This request is processed by the onboarding service that's part of the control plane. At some point in your onboarding flow, the service will invoke the Tenant Provisioning service, which owns responsibility for creating and configuring any infrastructure that's needed for the new tenant. For this example, we have basic and premium tier tenants, each of which require different infrastructure footprints.

This is where Helm and Argo Workflow come into the picture. Our Tenant Provisioning service will invoke a workflow that will be responsible for executing all the steps to complete the tier-aware provisioning of tenant resources (step 2). The workflow has two distinct toolchains it must use to get our tenant environment created. For one half of the process, it must use classic infrastructure automation tooling (Terraform, CDK, CloudFormation) to provision the non-EKS infrastructure resources. In this particular case, this means provisioning the different storage resources that are needed for our microservices. To achieve this, the workflow invokes an infrastructure automation tool, say Terraform, to execute this part of the process (step 3). The automation scripts and code employed here will invoke all the tier-contextual operations needed to create the siloed storage for any new premium tier tenant or it will provision just the one siloed RDS instance for any new basic tier tenant (step 4). If you recall, basic tier tenants are mostly pooled but offer siloed storage for the product services (shown at the bottom right).

Up to this point, we've mostly just executed a classic infrastructure automation process that happens to be triggered as part of an Argo Workflow. For the second half of this process, though, we're more focused on how to get the EKS cluster and tenant constructs configured. Here we'll rely heavily on the Helm charts to drive the configuration and creation of our tenant's EKS assets. First, we'll clone the baseline template that we used for all of our tenants (step 5). Then our Argo Workflow will generate a tenant-specific Helm release configuration, merging in the configuration settings for each individual tier (step 6). The end result is a tier-specific Helm release configuration that contains all the information/settings needed to onboard tenants for a given tier.

At this point, we have a Helm chart that represents the configuration we want for our tenant, but it has not been applied to our EKS cluster. This is where Flux comes into the picture. Once our Helm chart is ready, we can commit to our repository (step 7). Flux will be listening to that repository to detect any updates. When it sees the new Helm chart, it will use this configuration to create the EKS resources that are needed for my new tenant (step 8). This is where you'll see the creation and configuration of your namespace, microservices, and other EKS-specific constructs.

In reviewing this approach, you should be able to see how this moves much of the complexity of our tenant provisioning process into a set of tools that fit well with the needs of our tier-based onboarding experience.

Tenant-Aware Service Deployments

Getting tenants onboarded is only half of this story. Once we have these tenant-specific environments and resources, we still have to think about how the developer pipelines will incorporate support for these different deployment configurations. The release of an update to a microservice, for example, must include some ability to deploy that new microservice to multiple namespaces within your EKS cluster. It's here that you need to find a way to accommodate these multi-tenant deployment requirements without adding any burden to the developer experience. Developers should be able to simply build and release a new microservice without needing to be aware of these deployment complexities.

With EKS tooling you do have access to constructs that can help automate these deployments. Figure 10-12 provides a conceptual view of how Helm and Flux can support your deployment of services.

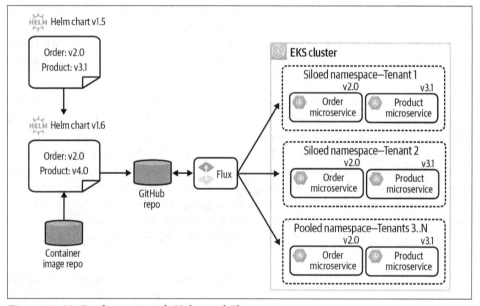

Figure 10-12. Deployment with Helm and Flux

Let's start by looking at the righthand side of this diagram where we have a cluster with multiple tenants onboarded. There are two premium tier tenants that are running in separate namespaces (Tenants 1 and 2). And we have a pooled namespace that's running all the basic tier tenants. Each of these namespaces are all running the same Order and Product microservices that have specific versions (shown at the top right above each microservice).

Now, imagine you're a builder who's rolling out a new version of the Order service, moving it from v3.1 to v4.0. As a developer, I just want to build it, test, and release it. However, something needs to deploy this updated service to each of the three namespaces on the right. This is where Flux can deal with 1-to-many mapping and address the rollout of the new version of the Order service.

Making this work first starts with the Helm charts illustrated in the top left. Within these charts, there are references to the microservices that need to be deployed. My build process can clone the current chart, update the product microservice version, and update the version of the Helm chart to indicate that there are changes that need to be applied. When this updated Helm chart (v1.6) is packaged and checked into the repository, our Flux process will detect the presence of this new version. It will then determine how to apply this updated chart to all of the environments that are running the previous version, moving all of them to the v1.6 configuration. The end result will be that my new v4.0 Order service will be deployed to all namespaces.

For this particular example, I focused on updating the microservice. However, there are other settings that can be configured with Helm charts. This same mechanism can change any number of different settings that are part of the EKS environment.

 The challenge of digging into this EKS DevOps space is that there are simply too many tools and options to consider. For this chapter, I tried to give a sense of the multi-tenant DevOps challenges, providing a glimpse into how some of the common tools can address your multi-tenant deployment requirements. However, I would encourage you to dig more deeply into the options and assess which tools and strategies are going to best fit the profile of your team and solution. The broader takeaway here is that the tiering, deployment models, and general nature of multi-tenant environments may require targeted approaches to automate the onboarding and deployment of your SaaS environment.

Tenant Isolation

In a multi-tenant EKS environment, we have lots of new constructs and mechanisms that describe how our compute is deployed. Now we need to think about what it means to layer tenant isolation on top of these constructs. How and where do we insert policies into an EKS cluster to ensure that one tenant can't access the resources of another tenant?

As you might suspect, there are multiple dimensions to the EKS isolation story. To get a better sense of the fundamentals of the EKS SaaS isolation strategy, let's start by looking at a more conceptual view of the fundamental isolation boundaries of the environment (shown in Figure 10-13).

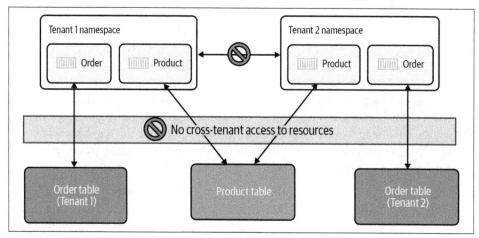

Figure 10-13. EKS SaaS isolation boundaries

In this diagram, there are essentially three flavors of isolation. At the top, where I have the different siloed tenant namespaces, I need some isolation construct that can ensure that microservices running in one tenant namespace can't access the microservices running in another tenant namespace. Isolating at this level can be achieved fairly easily through the use of natural Kubernetes constructs. When each namespace is provisioned for a new tenant, the onboarding process will configure a network policy for the namespace that limits its ability to access other namespaces. Here's a sample policy that can be applied when provisioning tenant namespaces:

```
# tenant-service-policy.yaml
kind: NetworkPolicy
apiVersion: networking.k8s.io/v1
metadata:
  namespace: TENANT_NAME
  name: TENANT_NAME-policy-deny-other-namespace
spec:
  podSelector:
    matchLabels:
  ingress:
  - from:
    - podSelector: {}
```

The area to focus on here is the metadata, which has placeholders for the name of the tenant namespace and the policy name. This policy essentially prevents any tenant from another tenant namespace from accessing the namespace we're creating for this new tenant.

In Figure 10-13 we have also introduced policies to isolate the storage being accessed by our microservices. In this scenario, you'll see that I have introduced two microservices, one that uses pooled storage (product) and one that uses siloed storage (order). These siloed and pooled storage models require different isolation constructs to prevent cross-tenant access.

Let's start by looking at how we'll isolate the order table. For this data, we know that each tenant will have its own dedicated table. This means that we can use a deployment-time isolation approach that configures our isolation when each tenant namespace is provisioned. To get a better sense of how this isolation works, we need to start with the policy that will enforce the siloed isolation of our order tables. The following policy represents the template that is populated with tenant context and applied as each order table is provisioned for a new tenant:

```
{
  "Version": "2012-10-17",
  "Statement": [
    {
      "Sid": "TENANT_NAME",
      "Effect": "Allow",
      "Action": "dynamodb:*",
      "Resource":
          "arn:aws:dynamodb:us-east-1:ACCOUNT_ID:table/Order-TENANT_NAME"
    }
  ]
}
```

This represents an AWS Identity and Access Management (IAM) policy that declares the privileges for a resource, in this case a DynamoDB table. Here, we're essentially allowing our tenant's Order microservice to have access to its corresponding order table. Again, this file represents the template. The TENANT_NAME placeholders will be replaced with specific tenant values when the tenant provisioning process creates a tenant namespace.

This policy is applied to our tenant namespaces using what is labeled as IAM Roles for Service Accounts (IRSA). The idea is that the populated IAM policy will be attached to the service account associated with its target tenant namespace (as shown in Figure 10-14).

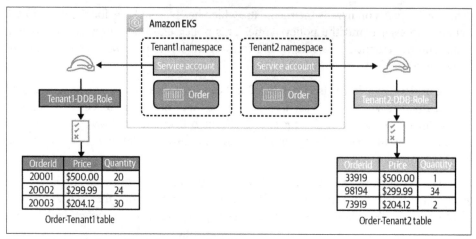

Figure 10-14. Order table isolation with IRSA

At the top of this diagram, you'll see Tenant 1 and Tenant 2 namespaces, each running the Order microservice. Within each namespace, there are references to service accounts. These service accounts are configured with the tenant-specific order IAM policies that were defined earlier. The configuration of these policies is applied when these namespaces are provisioned as part of tenant onboarding.

Now, when an Order microservice attempts to access the Order table, the tenant-scoping of our namespace's service account will automatically enforce the policies that are associated with that namespace. This means that Tenant 1 can only access the Order table associated with Tenant 1. Any attempt to access Tenant 2's Order table will be prevented. Here, we're getting the full benefits of deployment-time isolation, which means our isolation policies are applied entirely outside the view of the Order microservice builder.

This strategy works well for our siloed order tables. However, for our pooled Product table, we have to look at how we can implement item-level isolation since our tenant data is commingled within the same DynamoDB table. It's here that we have to adopt a runtime enforced isolation model that examines the tenant context of each request, using this context to determine which policies must be applied to prevent cross-tenant access to the tenant items within the Product table. Figure 10-15 provides an example of the moving parts of the Product table isolation that could be applied as part of your multi-tenant EKS architecture.

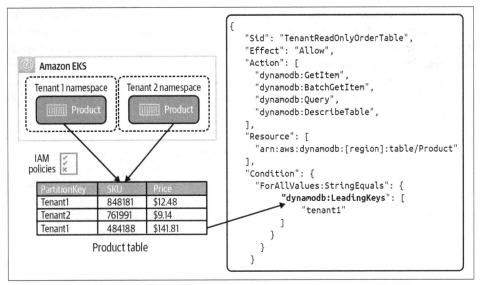

```
                                              {
                                                "Sid": "TenantReadOnlyOrderTable",
                                                "Effect": "Allow",
   Amazon EKS                                   "Action": [
                                                  "dynamodb:GetItem",
 Tenant 1 namespace   Tenant 2 namespace          "dynamodb:BatchGetItem",
                                                  "dynamodb:Query",
      Product             Product                 "dynamodb:DescribeTable",
                                                ],
                                                "Resource": [
 IAM                                              "arn:aws:dynamodb:[region]:table/Product"
 policies                                       ],
                                                "Condition": {
 PartitionKey   SKU      Price                    "ForAllValues:StringEquals": {
 Tenant1       848181   $12.48                      "dynamodb:LeadingKeys": [
 Tenant2       761991   $9.14                          "tenant1"
 Tenant1       484188   $141.81                      ]
         Product table                            }
                                                }
                                              }
```

Figure 10-15. Item-level isolation with the Product table

On the top left of this diagram, I've shown our Product microservices running in separate, siloed namespaces. The compute may be siloed, but the diagram also shows a shared Product table that stores data for all tenants. Because this data is pooled, we cannot use the IRSA mechanism that was used to isolate our order tables. Instead, the code in our Product microservice is required to examine the tenant context of each request and acquire tenant-scoped credentials for that tenant that constrain its view to just those items in the table that belong to the current tenant.

Acquiring these credentials is achieved by assuming a role based on the policy you see on the righthand side of this diagram. Here, we have another IAM policy for our DynamoDB table, but this version has a "Condition" section that limits access to items based on a leading key. This leading key is populated, contextually, based on the current tenant (in this example, it's populated with Tenant 1).

As you can imagine, there are multiple ways that you can implement your runtime isolation. You might, for example, use shared libraries that will capture the tenant context, map to the appropriate policies, and assume a role that is valid for the current tenant. Generally, for any runtime isolation model, we'd like to find some way to move this resolution of the isolation policy outside the view of developers.

EKS includes another construct that can be used as part of a runtime isolation strategy: sidecars, which are separate processes that can run alongside our services within the EKS network. The mental model is that of a motorcycle that has a sidecar attached. For our discussion, the value of the sidecar is that it sits between our microservices as a proxy, allowing us to collect telemetry, apply policies, and so on. Figure 10-16 provides an example of a sidecar applied to our tenant isolation problem.

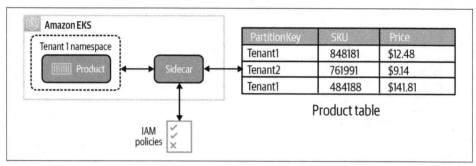

Figure 10-16. Runtime isolation with a sidecar

In this diagram we have the same Product microservice (for Tenant 1) that consumes the same pooled table that holds all product data for all tenants. What's different is that I've introduced a sidecar into the equation. It sits next to my Product service and intercepts all the traffic flowing from it. Now, when my Product service requests data, the sidecar can assume a role using the appropriate IAM policies to restrict access to just those items in the table that belong to Tenant 1.

The beauty of this approach is that it sits in the middle of all the interactions with our microservice, serving as the perfect traffic isolation cop. For many, having isolation sit at this level can be very appealing. Now, what's less obvious is how the sidecar interacts with the storage. In the model I proposed, the calls to the Product table would have to originate from the sidecar since it needs to apply the scoped credential to the request. This would essentially mean that you would need to put a data access library in the sidecar to make this work. That may not be the best division of labor or how you want your microservice code distributed.

An alternate approach would be to have the sidecar acquire the scoped credentials and return them back to the microservice. Then, the microservice would use the credentials. With that approach, though, the sidecar is more of a glorified library. So, while I think sidecars have a place here there's more work to be done to figure out how best to apply them to this isolation problem.

The examples we reviewed here provide a sampling of the various isolation techniques that are available with EKS. You'll likely find yourself applying a mix of these strategies to cover the varying needs of your solution.

When we talk about isolation in any multi-tenant container environment, it's natural for teams to have questions about whether the "escapability" of containers will impact your overall isolation story. This is a basic security concern for any container-based solution. The focus is on the impact of malicious code escaping the container and gaining access to resources and operations that should not be accessible. The technologies and strategies used to mitigate this risk go beyond the scope of this chapter. To me, it's something to be aware of as you assess the overall security footprint of your environment.

Node Type Selection

Within our EKS cluster, our pods are always running on compute nodes that must scale to meet the needs of your multi-tenant workloads. The nature and configuration of these nodes is part of what you configure with your EKS cluster. Do you need CPU- or memory-intensive nodes? Do you need GPUs? This notion of selecting a node type represents yet another variable in our overall multi-tenant compute strategy. If you're landing in an EKS environment, it will be your job to figure out which combination of node types best align with the workloads imposed by your tenants.

One approach to this could be to hand-pick different nodes for the different services that are part of your application. You could look across the services of your application and decide certain services might map better to a specific node type. If you take this approach, you'd need to configure your cluster to launch multiple node types and then associate these services to their target node type (as shown in Figure 10-17).

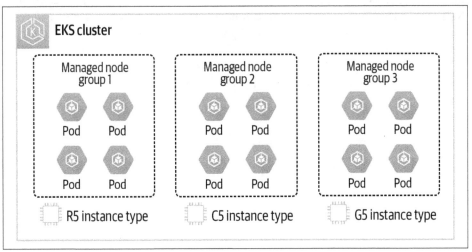

Figure 10-17. Mapping workloads to node types

For this example, I've created three separate managed node groups. The grouping construct lets me configure the profile of a set of nodes within my cluster, which includes defining the EC2 instance type that will be associated with each group. To illustrate the extremes, I've selected a range of different AWS instance types for each of these node groups. One group is using an R5 instance type that is optimized for memory. The next uses C5 nodes, which are optimized for compute. Finally, the last group is using a GPU instance type (G5).

The assumption here is that the workloads running on the pods within these node groups are aligned well with the capabilities of each instance type. While I think this is a strategy that has some merit, I'd also be careful to be sure that you have a clear set of requirements that justify the extra complexity that comes with adopting this model. It may be that you'll have a handful of key services that happen to need a targeted instance type. Then, the rest of your services can run with one common instance type that can effectively support your remaining workloads.

There are, however, other more creative ways to determine which instance types are needed to support your system's workloads. In an ideal scenario, you could have this whole notion of node type selection be a more dynamic process that examined real-time activity and determined node types on the fly. This is where Karpenter comes into the picture. With Karpenter, I can configure a set of node types that are available to my cluster without connecting them to any specific node or managed node group. Figure 10-18 provides a view of how Karpenter can optimize the alignment between my cluster and the activity of my tenants.

In Figure 10-18, I have two running nodes, both of which were launched with a C5 instance type. Now, as part of setting up my environment, I also configured Karpenter, providing it with a list of candidate node types that I've deemed as being valid for my cluster (shown at the top right). This means that Karpenter can assign any of these instance types to a node; which instance types get assigned becomes the job of Karpenter. It will evaluate and profile the current activity in the system and decide which instance types should be assigned to individual nodes.

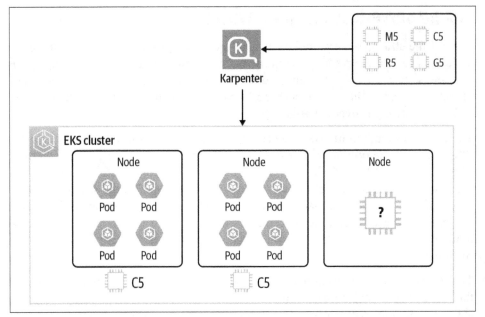

Figure 10-18. Optimizing node types with Karpenter

This is a powerful construct on its own and can be especially useful in a multi-tenant context where the activity of your cluster can vary wildly. Being able to push the node selection to Karpenter frees you up from trying to define your own strategies that associate workloads with instance types. It can also yield optimizations that could bring greater efficiencies to your SaaS environment.

The node selection and optimization strategies are powerful, but this approach still requires you to define the policies that will determine how your cluster will scale these nodes. This adds a layer of complexity to your EKS architecture and, in some cases, can lead teams to overprovision the nodes in their cluster. This can impact the cost efficiency of your environment and undermine your economies of scale.

Mixing Serverless Compute with EKS

Most of the strategies we've looked at here are centered around a model where the nodes in your cluster are very much in your view. Node selection, for example, was very much focused on optimizing node and workload alignment. Across all these models, you must still have policies and strategies that determine how these nodes will scale to meet the overall needs of your environment.

There is, however, another compute strategy that you can pick for your EKS cluster. EKS gives you the option of choosing AWS Fargate as the compute model for your EKS environment. Fargate allows you to adopt a serverless compute strategy, removing any awareness of the nodes in your cluster. This simplifies the scaling compute model of your EKS environment, allowing you to lean on Fargate's managed compute model to deliver the compute resources required for your environment. It can also limit overprovisioning concerns, allowing you to only pay for the compute you consume.

The real challenge is figuring out which of these compute strategies will best support the needs of your environment. For some, Fargate may be a perfect fit. For others, the ability to have more control over the nodes and instance types could represent a more compelling option. In reality, you'll have to weigh the cost and other considerations to figure out which option is best for your architecture and operational model.

An EKS SaaS Reference Solution

This chapter looked more broadly at the general patterns and considerations that you can apply when architecting your own EKS SaaS solution. The team I work with at AWS, the SaaS Factory, has also produced an EKS SaaS reference architecture that grants access to the code of an end-to-end working multi-tenant EKS environment. It provides you with a more concrete view of some of these strategies in action.

I've placed the code in a GitHub repository (*https://oreil.ly/s9qDg*). The strategies and techniques that are referenced in this repository represent a single example that doesn't cover the full spectrum of topics we've explored in this chapter. The nature of the solution also continues to evolve to support new approaches. So, some of what's in the solution might be a bit behind the curve. Still, overall, you may find the resource valuable if you're interested in getting into the next level of detail. Just know that what we covered here is meant to expose you more to patterns, while the reference architecture represents a sample implementation that provides a view of one specific approach.

Conclusion

This chapter provides you with your first look at the intersection between some of the core SaaS principles we've been discussing and the possibilities introduced by the EKS technology stack. By looking at SaaS through an EKS lens, I was able to highlight some of the key areas where the features of EKS could be used to describe, configure, and deploy a multi-tenant environment. This process should have also surfaced some of the power and elegance that EKS enables for SaaS builders, equipping them with a diverse set of tools and constructs that give them a broad palette of options. This review of EKS and SaaS should also make it abundantly clear why there is simply no one blueprint for building SaaS on EKS.

Our exploration of the EKS SaaS strategies started with a high-level look at the fundamental alignment between SaaS and EKS. I included this to emphasize the strengths of EKS and outline some of the areas that make it particularly compelling for some SaaS teams. From there, I picked a few key areas where I thought EKS surfaced new possibilities and considerations that could shape how you approached fundamental aspects of your SaaS architecture. This started with a look at deployment models where I went through a range of different strategies that could be used to describe how tenant workloads could be deployed using various siloed and pooled models and constructs. This also included a brief look at tenant-contextual routing, reviewing some of the tools and mechanisms that could be used to route tenants within clusters.

A big part of the chapter focused on deployment and onboarding automation. To me, this is an area where EKS shines. By looking at one flavor of the EKS DevOps tool experience, I was able to provide a glimpse into the rich set of mechanisms that can address some of the key challenges that come with automating onboarding and deployment in a multi-tenant environment. I really only scratched the surface here, but my hope is that the insights we covered will inspire you to dig deeper into the EKS community and tools that can be applied to the SaaS DevOps domain.

The last bits of the chapter looked at tenant isolation and node selection. For tenant isolation, I focused on the nuances of how EKS can influence the isolation model of your SaaS architecture. This meant looking at how we could isolate EKS compute resources, limiting any cross-tenant access between dedicated tenant namespaces. This also included a look into how you could introduce dynamic policies via classic techniques as well as sidecars. Finally, I wrapped up by looking at how node selection could better align your EKS cluster's node types with your tenant tiers and workloads. This mechanism provides a view into how you might tune and optimize the compute profile of your architecture.

EKS tools and constructs allow me to move up a level from the underlying infrastructure, equipping me with logical grouping, management, and deployment mechanisms that seem to be well-positioned to address many of the needs I have in a multi-tenant environment. Namespaces, service meshes, ingress controllers, sidecars—the list of options seems to be long and continually growing. This depth and diversity paired with a vibrant community is likely to continue to represent a compelling option for many SaaS builders.

Now that you have a sense of the EKS possibilities, I want to look at how these same concepts might be applied with a different technology stack. In the next chapter, we'll explore the nuances associated with building SaaS solutions with serverless technologies. The serverless model brings new tools, strategies, and considerations to the table. Seeing the influence of serverless will broaden your perspective and equip you with a view of how core multi-tenant SaaS principles are realized through the constructs and mechanisms enabled by a different technology stack.

## CHAPTER 11

Serverless SaaS: Architecture Patterns and Strategies

The serverless computing model has become quite popular with builders. Consuming compute in an entirely managed model where there are no servers enables SaaS builders and architects to shift their mindset away from chasing elusive scaling and cost optimization strategies. The function-centric nature of serverless compute can also influence how you approach the design and implementation of your multi-tenant SaaS architecture. For these reasons, I thought it made sense to devote a chapter to looking at how multi-tenant strategies are realized within a serverless compute model. The goal here is to dig into the specific nuances and implications that come with building a SaaS environment that delivers its application services via a serverless compute. To make this more concrete, I'll map these strategies to the AWS Lambda service, which provides the managed compute capabilities that will configure, host, and scale the functions of our environment.

At the outset of this chapter, I will start by outlining the natural alignment between the profile of SaaS environments and the serverless model. We won't spend too much time here, but I think it's essential for SaaS architects, builders, operations, and business stakeholders to understand the broader value proposition that serverless represents for SaaS providers. I touched on this briefly in Chapter 8 as part of looking at how serverless can influence storage. Now, though, I'll go deeper and examine some of the dynamics and efficiencies that can be achieved through the adoption of a serverless compute model.

Once I've established the value proposition, I'll start looking at how the function-based nature of serverless compute influences our approach to creating tier-based deployments. The focus will be on exploring what it means to create pooled and siloed tenant environments with serverless functions. This will include an examination of the different patterns and approaches that can determine how and when you might silo tenant functions. From there, we can then start looking at what it means to contextually route tenants in a serverless compute model. This will build on the deployment model discussion, highlighting the mechanisms that can be used to map tenant requests to the functions that are part of their environment.

I'll also use this chapter to review the onboarding and deployment automation nuances that come with the serverless model. Here you'll see the unique set of challenges that come with building a tier-aware onboarding and deployment automation. While there are good tools available to help bring this to life, you'll also see that you may need to introduce your own constructs to address the realities of a multi-tenant environment.

The next part of the chapter will look at some of the twists that come with introducing tenant isolation in a serverless environment. Here you'll see some of the serverless-specific techniques and constructs that are used to prevent cross-tenant access.

I'll close the chapter out with some higher-level serverless design considerations. I'll look at how we can configure the scale profile of our managed functions, using reserved concurrency to configure how workloads will be scaled across the different Lambda functions that are part of a multi-tenant environment. Finally, to close things out, I'll also touch briefly on the bigger picture implications of serverless, exploring what it means to apply serverless across all the layers of your architecture.

This chapter intentionally sits alongside the Chapter 10 discussion of EKS. The goal is to illustrate how serverless and EKS achieve similar goals with, in some cases, very different approaches and tool chains.

The SaaS and Serverless Fit

For many organizations, adopting a SaaS model is all about achieving economies of scale that can fuel their growth, efficiency, and innovation. At the core of this mindset is the underlying need to build a SaaS environment that aligns the profile of tenant activity with the consumption of infrastructure resources. While it's our goal to achieve this alignment with whichever technology we're using, there are some technologies that can simplify the level of effort that's required to achieve this goal. This is precisely where serverless compute strategies shine. To better understand why, let's start by considering the dynamics that teams face as they're building out their SaaS environment (shown in Figure 11-1).

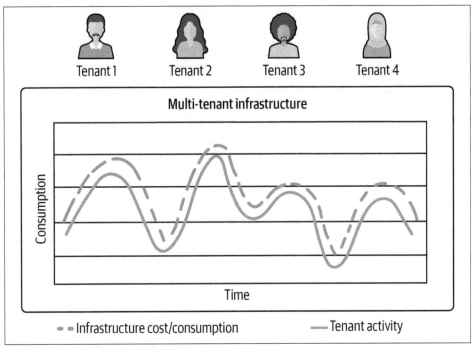

Figure 11-1. Serverless SaaS: aligning activity and consumption

In this diagram, I've tried to represent a conceptual view of how you might profile the activity within a SaaS architecture. This graph is meant to represent an operational view into tenant infrastructure consumption (the dashed line) and tenant activity (the solid line). The tenant activity attempts to convey just how unpredictable tenant activity can be. This unpredictability is driven by a number of different factors. The number of active tenants, the variable nature of tenant workloads, and a host of other factors can make it quite difficult to anticipate how much compute infrastructure is needed to meet the continually evolving needs of your tenants. This is further complicated by the fact that tenants may be onboarding and exiting throughout the life of your system.

Even though it can be difficult to precisely anticipate tenant activity, we still have a clear goal of minimizing the overprovisioning of resources. In the diagram, I've represented the fantasy version of how infrastructure consumption would ideally track tenant activity within our environment. In this example, the infrastructure consumption graph mirrors the tenant activity, delivering just enough infrastructure to meet the demands of tenants at any given moment in time. While this may not be entirely practical for every solution, it is still the mental model that SaaS architects are trying to follow when designing their systems. They want the system to respond as dynamically as possible, optimizing the infrastructure costs and enabling the economies of scale that are essential to building a successful SaaS business.

Now, this might be where you would view cloud elasticity and the idea of horizontal scale as the answer to this problem. And, for the most part, that's a perfectly reasonable expectation. However, most horizontal scaling technologies are implemented via scaling policies that determine how and when your environment should scale. This is where things get challenging. Even though compute can be dynamically scaled, someone (you) still has to define how and when the system will need to scale up and down. You have to write and apply these scaling policies and hope that you've identified a strategy that will be both efficient and reliable. If your environment has somewhat predictable workloads, this approach can work well. However, in a multi-tenant environment (as discussed earlier), it can be quite difficult to build a set of policies that can universally address the unpredictable nature of tenant workloads. This generally leads to scenarios where teams will opt to overprovision resources and adopt more pessimistic scaling policies to limit their exposure to noisy neighbor, performance, and resilience issues.

These challenges are all rooted in the idea that the compute resources of your environment are your responsibility. Yes, they can come and go based on your policies, but you still have to ensure that the right level of compute resources is available when needed. With serverless computing, as the name implies, you're completely taking away any notion of servers. Your code is simply executed by a managed service that assumes responsibility for delivering the compute resources your system demands. This allows you to push all the responsibility for scaling to the managed service (in this case, AWS Lambda). To me, this is a game changer for SaaS architects.

In this model, you are no longer responsible for chasing the elusive set of scaling policies. This frees SaaS teams up to focus more of their time on features and functions, removing so much of the heavy lifting that comes with building an effective and efficient scaling strategy. The other piece of the puzzle here is cost. In a serverless model, you'll typically only pay for actual execution of your code. There's no need for any overprovisioning or idle capacity that's waiting for spikes that may or may not happen. With serverless, you only pay for actual invocation of individual managed functions. If a function is never called, it incurs zero costs.

Imagine how these dynamics influence the graph that we started out with (Figure 11-1). If we're focused purely on compute and are trying to align consumption with activity, serverless now makes this a much more achievable goal. In the pay-as-you-go model of serverless, your compute infrastructure consumption in the graph should match the activity of your tenants. And, to top it off, you'll be realizing this efficiency without any real dependency on policies. The managed service, by its very nature, will ensure that compute consumption and costs are optimized.

The function-centric nature of the serverless computing model also brings some potential additional value that goes beyond efficiency. Generally, with functions being the unit of deployment, your environment will have a much more granular deployment model. This allows you to push out changes and updates that have a much smaller blast radius. This can be especially useful in a multi-tenant environment where there's added emphasis on achieving zero downtime. The smaller deployment units of a serverless model give you a better opportunity to minimize the scope and impact of newly released code.

The serverless computing model can also open up simpler paths for attributing consumption to individual tenants. Since each function can only be invoked and consumed by one tenant at a time, it becomes much easier to attribute compute consumption to individual tenants. This same dynamic also creates new opportunities to capture and profile compute telemetry data on a tenant-by-tenant basis. Overall, these factors can make it easier to build out a tenant-aware operational experience for the compute layer of your multi-tenant architecture.

While most of my focus will be on the use of managed functions to scale your application's services, the alignment between SaaS and serverless goes well beyond managed functions. Serverless has found its way into a growing list of additional infrastructure services. Messaging, analytics, storage, and a host of other managed infrastructure services have begun to incorporate serverless capabilities into their compute models. This allows you to bring the value proposition of serverless to more layers of your SaaS architecture. This has been particularly significant for designing multi-tenant storage strategies where teams are constantly struggling with how to rightsize the compute footprint of their databases. In Chapter 10, we also saw how the AWS Fargate compute model allowed organizations to realize the benefits of serverless computing in a container-based environment. In general, this move to more and more serverless-based computing models is going to enable builders to further maximize the efficiency of their SaaS environments.

 While this chapter focuses on designing and building solutions with serverless computing, it's important to recognize that serverless may not be a fit for every part of your system. Certain workloads may still be better suited for containers or other computing technologies. If, for example, you have parts of your system that can and must use long-running tasks, then you may choose to adopt a different compute model for these use cases. In general, we don't want to view any compute strategy as an all-or-nothing choice. Instead, you should be finding the mix of compute models that best align with the workloads and goals of your system.

Deployment Models

Let's shift to looking at what it means to actually build a multi-tenant environment using AWS Lambda as our managed compute service. The logical place to start is with deployment models. We generally need to get a good handle on what it looks like to use Lambda to deploy the different services of our tenant environments in siloed, pooled, and mixed mode models.

Before we can dig in, though, we need to have a common understanding of how our application's microservices will be represented in a Lambda environment where all of our code is written and deployed as individual functions. To help with this, I've provided a view of the basic moving parts of a Lambda microservice (Figure 11-2).

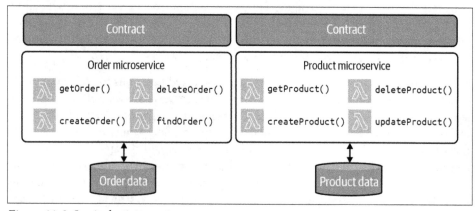

Figure 11-2. Logical microservices

This diagram includes two simple examples of Order and Product microservices, each of which supports a handful of operations. The services expose an entry point (typically an API) that represents their contract with the system. The underlying implementation of a service is allowed to change freely as long as it doesn't break this contract. These services often reference, encapsulate, and own storage resources. These are just the basic principles of microservices, where we create autonomous services that can be built and deployed independently.

Now, this gets more interesting when we look inside these services. Each of the operations within these microservices is associated with a separate Lambda function that is responsible for implementing the functionality for that operation. Together, these functions are responsible for implementing the contract of the service. At the same time, the Lambda managed service has no real awareness of any relationships between these functions. This is why I'll often refer to these services as logical microservices. While Lambda makes no binding between these functions, our teams will still view them as a grouped set of functions that are mapped to the contract and implementation of our overall microservice.

The builders that work on these services will typically work on them collectively. They will version, deploy, and test them as one unit. We're essentially bringing all the value systems that come with the microservice model and assembling a view of our functions that is consistent with these fundamental microservice principles. Even though your microservices are often likely to be represented as a collection of functions, It is possible that you could have a service that is represented by a single function. The key is that you do not need to view microservices as having a one-to-one mapping with functions.

Of course, this whole discussion of logical microservices has a direct mapping to how we think about our multi-tenant deployment models. As we start describing the signature of our deployments, they won't just be functions—they'll be represented as logical microservices that are deployed as a group of functions that implement the microservice's contract/functionality.

Pooled and Siloed Deployments

The idea of implementing siloed and pooled deployments looks a little bit different when you're using serverless functions. With other stacks (like EKS), you are often given grouping constructs that can define how compute resources are deployed, drawing boundaries around compute resources. However, with Lambda, there really aren't mechanisms that allow you to place functions into specific groups (other than tags, which don't really fit well with the multi-tenant grouping we're trying to create).

This means that our deployment models are really implemented by deploying separate function groupings for tenants and using routing mechanisms to connect tenants with their functions. This makes the deployment part of this story relatively straightforward. Figure 11-3 illustrates what it might look like to have your application's serverless services deployed into pooled and siloed models.

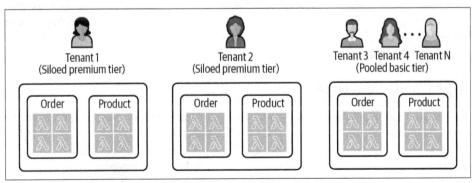

Figure 11-3. Supporting serverless siloed and pooled deployments

On the left and in the center of this diagram are two premium tier tenants that have siloed serverless compute resources. This basically means that I have provisioned and deployed separate copies of the Order and Product functions for each of these siloed tenants. The functions that are in these silos are entirely dedicated to these premium tier tenants. On the righthand side are our basic tier tenants running in a pooled model. These functions will be shared by all of the basic tier tenants. It's important to note that, even though we have separate deployments for each of these experiences, the functions for each of these tenants are all running the same version of your code. In fact, if you were to update a function, a separate copy of that function would need to be deployed for each of these tenants.

In looking at these deployment models you might be wondering if supporting siloed Lambda functions really adds any value. Lambda functions, by definition, are never shared. If a tenant invokes a function, the scope and life of the functional call will be dedicated to that one tenant. If multiple tenants are calling that same function, Lambda will add more instances of that function to meet your demands. This means that Lambda functions are inherently siloed already. So, what value do we get from supporting separate siloed deployments?

There are multiple advantages that can still come with deploying siloed tenant functions. Noisy neighbor is certainly a big part of this story. Even though Lambda scales our functions it still has concurrency limits that can impact how many simultaneous executions are allowed for a function. If I simply have one function that is deployed and shared by all tenants, there is the potential for me to exceed Lambda's concurrency limits. This could trigger throttling and lead to noisy neighbor conditions. By deploying separate, dedicated functions for my siloed tenants, I can ensure that only one tenant will be invoking its functions. This enables me to apply separate concurrency policies for my siloed and pooled deployments. It also gives me greater control over how tenants are allowed to consume these functions.

Siloing functions can also influence the tenant isolation model of our environment, enabling you to attach isolation policies at deployment time. This can simplify how isolation is applied, reducing the effort and complexity that comes with defining your serverless tenant isolation model. I'll go deeper into the trade-offs when we review different serverless tenant isolation strategies later in this chapter.

Mixed Mode Deployments

As we've seen throughout our discussion of deployments, siloing and pooling resources does not have to be an all-or-nothing proposition. With serverless, we certainly have options to selectively silo a subset of tenant functions (microservices) to address noisy neighbor, tiering, isolation, and other requirements. With serverless, this really just means we can take a more fine-grained approach to determining how our functions are deployed. Figure 11-4 provides one example of how you might apply mixed mode serverless deployments in a multi-tenant architecture.

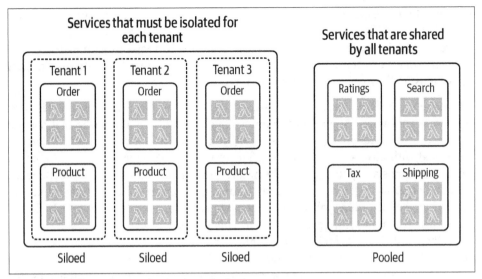

Services that must be isolated for each tenant

Tenant 1	Tenant 2	Tenant 3
Order	Order	Order
Product	Product	Product

Siloed · Siloed · Siloed

Services that are shared by all tenants

Ratings · Search

Tax · Shipping

Pooled

Figure 11-4. Serverless and mixed mode deployment

In this example, I have selected a set of serverless microservices that will run in a siloed model (shown on the left). The idea is that the Order and Product services represent key areas where the business determined that there's value offering this functionality in a siloed model. Meanwhile the rest of our services (shown on the right) are able to be run in a pooled model.

We've talked about this mixed mode before. Serverless adds a bit of a new wrinkle, though. With traditional compute, you'd need to be weighing the value, cost, and complexity that would come with provisioning per-tenant resources for each of these siloed tenant environments. You might also need to consider how the pooled compute resources would be effectively scaled to meet the multi-tenant demands of your tenants. The factors are less relevant when you're using serverless compute. Regardless of what's siloed and what's pooled, for example, you'll only end up paying for what you consume. There's also less effort that will go into determining how these siloed and pooled functions will need to scale. Instead, you can lean more on the Lambda service to efficiently scale your compute.

The simpler cost and scaling story of serverless computing can make this more inviting for some teams. At a minimum, serverless reduces some of the friction and challenges that can be associated with supporting a mixed mode deployment model.

More Deployment Considerations

There are a few nuances of serverless deployment models that might influence your approach to selecting which compute resources are siloed or pooled. To understand your options, we have to start by looking at the lifecycle of the functions being managed by the Lambda service. Each time you invoke a function, Lambda has two possible paths. If you're invoking a function for the first time, Lambda will need to create the first instance of that function. Then, after your request is completed, a subsequent request can reuse that function. The idea is that Lambda is getting efficiency out of reusing the instances that have been recently executed.

There are two specific dimensions of this lifecycle that we want to focus on. The first of these is cold starts. A cold start describes the invocation of a function that has not been recently executed. In these instances, you may see some slight added latency associated with processing this request. The impact of this latency will vary based on the technology stack you're using, the nature of your function's code and dependencies, and other factors. For a pooled environment, the impact of cold starts is likely to be negligible since there will be many tenants exercising the system, which should limit the frequency of hitting any cold start conditions. However, for a siloed environment that's only being exercised by a single tenant, you may see more instances where cold start could impact your tenant's experience. This could influence what you choose to silo and it could lead to the introduction of targeted warming strategies that reduce the impacts of cold starts.

The other lifecycle issue relates to state residue. Each time Lambda processes a function invocation for a tenant, that function will be executed for that tenant only. Lambda will scale to meet the needs of multiple tenants by spinning up more instances of a given function. While there may be multiple copies of a function running, each invocation is still mapped to a single tenant. This is mostly a good thing. However, once a function has completed processing a tenant request, the system can then reuse that instance to process a request for another tenant. For the most part, this all works fine and the reuse of a previously executed function shouldn't cause any issues. However, if the implementation of your function somehow holds or references state information that is not released upon completion, that state could be accessed by a subsequent tenant request. This is especially essential to pooled environments where your functions will be heavily shared between tenants. Ideally, your code should not be employing any constructs that would allow state to be carried over from one request to the next. However, given the potential exposure here, your functions should leverage policies/libraries that will ensure that state is cleared when they are done executing.

Control Plane Deployment

With serverless (and all of our SaaS deployment models) we have to decide how and where we want to land the control plane elements of our multi-tenant architecture. The options you have are really dictated by the different constructs that are part of your broader environment, In a Lambda environment, our choices are mostly limited to the higher level, coarse-grained mechanisms that are used to group and isolate any cloud resources. In Figure 11-5 I've shown two possible strategies for deploying a control plane in a serverless model.

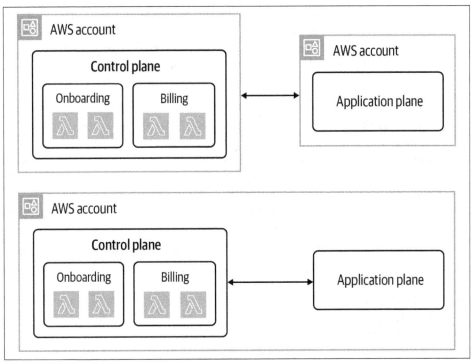

Figure 11-5. Deploying a serverless control plane

For the most part, your options come down to determining which AWS account will house your control plane. At the top of this diagram, the control and application planes are deployed into separate accounts. You might choose this option if you have security, compliance, or other factors that require a more absolute boundary between your control and application planes. There may also be performance and security requirements that lead you to land your control functionality in another account, limiting your control plane's ability to impact any concurrency requirements that are associated with your application plane. This, of course, is a bit of a heavier lift and would require cross-account access to be configured to enable interactions between the control and application planes.

At the bottom of Figure 11-5, we see the simpler version of this where the control plane lives in the same AWS account as your application plane. This model essentially has you deploying your control plane functions and supporting infrastructure along-side the functions and infrastructure that are running your application plane. This certainly simplifies the deployment and configuration of the control plane. However, with this approach, you would have to be comfortable with the security, concurrency, and isolation model considerations that come with this deployment pattern.

As you might imagine, I've really just scratched the surface here. There are other AWS technologies that can influence how you might choose to deploy your serverless control plane. The main takeaway is that this needs to be on your radar as you think about the overall deployment footprint of your serverless architecture.

Operations Implications

Any time we distribute the footprint of our SaaS architecture, we must also consider how this more distributed signature can impact the overall operational complexity of our SaaS environment. This idea of having multiple copies of our functions deployed in these siloed and pooled configurations can certainly raise questions about how this impacts the operational footprint of your solution. For some, a propagation of per-tenant copies of functions could be seen as adding complexity to the management and deployment of your environment.

This is a general problem that applies universally to any environment where we have distributed deployments. However, I feel like serverless magnifies the potential impacts of this problem. With serverless, we can have much more fine-grained units of deployment and management. As an example, in a traditional compute model, my unit of management and operational visibility tends to be more at the microservice level where the microservice represents the composite of all the operations that are supported by that service. With serverless, each of those operations could correspond to individual functions. Now, layer on that the need to support for multiple tenant environments and you can imagine how this could rapidly grow the operational complexity of your environment.

These factors don't suggest that serverless is a bad idea. They do, however, suggest that you may need to expend more energy to arrive at an operational experience that accounts for this more granular view. You'll want your operational telemetry to allow you to focus on the individual functions of your system. Being able to pinpoint health, availability, and scale issues means having richer insights into how these individual functions (not just services) are performing. The mechanisms and tools are there to make this work, but it's something that should be on your radar as you architect your system. This is especially true if you're expecting to support a large population of tenant environments.

Routing Strategies

If you're planning to support a range of deployment models, you must also consider how you will contextually route traffic to the functions that are associated with different tiers and deployment profiles. The mechanics of enabling your serverless routing model are relatively straightforward. There are, however, different routing patterns you might adopt based on the needs of your solution. Figure 11-6 provides a conceptual view of the simplest routing model.

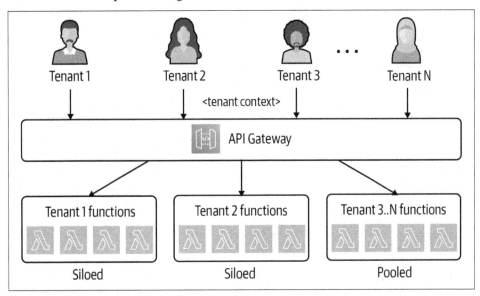

Figure 11-6. Routing to tenant deployments

At the bottom of this diagram I've introduced a range of tenant environments that are using different deployment models. There is one universal set of functions that represent the implementation of our application plane service. Here, I needed to create three separate copies of these functions to support the deployment requirements of my tenants. Now, as requests flow into my system, I need to be able to use tenant context to route these requests to the appropriate Lambda function. For this example, you'll see that this function mapping is defined by the API Gateway.

For this particular solution, I've shown a single instance of the API Gateway that serves as the entry point to all of my functions. That means that I'll have to define separate routes for each of the functions that are part of my tenant deployments. While it's handy to have all of this routing resolved via a single instance of the API Gateway, there could be a point at which this could get unwieldy. The number of tenants you need to support, the number of routes you're mapping—there are multiple factors that might suggest you may need another approach.

One way around this would be to consider supporting separate instances of the API Gateway for each of the tenant deployments. Figure 11-7 provides a conceptual view of the moving parts that would come with introducing separate API Gateways.

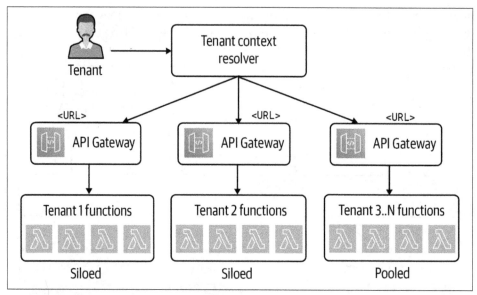

Figure 11-7. Separate API Gateway instances for each tenant

In this model, I have separate API Gateways instances that are scoped to each tenant. This means that each API Gateway will only be responsible for processing and routing requests to a single set of functions for a given tenant silo or the pooled tenants. This creates a bit more of a logical binding between each API Gateway and the individual functions that belong to each deployment. It also enables more granular control over the policies that might be implemented at the API Gateway level for each deployment.

While this model has its upsides, it does require you to create some mapping between tenants and their corresponding API Gateway URL. As each tenant submits a request, you'll need to use the tenant context and tenant tier to determine which API Gateway should process the request. This added level of indirection, for some, can feel unnatural.

Cost should also be a factor when choosing your routing strategy. It's true, for example, that we could add separate API Gateways for each tenant. This may be a perfectly reasonable strategy if you have a smaller number of siloed tenants that have their own API Gateway. However, if you attempt to scale this to hundreds or thousands of tenants, it could impact cost, operations, deployment, and a host of other dimensions of your SaaS environment.

Onboarding and Deployment Automation

The onboarding, provisioning, and deployment strategy for serverless environments typically rely on the traditional tools that provision and configure your per-tenant infrastructure. If you're running AWS, which is where I'll be focused, this usually is achieved through a combination of DevOps tools, including the CDK, CloudFormation, Terraform, and so on. AWS also provides a variety of build and deployment orchestration tools that can automate these processes (CodeBuild, CodePipeline, and CodeDeploy). In addition to these tools, there's also the Serverless Application Model (SAM) that is targeted specifically at the serverless configuration and deployment experience.

Let's start by looking at onboarding. As you can imagine, the nature and complexity of your onboarding experience is directly influenced by the deployment and tiering strategies you've selected for your system. If everything is pooled, this is pretty straightforward. However, if you support a tiered model, you have significantly more moving parts in your deployment. This, of course, is true for any SaaS architecture. What I want to focus on is the bits of automation that relate more to the serverless dimensions of this automation problem.

While we have multiple tools available to implement onboarding, I'm going to focus on SAM since it's purpose-built for configuring, provisioning, and updating serverless architecture. Figure 11-8 provides a view of how we can use SAM to describe the configuration of each of our tenant tiers.

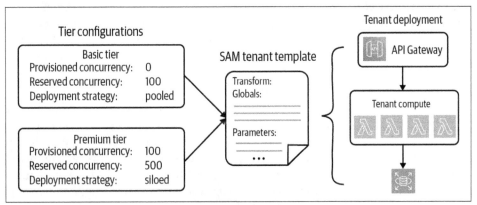

Figure 11-8. Defining serverless tiered environments

At the right of the diagram, you'll see a tenant deployment. This is a conceptual place-holder that is meant to represent the universal template for the infrastructure and resources that are needed to support tenant deployments (as part of the application plane). For this example, each deployment includes an API Gateway, a set of functions that implement our application plane microservices, and storage (in this case, an RDS database). Our basic and premium tier tenants will each have deployments that match this architecture. They may be configured differently, but they share a common footprint. The key takeaway is that, as we onboard tenants, we'll need to either provision a new deployment (premium tier) or configure tenants to be added to an existing deployment (basic tier).

Provisioning and configuring these jobs will be handled by the SAM template you see at the center of the diagram. This baseline template describes all of the infrastructure that will be included in each tenant deployment. In this case, it will be responsible for configuring and deploying all the infrastructure shown on the right (in the tenant deployment). It will set up the API Gateway, deploy the Lambda functions, configure the routes, and provision the RDS database used by our system. It's worth noting that a more realistic example would have multiple microservices, each of which could have its own storage infrastructure.

On the left, you'll see where I've created separate tier configuration files that supply all the parameters that are used to define the variations associated with each tier. For this example, I've included basic and premium tiers. This somewhat simplified model focuses on setting specific performance and scaling parameters for each tier. You'll see that each set of parameters reference provisioned and reserved concurrency settings, both of which will influence the scale and performance profile of each tier. The provisioned concurrency setting is used to control the number of pre-initialized execution environments you want in your Lambda environment (tier). For basic tier tenants, I've set this to zero with the assumption that the concurrent activity across multiple tenants will keep most functions warm, reducing the need to pre-warm any of the basic tier functions. Meanwhile, for premium tier tenants, I've opted into using some level of provisioned concurrency to overcome the cold starts that could show up more frequently in a siloed environment. The data in these configuration files is used as input to your SAM template, feeding in and configuring the parameter place-holders that exist in the template. It's fair to say that there would likely be more moving parts to this in a fully formed environment where your tier configurations might require more elaborate constructs to define more complex siloed and pooled deployments.

While Figure 11-8 provides us with a view of the key components of this onboarding experience, it doesn't explain how you would introduce the tools and processes that would apply these constructs as part of a fully automated onboarding experience. In Figure 11-9 I've provided an example of how you might incorporate these concepts into your onboarding flow.

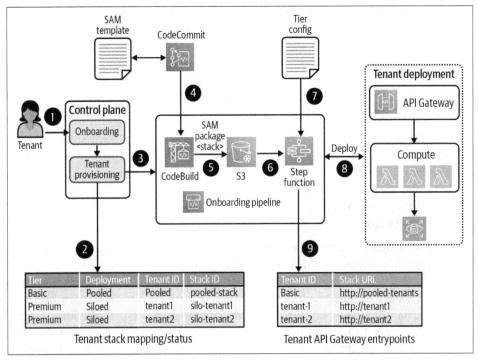

Figure 11-9. Onboarding orchestration

Clearly, there are lots of moving parts to this experience. Let's work from left to right, starting with our tenant triggering the onboarding process (step 1). The control plane's onboarding service will handle all the basics associated with creating a new tenant, identity, and so on. It will also invoke the Tenant Provisioning service, which is responsible for creating and configuring any per-tenant resources.

Now, at the bottom left of the diagram, I've introduced a new table to support the onboarding experience. This table is essential to this particular serverless onboarding process. It is used to keep track of the different tenant deployments that are part of our serverless environment. It is the mechanism that associates a tenant with its corresponding infrastructure stack and Lambda function. Tenant provisioning consults this table during the onboarding (step 2). If the tenant being onboarded is a basic tier tenant and that tenant is the first basic tier tenant to be added to our environment, the provisioning service will insert a new row into this table (shown here as the first row). For this example, I've shown the table in a state where the first basic tier has already onboarded, leaving behind the first row shown in the table. The deployment column for this row also indicates that this stack is using a pooled model. Since a pooled model will apply to multiple tenants, the column has no specific tenant ID. Instead, the tenant ID column has a value of "pooled" indicating that this entry corresponds to all basic tier tenants.

After this entry is created, the Tenant Provisioning service will invoke our onboarding pipeline, which uses AWS CodePipeline to automate the onboarding flow (step 3). This code pipeline uses AWS CodeBuild to retrieve and process the universal SAM template that describes our tenant environments. For this example, the template is retrieved from an AWS CodeCommit repo (step 4). Our build process will then package our template and deploy it to an S3 bucket so it can be referenced from a standard, accessible location going forward (step 5).

The last step in this process is to actually execute our packaged SAM template. This is achieved by invoking a Lambda step function (step 6). This step function retrieves the tier configuration settings that we discussed earlier, sending them as parameters into a SAM deployment request that references the packaged S3 template (step 7). Executing this deployment will result in the creation of our first basic tier, pooled tenant environment (step 8).

I did want to highlight one last dimension of this process. At the bottom right of the diagram, you'll see that I've shown a table with tenant API Gateway entry points. For this solution, I've opted to use a separate API Gateway for each deployment. For this to work, I'll need to keep track of which API Gateway URL maps to each tenant or tier. This data will be used to route tenant requests to each tenant's function. To make this work, we need to track and store this mapping information. Our onboarding automation must include a process that stores this data in the mapping table (step 9). Basic tier tenants will share an API Gateway entry point and premium tier tenants will each get a separate entry in this table.

At this point all the infrastructure that's needed for our basic tier tenants is in place. However, what would it mean to onboard another basic tier tenant (since these tenants are running pooled infrastructure)? When the process executes for the next basic tier tenant, the Tenant Provisioning service will see that a basic tier entry already exists in the tenant stack mapping table. So, instead of redeploying the infrastructure again, it will only introduce the incremental configuration entries that are needed for this new tenant.

Now, let's consider how onboarding siloed, premium tier tenants would fit into this flow. Most of the end-to-end process is very much the same. The key difference here is that a siloed tenant will end up with its own unique entry in the tenant stack mapping table. This allows us to have a completely separate stack that can be tracked and updated for the tenants that have dedicated infrastructure and Lambda functions.

This covers the basic moving parts of onboarding automation in a serverless environment. The other piece of the puzzle is the deployment of updates. Once these environments are all up and running, we'll still need some way to push out changes to our serverless architecture that has awareness of the different tiers and deployment models. Figure 11-10 provides a view of how you can automate the rollout of new features and updates.

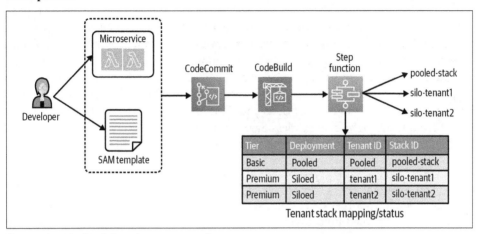

Figure 11-10. Applying tier-aware updates

This diagram is focused on the developer update experience. On the left you'll see a developer that's introducing a new microservice into an environment where we've already deployed a number of tenants with different tiers. For this to work well, the developer should be able to simply build and check in their microservice code without worrying about how this code will get deployed to all the tenant environments. We'll also need to update the SAM template to reflect the presence of the new microservice. I've shown both being checked into a CodeCommit repository.

From here, we'll use CodeBuild to package our updated template. Then, our step function will iterate over all the entries in the tenant stack mapping table to apply this updated template to each of our tenant environments. This, to me, is one of the essential and often overlooked pieces of the serverless deployment automation puzzle. There are no built-in constructs or tools that can directly support this need to keep track of tenant stacks and apply the updates across all of your different environments. Is a step function and a table the right way to implement this? Maybe. This happens to be how I've shown it here, but there may be other options that might better fit your overall automation experience. Ultimately, though, something will have to track this tenant stack mapping information and weave it into your deployment strategy.

It's also worth noting that this same mechanism could be used to stage rollout of fixes or new functionality. You could augment this tenant stack mapping table, adding additional flags that could indicate how and when tenants would have updates applied. This could become part of a canary or wave deployment strategy.

Tenant Isolation

While the principles and general sentiment of tenant isolation remain unchanged in a serverless environment, there are specific serverless isolation nuances that need exploring. With serverless environments, isolation strategies can be applied at multiple layers in your multi-tenant architecture. For example, you can introduce isolation policies at the API Gateway layer, observing inbound tenant requests and controlling the functions and operations that can be invoked by each tenant. There are also opportunities to attach isolation policies directly to functions. The point is that you'll want to evaluate each of these options and figure out which flavors of isolation might best fit the needs of your serverless SaaS architecture. The sections that follow will outline the moving parts of each of these serverless isolation models.

Pooled Isolation with Dynamic Injection

Isolating tenant resources in a pooled environment is always more challenging. Generally, with any pooled model, you'll need to leverage some form of runtime-applied policies as part of your isolation model. With runtime policies, this means that your developers will need to introduce bits of code that will apply your isolation policies to each tenant request. Of course, we'd like this process to be as simple and as straightforward as possible, limiting our dependencies on teams to comply with complex isolation mechanisms. We also want our policies to be centrally managed outside of the developer's view.

One way to approach this problem is through isolation credential injection. This strategy moves most key parts of the pooled isolation implementation out to the API Gateway as a preprocessing step that is applied to each inbound request. We talked about injecting credentials as a general technique in Chapter 9. However, I want to look more closely at the specifics of how this strategy could be applied in a serverless environment. Figure 11-11 provides a high-level view of the serverless credential injection model.

For this example, we have an Order service that relies on a DynamoDB table to store its order information. This Order table uses a pooled storage model that commingles the data for all tenants within the same table. The table puts tenant identifiers in its partition key to associate items in the table with individual tenants. With injection, our goal is to generate the isolation credentials before the request makes its way into the Order microservice. The microservice would just receive the credentials and apply them to its Order table interactions, limiting its access based on the tenant context of the injected credentials.

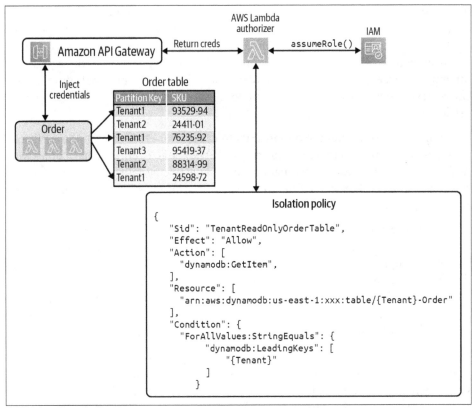

Figure 11-11. Serverless isolation with credential injection

All of the moving parts of this injection mechanism are implemented at the API Gateway layer of your architecture. In Figure 11-11 you'll see that I've attached a Lambda authorizer to the API Gateway. This authorizer function extracts the tenant context from the request, determines the nature of the operation being performed, and identifies the isolation policy that will be used to scope access. Here, I've shown a sample policy at the bottom right of the diagram that scopes access to the Order table based on the current tenant context. This policy is populated with the tenant context and sent into the identity and access management (IAM) service via an `assumeRole()` call. The role takes the policy/tenant context and generates a set of credentials that constrain access to the scope defined in the policy.

The credentials returned by this process are then injected into the header of the request being sent into the microservice. The service will still have some responsibility for applying these credentials. For this example, the credentials would be used when initializing the database (DynamoDB) client and applied to each request that attempts to access the data in the Order table. This places minimal effort on the microservice developer, allowing them to simply acquire and apply the injected credentials.

This approach also creates the opportunity to cache your credentials at the API Gateway, helping teams overcome some of the latency and overhead that comes with acquiring credentials for every tenant request. This is especially relevant in a serverless environment where your functions are not meant to hold state across different tenant requests.

The particular approach to isolation moves your policies away from your microservice. They're now centrally managed and processed at the API Gateway level. This also creates opportunities for optimizing your isolation model. Here, you can now cache the acquired tenant credentials and reduce the overhead associated with running `assumeRole()` on every request. You could also leverage the time-to-live (TTL) of the gateway to control the caching lifecycle of your credentials. The performance gains that come with this could be critical for some environments.

While there is a lot of upside to this approach, it does come with some downside. Some teams prefer to see these isolation policies owned, versioned, and managed by each microservice—especially since the policies are often tightly connected to the individual microservices. The alternate approach, one we discussed in Chapter 9, is having each microservice own responsibility for defining policies and generating its credentials. You could certainly argue that the policies should be encapsulated by the service and viewed as part of its underlying implementation. With this approach, your implementation would flow the tenant context into the serverless functions, and each function would include the code needed to acquire the tenant-scoped credentials.

Deployment-Time Isolation

Applying isolation to siloed functions is a much more straightforward story. If you've opted for a siloed model, this means that these siloed tenants will have dedicated functions that can only be executed by one tenant. Given this reality, we can take a much simpler approach to defining our functional isolation model, attaching isolation policies to your dedicated tenant functions when they are deployed. Here, your DevOps tooling would assume responsibility for configuring a function's isolation policies during the onboarding of a siloed tenant. Figure 11-12 illustrates how this deployment-time isolation model works in a serverless architecture.

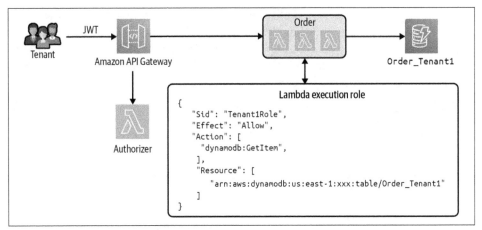

Figure 11-12. Deployment-time siloed isolation with Lambda functions

Figure 11-12 includes the same Order microservice that was in the prior example. The only difference now is that it is deployed in a siloed model. When the provisioning process creates this microservice, it attaches a Lambda execution role to each of the functions in that microservice. This execution role references the policy that you see at the bottom right of the diagram. This policy restricts this function's access to the Order_Tenant1 table. Any attempt to access another tenant's table will be denied.

This, as you can see, has genuine advantages over any runtime isolation strategies. Gone are all the injected credentials and special handling that was required for our pooled tenants. Now, everything happens during deployment and, for the life of these deployed functions, the microservice is constrained to Tenant 1's order table. This is simpler to build and has less runtime overhead. Another upside is that your isolation policies can be scoped at the function level, meaning they can be more fine-grained and focused exclusively on implementing the isolation needs of individual functions. In other compute models, your policies may span all the operations that are part of a microservice. This isn't a huge advantage, but it does give you another level of control over the scoping and management of your isolation model.

Simultaneously Supporting Silo and Pool Isolation

We've seen two different approaches that are quite different for siloed and pooled deployment models. What may be less obvious is the fact that a single function may be deployed into both pooled and siloed environments. This function could be accessing a pooled DynamoDB table for basic tier tenants and a siloed Order table for premium tier tenants.

The challenge is that each tier could employ different isolation schemes. This means that the common code in your functions would need to contextually support different approaches to accessing data and applying isolation policies. To better understand how this might work, let's look at a snippet of code that is used to access order data that may be siloed or pooled (depending on the context of the tenant's tier):

```
def __get_dynamodb_table(event, dynamodb):
  if (is_pooled_deploy=='true'):
    accesskey = event['requestContext']['authorizer']['accesskey']
    secretkey = event['requestContext']['authorizer']['secretkey']
    sessiontoken =
      event['requestContext']['authorizer']['sessiontoken']
    dynamodb = boto3.resource('dynamodb',
      aws_access_key_id=accesskey,
      aws_secret_access_key=secretkey,
      aws_session_token=sessiontoken
    )
  else:
    if not dynamodb:
      dynamodb = boto3.resource('dynamodb')
    return dynamodb.Table(table_name)
```

This code represents a helper function that's part of the Order microservice. Its job is to determine which flavor of Order table is being accessed. If this is a pooled tenant, then the database (DynamoDB) client will need to be initialized with the credentials that were injected by the API Gateway. However, if this is a premium tier tenant (siloed), there is no need to use these injected credentials.

If you look at the helper function, it's doing precisely what I've described here. It has two distinct branches, both of which return a table object that is used to access data. At the top of the function, the code checks to see if this is a pooled tenant. If it is pooled, it will use the credentials that were injected to initialize the database client. If it is siloed, the database client is constructed with the default credentials, which means it is not scoped down to a specific tenant. It doesn't need to be scoped in the code since the execution role that was attached at deployment time will ensure that the function is scoped to the appropriate tenant. Essentially, the scoping has already been applied during the deployment of the function. The database client that was initialized on either of these two paths is then used to create the table object on the final line of the function.

While I'm covering this in the context of our serverless isolation patterns, it's worth noting that this code would look similar in other non-serverless environments. I mostly included it here to give you a better sense of how you'd use deployment- and runtime isolation policies within the same serverless function.

Route-Based Isolation

Any time you're trying to secure an environment, you should be thinking about the various layers at which you can limit control access. This mindset also applies to our serverless tenant isolation model. Yes, we can and should be using the deployment- and runtime isolation models I described earlier. At the same time, you can also introduce more traditional protections at the API Gateway level of your serverless SaaS architecture. Figure 11-13 provides one example of how you might introduce controls at the API Gateway level as an extension of your isolation model.

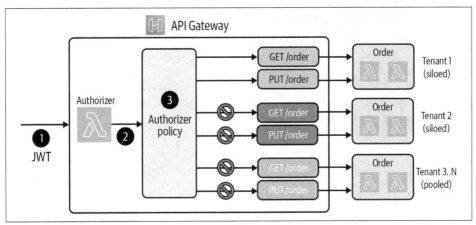

Figure 11-13. Controlling access at the API Gateway level

For this example, I've shown some of the different mechanisms that can be used at the API Gateway level of our architecture. If we work this diagram from left to right, you'll see that this starts with the inbound request that includes a JWT with tenant context (step 1). This JWT enters the API Gateway and is processed by an authorizer. This authorizer will extract the tenant context from the JWT and use this context to configure an authorizer policy (step 2). This policy can configure the behavior and enable API Gateway routes.

To better understand how this could be used, imagine we have a series of REST paths being managed by our API Gateway. These paths are routing our tenant requests to the appropriate tenant functions (services). For this example, I've shown three different deployments of the Order service for different tenant tiers or profiles. When a request comes in from Tenant 1, I'd like to ensure that this request is only routed to valid Tenant 1 functions. It's here that my authorizer policy is configured to block access to the routes that are accessing the paths that belong to other tenants (step 3).

You could also consider applying another variation of this model to serverless environments where you have separate instances of the API Gateway for each of your function groups (siloed and pooled deployments). Figure 11-14 highlights how you might use the presence of these separate API Gateways to control tenant access with a more coarse-grained approach.

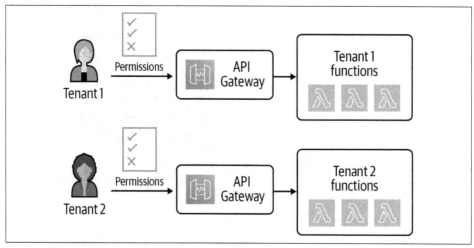

Figure 11-14. Limiting access via separate API Gateways

In this diagram, we have two siloed tenants. Each tenant has its own set of dedicated functions that are accessed via a dedicated API Gateway. Now, with this model, you can apply isolation policies directly to the API Gateway, attaching tenant-specific policies to prevent cross-tenant access. It's important to note that you'd want to apply the API Gateway per tenant with some caution.

The main takeaway is that there can be more nuances to the isolation story. While we know you need to protect resources at the point they're being accessed, you can also introduce controls at different layers of our multi-tenant architecture that can enhance the overall isolation profile of your SaaS environment.

Concurrency and Noisy Neighbor

With every compute model you must consider how it will control the load that tenants can place on your system. The serverless model is no exception. It might be tempting to assume that the managed nature of Lambda functions means that there's no need to worry about tenants saturating your functions or creating noisy neighbor conditions. Of course, we know that's not practical. Every compute model must impose constraints to ensure its scale, health, and resilience. The real question, then, is what constructs and mechanisms does Lambda give us to configure and control the consumption of functions?

To better understand how Lambda addresses this topic, let's start by looking at how Lambda scales its functions. Figure 11-15 provides a conceptual view of Lambda scaling for the getOrder() function.

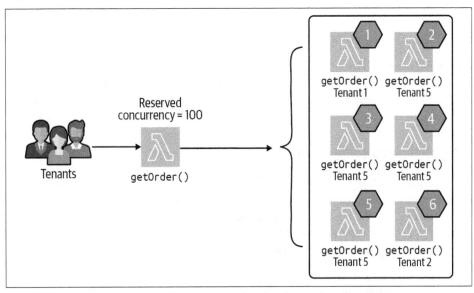

Figure 11-15. Managing the concurrency and scale of serverless functions

On the left of this diagram, you'll see that I have a group of tenants that are consuming the getOrder() function. Each time a request is made to this function, Lambda will execute a unique instance of that function. This means that, at any given moment in time, there could be multiple instances of this function running. For this example, six instances of the function are running concurrently; in a real-world scenario, you could imagine there being a much larger population of concurrent instances of this function.

Since Lambda can't infinitely scale the number of instances concurrently, we need to think about how we could limit the number of concurrent instances that would be allowed for this function. This is where Lambda's notion of reserved concurrency comes into the picture. In this example, I've set that reserved concurrency to 100, indicating that there can be no more than 100 concurrent instances of that function running at a moment in time. You can imagine how this mechanism introduces a range of configuration options in your serverless SaaS environment. It could, for example, be applied strategically across the microservices of your solution, allocating greater levels of concurrency to key, high-volume parts of your system. It could also be connected to SLAs, ensuring that elements of your system are able to provide the throughput that's required.

This same mechanism can be used to shape the tiering strategy of your application. You could, for example, assign different reserved concurrency settings to each of the tiered function deployments in your multi-tenant environment. You might, for example, put greater reserved concurrency constraints on Basic tier tenants to prevent them from imposing load that would impact premium tier tenants. This is covered in more detail in Chapter 14.

The key takeaway is that reserved concurrency represents yet another tool in your multi-tenant serverless tool bag. As you design your serverless SaaS architecture, you should be developing a general concurrency strategy to determine how best to allocate the concurrency across functions that are part of your system.

Beyond Serverless Compute

Up to this point, the bulk of my focus has been squarely on building out your serverless application services. In reality, the scope of the serverless topic is much broader than Lambda, extending into a wide range of services that are part of the AWS stack. Storage, messaging, analytics, and a host of other services in the AWS stack have been actively adding support for serverless functionality.

Traditionally, many of the services that run on AWS have required builders to select and size the compute resources for the particular instance of that service. Some databases, for example, require you to predetermine the compute footprint of your database. This would typically lead teams to overprovision their database to ensure that it could meet the shifting database consumption patterns of their tenants. This represents a real challenge for SaaS organizations and generally undermines the cost and operational profile of your system. Now, with a serverless option, these same services can reduce the need to bind to any specific compute size or profile. Instead, the compute becomes a managed layer of the service, scaling and sizing based on the actual workloads being placed on the service. The goal is to bring the value of the serverless model to a broader range of services, enabling you to bring the advantages of serverless to more dimensions of your SaaS architecture.

A Serverless SaaS Reference Solution

This chapter looked more broadly at the general patterns and considerations that you can apply when architecting your own serverless SaaS solution. The team I work with at AWS, the SaaS Factory, has also produced a serverless SaaS reference architecture that lets you have access to the code of an end-to-end working multi-tenant serverless environment. It provides you with a more concrete view of some of these strategies in action.

I've placed the code in a GitHub repository (*https://oreil.ly/jo0u6*). The strategies and techniques that are referenced in this repository represent a single example that

---

doesn't cover the full spectrum of topics we've explored in this chapter. The nature of the solution also continues to evolve to support new approaches, so some of what's in the solution might be a bit behind the curve. Still, overall, you may find the resource valuable if you're interested in getting into the next level of detail. Just know that what we covered here is meant to expose you to patterns, while the reference architecture represents a sample implementation that provides a view of one specific approach.

Conclusion

This chapter allowed us to dig into the patterns and strategies associated with using serverless compute in a multi-tenant environment. My goal was to try and identify the specific areas where serverless compute influences how you approach the deployment, onboarding, isolation, and noisy neighbor footprint of your solution. Highlighting these nuances should equip you with a better sense of the constructs and mechanisms that come into play when you're building your architecture based on a serverless compute model.

I started the chapter by looking at the fundamental value proposition of the serverless compute model, highlighting the natural intersection between the profile of serverless compute and the efficiencies you're trying to achieve as a SaaS business. I highlighted the natural intersection between serverless and the scaling and workload challenges that surface in multi-tenant environments. As part of this, I also looked at how serverless removes some of the typical challenges that come with defining scaling policies in a traditional environment.

Deployment models were next up in our exploration. This part of the chapter focused mostly on how you could use serverless deployment models to support a range of tiered experiences. This included exploring patterns for deploying serverless functions into different tenant environments that supported pooled and siloed deployments. A key here was to highlight some of the scale and isolation considerations that could be enabled through siloing serverless functions.

The next part of the chapter shifted to the onboarding and deployment automation aspects of serverless environments. To me, this represents an area that can easily get overlooked when building out your environment. The goal was to examine how serverless shapes the automation of onboarding strategies of your SaaS architecture. This was followed up by a review of serverless tenant isolation models where I reviewed some of the unique aspects of implementing isolation in a serverless multi-tenant architecture.

The last bits of the chapter focused on some of the broader serverless considerations. I wanted to be sure we took time to explore some of the configuration strategies you can use to manage the consumption of serverless functions. We looked at how the use of reserved concurrency could influence the tiering, availability, and general footprint of your multi-tenant architecture. I also discussed what it means to extend the reach of serverless into more layers of your architecture, leveraging its strengths as part of storage, messaging, and other aspects of your SaaS environment.

My broader hope is that I've made it clear how and why serverless technologies can simplify aspects of your multi-tenant architecture. Serverless moves parts of your system to more of a managed experience where the footprint of the infrastructure is less complex and the scaling options become much more manageable. It also gives you new ways to think about how you compose a system and how you can use the strengths of serverless to enrich your impact on the business, potentially enhancing the margins, agility, and efficiency of your offering.

Now that we've covered the core concepts and reviewed working examples, we can start thinking about the operational side of SaaS. In the next chapter, we'll dig into how you build out a multi-tenant operational experience that deals with the specific challenges that come with supporting, managing, and operating a SaaS environment. The goal will be to highlight some of the strategies and considerations that go into creating a best-of-breed SaaS operations experience.

## CHAPTER 12

Tenant-Aware Operations

When you create a multi-tenant environment, a big part of your focus is on creating a unified experience that allows you to manage, operate, and deploy your environment through a single pane of glass. You want and need efficient, automated, repeatable mechanisms that are purpose-built to address the unique profile of multi-tenant environments. You want to be that SaaS company that takes pride in its ability to manage and operate your environment with a small, focused operational team. In many respects, this operational view of a multi-tenant solution provides the greatest insight into whether you've built a system that achieves the agility, innovation, and efficiency payoff of the SaaS model.

The goal of this chapter, then, is to go deeper into the SaaS operations space and look at the mindset, strategies, and considerations that go into building a best practices operational experience. This means challenging and expanding on the traditional notions of operations, looking more closely at how multi-tenancy influences the operational profile of the entire business.

I'll start by laying a foundation that explores the fundamentals of the SaaS operations mindset. The goal will be to examine the operations landscape and outline the mental model that teams often adopt when designing and building their operational tooling and experience. You'll see the intersection between the zero-downtime nature of SaaS and the broader needs for data that can drive current and long-term strategy for the business.

From here, we'll shift into exploring the metrics data that is at the core of delivering the business and technical insights that are used to analyze every aspect of a SaaS business. We'll look beyond the traditional infrastructure metrics, highlighting the wider-reaching set of metrics that are used to measure and analyze every dimension of tenant activity, business health, operational health, agility, and so on. Exploring these different types of metrics will give you better insights into the overall analytics profile that SaaS teams rely on to assess the state of the SaaS business. As part of this, we'll also look at cost modeling strategies that enable you to associate consumption and cost with individual tenants.

We'll also use this chapter to review different strategies that you can leverage to implement this operational model, outlining different tools, techniques, and technologies that are used to capture, publish, and aggregate metrics. This will transition naturally into exploring how these metrics and insights are surfaced through your operational console. Here, I'll focus heavily on the nuances of building out your own tenant-aware console that supports specific multi-tenant capabilities that are essential to managing and operating a SaaS environment.

To wrap up, we'll examine how the build and deployment aspects of your environment are influenced by the various multi-tenant deployment models you may be required to support.

The SaaS Operations Mindset

Operations tends to have a pretty well understood scope for many software organizations. However, in SaaS environments, I believe that successful teams are better off when they adopt a broader view of the scope of their operational model. This is all part of the shift from a product to a service mental model that requires organizations to focus more heavily on the entire end-to-end customer experience as part of their operational model. In this mode, you're thinking about every step in the customer journey and continually monitoring, measuring, and analyzing the quality of the customer's service experience wherever they may have a touchpoint with your system. This may already be the case for some teams. However, as we dig into the details of this operational mindset, you'll see how this model has a distinct impact on how teams apply the concepts within an organization. It's not about giving people new titles—it's a mindset that should have a cross-cutting impact on how the different roles in your organization incorporate SaaS operations principles into their overall approach.

To better understand this broader operations model, let's look at how SaaS influences the mindset of different parts of the organization. The easiest place to start is with the "classic" view of operations, where a tech-focused team is on the frontlines of monitoring and measuring the activity, scale, and health of your SaaS application. This team faces a set of new challenges in a SaaS environment, where any outage or performance degradation could have a cascading impact across all the tenants that are part of your system. Instead of operating a series of standalone customer environments, these teams will be working with infrastructure that is shared by some or all of your tenants. This dynamic adds a new dimension to the operational experience, requiring new tooling, instrumentation, and constructs that can analyze system activity and health. Fundamentally, teams need much more tenant-aware views into their environments that allow them to effectively identify, react, and respond to operational events.

Where this gets more interesting is when we look at operational considerations that are outside of the traditional view. Here, we shift away from the urgency of creating a zero-downtime environment, focusing more on the customer's experience. The idea is that we must identify and surface data that can tell us more about the overall experience of tenants. For example, tenant onboarding represents a significant operational moment for a SaaS provider. We want to be able to have customers move through the onboarding process with as little friction as possible, moving them from onboarding to extracting actual value in a timely manner. This is part of the operations experience of your SaaS environment. Your teams and multiple roles in your organization should have insights into this onboarding experience that allow them to assess the quality of the tenant experience as they begin exercising the moving parts of your system. Multiple customers struggling to get traction would represent a significant operational event that would need attention.

This same mindset can be extended to the other aspects of your organization. Your Customer Success team, for example, should have access to insights that allow them to monitor the customer's ongoing activity, which features they're using, where they might be getting stuck, and so on. These insights enable teams to create a better overall service experience for the customer, using data to profile and identify tenant patterns that may need to be addressed by the engineering teams. Product management teams are also connected to this operational story. They may, for example, need access to data on tenant consumption trends that could shape the tiering and pricing experience of your environment. They may want to employ canary releases to test features out on specific tenant populations or assess interaction patterns to find points of friction in the user experience.

A big part of this mindset is focused on creating a proactive model where the operational mechanisms and culture put greater emphasis on identifying trends and issues before they might be impacting tenants. This is easy to understand when we're talking about system health, where the value of proactively detecting and resolving issues has a clear impact on your SaaS business. This same proactivity, however, is also important to the other operational views of the business we've talked about here. Identifying a tenant that's having a bad onboarding experience is also essential to your operational success. The same applies to customer success, product management, and other parts of the business that may need to proactively identify trends that need addressing.

The key takeaway is that SaaS operations should be viewed as a more holistic experience that spans multiple roles in an organization. This, of course, relies on a fairly significant shift in the culture of some organizations. In many environments, operations has often existed in a bit of a silo where it's treated purely as a technical domain.

Now, with this extended model, we're asking other parts of the business to have a more vested interest in the service experience of the business. That means asking people to think somewhat differently about the scope of their roles and how they contribute to the overall operational profile of the business.

For some, taking on the added operational perspective may not be natural. This is where leadership needs to play its part in setting the right operational tone for the organization. In some instances, I've seen leadership assign teams shared operational goals. This can help teams better prioritize their investment in operational tools, mechanisms, and deliverables. Having a top-down, leadership-driven view of shared goals can better emphasize the commitment the business is making in driving this service-focused operational model.

All of this discussion of operations and new mindset may seem relatively straightforward. Generally, it's not hard to get teams to agree on the importance and value of taking this broader view of operations. Despite having the philosophical alignment, a number of the organizations I've worked with haven't fully adopted these concepts. The rush to build features and capabilities seems to continually push these operational needs to the background. They become "we're planning to get to it" areas that never get the full attention they need. To me, if you're really focused on building a rich SaaS service experience, your business should give priority to building the operational foundation and culture that can drive the growth and success of your SaaS business. Your teams and your organization should be leaning into the operational capabilities of your service—even at the expense of features and functions.

It's important to note that operations should not be viewed as a static, one-time investment. As your tenant requirements, architecture, market, and teams evolve, you should be continually reevaluating the operational tooling, mechanisms, and metrics that are used to manage and analyze the operational state of your business.

Multi-Tenant Operational Metrics

As a SaaS business, it's essential for you to have your finger on the pulse of your service. SaaS teams are generally hungry for data and insights that span the full spectrum of business and technical insights. Product owners, architects, builders, marketing, CEOs—they should all have a vested interest in being metrics driven, using data to continually evaluate how the business is performing and meeting the needs of tenants. This data is used to shape architecture decisions, product backlogs, tiering models, onboarding, architecture strategies, and a host of other aspects of the business.

I've classified all of this data as "metric" data. I put any data that is used to analyze infrastructure, tenant, and financial activity into this bucket. This data, which could come from application and business sources, is used to drive operational and strategic decisions across a broad range of roles and use cases. I distinguish this from "metering" data, which is used to track the data that's needed to generate a tenant's bill. These two areas can overlap in that the metrics data could also be used in a metering context. The key is that metrics and metering are driving two separate use cases.

To better understand this, let's start looking at some of the different types of data that could be collected as part of your solution's metrics model.

Tenant Activity Metrics

Within a SaaS environment, your team will need insights into the specific activities of individual tenants. This data will help you construct a more complete view of how tenants are exercising the elements of your environment and, in some cases, correlate that activity with other metrics that might uncover interesting patterns and trends. Figure 12-1 provides a view of some of the metrics that fit into this category.

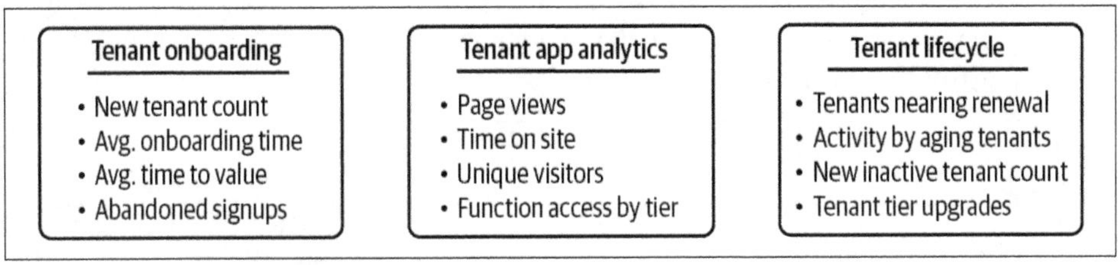

Tenant onboarding	Tenant app analytics	Tenant lifecycle
• New tenant count • Avg. onboarding time • Avg. time to value • Abandoned signups	• Page views • Time on site • Unique visitors • Function access by tier	• Tenants nearing renewal • Activity by aging tenants • New inactive tenant count • Tenant tier upgrades

Figure 12-1. Examples of tenant activity metrics

You'll see that I've broken tenant activity metrics into three separate categories to give you a better sense of the scope that's covered by tenant activity. At the top left, you'll see tenant onboarding. The metrics captured here are used to profile the tenant's overall onboarding experience, identifying potential bottlenecks within the flow that might be impacting the tenant's ability to get their environment up and running. While the importance of having a robust, efficient onboarding experience is recognized by most teams, many do not expend the effort to capture metrics in this area. Measuring the repeatability, stability, and scalability of onboarding is critical to assessing the state of your SaaS business. It also represents the first impression you might be making with the new tenant.

Onboarding metrics have added importance in any self-service onboarding flow. Even with an internally managed process, you're going to be interested in introducing metrics that capture key data about the tenant's onboarding experience. This is often where you'll see lots of focus on measuring each tenant's time to value. This is a measure of the time between initiating the onboarding flow and actually beginning to realize the value proposition of your solution. If the steps in your solution make this process too cumbersome, it could degrade tenant adoption or even lead to tenants abandoning the service.

The next category of tenant activity metrics, tenant app analytics, is shown in the middle of the diagram. This represents the classic metrics that are used to track a tenant's interaction with the actual application (think web analytics). Here we're assessing how individual tenants are navigating through the application, identifying potential areas where the user experience might be impacting a tenant's productivity or overall experience. This is a well understood area, but the idea of capturing this on a per-tier or per-tenant basis adds a new layer of considerations.

Finally, on the far right of the diagram, you'll see tenant lifecycle metrics or events. Here, the system is capturing data about tenants that may be approaching or going through different state transitions. Imagine, for example, having a metric that told you that a tenant's overall usage of the system was slowing. This, connected to the fact that they're approaching renewal, would help your team identify tenants that are considering leaving the system.

Used together and in combination with other metrics, this data can provide insights into key, actionable moments in the life of a tenant. Figure 12-2 illustrates one example of how this data could be used.

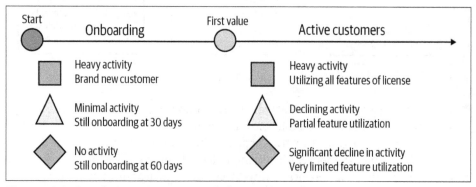

Figure 12-2. Correlating tenant activity to business events

Across the top of this diagram, I've shown examples of the two tenant states. On the left is the onboarding state, which represents newly onboarded tenants. Under this heading, you'll see a series of metrics that are used to classify the success of their onboarding experience. The level of activity of each tenant and the features they're accessing would be used to profile their progression through the onboarding experience, assigning red (square), yellow (triangle), and green (diamond) states to tenants that are in different stages of their onboarding experience. Those tenants that are getting value and exercising the system's functionality are assigned a "green" state and others who are making less progress might be yellow or red. These indicators let us identify tenants that may need some outreach.

On the right, I have tenants that have been in the system for some time and I'm using tenant activity to profile their ongoing use of the system. This is where tracking activity takes on a different role, providing insights into tenants that may be reducing their level of activity. This could be related to new challenges or it could be that the team is reducing its dependency on our solution. Either way, this state also identifies tenants that could be candidates for additional outreach.

Agility Metrics

Agility may not feel like something that can be measured. However, when you look at the spectrum of operational activity, you'll find that there are opportunities to surface data that you can use to characterize the agility of your environment. If, as an organization, you are making investments in mechanisms that are focused on maximizing agility, then you should also be equally invested in identifying the metrics that will be used to measure your progress toward that goal. SaaS business and technical leaders should be using this data to continually assess agility trends and patterns, identifying any emerging or persistent challenges that might be undermining the operational efficiency of the business.

Agility is used to pose any number of operational questions. How poised are you to take on a burst of new tenants? How effectively are you rolling new features and capabilities? How quickly and proactively can the team respond to performance, scale, or functional issues? These are all areas where the mechanisms and tools of your operational experience are meant to shine. Now, you just need to add the metrics that equip the business with data that can measure how these constructs are performing. The following is a list of some of the key metrics you can use to measure your operational agility:

Availability
> Measuring operational agility starts with the most fundamental of metrics: availability. Issues with uptime will undermine every other aspect of your agility story. Teams with availability or stability challenges are more prone to limit releases out of fear that introducing any new functionality might also translate into more outages. Availability, in some instances, is also a measure of the multi-tenant scaling policies that you've adopted. Your architecture will need to employ policies and strategies that can withstand the introduction of new tenants, noisy neighbor conditions, and a variety of shifting tenant consumption patterns without missing a beat. Tracking this data and measuring the system's response will allow you to assess your system's ability to detect and respond to challenges before they disrupt tenants.

Deployment/release frequency
> In a multi-tenant environment, build and deployment often present new challenges. The siloed and pooled footprint of your tenant resources means that your deployment tooling will need to consider how to contextually deploy updates based on the unique infrastructure profile of each tenant's environment. This can

be tricky and can introduce issues if there are weaknesses in your deployment automation. This includes considering how you might apply configuration or schema changes to tenants in a zero-downtime environment. The more confident you are in your release tooling, the more likely it is that you'll embrace the continual release of new features without fear of impacting the stability of your environment. This is where you'll see overlap with the DevOps Research and Assessment (DORA) metrics that many refer to when measuring the efficacy of your DevOps footprint.

Failed deployments

There may be instances where you attempt a deployment and something within your deployment tooling or automation fails. This may or may not be directly visible to tenants, but it still represents an important agility metric for your SaaS organization. It provides you with a more concrete assessment of the stability of your deployment automation, potentially highlighting issues that can or are impacting the overall availability of your environment.

Cycle time

If you've built an agile operational environment and you're able to release frequently, then you should also be able to operate in more of a fail fast mode. Cycle time is the key measure of this dynamic, measuring the time between having an idea for a new feature and the time when that feature lands in the hands of customers. The idea is to rely on your agility to experiment and try new ideas with customers, knowing that you can pivot rapidly based on their feedback. This promotes innovation and, ultimately, can drive greater loyalty with customers who see more immediate response to their feedback.

Mean time to detection/recovery

A key element of agility is also focused on your ability to rapidly detect and recover from issues. If some issue finds its way into the system, you'd like your tooling and mechanisms to detect these issues as fast as possible, employing constructs that can rapidly repair the environment. This might be a rollback or it might be the release of a patch. The key is: how quickly is your tooling and automation able to effectively address the issue and return the system to a healthy state? This is often a big ask for any environment and it can be especially challenging to implement in a multi-tenant setting.

Defect escape rate

Testing plays a significant role in the overall agility story of your SaaS environment. The all or nothing nature of a multi-tenant model can require a greater level of investment in the overall testing footprint of your environment. By measuring the defect escape rate for your environment, your teams will have a much clearer view into how effectively their testing constructs are capturing and identifying issues before they find their way into the wild. With or without robust testing in place, your teams will want to continually measure and evaluate trends for your defect escape rate. Spikes in this rate may surface some broader issues that need more immediate attention.

This is just a sampling of some of the common areas I see teams focusing on as part of looking at measuring agility. This list mostly looks at the friction, stability, and reliability of your overall operational experience. Certainly, being agile in a SaaS environment is heavily dependent on building confidence in your tools and mechanisms, which allows teams to get comfortable pushing out new releases on a regular basis. This can represent quite a shift for some teams and requires a willingness to work through some of the natural challenges that show up when you're bringing your environment to life. There's no magic bullet to make it all perfect on day one. Instead, you have to be committed to rapidly evolving your culture and tooling.

Consumption Metrics

For multi-tenant environments, operational teams must have insights into how tenants are consuming the resources that are part of their environment. Having visibility into this consumption data will allow teams to assess the patterns of consumption associated with individual tenants and tiers, enabling them to assess how the system responds to different tenant profiles, workloads, and use cases. These metrics will be essential to analyzing scaling policies, profiling infrastructure consumption efficiency. It is also likely to influence your tiering and throttling models. In many respects, this data gives you a view into how your architecture and deployment choices are meeting the consumption needs of your tenants.

Consumption metrics are valid for any and all SaaS deployment models. However, they have added importance for pooled resources. When you have siloed tenant resources, you can more easily map consumption to individual resources. With pooled resources, where tenants are sharing a resource, it's much more difficult to attribute a percentage of consumption to an individual tenant. There are typically no ready-made tools that can provide a more granular, tenant-scoped view into how much of a resource was consumed by a given tenant at a moment in time. Instead, this is an area where you'll need to introduce your own constructs that can capture and attribute consumption to tenants. Figure 12-3 provides a conceptual view of the challenges associated with profiling the consumption of pooled resources.

In the middle of this diagram, I have shown a simple example of some infrastructure that could be part of your multi-tenant environment. I have pooled container compute resources presumably running the microservices of my application. These microservices are interacting with a pooled relational database.

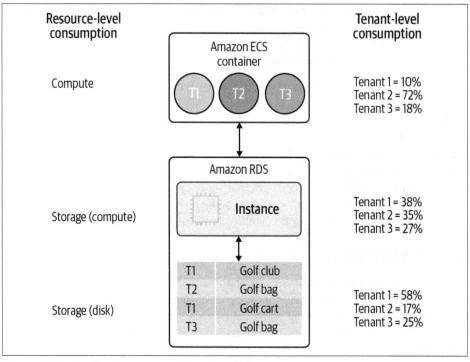

	Resource-level consumption		Tenant-level consumption

Resource-level consumption ... **Tenant-level consumption**

Compute

Amazon ECS container

T1　T2　T3

Tenant 1 = 10%
Tenant 2 = 72%
Tenant 3 = 18%

Storage (compute)

Amazon RDS

Instance

Tenant 1 = 38%
Tenant 2 = 35%
Tenant 3 = 27%

Storage (disk)

T1	Golf club
T2	Golf bag
T1	Golf cart
T3	Golf bag

Tenant 1 = 58%
Tenant 2 = 17%
Tenant 3 = 25%

Figure 12-3. Attributing consumption of pooled resources

Now, there are two ways we can look at consumption. On the left is the traditional resource level view of this infrastructure consumption. Here, your environment can tell you how much of a resource has been consumed over a given window of time. This gives me access to the total consumption, but doesn't associate any of this consumption with individual tenants. On the right is the tenant-level consumption view. This is where I can, for a given resource, understand what percentage of a resource was consumed by individual tenants. This includes breaking out consumption for the compute and storage of the relational database.

There is a wide array of different strategies that you can use to capture this data. Your approach will certainly vary based on the nature of your solution. It's often easiest to start by thinking about the different layers of your architecture and where you might want to introduce the instrumentation that would capture and publish your consumption metrics data. Figure 12-4 provides an example of this layered model.

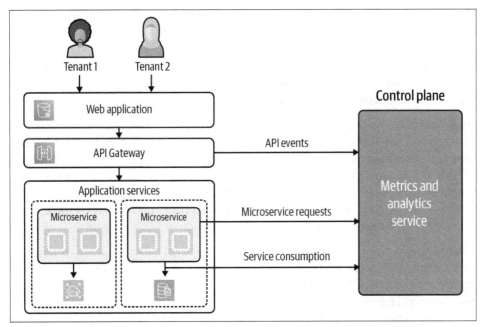

Figure 12-4. A layered approach to gathering consumption metrics

On the left of Figure 12-4, I've shown a sample SaaS application architecture that has a web application that calls the application's microservices via an API Gateway. These microservices then call various AWS services. On the right is the metrics and analytics service within the control plane that is responsible for ingesting and aggregating consumption metric data.

With these fundamentals in place, we can now look at how you might capture consumption metrics at the different layers of our architecture. The first layer you might look at could be the API entry point into your microservices. Here, you'll see that I've shown API events being published as consumption metrics. This definitely represents the simplest and most lightweight place to capture this data. However, API requests may not offer enough detail or insights to accurately breakdown tenant consumption. Number of requests, for example, could be useful. However, it may be that some aspects of your tenant workloads could require fewer requests but consume more resources.

The next layer is at the microservices level. Here, you can look at consumption through the lens of individual microservices and publish consumption based on the profile and workloads being processed by a given microservice. This gives you a way to be more contextual and precise with your consumption metrics. Now, you have the option to introduce different patterns for capturing consumption based on the workloads and profile of individual microservices.

In the last layer, we go a level deeper, profiling the consumption of specific infrastructure services. So, if my microservice works with a database, a queue, or other infrastructure resources, I can capture and publish tenant consumption data at this level. Again, this is about getting access to more granular data that allows you to attribute tenant consumption for an individual infrastructure service. Here again, we have the option to decide how best to attribute consumption based on the nature of the workload and the infrastructure resource being consumed.

These layers are not mutually exclusive. They highlight different areas within your architecture that could represent good candidates for capturing different types of consumption metrics. It's really your job to develop a strategy that best addresses the realities of your environment. It's also important to note that you may choose to limit your consumption metrics to specific high-value areas of your system as a starting point, then add more detail as you begin to better understand where you might need more precise insights.

Overall, this may feel like a bit of a heavy lift. However, having this data is essential to building and evolving the footprint of your SaaS environment. It has far-reaching value and impact that can shape operational efficiency, cost efficiency, scaling, and tiering considerations.

Cost-per-Tenant Metrics

As part of looking at consumption, we must also consider how a tenant's consumption might correlate to costs. The goal is to essentially associate a cost with each tenant and tier and use that data to better understand how the infrastructure costs of tenants map to the pricing and tiering strategies of the architecture, giving you a better view into the real margins of your SaaS environment.

This data is what I refer to as cost-per-tenant metrics. We'll build on the consumption metric data discussed earlier, connecting each tenant's consumption data with the infrastructure costs that are associated with that consumption to arrive at a cost-per-tenant allocation that gives you a sense of how a tenant's consumption is influencing the cost profile of your SaaS environment.

There are multiple areas where cost per tenant can add value. Let's look at one scenario that highlights how cost per tenant can impact a SaaS business (visualized in Figure 12-5).

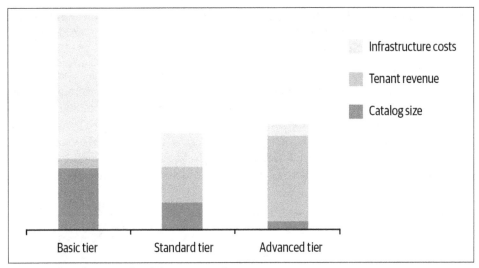

Figure 12-5. An example of the impact of cost per tenant

In this example, you'll see a graph that provides a profile of the three different tenant tiers that are part of an ecommerce SaaS environment. For each tier, I've broken out three different metrics that are mapped to the tenant tiers: infrastructure costs, tenant revenue, and catalog size (number of products being sold). The proportion of each of these metrics is represented by the size of the stacked bars for each tier.

Now, if we start with the basic tier tenants, you'll see that they have very large catalogs and generate very little revenue for the business. Meanwhile, the standard tier tenants are more of a 50/50 split between catalog size and revenue. The advanced tier, however, has very small catalogs, but is selling those products very successfully and generating a much larger proportion of revenue.

The key takeaway is that the standard and advanced tier tenants are clearly contributing way more revenue to the business. However, when we look at cost-per-tenant data for the tenant infrastructure, it turns out that our basic tier tenants are contributing the most to the infrastructure costs of our environments. This presents a real problem for the business. Essentially, our lowest tier tenants are paying us the least while generating the greatest infrastructure costs for our business. There's essentially nothing in our tiering and pricing strategy that ensures that our basic tier tenants don't end up adversely impacting the margins of our business.

This example provides just one simple illustration of how cost-per-tenant data could have a significant impact on the strategy of your business. It's this data that helps the team figure out how and where their tiering and pricing policies align with the overall infrastructure costs of their environment. More broadly, teams need access to this data to continually profile the costs as new features and capabilities are introduced to the environment. Product owners, for example, should be interested in assessing the expected cost-per-tenant impacts of each new feature they might be considering and weighing where this fits into their tiering strategy.

To calculate this cost-per-tenant data, you'll need to add additional capabilities to your system's metrics and analytics service. Once you have the consumption data (discussed earlier), you'll need to have access to your infrastructure billing information. Where this data comes from will depend heavily on the nature of your environment. However, even if you're hosted on-premises, you should be able to assemble some notion of costs that can be used as inputs to your cost-per-tenant calculation. Figure 12-6 provides a conceptual view of the key moving parts of this experience.

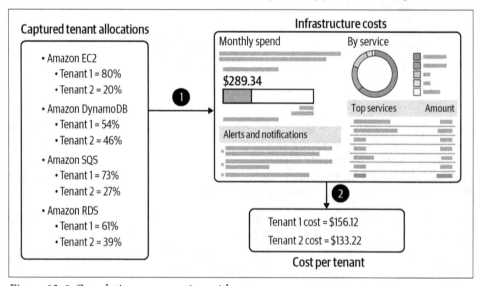

Figure 12-6. Correlating consumption with costs

To make this more concrete, I've shown an example of an AWS-hosted SaaS environment. On the left, you'll see the raw tenant consumption metrics for the different AWS infrastructure resources that are part of the environment. It shows how we've attributed consumption to two tenants across these services. This data, as mentioned earlier, has its own operational value—with or without cost correlation.

Now, to get to cost-per-tenant, we have to ingest the billing information (step 1). For AWS, this could be done by accessing the raw billing information or it could be done through one of the third-party cost tools. Once you have the aggregate of this cost data, you can then use the consumption data to apportion these costs to individual tenants to arrive at a net cost per tenant (step 2). You have many choices here. You could break this down by service, sum it all up as an average across services, or some mix of the two.

It's important to note that the cost-per-tenant metric is meant to represent an approximation of costs. This is not an accounting function or a way to generate a bill for a customer—it's a way to provide an operational view into tenant costs that can inform the architecture, pricing, and tiering profile of your environment. There will certainly be a margin of error within this data, but it should still be useful to the business.

For many, the cost-per-tenant strategy can be directly influenced by the overall cost profile of your infrastructure. If compute represents 80% of your bill, for example, then it's easy to justify investing heavily in capturing cost-per-tenant details for the compute portion of your bill. However, if object storage and messaging only represent 2% of your bill, you may opt to avoid investing in detailed cost profiling for these elements of your infrastructure.

Business Health Metrics

The most commonly discussed metrics in the SaaS space are more centered around profiling what I've loosely labeled as business health. These metrics look more at revenue, marketing, and macro tenant information that can evaluate trends that impact overall business health. Since these numbers often have the greatest immediate correlation to profitability and sustained growth, they deserve lots of attention. At the same time, they have little direct correlation to the technical strategies that we're covering here. Still, I think it's worth highlighting some of these key data points to round out our view of metrics.

Many of the metrics in this space have a stronger mapping to the B2C SaaS domain where there is huge marketing spend and lots of activity with tenants entering and leaving the environment. Still, even in B2B settings, teams will focus on these numbers as well. The following provides a quick review of a few of the key metrics that I thought might be worth surfacing here:

Monthly recurring revenue (MRR)
> Most SaaS businesses focus on MRR as a key measure of financial health. It represents the clearest view into how revenue is trending for the organization.

Churn
> In environments where tenants are onboarding and, potentially, leaving on a somewhat regular basis, you'll want to track your overall churn rate to continually assess the rate at which tenants are turning over within your environment.

Customer acquisition costs (CAC)
> This is a classic business measurement metric that evaluates the cost associated with acquiring new customers. In an environment where you're investing heavily in marketing your SaaS offering, you'll want to have some sense of the average cost associated with acquiring each customer.

Customer lifetime value (CLTV)

This metric is used to measure the average amount of income you'll get from a customer over their lifetime using your system.

CLTV/CAC ratio

Here you're evaluating the mix of the cost of acquiring a customer with the overall value they deliver to the business. A 1:1 ratio, for example, would suggest that money you spend to acquire one customer is equal to the amount you will make from that customer. Obviously, that's not the goal. It's your job to figure out what ratio makes sense for your business. Some say 3:1, but there's certainly debate about what this target should be.

The interesting aspect of this data is that much of it doesn't actually come from your application, your architecture, or any profile of the runtime activity of your tenants. Instead, the data might come from accounting systems, customer relationship management (CRM) tools, and so on. How you choose to aggregate and surface this data will depend heavily on how you source the information. There are systems that directly target this space, and in some cases, you may need to build your own solution.

Composite Metrics

Many of the metrics we've covered represent baseline, foundational data that is used to profile a SaaS environment. While these metrics can be valuable, it's also likely that you'll need to develop and introduce your own metrics that map to the specifics of your solution or domain. These metrics may exist entirely on their own, or they may be created as a composite of other metrics. You might, for example, have some formula that takes in a tenant activity metric and a resource consumption metric to calculate some new derived metric that has specific meaning or value for your domain.

The key takeaway is that metrics don't always correlate directly to some tenant activity or infrastructure consumption. Some of the best metrics you might introduce will come from the mechanisms you create to profile workloads, logical business events, or other higher-level activities that are part of your environment.

Baseline Metrics

The metrics we've been discussing are intentionally focused on areas that have specific meaning and value to a SaaS operational experience. There is, however, a collection of more general metrics that are also part of this experience. Your infrastructure will naturally emit metrics that provide fundamental insights into how the moving parts of your architecture are performing. The compute of your environment, for example, would naturally emit data about CPU activity, memory consumption, and so on.

This data should still be considered part of the scope of this metrics story. You'll still want to ingest it and set it alongside your other metrics data, using it to correlate tenant patterns with these other metrics (where it makes sense). The challenge of these baseline metrics is that they can't always be connected to individual tenants. Still, the data does have a clear role in this broader metrics story.

Metrics Instrumentation and Aggregation

Introducing the metrics I've outlined requires you to touch two distinct areas of your SaaS environment. First, you'll need to introduce instrumentation into your application services that will publish the metrics to your control plane. How and where you do instrument will vary based on the nature of your technology stack and where you've chosen to capture metrics data. We looked at aspects of this instrumentation process in more detail in Chapter 7.

The other half of the metrics story is the ingestion and aggregation of metric data. It's here that you'll identify the tools and technologies that will be used to process and house this metric data. As you can imagine, the list of tools that are used to build out this ingestion and aggregation is quite long. Data warehouses, search technologies, object storage, analytics tools—the options are extensive. Figuring out which flavor of these tools best fits the profile of your target experience may include considering the different personas that may be analyzing this data. Figure 12-7 provides a sample of two ways you might implement your ingestion and aggregation.

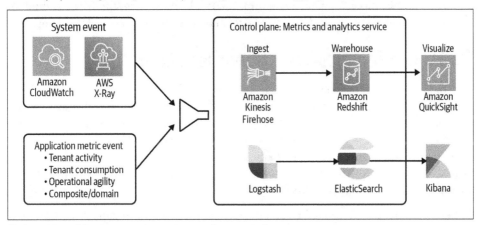

Figure 12-7. Metric event ingestion and aggregation

On the left of this diagram, I've shown the various sources of metric data. At the bottom left are the different categories of metric data that you'd instrument into your SaaS application. I've also represented what I've labeled as "system" events to fold in the other built-in events that will be generated by your infrastructure services. This is where common, baseline metric concepts (CPU, memory, etc.) are captured and published along with your other metrics.

This data will be published to your control plane's metrics and analytics service, which will include tools and services that are used to ingest and aggregate this data (shown in the middle of the diagram). Here, I showed two different tool chains that could be used to implement this service. At the top, I've shown Amazon Kinesis Firehose as the ingestion mechanism. This service ingests the data at scale and moves it into Amazon Redshift, a columnar database that's well suited for this use case. Then, Amazon QuickSight's analytics dashboards could be used to construct the operational views of the metrics (on the far right).

At the bottom, I've shown how Logstash could be used to ingest the data and publish it to Elasticsearch, a search engine that can be used to analyze your metrics data. This set of tools is combined with Kibana, which would be used to construct the different dashboards that enable you to analyze the data (on the far right).

It's important to note that the data that's aggregated here could be used in multiple contexts and by multiple roles in your organization. Product owners, architects, operations teams, and leadership may all be interested in creating their own views of the data to answer the questions that are most important to their respective roles. The key is that you should not view this metrics data as being exclusively owned by the technical teams.

As part of this model, you'll also want to decide how long this data should be retained. The lifespan of the data will be driven by the specific needs of your business.

Building a Tenant-Aware Operations Console

I've talked a lot about what goes into creating a rich SaaS operations model. More specifically, I've talked at length about the metrics that are used to continually evaluate the operational state of a multi-tenant environment. However, I haven't really touched on what it means to put these concepts into action. Now, I want to look at how you might bring these metrics and data to the surface, creating the tooling that will allow teams to create a management experience that addresses the unique demands of a multi-tenant solution.

When I talk to teams about building SaaS operations consoles, many assume they already have tools that will fill this gap. There are myriad ready-made tools that allow operational teams to view logs and get insights into core metrics for their system. While these tools can absolutely provide value in a SaaS setting, they typically don't include any notion of tenant context of tiering as part of their solution. This is generally where I see teams needing to customize existing tools, build their own console, or use some combination of these options to create a true, tenant-aware operations experience.

To help clarify this point, let's consider the day-to-day experience of the operations team that's charged with proactively managing the health and state of your SaaS environment. Yes, this team would need some global view into the overall state of the system in order to identify any potential global health or activity issues. Where this gets more interesting is when you consider how you might deal with more tenant- or tier-focused challenges.

Imagine a scenario where the global view of your system health is showing "green." On the surface, all the key health indicators suggest that the system is not experiencing any performance, scale, or failure conditions that require your attention. At the same time, you get word that a single tenant is reporting performance problems. Now, let's assume this same tenant is running with pooled infrastructure that seems to be working well for other tenants. What tool or mechanism do we use to figure out what might be causing issues for this particular tenant?

To effectively support this and other tenant-aware operations scenarios, you'll need tooling and mechanisms that allow you to interact with our operational data through the lens of individual tenants and tiers. There's any number of tooling experiences you may need within your console to enable these tenant-contextual operational views. Figure 12-8 provides a conceptual example of one way you might see this tenant awareness injected into your operational tooling.

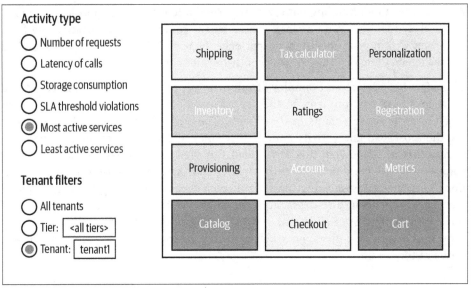

Figure 12-8. Adding tenant context to your operations console

This example provides a microservice-centric view of your operations experience, using a heatmap on the right side of the diagram to illustrate the health of individual services. The idea is that these boxes will change colors based on their health, with colors spanning shades from green to yellow to red to reflect the current health of the service.

On the left are a highly simplified set of toggles that are used to select the scope of the health that's showing for these services. At the top left, you'll see that I've selected the "most active services" option to narrow in on services that may be experiencing the heaviest activity. Then, below that, you can see where I have various options for refining the scope of tenants that are included. I can select all tenants, a specific tier, or an individual tenant to change the scope of the data being evaluated. Here, I have selected tenant1 as my filter and the view is showing me the state for this specific tenant. From here, I could identify any services that are red for this tenant and drill into each service to get more context on how or why this tenant might be experiencing problems.

This is a highly simplified example, but it's meant to illustrate the importance of having tenant and tier awareness baked into your operations experience. Without this ability to view operational data with a tenant context, it would be very challenging to easily pinpoint any tenant-specific issues. This, in a multi-tenant operational setting, is where you need tools that will let you detect and resolve these issues in a timely manner, heading off challenges that could have a cascading effect across multiple tenants.

As you think about building out (or configuring) a tenant-aware console experience, you'll likely identify plenty of areas where tenant context can be surfaced as a first-class view within your operational experience. Figure 12-9 provides a small sampling of how tenancy could surface in your multi-tenant operational dashboards.

This view includes three examples of multi-tenant operational data that could add value in a SaaS environment. In the top left, you'll see a list of tenants that represent the most active tenants in the system. These are the tenants that are generating the most load and activity and, as such, may also be most prone to experience technical issues. Knowing this, I've added this view as a top-level construct in my console that lets me quickly identify tenants that may need more immediate attention. There's a status showing the state of each tenant, indicating whether a tenant may be experiencing any degradation or issues. A more sophisticated version of this console might even allow me to click on one of these tenants and immediately drop into a view that gives me a quick, contextual look at the current activity and status of the tenant.

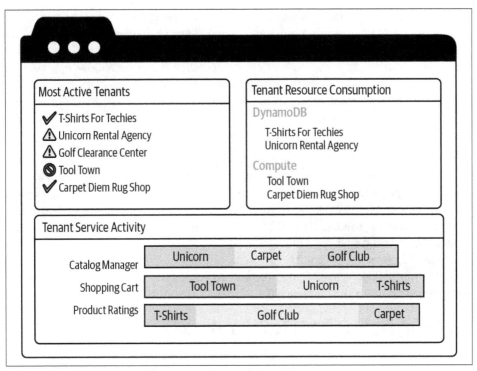

Figure 12-9. Surfacing tenant-aware operational insights

On the top right I have another view that shows me how tenants are consuming individual infrastructure services. The idea is that I can easily see how the load for tenants is being distributed across the key infrastructure services that are part of my environment. This would allow me to easily identify scenarios where a tenant may be consuming a disproportionate amount of a given service. This could point out a potential near- or long-term issue with how this particular infrastructure is scaling, highlighting our need to dig into the tenant workloads and trends that might be triggering the excess consumption of a given service.

Finally, at the bottom, we have a diagram that illustrates tenant activity across some of the high-profile microservices that are part of my solution. The horizontal bars show the levels of microservice consumption for specific tenants. This might help you evaluate how tenants are consuming microservices and identify scenarios where a microservice is not scaling effectively to meet the SLAs of your tenants or tiers.

As part of this discussion, you'll notice that I've included tiers as part of the operations story. Tiers are not just a billing construct. They have operational implications, and our environment is often configured to offer distinct experiences to different tiers. This means that, for some part of our operational experience, we may need to view system activity and health through the lens of individual tiers. I might, for example, want to view microservice health and activity for the advanced tier to see if my architecture is effectively preventing these tenants from being affected by noisy neighbor conditions.

The examples we've reviewed here are just beginning to scratch the surface of possibilities. The goal was to emphasize the need to create tenant-aware operational tooling that supports the unique needs of multi-tenant environments. Trying to piece together operational insights by sifting through piles of data simply won't cut it in a SaaS environment. You need a dashboard and analytics tools that put tenant and tier context front and center, providing carefully crafted views that allow you to rapidly evaluate and traverse operational data with tenant awareness. The more you invest here, the more likely it is that you'll be able to proactively identify challenges before they might surface to your tenants.

Combining Experience and Technical Metrics

When you're creating a SaaS operations console, you need to make choices about which data belongs in this experience. In a multi-tenant environment, there's a pretty wide spectrum of data that could be used to enrich the operations experience. The question is: do I fold more general technical data into my console that surfaces data that doesn't necessarily correlate directly to tenant activity? CPU, memory, latency—there's a whole list of general system performance and consumption data that could be candidates for your operations console. There are also business metrics that you might be measuring (agility, time-to-value, etc.). Do you bring all these metrics into your console or leave them in other tools you might be using?

I do see value in selectively incorporating some of these metrics to a broader operational view of your environment. Bringing this data into your console may allow you to make natural correlations between business and technical events. A new feature, for example, could introduce a performance issue that is impacting onboarding times. Being able to see these broader SaaS metrics alongside your classic health and activity metrics could allow you identify patterns that might otherwise go undetected. It also helps reinforce the idea that your operations team is doing more than monitoring health. Surfacing and having access to these metrics puts greater emphasis on the need for operations to extend its view of health to include analysis of these broader SaaS operational considerations.

Tenant-Aware Logs

I haven't really mentioned logs yet. They are an essential part of the overall operational tooling model, and this represents yet another area where you'll want to be able to easily access logs with tenant and tier context. There are two dimensions to the problem. First, your microservices need to ensure that they are generating logs that include all the tenant context that's needed by your system. We explored how these logs might be introduced into your multi-tenant microservices in Chapter 7.

If your logs include tenant context, then the other half of this challenge is figuring out how you want to support access to these logs. Some teams will build log views directly into their console, providing users with the ability to easily filter and view log activity based on tenant- or tier-specific criteria. Others will defer to existing, ready-made tooling that's purpose-built for log analytics. Both approaches are valid. The key is to be sure your tooling provides an easy way to apply tenant and tier context.

Creating Proactive Strategies

In a multi-tenant environment where we're taking every measure we can to avoid outages, teams will often put greater emphasis on implementing proactive operations strategies that attempt to detect and resolve issues through automation and policies. This might come in the form of alerts that bring more immediate attention to conditions that require human intervention, or it might come in the form of proactive detection of performance degradation that proactively adjusts the scaling of your environment to limit any impact to tenants.

Where and how these policies are introduced can vary significantly from one environment to the next. The nature of the technology stack, the deployment model you're using, and the nature of your solution could all influence your approach to building out your proactive strategies.

Persona-Specific Dashboards

This discussion of metrics and the operations console may make it seem like the operations team and this console provide the one and only view into metrics. In reality, there may be multiple views into this data for the different roles that are part of the business. I prefer for teams to view all of this metric data as landing in a shared warehouse that can be consumed in multiple contexts (as shown in Figure 12-10).

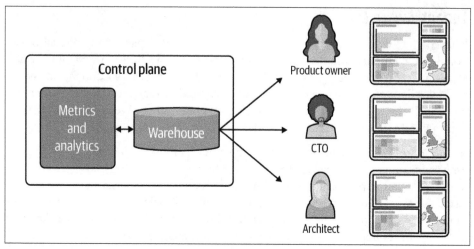

Figure 12-10. Metrics for multiple personas

You can see the mental model I'm suggesting for the scope and role of your metrics data. In an ideal world, you'd see various roles across the business leaning into the metrics data of your system, using it to develop their own dashboards with their own views into the trends and patterns that add strategic value and insights into their specific area. This plays a big part in promoting the shared operational responsibilities of the various roles in a SaaS organization. As more teams lean into this, you'll likely see greater demand for adding new metrics and insights to your solution.

Multi-Tenant Deployment Automation

Automating the configuration and deployment of multi-tenant environments is a key part of the overall SaaS operations story. It's this automation that plays a pivotal role in ensuring that your environment can onboard new tenants and release new features that support the specific needs of a multi-tenant model. Your approach to implementing this automation will inevitably have a significant impact on the agility, innovation, and availability profile of your SaaS business.

The nature, scope, and role of infrastructure automation in a multi-tenant setting often requires teams to evolve their thinking to support the unique blend of SaaS configuration and deployment models. Multi-tenancy may require you to decompose your automation differently, separating out parts of the automation to align with the flows and patterns that make up your overall SaaS DevOps experience.

To get a better understanding of the nuances here, let's consider a few pieces of automation that could be needed in a multi-tenant setting (shown in Figure 12-11).

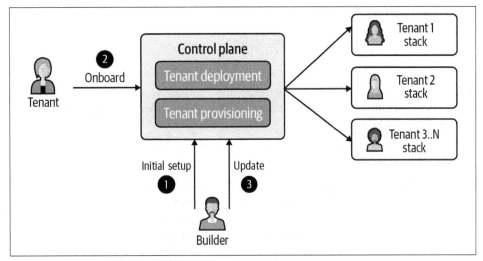

Figure 12-11. Multi-tenant configuration and deployment automation

I've shown an example where your operational tooling would need to support tenant-specific provisioning and deployment requirements. There are basically three distinct elements of the infrastructure provisioning lifecycle. First, there is the initial setup of your environment, where you provision any baseline infrastructure and any pooled tenant resources (step 1). If you're running a fully pooled model, all the tenant infrastructure could be provisioned at this point.

Once the environment is set up, our provisioning must then look at what automation and configuration would be applied during the onboarding of tenants (step 2). As we've seen in other examples, onboarding is triggered as a runtime process that takes a tenant's parameters and provisions and configures resources based on the tenant's configuration. During this process, the system executes any automation required to provision and configure each tenant's infrastructure.

There's one last part of the DevOps story here. We still have to think about how the presence of per-tenant infrastructure will influence the deployment of application updates (step 3). This is less about provisioning infrastructure and more about having a process that knows how to map deployment of updates to each tenant's resources. Your deployment process may deploy services multiple times to cover all the different pooled and siloed tenant infrastructure.

We saw bits of this in the serverless SaaS architecture. However, I wanted to call this out as a key piece of a multi-tenant operations footprint. Having per-tenant infrastructure that is being added dynamically at runtime represents a new twist for many teams. This, given our uptime and resiliency goals, means our infrastructure automation code will need to meet a very high quality and reliability bar to ensure that onboarding and updates aren't somehow compromising the health and performance of our overall environment.

Scoping Deployments

In SaaS environments, teams are often looking for creative ways to control how features and capabilities are rolled out to tenants. This is where concepts like feature flags and canary releases come into play. Feature flags let us enable or disable individual features within a release and canary releases let us roll out versions of a service to a select set of tenants.

You can imagine the value these concepts can offer in a SaaS setting. With feature flags, a team can selectively turn on features for specific tiers of tenants, for example. This allows you to avoid any one-off deployments for tenants and continue to manage and operate your solution through a single pane of glass.

Feature flags can represent a point of tension for some organizations. Some teams will view them as a way to create one-off features for individual tenants. This can be a slippery slope. If you think of our broader multi-tenant SaaS goals, we're intentionally trying to move away from any notion of per-tenant customization. If you end up with 100 different tenants, each with their own custom feature flags, this could undermine the agility and efficiency goals of your organization. You want to avoid the temptation of viewing feature flags as a way to work around the tenets of SaaS, doing what you can to have one system that's available to all users and doesn't require one-off support to handle each tenant's customizations. Regardless of where you land on this, you need to be sure that your feature flags are implemented as a global mechanism that is available to all tenants. This will allow you to continue to have one deployment for all tenants. In an ideal case, feature flags would be assigned at the tier level to distinguish different experiences, and any one-off, per-tenant flags would be the exception instead of the rule.

Targeted Releases

By default, when you're rolling out new releases in a SaaS environment, you're essentially pushing your updates out to all tenants in one move. For some organizations, this can be a bit scary. If you've modified some feature or added some new flow into the system, you could easily upset your entire tenant community if they are unhappy with the changes you've introduced. If there are issues with a release, you may be collectively exposing all of your tenants to this issue at the same time. Both of these scenarios can represent tough moments for the operations side of your SaaS organization. They can also undermine the trust and loyalty of your tenant community.

This is where teams look at ways to roll out targeted releases where updates are released to a subset of tenants to gauge the response and impact of a new release. In the DevOps world, this has been achieved through canary releases, where you identify a select group of tenants and deploy to them as a way to collect feedback or assess system impacts without impacting all tenants. This technique has existed in the DevOps world for some time, and it represents an especially powerful construct for SaaS environments where the scope and potential of a deployment can have such a profound impact on the business.

The idea of canary releases gets more interesting when you think about siloed and pooled environments. What does it mean to do a canary release to a pool environment where tenants are running in shared infrastructure? Does this mean you need to spin up a parallel pooled environment for the canary release? Or, if this is just about code and features, could some tenants in the pool be running the new branch of code while others are running the current version? The answer, as you might suspect, is that it depends. The nature of any given release could impose different requirements on your canary release, and if the effort here is too high or too complex, it could undermine the value of the canary release. This is also an area where you might fold in feature flags, turning on specific functionality for the tenants in your canary release.

The moving parts of this are pretty straightforward and conform to the typical targeted release strategies that are employed by some teams. Figure 12-12 provides a conceptual view of how targeted deployments might surface in a multi-tenant environment.

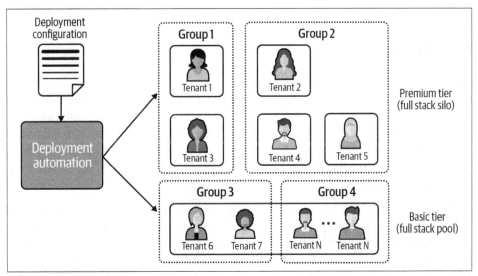

Figure 12-12. Targeted deployment in multi-tenant environments

On the right of this diagram, you'll see a multi-tenant environment that has a tiered model, deploying tenants in a mix of siloed and pooled models. On the left are placeholders for my deployment automation. Here's where we could find any number of different DevOps tools and mechanisms that deploy updates to our tenants. There's a configuration represented as part of this experience. It describes the structure of the deployment strategy, outlining the details of how our releases will roll out to our tenants.

For this example, I've created some tenant groupings (on the right). The groupings represent the different sets of tenants that are referenced in the deployment configuration. The groupings were presumably picked based on some specific operational and release goals. I might say that Group 1 represents our "friendly" tenants that are good candidates for getting the first rollout of updates. Or, it could be that we'll roll out to Groups 2 and 3 first to avoid impacting our pooled tenants, which could have a bigger business impact if we uncover issues. The main idea is that you will create a strategy for grouping releases based on the profile and needs of your business.

You can imagine how this model maps to the various targeted release strategies that I've been outlining. It fits nicely with the idea of selectively deploying your updates to a subset of tenants. These groupings, for example, would be used to implement a canary or wave release strategy, staging the rollout of changes and limiting the scope of potential operational impacts.

The key takeaway is that DevOps gives us a number of different tools and strategies that can fit nicely with the needs of your SaaS deployment model. How or if this fits will depend on the size and profile of your tenants and the deployment model of your SaaS environment.

Conclusion

After reading this chapter, I'm hoping that you have a clearer view of the broader role that operations plays in a SaaS business. SaaS companies are built around the idea of moving fast and being efficient. This means creating an operational footprint that enables frequent releases, zero downtime, and the flexibility that allows the business to grow and pivot based on the shifting needs of tenants and the market. That footprint is often the engine at the core of building a service that realizes the full promise of the SaaS delivery model.

To bring this into better focus, this chapter started by reviewing the general SaaS operations mindset, highlighting the foundational principles associated with creating an operational culture and approach that reaches across the different roles within a SaaS business. The idea is to move operations away from being a purely technical, siloed model. With SaaS, operations needs to consider every dimension of the experience, creating more collaboration between the different parts of your organization. The service experience of your tenants should be of interest to most roles in the organization. How efficiently they onboard, the throughput they see, the efficacy of their tiering strategy—these are just examples of tenant experience that should be of interest to product owners, strategic leaders, and so on.

With these core principles in place, I turned my attention to the metrics of SaaS. This goal was to draw attention to just how vital it is to be data driven in a multi-tenant setting. Generally, when you're operating and managing these tenants collectively, you need access to data that gives you rich insights into how tenants are exercising the moving parts of your service. It's this information that will provide the full spectrum of data that can support the more immediate needs of operations teams while also providing the broader insights that are essential to shaping the overall strategic footprint of the business.

The next step was to consider how these concepts come to life in a working SaaS environment. This is where I started looking at what it means to create a tenant-aware operations console that supports the unique needs of a multi-tenant solution. Here, I reviewed how multi-tenancy can end up directly impacting the features and capabilities that operations teams may need to identify, analyze, and troubleshoot tenant or tier issues. As part of this, I also looked at some examples of custom, multi-tenant operational views that provided examples of how you might surface tenant trends and patterns that could provide more direct insight into how tenants are imposing load on your system. The overall emphasis was on highlighting the unique set of multi-tenant operations challenges that require a more targeted, more tenant-aware approach to creating the operational experience that your SaaS environment demands.

Finally, I wrapped up the chapter with a brief look into the infrastructure automation elements of SaaS operations. This was more about reviewing the key role that provisioning, configuration, and deployment plays in creating an operational model that supports the specific needs of a SaaS environment. The unique deployment requirements of SaaS environments and the onboarding automation both play a big role in creating an operational foundation that can support the agility, efficiency, and innovation needs of the business and its tenants.

When working with SaaS architects and builders, my biggest concern is that they'll de-prioritize their investment in these operations constructs. I prefer to see teams going after operations and application architecture design in parallel, viewing them as one combined deliverable that, together, enables the business to grow and thrive. Generally, deferring the investment in operational tooling and instruments tends to have a significant impact on the success of a SaaS business. It takes tools out of your organization's hands that are essential to shaping the technical and business strategy. SaaS, as a rule of thumb, is a metrics-driven universe and that starts with having teams and leadership committed to making metrics a priority—in some cases ahead of features and functions. You are building a service and you need rich operational insights to be able to have insights into whether you're delivering on the promise of your service experience.

This coverage of SaaS operations connected the architecture principles to the operations mindset and experience. Up to this point, the concepts we've covered could mostly apply to customers in any stage of adopting a SaaS delivery model. Now I want to begin to look more specifically at what it means for a company to migrate an existing solution to SaaS. The goal is to give you a better sense of the strategies and patterns that can be implemented to move your solution to a multi-tenant model. This will be the focus of the next chapter, where I'll explore the technical and business considerations associated with migrating to SaaS. This should provide you with a range of options that can be factored into developing your own migration strategy.

CHAPTER 13

SaaS Migration Strategies

The path to SaaS doesn't always start with a blank canvas. The reality is, there are many instances where organizations have existing solutions that they want to move to a SaaS delivery model. A number of factors may motivate this move. For some, adopting SaaS may be focused exclusively on overcoming cost, operational, and scaling efficiency challenges. Others might be feeling pressure from emerging SaaS competitors. In other instances, this could be driven by a desire to use the economies of scale of SaaS to grow their business and reach new market segments. Customers might be in this mix as well, pushing companies to make their solution available in a SaaS model.

While the appeal of getting to SaaS is well understood, determining how best to make this move can be more challenging. When you have an existing offering with customers and revenue, making this move comes with natural concerns. It will mean striking a balance between the old and the new and finding a path that blazes a new trail without entirely disrupting the business. For publicly traded companies that face quarterly earnings reports and revenue expectations, this can be especially tricky to navigate. The nature of your domain, the profile of your tenants, and potential compliance considerations could also be imposing constraints that will complicate a move to SaaS. This is precisely why there is no one universal path to SaaS. SaaS migration is about finding the path that best balances the realities of your business.

In this chapter, I'll review the factors, patterns, and strategies that you'll want to consider as part of picking a migration path. We'll start by discussing some of the bigger picture dynamics that are part of the migration puzzle, looking at the tensions that teams face as they seek to strike a balance between near-term pressures, market factors, operational challenges, cost efficiency, team skills, and a host of other variables that are part of the migration puzzle.

With those strategic considerations out of the way, the chapter will shift to reviewing common migration patterns. The goal is to highlight the specific migration models that can address the different migration priorities and business implications. These patterns will expose you to a range of migration possibilities, highlighting the merits of each of these options. While these are just samples of the possible patterns, they should give sense of the trade-offs and provide insights that will guide your migration roadmap. This will include strategies that offer different approaches to incrementally modernizing your SaaS offering as part of the overall migration process.

In the last part of the chapter, I'll get into the details of how you'll sequence the steps of this migration journey. To me, the initial choices you make as you head down this path set a tone for the values and principles that are going to shape the foundations of your multi-tenant model. This is where we'll look at how to start introducing the foundational multi-tenant constructs that will be essential to achieving your architecture and operational goals—regardless of which migration patterns you adopt. This is also about establishing some of the core values of your SaaS culture that will be essential to transitioning your entire organization to a SaaS mindset.

While there's no one-size-fits-all model for migration, the strategies that I'll be covering should expose you to a spectrum of possibilities and should allow you to assemble a migration approach that best aligns with the business and technical realities of your environment.

The Migration Balancing Act

It's tempting for many organizations to view migration through the lens of technology. To me, this represents the big trap of migration. While we'll certainly focus the bulk of our energy on the technical nuances of migration, the migration strategy you select should be directly shaped by an evaluation of the business, market, and operational parameters that are motivating your move to SaaS. Time frames, market factors, operational costs, and other considerations should all directly shape your approach to migration.

For many, this is a classic software problem where we're fighting between the competing forces of business and technology. Figure 13-1 provides a conceptual view of the balancing act that comes with picking a migration strategy.

On the left of this diagram are some of the attributes that are drawing us into the SaaS model. Teams want to immediately begin to realize the agility, cost efficiency, operational benefits, and general value that comes with building a modernized, multi-tenant version of their solution. It's natural for teams to want to go after all the shiny objects of this new model and focus on erasing the technical debt that's been hanging over their heads for years.

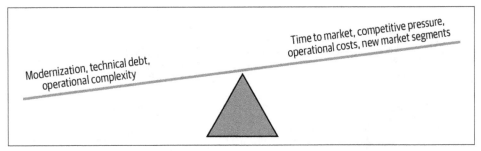

Figure 13-1. The migration balancing act

The right side of the diagram represents the business migration motivators. Here, there could be a wide range of pressures that are driving the move to SaaS. There may be new SaaS offerings showing up in your domain that are beginning to take market share. Operational costs could also represent a significant motivating factor. It's not rare to find software businesses that have reached a point where the operational overhead of each new customer is so high that it's eroding their margins and limiting the growth of the business. The move to SaaS could also be inspired by a desire to accelerate growth by reaching new market segments. These are just a few examples of the business factors that you may need to evaluate when you're determining your migration strategy.

Ultimately, a good migration strategy ends up requiring a mix of business and technical trade-offs. In fact, the process of selecting your migration strategy can represent the first step in an organization's SaaS cultural migration, bringing product, operational, and technical teams together to play a more collaborative role in defining the overall migration model. Done right, this will make it clearer to technical teams that they need to have a more business-focused approach to aspects of their technical strategy. At this same time, this process will likely have a transformative effect on business leads, exposing them to the potential business impacts and possibilities that could be enabled through different technology models.

Timing Considerations

As you think about how to balance these competing forces, you have to think more holistically about how the transformation will play out over a longer time horizon. To better understand this, imagine two migration extremes: one where you move to SaaS as quickly as possible and one where you take more time to create a more modernized SaaS offering before going to market. Both of these strategies have distinct merits and trade-offs that could affect the business and the success of your SaaS offering. Figure 13-2 provides a view of how these two approaches might influence your overall transformation.

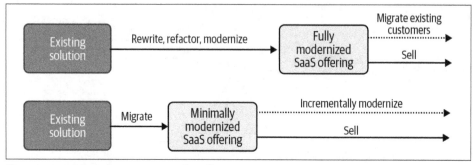

Figure 13-2. Migration timing trade-offs

I've shown two paths that a company might take as part of its SaaS migration. At the top is a model where we delay our release, putting more energy into rewriting and refactoring bits of our system to achieve some of the broader benefits of SaaS (economies of scale, higher availability, better agility, and so on). This path doesn't presume that you're completely rewriting the solution, just investing more time and energy to move the modernization needle before bringing a SaaS offering to market. This approach puts a higher premium on getting to a modernized version sooner instead of later.

The second path (at the bottom) is more of a "SaaS now" model where the team makes modernization compromises to bring their solution to market as soon as possible. This doesn't presume that you won't be investing in new code and foundational multi-tenant constructs to get this up and running. It just means that—for your initial rollout—you're avoiding refactoring your application's code as much as possible. Here, we're trading speed to market for some of the efficiencies we might get out having a fully modernized SaaS offering.

The pros and cons of these two approaches should be pretty clear. With the top model, you are modernizing without the extra burden of making these changes against a released version of the product. This provides greater freedom, mobility, and less need to carefully consider how each step toward modernization can be introduced into a deployed version of your working solution. The second model gets you to SaaS sooner, but does so at the expense of making future incremental modernization slower and more complex.

What gets missed in weighing these trade-offs, though, is the value of customer feedback. With the top model, you will have some long stretch where you're not getting feedback from your customers. You're assuming the choices you're making during this time will meet their needs and that the needs of the market won't be evolving significantly in that window. This could work, but it certainly comes with real risks that can be easily overlooked.

It's also important to note that migration isn't just about migrating your technology. When teams choose to make the move to SaaS, they're often choosing to fundamentally change how they approach their jobs. Support, operations, sales, product management—all of these roles may, in some way, be reshaped based on the move to a SaaS delivery model. The outward-facing view of your business will also go through changes, altering how you engage your customers.

You can imagine how these changes to your team's roles, interactions, and responsibilities could influence the structure of your organization. You'll need to factor these transformation considerations into your migration model. Each of the models shown in Figure 13-2 would likely yield different transformation paths. Generally, when teams take the "modernize now" approach, this tends to put the broader business transformation on the back burner. The rest of the organization will essentially wait until much later in the process to begin thinking about how they will transform the nature of their roles. In contrast, the "SaaS now" model provides a bit of forcing function, requiring the organization to begin to tackle all the aspects of transformation much earlier in the process.

While both of these models are valid, you might guess where I lean. As a general rule of thumb, I prefer migration strategies that put more emphasis on operating as a SaaS business as soon as possible. The combination of getting feedback sooner and transforming the entire business sooner seems to offer more value than focusing on modernization up front. For many, this is about not missing a window of opportunity. From some, though, the technical debt and other limitations could tip the scales toward an incremental modernization-first strategy.

Again, this is just one more example of the balancing act that's part of migration. I've presented these two extremes to give you a better sense of how this mix of business and technical considerations might shape the trajectory of your migration. The reality is, your path might be somewhere else along this continuum. Your business parameters might allow you to modernize more or require you to get to SaaS faster. The key is to avoid weighing these options purely as technical trade-offs. If I'm an architect and I'm asked to develop a migration strategy, I'm going to ask lots of business and product questions to help the company determine which option best suits the broader needs of the organization. As part of that, I'm going to think about the overall transformation of the business, considering how delays could impact my ability to get feedback and exercise all the moving parts of our SaaS business.

What Kind of Fish Are You?

As part of migrating, you'll want to have a clear notion of how this move could influence both cost and revenue streams for the business. These are both areas businesses classically consider with any strategy. The move to SaaS can have a profound impact on the fundamentals of the business, causing shifts in key economic dynamics. The initial investment in transforming to SaaS, moving customers to new monetization strategies, and the economies of scale of SaaS can all influence the financial trajectory of a SaaS business. There are plenty of examples of organizations that navigated this economic shift, and they highlight the financial dynamics associated with moving from classic long-term contracts to subscription or other flavors of SaaS pricing strategies.

For many, the economics of this migration effort can be challenging. Imagine you're a publicly traded company and you're making the move to SaaS. How will you explain to stockholders that your costs may go up and your revenue might go down during your transition to SaaS delivery? That message is not likely to go over well.

The *Technology-as-a-Service Playbook* (Baker & Taylor), authored by Thomas Lah and J.B. Wood, describes this dynamic with a diagram that brings these migration economics into better focus (Figure 13-3).

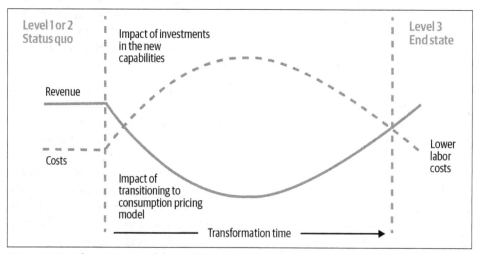

Figure 13-3. The migration fish model

This diagram, based on its shape, is referred to as the fish model. It juxtaposes revenue and costs, showing how they can trend over the life of your transformation to a SaaS delivery model. The dashed line at the top of the fish correlates to costs. When you're migrating, your teams will be responsible for building out new constructs to achieve the operational, agility, and cost efficiency goals of your offering. This effort, for some, could translate into additional incremental costs. These costs might be related to new people, new tools, new technologies, and so on.

The solid line at the bottom of our fish corresponds to revenue. As part of transitioning to new pricing and monetization models, you could see a dip in the revenue for your business. This could be the side effect of shifting to a pay-as-you-go pricing model or some other pricing strategy that, in the near term, could cause your revenue to decrease. The general idea here is that there is likely some added overhead associated with building all the plumbing that's needed to support your SaaS offering.

This is naturally intimidating to many companies that are migrating. They generally want this fish to be as skinny as possible. The good news shows up on the right side of the diagram. The expectation is that as you build out all the efficiencies and mechanisms that will create a highly agile multi-tenant environment, you'll eventually see your costs trending downward. At the same time, as you transition customers over to your new pricing model, you'll be able to lean on the efficiencies and agility of SaaS to take advantage of these economies of scale. Ideally, you'll also be able to reach new customers and market segments, accelerating the growth of your business.

It's at this point of inflection where you see revenues spiking back up and your costs trending downward, yielding the true payoff of this transformation. This is where the sweet spot of the SaaS model thrives, enabling organizations to leverage the strengths of SaaS to maximize margins and efficiently grow the business.

So, as I sit down with businesses that are beginning their SaaS journey, I often reference this fish model. It's not that I expect every business to fit the fish model. In fact, there are plenty that don't. The key, though, is to use this model to ask them what kind of fish they want to be. This helps frame the overall migration discussion and certainly impacts the overall mindset of the transformation effort.

Thinking Beyond Technology Transformation

I've made it clear that SaaS migration is very much about transforming from a product-centric experience to more of a business and service-focused mindset. For the scope of this book, however, I'm not going to dig into the weeds of how the transformation affects these other parts of the business. In reality, that's likely an entire book on its own and we're here mostly to consider how the business bits influence the technical approach.

At the same time, I think it's worth noting that your migration strategy should be looking at how it impacts all the other disciplines within your organization. Sales and marketing teams, for example, will definitely need to consider how the fundamentals of marketing and selling a product will change with a SaaS model. Customer support typically undergoes a transformation, adopting more of a Customer Success model that shifts the mindset from addressing customer issues to proactively engaging customers and shaping their experience. Pricing and billing will also be part of the transformation process, requiring you to consider how SaaS will influence the overall monetization model of your business.

These are just examples of how the business changes during your transformation. The key takeaway is that this organizational and cultural transformation of your business needs to be woven into your overall migration story. These are not areas where you build a SaaS offering first, then think about how these other parts of the organization will be folded into the SaaS model. Instead, these parts of the organization should be active participants in the overall migration journey.

Migration Patterns

Once you've established the basic parameters of your migration strategy, you can then start looking at specific architecture patterns that you can use to move an existing solution to a multi-tenant model. The patterns we're going to explore are meant to represent different approaches that could be executed in isolation or as part of a phased modernization strategy.

Each pattern has a distinct strategy that targets a specific migration use case with its own set of pros and cons. You'll see that these patterns can also be correlated to the different migration strategies discussed earlier. Some are clearly better for rapid migration and others fit better with a model that puts more early emphasis on moving to a modernized SaaS architecture.

It's important to note that none of the patterns advocate a big bang migration where you go away and rewrite most of your solution. That would not be consistent with a migration mindset. It's also not a strategy that I would advocate. The move to SaaS has lots of moving parts and taking a more incremental approach allows teams to evolve their strategy based on the data they get from seeing bits of their solution come to life in a working environment. The incremental approach also allows you to see the operational and application elements of your environment emerging in parallel, enabling you to see how your strategies are addressing the functional and operational needs of the service. The key is to get immersed within the details of the different patterns then figure out which aspects of these patterns best align with your migration strategy.

The Foundation

Before we get into the details of individual patterns, I want to start with one core foundational concept that spans all of the patterns. Every migration—regardless of the strategy you choose—includes the introduction of a control plane. The control plane, as you've seen throughout this book, provides all the shared services that support the centralized functionality that enables you to manage and operate your solution in a multi-tenant model.

This is especially important in a migration scenario since the control plane represents a completely new and separate area that the business must build as part of moving to a multi-tenant architecture. This control plane is what allows us to introduce the fundamental notion of tenancy into your environment, providing the constructs that allow you to manage and operate your tenants through a single pane of glass.

So, the first step in your process is to determine which control plane capabilities you'll need to support the initial requirements of your SaaS offering. In a migration mindset, this likely will start as a narrower set of services that give you baseline support for multi-tenancy without building out all the depth that you'll ultimately want to live in the control plane. The idea is to get the fundamentals up and running and have the shell of your control plane experience in place. Then, you can allow the control plane to evolve incrementally as your solution matures. This is all part of the balancing act that comes with migration. You want to build just enough to establish the principles and key placeholders, then add depth as you go. Figure 13-4 provides a familiar snapshot of the spectrum of control plane services that you'll want to consider as part of scoping out your initial control plane functionality.

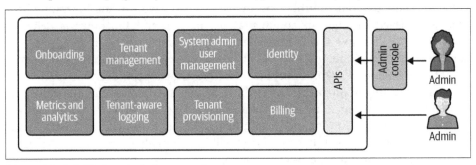

Figure 13-4. Initial control plane services

The services illustrated in Figure 13-4 have mostly been part of our broader control plane discussion. If you look at these services through the lens of migration, you can imagine what an initial, lighter weight version of these might look like. The services that are focused on orchestrating onboarding and creating tenants are big focal points, supporting the provisioning of tenant resources, creation of tenants, and establishing the core elements of your SaaS identity model. This is also laying the foundation for tenant authentication and the injection of tenant context into your application request. Having all this in place will require your application to handle the introduction of multiple tenants. It will also support tenant context to drive routing, logging, and so on.

The migration of your identity model can require a bit more thought. The legacy solution that you're migrating is likely to already include support for some notion of authentication. So, do you move identity into the control plane and make the commitment to potentially reworking part of your migration story? Or, are there more obstacles and challenges in your current environment that may have you deferring moving this to a new model? Timing, complexity, and long-term requirements will all play a role in how you might approach the identity migration of your experience. The key, though, is that even if you stick with your current identity model, you'll have to determine how your authentication experience will be expanded to support tenant context.

Other services (metrics and analytics, tenant-aware logging, and billing) may be key to the long-term needs of your multi-tenant environment. However, you might put simplified versions of these in place to establish the concept, then enhance them as the system and your needs evolve. Even if these have minimal use at first, I prefer to see them show up and offer some points of integration to begin to establish the commitment to capturing and surfacing tenant-aware operational insights.

Finally, you'll see an admin experience on the right of the diagram. This is meant to serve as a placeholder for whatever management and configuration experience you're going to expose for your control plane. I've shown two flavors of administration here. One is achieved through an administration console, and the other is delivered through API calls. How this is implemented is less important than simply making some level of commitment to putting this in place as part of the foundation of your operational experience. It's essential that you have some aspects of this in place at the front of your migration path. This will force you to exercise the system admin authentication experience and allow you to surface key multi-tenant insights that will help during your migration. Specifically, being able to access tenant state here and view logs and metrics with tenant context will be especially useful to teams that are testing and building out a multi-tenant environment.

As we move forward and start looking at patterns, I'll include a placeholder for this control plane in each of the migration strategies. This control plane is conceptually the same for all of the patterns that I'll cover.

Silo Lift-and-Shift

The first pattern we're going to look at is what I've labeled silo lift-and-shift. This pattern, as its name suggests, is focused squarely on getting an existing workload moved into a SaaS delivery model with as little refactoring as possible. In this mode, you are lifting your existing code and shifting into an environment where you can begin to operate your solution in a multi-tenant model (using our expanded definition of multi-tenancy). Figure 13-5 provides a conceptual view of the moving parts of this model.

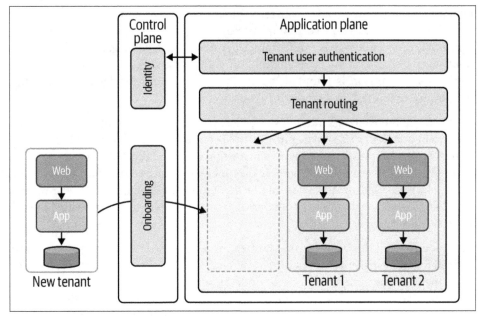

Figure 13-5. Silo lift-and-shift migration

With silo lift-and-shift, we're essentially adopting a full stack tenant deployment model where each tenant runs an entirely separate, siloed stack of infrastructure. The idea is to take a single stack that is not multi-tenant today and drop it into a multi-tenant environment that provides all the surrounding constructs to manage and operate these tenants collectively.

Let's look at how this lands in the diagram. You'll see that I've shown the application plane in the middle. This is where each of the full stack silos of our legacy environment will land for each tenant. I've represented this at the bottom of the application plane, showing stacks where Tenants 1 and 2 deployed to the environment. For the purpose of this discussion, I've shown these as n-tier apps. However, the legacy stack you're bringing in could come in many shapes and sizes. The key is that each tenant stack be created by a fully automated onboarding process that essentially provisions, configures, and deploys these tenant silos into your application plane. This experience is shown on the left of the diagram, where a newly onboarded tenant uses the onboarding capabilities of your control plane to automate this process.

This deployment automation represents an essential aspect of your SaaS migration. It is, in some respects, what enables your migrated solution to realize some of the key benefits of what it means to be SaaS. It also sets the stage for future evolution of the stack, demonstrating your commitment to having a single, unified onboarding experience for all tenants.

One key caveat that may be less obvious is that every tenant in this silo lift-and-shift pattern is running the same version of your application. This, in fact, can be a significant point of tension in your shift from a per-tenant installed legacy model to a full multi-tenant environment. Resisting one-off variation and requiring every tenant to run this same version is foundational to achieving the efficiencies and agility that have been emphasized throughout this book.

As you move these tenants into full stack silos, you must think about how you'll manage tenant access to these environments. I've represented this conceptually at the top of the application plane. Here, I have tenants that are authenticated just as they would be in any SaaS environment. Then, as they make requests with tenant context, this context will be used to direct tenants to the appropriate tenant stack. The routing could be implemented with subdomains or through context that's embedded in each request.

The good news of this model is that it often represents the fastest, least-invasive path to SaaS for some organizations. Once completed, you'll be in a position to begin realizing many of the benefits of a SaaS model. It also positions you to begin thinking about how you can start incrementally advancing the environment to achieve greater cost and operational efficiencies. This can all happen while you're functioning and operating as a SaaS business.

While this can be a somewhat low-impact move, it's important to note that your current environment will require changes to participate in this multi-tenant model. Minimally, you'll want your existing design to add support for sharing tenant context across the code in your environment. This context should be added to logging and other operational insights to help teams centralize tenant insights and provide a universal approach to troubleshooting issues with tenant context.

Layered Migration

The next variation of migration begins to shift toward introducing hints of multi-tenant optimization into your overall migration process. The key difference here is that, as part of migrating, you're choosing to dig a bit more into the code to introduce targeted bits of optimization that will allow you to realize some cost and operational efficiencies during the migration. In this mode, you're still not attempting to go after a full modernization. You're just identifying candidate areas within your existing architecture where you might be able to get some upside from sharing layers of your architecture, achieving better alignment between tenant activity and infrastructure consumption.

How or if you can use the layered migration model really depends heavily on the architecture that you're migrating from. Some architecture patterns fit better with the layered model than others. Figure 13-6 provides an example of how you might apply layered migration in a classic n-tier architecture.

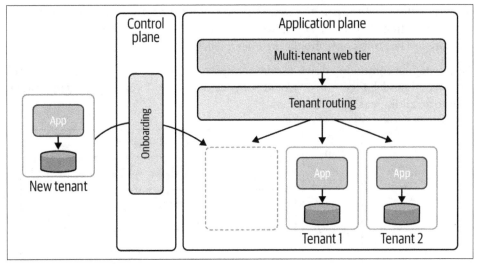

Figure 13-6. A layered migration of the web tier

The themes here should look familiar. We're still creating a control plane and automating all the onboarding of tenants via that control plane. All the values and principles that I outlined around silo lift-and-shift come forward with us. We still want to have a single process for introducing tenants and the expectation is that all tenants are running the same version of the product.

What's different is that I have moved some layers of my application stack into silos. However, you'll also see that the web tier of our n-tier architecture is not included in the silo or as part of onboarding. Instead, with this layered approach, I have migrated the web-tier layer to a shared, multi-tenant model (shown in the upper part of the diagram).

Here, I determined that the implementation of my web tier did not include lots of binding to tenant context. It was mostly processing requests and redirecting to my application tier, where the bulk of the business logic resides. Knowing this, I decided I could move the web tier of my application to a pooled model where it would be shared by all tenants. What made this possible (for this example) was that the move to a pooled model could be achieved without any significant refactoring. If more significant changes are required, the layer may not represent a good candidate for migration.

By moving the web tier to a shared layer, it can now scale based on the actual load of tenants, allowing the business to take advantage of the dynamically scaling infrastructure concepts across the entire multi-tenant workload. This could reduce cost, simplify deployment, and achieve some additional degree of operational efficiency. We still haven't modernized our architecture, and this layer still represents a significant point of failure, but the benefits could be compelling enough to make this intermediate optimization. This move also means that my onboarding gets moderately simpler. It no longer needs to configure the web tier as each tenant is onboarded.

Now, imagine continuing down this layered path, migrating more layers of our stack to a shared model. Figure 13-7 provides an example of how you might extend migration to an additional layer of your stack.

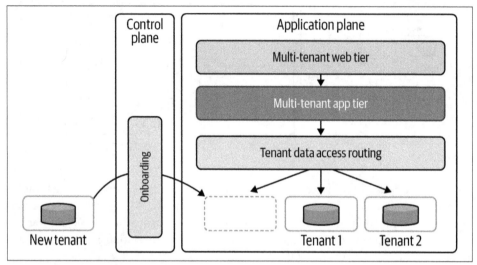

Figure 13-7. Migrating the application layer

For this example, I've moved the application layer into a pooled model alongside our web tier. This essentially moves all the business logic of our application services into a shared infrastructure model that scales dynamically based on the workloads of our tenants. This allows the application tier to take advantage of the efficiencies that we discussed with the web tier. It also inherits the same challenges.

Now, for some, making this move could be much more extensive than moving a web tier. There could be dependencies and logic in your existing app tier that may not easily convert to a multi-tenant model where the code would be able to access and apply tenant context to each request. This could mean that the level of effort here would be too high, making it impractical to migrate this layer of your architecture. However, if it is possible and the investment and effort math makes sense, this could represent another valuable step in your migration path.

Assuming this did fit your environment, your onboarding would now only be required to provision new storage for each tenant. Your app tier would now use the incoming tenant context of each request to connect the application call with the appropriate tenant storage resources.

While this is clearly not a path to a modernized SaaS architecture, the layered model could represent a good starting point for some SaaS vendors. Yes, there are clear weaknesses to this model that could, eventually, be overcome by further decomposing your system into smaller services. Still, the economies of scale with this approach could be acceptable for some teams (if your scaling policies are dialed in). At a minimum, this can be a reasonable compromise that lets you achieve some initial efficiencies without a major rewrite, giving you a solid first evolutionary step in migrating your SaaS environment.

Service-by-Service Migration

Some teams have a greater focus on migrating to a modernized architecture. These teams are looking for a more direct and immediate path to an architecture that maximizes cost efficiency, agility, innovation, and the operational profile that represents a best-of-breed multi-tenant environment. The expectation is that teams can absorb a bit more complexity in exchange for being on a path that lets them step more squarely into a modernized environment. Any number of factors could be motivating this approach. Teams may feel they have more time, or they may be facing challenges with their current design that demand a more immediate rewrite.

Even in this mindset, though, it's important to note that we're not really targeting a full modernization of the system. Any path to modernization should still have some degree of urgency that steers teams toward finding ways to incrementally modernize their solutions as part of the journey instead of a one-time rewrite. This goes back to some of the thinking outlined at the outset of this chapter where I highlighted the importance of focusing on time-to-market (for any migration strategy).

A commonly used pattern to support this modernization-focused model is referred to as the service-by-service migration strategy. This pattern takes the approach of incrementally modernizing individual services of your architecture, running the existing code alongside new, modernized microservices. Figure 13-8 provides an example of this service-by-service model in action.

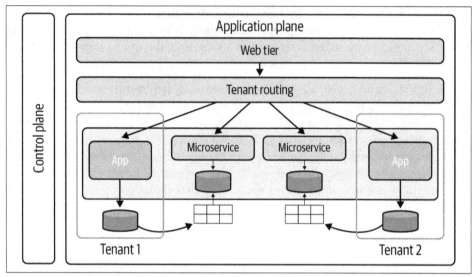

Figure 13-8. Service-by-service migration

For this example, I'm sticking with the same siloed stack starting point that was discussed with the other patterns, moving an n-tier application into our migrated SaaS environment. I did take one shortcut, extracting the web tier and moving it to a pooled model (like you saw in the layered example). I did this to put more of the migration focus on the application tier. Here, instead of moving the application tier into one shared layer, I'm going to start by modernizing the functionality that lives in that application tier, incrementally extracting functionality from these siloed application tiers and moving this functionality into pooled multi-tenant microservices.

Often, the hardest part of this model is identifying the first service(s) that can be extracted from the application tier. You might pick an area of the system that has the least potential for disrupting the business or an area that represents a key bottleneck that needs more immediate attention. There are no absolutes here.

Regardless of where you start, teams generally find it quite challenging to identify functionality that can be easily removed from the application tier. You can imagine how the application tier code has evolved over the years and how tightly coupled the different bits of functionality might be. Without hard boundaries, builders may have taken advantage of having open access to any part of the application tier. These environments will often include a single monolithic database that is shared across any and all parts of the application tier.

You can see how these factors can make it really difficult to find a good starting point. While this can be challenging, it's also part of the natural tension that comes with getting your migration off the ground. For some, this will mean making compromises around these first services to start pulling your application tier apart. That could require you to start with services that are more coarse-grained than you'd like. The idea is that we need to begin to extract services to get the foundations in place, knowing that you're finding a balance that lets you move forward. It's about creating momentum. As you begin to move more bits out of the application tier, this will get easier. Then, once you have these services in place, you can use real workloads to find the best places to further decompose your system. In some cases, you may find that not every service needs to be decomposed into a smaller representation.

These first few services you build should be implemented as first-class multi-tenant microservices that will run alongside your existing app tier. I've shown this in Figure 13-8, with two tenants having app tier and storage deployments. Then, in the middle, I've shown two microservices that represent functionality that I've extracted from the application tier and deployed as microservices. A big part of creating these services is also focused on pulling the data out of your tenant silos, creating new multi-tenant storage models. With your new microservices, you will be moving your data into multi-tenant pooled or siloed storage based on the needs of your service. The key here is that this moves compute and storage to microservices that encapsulate the data that they manage. This gives our microservice the autonomy it needs and lets us manage all access to the data through the contract of the service. Pulling this data out can, in some instances, be even more difficult than the efforts to extract the code.

In addition to carving out microservices, you also have to consider how migration will influence the tenant routing strategy of your application. There are two dimensions to this problem. One is shown in Figure 13-8, where you'll see a routing layer that uses tenant context and the nature of a request to determine how the request will be routed. Some requests will go straight to the old app tier and some will go to the new microservices. The other layer of routing and integration that happens here is a bit less obvious. As you're carving out your new microservices, you'll discover that you need to support some interim interaction directly between the application tier and your new microservices. Figure 13-9 provides a conceptual view of these interactions.

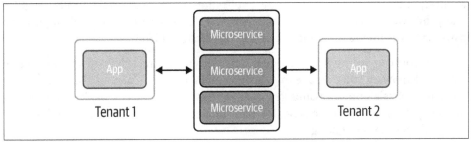

Figure 13-9. Integrating the app tier with new microservices

I've shown two different tenants, each with their own app tiers. The app tier may, as part of processing requests, need to call one or more of your new microservices, or your microservice may need to call the app tier as part of processing one of its requests. The key point is that while you'd like to minimize these dependencies, they will happen. Ideally, you'll be able to limit the effort needed to support these interactions to prevent old dependencies from finding their way into your new code.

After you've got the fundamentals of this model in place, much of the focus will be on spinning up the next set of microservices. The nice part of this approach is that it puts you on the path to modernization and forces you to begin tackling your multi-tenant realities sooner instead of later. Also, once you're done, you'll find that the remnants of your legacy architecture will fade away and you'll be left with a fully modernized architecture footprint. I've shown a conceptual view of this end state in Figure 13-10.

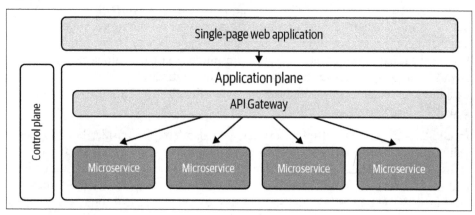

Figure 13-10. A fully modernized end state

You'll see that I've completely removed the app tier from the architecture. What's left are all the successfully migrated multi-tenant microservices. I've also presumed a natural next step, eliminating the web tier and moving the client to a single page web application that's hosted outside of the application plane. This would be a big step for many, but would represent a natural evolution, leveraging modern web application patterns to streamline the signature of your application plane.

Overall, you can see how this strategy sets you on a direct path to modernization while still allowing you to make this move in an incremental fashion. This model puts greater emphasis on addressing key multi-tenant architecture considerations earlier in your process and sets the stage for introducing your next-generation architecture alongside your existing design.

Don't compromise on new microservices

The new microservices you introduce during your migration are meant to be built as fully modernized services. These services should not make compromises that could undermine your modernization goals. This can seem like a high bar, but it's essential to getting the payoff that comes with going down this more modernization-focused path.

So, what does this mean? Well, the guidance I give is to build these microservices as if they were being created for a greenfield environment. I would design, implement, and deploy these microservices using the best practices strategies and patterns that will enable the longer-term efficiency, scale, and agility goals you have for your environment. There will be some areas where you may need to support slight, temporary variations to run alongside your legacy environment, but don't let those trade-offs creep too heavily into your design.

This is especially important for the first few microservices. These initial services are the blueprint for the next wave of services that you'll create, so you want to demand a lot of them. They should look to establish the foundational libraries that can be used by other microservices. You should be looking at how shared constructs and integration like token management, tenant-aware logging, billing, and metrics can be turned into reusable mechanisms (as covered in Chapter 7).

Ultimately, you don't want to find yourself returning to your new microservices to apply another round of refactoring to achieve your modernization goals.

Integrating legacy code with the control plane

In this service-by-service integration model, you'll have new and old code running side by side. The new code will have full multi-tenant support. This means that it will emit tenant-aware logs, integrate with billing, publish metrics, and so on. These new services will rely heavily on the cross-cutting capabilities of your control plane.

While these new services are built with these multi-tenant capabilities, they only represent part of the functionality of your system (while you're migrating). That means that your control plane will only get data and operational visibility into a subset of the overall system. The legacy bits of the application tier have no awareness of the control plane and, as built, don't have any notion of tenancy. This could mean that, during migration, the team would need to construct operational views from these two different elements of the architecture. This would place a significant extra burden on operations teams and make it generally difficult to monitor the state of your system.

This may lead teams to invest in creating new control plane integrations into their existing application tier code, knowing that this code will eventually be cycled out. You need to find a reasonable balance of investment and near-term value here. You'll certainly need to add extra instrumentation to your existing app tier code. Ideally, though, you can surface enough operational data to your control plane to make this work and not have it represent a huge diversion. A lot depends on where your technical stack will allow you to add this instrumentation without it being a huge diversion.

Comparing Patterns

There are clear strengths and weaknesses for each of the migration patterns that I've outlined. I've tried to highlight the business and technical factors that come with each of these patterns. However, I thought I'd provide a high-level summary of the pros and cons of these patterns, bringing more clarity to the trade-offs associated with each approach (Figure 13-11).

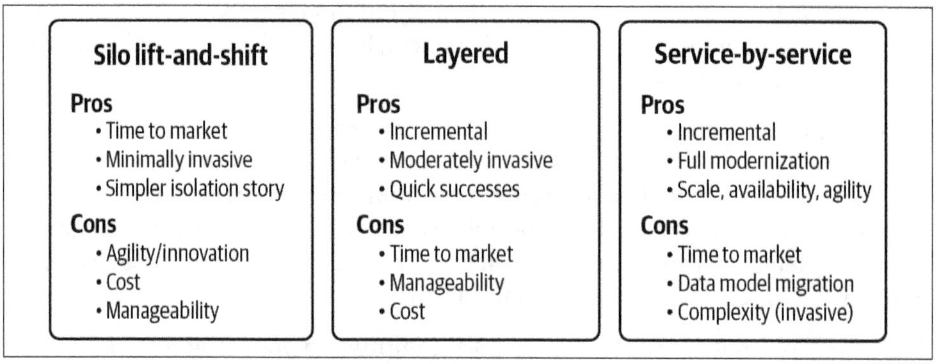

Silo lift-and-shift	Layered	Service-by-service
Pros	**Pros**	**Pros**
• Time to market	• Incremental	• Incremental
• Minimally invasive	• Moderately invasive	• Full modernization
• Simpler isolation story	• Quick successes	• Scale, availability, agility
Cons	**Cons**	**Cons**
• Agility/innovation	• Time to market	• Time to market
• Cost	• Manageability	• Data model migration
• Manageability	• Cost	• Complexity (invasive)

Figure 13-11. Migration pattern pros and cons

Clearly, the strengths of the silo lift-and-shift model are its speed and simplicity. The less invasive nature of this pattern makes it easier to get your system up and running without digging into your application code. Of course, this comes at the price of operational complexity, agility, efficiency, and cost. It will limit your ability to achieve some of the economies of scale that come with SaaS environments that pool resources. Still, if your target end state is a fully siloed model, this may not be so important.

The layered model represents a bit of a compromise. It's about letting you get some targeted efficiencies without leaning heavily into significant refactoring or rewrite. The upside is that it is only moderately invasive and it does put you on a path to some early successes. Naturally, any investment in refactoring will introduce some delay into your time to market. Also, while you'll get some efficiencies, they'll be somewhat constrained. You'll still face cost issues and management challenges with this model. The pooling of these layers can also introduce more single points of failure in your environment.

Finally, the service-by-service (strangler) pattern places a greater emphasis on achieving modernization sooner. It's still an incremental model, but the efforts and investment associated with cutting over to new microservices will be somewhat invasive. This will impact time to market and add layers of complexity to the overall migration process. The good news is that this is still an incremental model, so once the foundational bits are in place, you should be able to slowly move your environment to a fully modernized experience.

A Phased Approach

The patterns that I outlined in the previous sections are not meant to be viewed as mutually exclusive, and they are not meant to represent an exhaustive list of every flavor of migration. It's also worth noting that these patterns might be applied together as part of a phased approach where you move from one pattern to the next. Figure 13-12 demonstrates how you might combine these patterns in a phased approach.

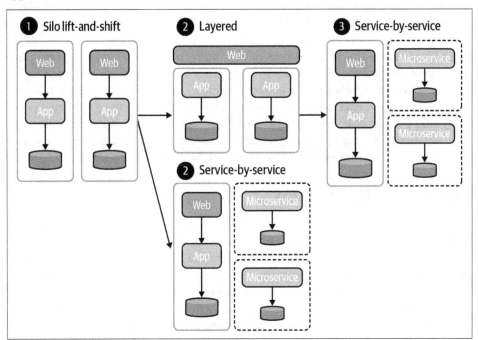

Figure 13-12. Combining migration strategies

For this example, the business started its migration journey with a clear need to get its SaaS solution to market as soon as possible. Knowing this, they opted to use the silo lift-and-shift pattern since it required the least effort to get their environment up and running (step 1).

Once the business was running in this new model and selling its offering to customers in a SaaS delivery model, they wanted to begin getting more cost and operational efficiency out of their solution. Here, within the patterns we've discussed, they could consider a layered model as their first wave of modernization or they could consider going straight to a service-by-service migration that put them more directly on a path to full modernization (both options shown as step 2).

Now, if the business chooses to start modernization with the layered approach, this could get them some immediate multi-tenant benefits as a first step in their modernization process. Then, after this, they could consider moving on to a service-by-service migration to begin fully modernizing their environment (step 3).

The key is not to view your migration process as a static, one-time migration. All of these strategies are about making some incremental step toward a modernized SaaS offering where there may be multiple phases to that journey. It's up to you to find the mix of business and technical considerations that can help you formulate a plan that best meets your needs. It's also worth noting that not every migration ends with a fully modernized experience. The level of modernization you are targeting might vary based on the parameters of your business. The deployment model of your tenants could also influence the path you follow. If your tenants will need siloed infrastructure, for example, you might stop at silo lift-and-shift. Modernization is always a good goal, but the nuances of the destination can be different for every SaaS business.

Where You Start Matters

I've laid out some patterns, but I still haven't said much about how this migration might unfold. Once you've picked your path and strategy, you still have options about how you might sequence the steps in your migration. My bias is toward having a migration strategy that begins with a clear focus on injecting tenancy and establishing the elements of the overall operational experience. I want teams focused on figuring out how tenants will get introduced into their environment, how they authenticate, and how they manage and operate these tenants once they're in the system.

To me, this always starts with creating the control plane. That doesn't mean building every element of the control plane. It's more about building in support for foundational constructs that will get your system running in a multi-tenant model from day one. This puts multi-tenancy front and center on day one and has a cascading effect across all the remaining steps in your migration process. Figure 13-13 provides an example of this approach.

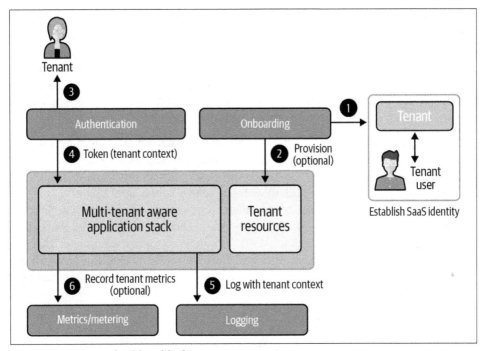

Figure 13-13. SaaS building blocks

Figure 13-13 provides insights into how these core multi-tenant principles land in your architecture from the outset of your migration. First, at the top right, you'll see the idea of establishing a SaaS identity. Your new environment must start by support-ing some clear way for tenants to onboard to your solution, create a tenant, create a tenant user, and bind that user to the tenant (step 1). These are all fundamental con-trol plane concepts that I've covered in detail throughout this book. There are not many corners you can cut when you're starting out your migration. There may be some scenarios that you may not initially cover, but you'll still need to be committed to creating a significant amount of your onboarding experience.

The other bit of onboarding I've shown is connected to the idea of provisioning and configuring infrastructure as each new tenant onboards (step 2). I've presented this as optional since some environments may not require per-tenant resource provisioning. However, if your solution is going to need per-tenant provisioning, you should be focused on wiring up this process from the start, providing a clear home for the pro-cess and a mechanism that will get exercised as your migration takes shape. The goal is to avoid having one-off runbooks or scripts that provision tenant environments while you're ramping by having provisioning woven into your onboarding all along the way.

In the top left of the diagram you'll see tenant authentication (step 3). This is also a foundational element that needs to be addressed at the front of your migration build. This connects to the onboarding work we've discussed, authenticating a user and getting their SaaS identity, which can then be passed into the application plane. Having this in place early forces teams to consider how they will process and apply tenant context as it flows into the backend services and architecture of your application plane (step 4).

Finally, at the center of our diagram are the services that we are migrating into this multi-tenant model. Some of these will be legacy services and some may be new, modern multi-tenant services (depending on which migration pattern you're following). Either way, these services will now receive tenant context and use this context to surface data and insights to your control plane. The data may be minimal at first, but you want to establish this end-to-end experience to lay the foundation for more comprehensive control plane interactions. Here, I've shown a simple example of applying tenant context in your application services. First, we see an illustration of logs being published with tenant context (step 5). This is key to ensuring that your environment, from the outset, includes support for surfacing system activity with tenant context. More importantly, it also exposes teams to this tenant context at the service level, driving home their need to think more in a multi-tenant mindset as they're implementing/migrating elements of the system.

The other example highlights the use of tenant context to publish metrics and analytics data (step 6). This is the data that provides business and operational insights into the health and activity of tenants. I've also presented this step as optional. However, I included it here because I believe that seeing teams integrating with the control plane and publishing some data (even if it's minimal) drives home the value and importance of investing in surfacing metrics that will have technical and business value.

Hopefully, you can see that my emphasis is on giving priority to those parts of the system that are less about the application and more about the constructs that allow the environment to function as a multi-tenant offering. The mere presence of these mechanisms will drive questions that need to be surfaced early in the migration of your solution. This prevents teams from viewing tenancy, tenant logging, metrics, and other key multi-tenant concepts as something you bolt on after your application is up and running. Delaying introduction of these core concepts will undermine your overall migration, causing you to undo and rework bits of your system to add support for tenancy.

Automation is also an essential part of this migration story. You want to be thinking about the tenant lifecycle from the beginning, introducing and exercising mechanisms that let you (and your QA team) experiment with the steps needed to create, validate, and authenticate tenants. Focusing on efficiencies and repeatability up front is core to making the shift to the SaaS mindset.

Conclusion

The appeal of SaaS has many organizations looking for strategies they can use to migrate their offerings to a multi-tenant model. While there is often a common set of factors that drive this need to migrate, it should be clear that there is no single, universal playbook for making the move to SaaS. The goal of this chapter was to highlight the different variables that might shape your migration strategy and outline the business and technical considerations that are often part of this exercise.

I started this chapter by focusing on the business dimensions of migration. There are a range of business parameters that can have a significant influence on the path and priorities of your SaaS journey. Time to market, competitive pressures, operational challenges, and cost concerns are all part of the migration business story. As an architect or builder, it's your job to lean into this business discussion and figure out how the strategy you land on will drive your technical migration strategy. The key takeaway was that SaaS migration represents a holistic transformation that touches all areas of the business. The teams that market, sell, operate, and support your offering will need to rethink and evolve their roles, adapting their approach to align with the core values of the SaaS delivery model.

With these foundational concepts and motivations laid out, I started digging more into the technical aspects of migration. Here, the goal was to outline a set of migration patterns, each of which took somewhat different approaches to migration. Some patterns leaned purely toward speed and others were a blend of speed and modernization. The idea was to expose you to a range of possibilities that have slightly different priorities and strategies. In some cases, your migration might map precisely to one of these patterns. However, you may find a blend of these patterns enables you to implement a migration model that balances the business and technical needs of your offering. Sometimes, the state of the stack you're migrating from can have a significant impact on the strategy you select. You may be facing performance, scale, or operational challenges that might put greater emphasis on getting parts of your system modernized. Or, your system and target state might favor a lift-and-shift model that gives less priority to more immediate modernization. The list of possibilities is quite long. Still, the themes that are covered by the different patterns we looked at do a reasonable job of covering this spectrum.

Finally, I wrapped up the chapter by looking at how you should start your migration. The choices you make at the outset of your migration can have a significant impact on the success of your migration. Putting core concepts like SaaS identity/authentication, tenant context, and tenant-aware operations up front forces teams to tackle fundamental multi-tenant challenges that will cascade across all layers of your architecture. In many respects, this serves as a forcing function that requires all moving parts of your SaaS environment to consider the impacts of building, deploying, and operating in a multi-tenant model. This may appear to slow your migration initially, but the investments will pay great dividends as your environment begins to mature.

I've seen teams go down a migration path where they defer taking on these core multi-tenant concepts. They'll create a system that targets a single first customer that has zero support for the horizontal multi-tenant concepts that are part of the control plane. Then, they attempt to add multi-tenant support later as new tenants are introduced. Inevitably, this exposes challenges that didn't show up in the single customer version and typically starts a painful path of retrofitting to try and bolt multi-tenancy onto an environment that was not built to support multi-tenant from the ground up.

Overall, my hope is that the spectrum of concepts that I covered here will provide you with a broader mental model that has you thinking about the full range of factors that go into building a successful migration strategy. It should also be clear that any notion of viewing migration as a tech-centric strategy would be a mistake. You're building a new service and transforming your solution to meet the as-a-service goals of that business.

For the next chapter, I'm going to shift gears a bit and look at how tiering and billing end up shaping the architecture of your solution. While I've referenced tiering throughout the book, I haven't really dug into the nuances of how tiering and billing directly influence your multi-tenant architecture. The key will be to provide a more holistic view of these concepts and highlight the strategies that are commonly used to support a tiered experience without undermining the efficiency and agility of your environment. This will give you a clearer picture of the different areas where tiering and billing need to be woven into your multi-tenant architecture.

CHAPTER 14
Tiering Strategies

For architects and builders, the mention of concepts like tiering and billing may elicit a less than enthusiastic response. The technical brain often assumes that anything related to how a product is priced or sold is outside of their realm. It's a natural reaction. Technical teams are often used to having a hard line between how a system is designed and how that offering is presented to customers.

In a SaaS environment—where we're constantly blurring the lines between business and technical domains—technical teams usually have a vested interest in understanding how the personas, packaging, tiering, and pricing of a service will shape the scale, performance, and experience delivered by the underlying architecture. In reality, part of the multi-tenant story is to create a range of experiences for different customer personas that enable the business to reach new segments that will give them the flexibility that will fuel the growth of the business. The ultimate goal is to create what I'll refer to as a "tiered" experience that makes an overt attempt to segregate your solution into different experiences that offer different levels of value at different price points.

You can imagine how this notion of tiering has specific mappings into the multitenant strategies that are applied to your solution. Deployment, throughput, isolation, noisy neighbor—the topics we've been talking about all throughout this book—all represent different knobs and dials that can be used to create different tiered experiences. This is where you, as the architect, can bring added value to your SaaS business. As a SaaS architect, you have unique insights into the various technical strategies and boundaries in your architecture that can be combined to stratify your SaaS experience. In reality, you may be in the best position to help the team understand which tiering models best support their needs. This includes helping them weigh and consider the trade-offs associated with the various strategies.

The business will also look to you to understand how these tiering models might impact the infrastructure costs and margins for your offering. Tiering can play a key role in maximizing margins, allowing the business to scale its reach without fear of the cost and operational impacts associated with this growth. It's here that we see tiering connecting to the broader economies of scale story, as it is one of the tools that is used to align operational and infrastructure costs with the load of your tenants.

For this chapter, I'm going to focus on some of the common areas where tiering will touch your architecture. We'll start by looking at some of the different tiering patterns that can shape and differentiate tenant experiences. I'll identify some of the common categories of tiering, outlining the general goals, value, and intent of each of these types of tiering. Then, with these concepts in place, I'll pivot to looking at how you implement these strategies, providing insights into the nuances that come with bringing tiering to life across different layers of your architecture and different technologies. Finally, I'll wrap up the chapter by looking at how tiering influences the operational footprint of your environment.

Overall, this chapter should provide you with a good sense of the options that you need to consider when thinking about how, where, and when tiering can be applied to your solution. It should also provide more insights into the value that tiering can play, offering the business new ways to package, price, and offer their SaaS solution.

Tiering Patterns

Before we get into how you can apply tiering in your solutions, let's come up a level and review some of the common techniques that are used to introduce tiering into a multi-tenant environment. I thought it would be useful to start by identifying and categorizing some of these tiering models, highlighting the different motives that are often behind the adoption of different tiering strategies. The goal is to find points of inflection in your offering where there are real value boundaries for the business and your tenants. These points of inflection might be connected to performance, cost, features, isolation, and other key parts of the service.

A big part of your job (as a team) is to identify these points of inflection and determine which combinations of these factors map best to the business and technical realities of your domain. Putting tiers in place purely to drive different price points isn't enough. Your tiering models should be defining boundaries that make sense to the business and its tenants. This is where the patterns I'll cover come in. The areas I'm outlining represent some of the typical areas where teams will find these boundaries. It's important to note that there may be tiering strategies that are more directly connected to the nature of your domain. If your SaaS service does video encoding, for example, you may have tiers that are very much focused on domain-specific models that are well understood by the customers in your domain.

While this chapter focuses on tiering strategies, it's important to note that tiering does not apply universally to every SaaS solution. There are definitely environments where the domain, pricing, or other attributes of your solution may not be presented to customers in a tiered model. At the same time, it's also worth noting teams often overlook the value and importance of tiering and the role it can play in shaping a business and technical strategy. Also, in some instances, the strategies I've outlined here might be employed as internal-only mechanisms that are simply used to control and optimize the operational and availability profile of your SaaS environment.

The sections that follow will look at how you can use different tiering patterns to define the tiering model of your solution.

Consumption-Focused Tiering

At this point, it should be clear that a big part of the SaaS value proposition is focused on aligning tenant activity with resource consumption. While this is a general efficiency goal for multi-tenant architecture, it also represents a natural place to think about how you might introduce a tiered consumption model. The graph in Figure 14-1 provides a view of how tiering can shape the consumption experience of your tenant personas.

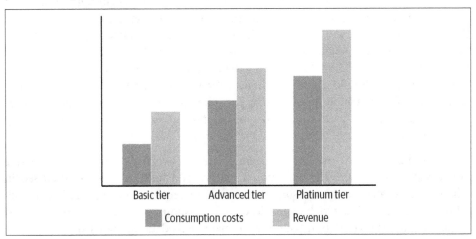

Figure 14-1. Aligning consumption with revenue

In this chart, you'll see consumption and revenue bars for three separate tiers. The goal of the chart is to illustrate the connection between the revenue generated by each tier and the costs associated with the tenants in that tier. If our tiering strategy is structured correctly, you should see a pattern that mimics what's shown in this graph.

The outcome we're looking for is one where the costs imposed by tenants, on average, do not exceed the revenue generated by those tenants.

Our consumption tiering policies, in this example, are presumed to be placing constraints on each tier to control or limit their consumption. For example, if we have a basic tier tenant that's paying $50/month, that tenant should not be able to consume resources at the same rate as our platinum tier tenants that are paying $5,000/month. This, again, is all part of creating a tiering model that can accommodate the varying tenant personas, using these price points and value boundaries to grow the business without eroding margins.

There are scenarios where you might intentionally allow tenants to consume resources in excess of their revenue. If you have a free tier, for example, that tier often provides a low friction path into your solution that will ultimately convert to a paying customer. This case represents an even stronger argument for consumption-based tiering. It's here that you'll absolutely need to associate consumption policies with this free tier to ensure that these tenants aren't consuming excess resources and inflating your costs (beyond what's anticipated).

With consumption-based tiering, the overall goal is to define a range of tiers that have clearly defined consumption policies that put constraints on the consumption activity of tenants. Where you decided to insert these policies and how they limit consumption will depend heavily on the nature of your domain and solution. As a multitenant architect, it's your job to work with the product owner(s) to figure out where there are specific points of inflection in your architecture that represent areas where the activity of tenants will create significant shifts in the infrastructure costs of your environment. It will be your job to find the data around these inflection points and surface them to the pricing teams, giving them a range of options that can create natural consumption boundaries that will drive the right cost and consumption dynamics for the different tenant personas that you'll be targeting. In many instances, there will be clear areas in your system that will stand out as candidates for controlling consumption.

You should also expect your consumption policies to evolve over time. This is where you'll really want to use the operational metrics and insights that we discussed in Chapter 12 to analyze the consumption trends of tenants and tiers. This data will allow you to assemble a richer profile of the consumption and infrastructure cost trends that are showing up in your environment. This data can be used to shape and evolve your consumption tiering model. Of course, you won't have all this data on day one. Instead, you'll have to work with estimates initially, then morph your tiering (if needed) based on the availability of insights that are extracted from your running environment.

Now, some teams that have a heavy emphasis on consumption-based pricing will presume they have no need for tiering. Instead, they will simply meter consumption and use this data to generate a bill, eliminating any need for tiering. In this mode, every tenant is treated the same. This is not uncommon and can work. However, it can also be a trap. If you have a purely consumption-based pricing model with no tiers, you're essentially saying that all tenants can impose whatever load they'd like on the system. So, for example, a tenant could make 10,000 API calls that are looking up configuration data and these API calls don't happen to be included as part of the consumption-based pricing model. In this model, I could still create noisy neighbor conditions and impact the experience of other tenants based purely on the bursting of API calls that are not metered or managed as part of your consumption-based pricing model. This is where you have to think beyond resource consumption of targeted resources and think more broadly about how tenants can impose load on your environment. If there are no constraints on their activity, you may also find yourself overprovisioning to accommodate sudden spikes of load.

The key with consumption-based tiering, from my perspective, is that we need ways to manage consumption that allow us to offer a range of experiences. So, even if I have consumption-based metering, I also want tiers attached to that experience that offer different levels of consumption based on the level of your tier. Without this, it can be difficult to distinguish the value proposition of your higher-level tenants. This circles back to the importance of connecting tiering to the business strategy, equipping the business with more tools that allow them to reach a broader range of markets and tenant personas.

Value-Focused Tiering

In many respects, everything we do with tiering is connected to value. However, for this discussion, what I'm labeling as valued-focused tiering is specifically targeting the way tiering is used to offer tenants experiences that translate into concrete value. When I say value, I'm talking about the kind of items you find on a list of direct benefits that are offered to each tier. This could be features, new capabilities, performance SLAs, and so on. The idea is that we're enabling access to functionality and experiences that allow tenants to have an enriched experience and extract more value out of your SaaS service.

This is a pretty broad area that includes a number of different mechanisms that can be correlated to direct tenant value. Performance represents one of the most common manifestations of value-focused tiering. Here, you're essentially indicating that tenants will get different levels of response and throughput for each of the tiers of your system. You can imagine how, for certain workloads, your system might offer better performance for a price. If, for example, you're running a video encoding service, you might provide a batch experience for basic tier tenants where their encoding jobs go into a queue and may have longer processing times. Meanwhile, that same system could offer more immediate processing and faster turnaround for platinum tier tenants. This provides tenants with a clear connection between value and the higher tier experience.

Value could also be connected to the functional capabilities of your solution. Specific features might be enabled based on your tier, providing higher tier tenants with access to additional functionality that is not available at lower tiers. You can also use other, more basic mechanisms to define tiers. For example, you could use the number of active users as part of your tiering configuration. You can imagine how the nature of your solution and the realities of your domain could play a big role in determining which flavors of value-based tiering might be applied to your multi-tenant architecture.

To support tiered access to different features, teams will often employ role-based access control (RBAC) or feature flags. A user's role (or tier in this case) might be used to selectively enable access to application features. In fact, the lines can get blurred here where a user's role within a tenant might control access to features and, in parallel, the tenant's tier will enable or disable access to specific features. The approach you take will be heavily influenced by the technology stack of your environment.

Deployment-Focused Tiering

While every SaaS solution must ensure that it isolates tenant resources, there are also domains and tenant personas that may impose specific deployment and isolation requirements on your solution. This may be driven by compliance and regulatory requirements or other domain factors that require elements of your system to be deployed in a dedicated model. You may find yourself using tier-based deployment to address specific performance and noisy neighbor conditions that are addressed through tier-based deployment strategies. There may also be certain high-value operations, for example, that some tiers expect to be fully isolated from any other tenant activity. Your goal is to find the specific areas where these deployment strategies might represent natural tiering boundaries for your offering. You can imagine, for example, offering dedicated resources for some or all of your offering as part of a premium tier that allows you to better correlate the added costs of dedicated resources to a higher price point.

The key is that you shouldn't view isolation as an all-or-nothing proposition that is applied equally to all tenants. Instead, you want to create an architecture that supports a range of isolation models that best aligns the pricing model of a solution with the different tenant personas that you'll need to support. Here, you can create unique tiers that mirror the needs of these different personas.

Figure 14-2 provides an example of how you might apply tiering to the different isolation and deployment models of your solution.

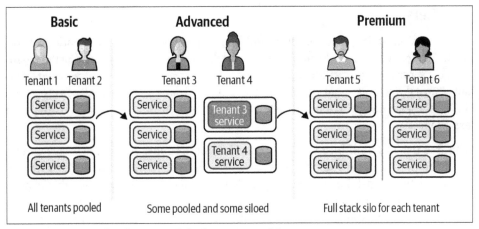

Figure 14-2. Tiered isolation and deployment models

I've included three tiers in this example, each of which employs a different deployment model. On the left I've shown the basic tier tenants. You'll notice that all the solution's resources are pooled for this tier. This means that tenants will be more exposed to noisy neighbor considerations and will rely on more complex isolation strategies. The advanced tier, shown in the middle of the diagram, takes a slightly different approach, carving out a specific service for each tenant in this tier. The idea is that you've picked some specific services that can offer tenants a different noisy neighbor and isolation profile for the functionality and data that's managed by these services. This can represent a good compromise, bringing the upside of siloed services to just those parts of the system where it has specific, targeted value that warrants a separate tier.

Finally, on the far right, you'll see the premium tier tenants. These tenants presumably have an even stricter set of siloed resource demands, requiring the entire stack for each tenant to be deployed in a full stack silo model where nothing is shared between tenants. Naturally, this tier would demand a much higher price tag and be viewed as a special case that enables the business to target these tenants that are willing to pay a premium to have access to a fully isolated environment. As I noted before, there are true scaling challenges that come with the full stack silo model, so you'll want to think carefully about how many tenants you'll allow to run in this model.

The primary point is that the deployment footprint of your application can play a key role in shaping the tiering experience of your solution. Again, this demands a more in-depth exploration between the product and technical teams, working together to identify the combinations of deployment models and tiers that are going to best meet the needs of your customer personas.

Free Tiers

No discussion of SaaS and tiering would be complete without some mention of free tiers. The free tier has traditionally represented a powerful construct for SaaS organizations, serving almost as a marketing and customer acquisition channel where tenants can take your system out for a spin without making any initial commitment. This is especially prevalent in B2C settings, but shows up across many SaaS experiences.

The free tier has both business and technical implications. Teams must give careful consideration to the operational, cost, and business impacts that come with supporting a free tier model. For many, the goal is to balance enabling a reasonable experience that will draw tenants without absorbing significant incremental costs or impacting the operational footprint of the environment. Some teams will carve out a free tier as a standalone experience. Others will have it behave as a first-class citizen, placing constraints on these tenants to limit their ability to consume excess resources. These are all the nuances that come with the free tier model. There are few absolutes here and how or whether your team uses this model depends heavily on the nature of your domain and the expectations of your customers.

If you do choose to support this tier, you'll need to figure out how this could impact the broader customer journey story for your solution. For example, will your tenants expect to have their data and configuration follow them if they move to a paid tier? If they're running in the same environment with paid tier tenants, this should be a natural transition. However, if you've carved out a separate environment for your free tier tenants, you'll need to figure out what it would mean to support a move to a paid tier. There's nothing particularly complex about supporting this transition; you just need to figure out what journey you're supporting for free tier tenants and include this as part of the overall lifecycle. As part of this, you may also need to have policies that will remove free tier tenants that are no longer active.

Composite Tiering Strategies

I've tried to categorize some of the different types of tiering that could surface in SaaS environments. However, this list is neither exhaustive nor mutually exclusive. In reality, organizations may choose to use a mix of strategies to arrive at an approach that best supports the consumption, value, and deployment requirements of their customers.

Generally, this is about finding the intersection between the factors that drive costs, the capabilities that can add incremental value, and the domain and market realities that could shape the deployment model of your environment. The goal is to weigh all of these options, lay them alongside the personas you'll be targeting, and find the combinations of tiering strategies that will make sense to your customers and allow the business to engage in a range of customer experiences that will enable both reach and growth. Finding the intersection of these needs and opportunities will allow you to identify the attributes that will drive the overall design and footprint of your SaaS architecture.

In some instances, teams may decide that there is no composite tiering model that meets their needs. Instead, they might opt to create a build-your-own tiering experience. With this approach tenants are presented with a menu of options when onboarding, selecting the combination of features that best map to their target experience. This option is powerful but it can also add complexity to the operational and implementation profile of your architecture. You'll want to carefully consider the trade-offs that come with adopting this model.

Billing and Tiering

The tiering strategies that we're discussing in this chapter are mostly focused on the architecture aspects of tiering. However, if you think about tiering, it's also very much part of the pricing story of a SaaS environment. A more complete look at tiering would also look at how you might connect tiers with specific billable units. For example, if you have a consumption-based tiering strategy, your system would need to measure and publish billable consumption units to your billing system. The bill will then be calculated using this information. This consumption price could be lowered as you move to higher tiers (where you're also consuming more resources). The reality is that there are any number of different ways that you might correlate tiers to your broader billing strategy, and this will influence how your architecture publishes and consumes this billing data. However, for the scope of this chapter, I'm intentionally steering away from going deep on the billing aspects of tiering. Instead, I've focused more on the builder and operational view of tiering, looking at how tiering strategies influence the shape of your architecture. This may overlap with the metering and metrics discussion that was part of Chapter 12.

It's also worth noting that tiering is often managed, in part, by your billing system. When you're setting up your billing system and defining the billing model, it's here that you may set up plans, tiers, or some construct that identifies the different billing models that are available. This notion of a plan or tier will be mapped back to your control plane and applied across your multi-tenant architecture. It may be used to throttle tenants, it may be used to measure and publish consumption, or it might be used to turn features on or off. This is an important dimension of the overall tiering story. However, the options vary significantly based on the tiering model you choose and the nature of your billing system. So, for this discussion, I'm going to focus more on how these tiers are defined and applied within your architecture and just assume that you'll also look into how these concepts get connected to your billing experience.

Tiering and Product-Led Growth

There's been quite a bit of attention centered around the idea of product-led growth (PLG) and SaaS. There are lots of dimensions to the PLG discussion that go beyond the scope of this book, but it does have some intersections with the notion of tiering and, as such, is worthy of discussing briefly.

In a traditional model, growth of a SaaS business would be driven by a combination of factors. Marketing, sales, acquisition, and a host of other mechanisms are used to engage potential customers and drive adoption. With the PLG methodology, there is a significant shift to placing the product itself at the center of customer expansion, conversion, retention, and acquisition. This puts a much greater emphasis on the overall experience supported by a SaaS application, requiring teams to think more about the surface of their experience, how frictionless and intuitive it is, and how successfully it connects tenants to the value of your offering. The product itself becomes the conduit for marketing and acquiring customers.

I've really just skimmed the surface, but you can see how this could end up at least partially influencing your tiering model. As you're choosing your tiering model, you may also need to consider how the pricing and packaging of your offering will support your overall PLG goals.

Implementing Tiering

At this point, you should have a good sense of the importance and role that tiering can play in a SaaS environment. It should also be clear that tiering can have a significant influence on the footprint of your multi-tenant architecture. Now, I want to start looking at how these tiering concepts end up being applied to the architecture of your system.

While the core principles of tiering apply to any technology, the specifics of implementing these strategies can be different for every environment. Your compute stack, your storage services, your API Gateway—these are all examples of areas where you'll see variation in how tiering is realized across different technologies and services. In some instances, you might implement tiering as a collection of different policies and techniques that span the layers of your multi-tenant architecture.

This list of options is too long to cover every possibility. Still, I thought it might help to connect some of these concepts to concrete technologies to give you a feel for what it means to bring these concepts to life within the different layers of your multi-tenant architecture. In the sections that follow, I will highlight some of the key ways that tiering is implemented across a range of infrastructure and application constructs.

API Tiering

In many instances, the services of your applications are going to support an API that's used to invoke different operations from your client or some developer SDK. This API often represents a natural place to introduce tiering constructs into your multitenant architecture. It's here that you have the opportunity to introduce policies that can shape, limit, and generally control how tenants interact with the services of your application.

The implementation model for these APIs can vary significantly. A common approach I see is one where teams use API management tools that provide a rich set of options for configuring and describing how traffic will flow into your services. Adopting these tools allows you to have a distinct entry point into your environment where you can introduce policies and other constructs that can be applied more universally to your SaaS environment.

There is a fairly broad set of tools that can be used to implement tiering at the API level. AWS has an API Gateway, Microsoft has API Management, and Google has Apigee. There's also open source tools in this space. Each one of these solutions adds its own twist to the tiering story. Still, most of these API management tools include mechanisms that allow you to define throttling policies that can be applied to each request.

Figure 14-3 provides an example of how tiers would be used to manage and control access to the services of your application.

This solution employs Amazon's API Gateway as the front door to our solution's services. All requests from your application will be passed through this gateway. Each tenant making a request will be associated with a tier, which will be used to apply your throttling policies.

On the righthand side of the diagram you'll see all the different usage plans (throttling policies) that are configured as part of the API Gateway. Each tier of this SaaS environment is assigned a unique policy that defines the throughput that will be supported in that tier. In this case, where we're using the API Gateway, we can configure the requests per second, the burst rate, and the overall request quota for the day. While this example illustrates API Gateway concepts, the strategies and mechanisms that are part of this experience typically map to similar constructs that are supported by other API management tools. Some offer more options and others have different ways of injecting the policies. The net effect, though, is usually similar to what I've shown.

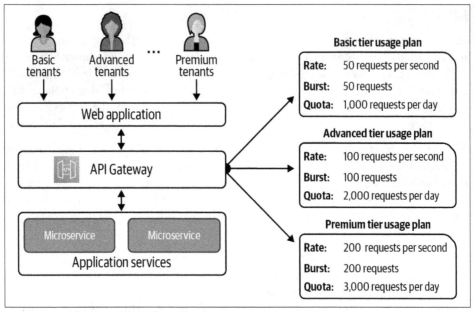

Figure 14-3. *Tiering applied to your API*

As part of defining your API tiering model, you'll also have to think about how you'll connect each request to a specific tiering policy. With the API Gateway, this is done with API keys. Each usage plan is associated with an API key. Then, as requests are made using a given API key, that key will be used to determine which tiering policy is applied. The question is: do you have to assign each tenant its own API key for this to work? This is certainly one way to make this work. However, this means that the clients of my API will need to use this key with every request that is made, which pushes more moving parts to my client. There is a more efficient way you can achieve this with the API Gateway, attaching a function (custom authorizer) to your API Gateway that is called each time a request is made. This function can extract the tenant's tier from the incoming request, determine which API key is associated with that tier, and process the request using the API key assigned by the function. This means that your client won't need to know anything about the API key. It also means you only need one API key for each tier.

This is just one approach to applying policies. Each API management solution has its own set of nuances to create the mapping between tiers and policies. Generally, I'm always going to be looking for strategies that allow me to configure these policies in one place and limit the client's need to inject or apply any throttling context.

Compute Tiering

Compute represents another layer where you can implement tiering. At the compute layer, you can introduce different scaling, throughput, noisy neighbor, and isolation strategies based on the tiering requirements of your solution. The options you have will vary based on the compute stack you're using, the deployment model of your solution, and a host of other factors. The key is that compute is often at the center of much of your solution's activity and, as such, it also represents a natural place to introduce tiering mechanisms.

Let's start by looking at how tiering could be applied in a serverless model. Generally, with serverless, our unit of scale is a function. These functions will need to scale out to support the varying workloads of our tenants. With the AWS Lambda serverless model, this scale is configured through its concurrency settings, which determine how many concurrent executions of a function are allowed.

Imagine, for example, you have a pooled environment where all of your tenants are sharing all of the serverless functions that implement your solution. In this scenario, there would be no way to offer your tenants any kind of compute-based tiering model. All tenants would be vying for the same collections of functions. If a basic tier tenant decided to submit a burst of requests that saturated the function concurrency, this would end up having adverse effects on premium tier tenants.

To address this, you need to create separate deployments of your functions with different concurrency configurations. Figure 14-4 provides a conceptual example of how you could address this by supporting different concurrency options for each tenant tier.

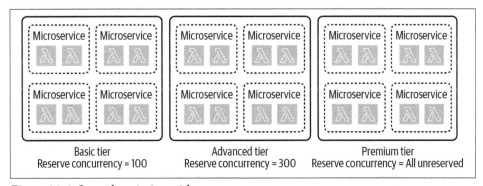

Figure 14-4. Serverless tiering with concurrency

Here we have three separate tier configurations where I've assigned separate concurrency values to each tier. With this approach, I have to deploy three separate copies of my solution's functions and, during deployment, I would configure them with different concurrency settings.

The basic tier tenants, on the left, have a concurrency setting of 100, which indicates that there can only be 100 concurrent function executions for all tenants in this tier. In the middle, the advanced tier is set to 300 concurrent executions. Finally, for the premium tier, you'll notice there is no concurrency value. This essentially means that any of the remaining concurrency that is available will be allocated to this tier. So, assuming there's a default upper concurrency limit of 1,000, my premium tier tenants would be able to have a concurrency of 600.

This, of course, is entirely focused on the serverless model. What would this look like if you were using containers to host your application's services? With containers, we have other constructs that can be used to manage the tiered scaling and consumption of our compute resources.

If we look at Kubernetes, for example, you'd see that we use a completely different set of constructs to manage and configure the tiering of your compute layer. Figure 14-5 provides an example of how you might use the Kubernetes quotas mechanism to implement a tiering strategy.

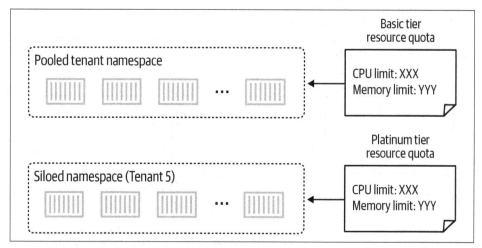

Figure 14-5. Tiering Kubernetes compute resources

In this example, I happen to have my tenants running in two separate namespaces. The one at the top employs a pooled compute model where the compute resources are shared by all tenants. The namespace at the bottom is using a siloed compute model where all the compute resources of a single tenant (Tenant 5) are running in a dedicated namespace. These two namespaces are associated with different tiers. My basic tier tenants are running in the pooled tier and the siloed namespace is associated with the platinum tier.

These two tiers or namespaces could require very different scaling profiles based on their tiering requirements. This is where resource quotas come into play. On the right of the diagram, you'll see that I have configured and associated two resource quota configurations with each of the namespaces. Teams can configure these quotas with different settings that will influence the scale and performance of the compute resources within a namespace.

These are just two examples of how you might apply tiering policies to the compute layer of your architecture. These policies might be used to support the different consumption and value tiering strategies of your solution. Even if your business hasn't adopted a tiering model, I would still look at how you might want to introduce policies that can prevent unexpected workloads from tipping over your system.

Storage Tiering

Storage represents another area where you might introduce tiering into the experience of your SaaS environment. Storage services—especially cloud-based managed storage—tend to offer builders a number of different knobs and dials that allow teams to configure the throughput and scale of your storage experience. This, of course, also represents an area where you might use these storage settings to define the different tiering models that are needed to support the requirements of your tenant personas.

With storage, tiering tends to be realized through two distinct approaches. If your storage is pooled, you'd be looking at how you might limit or constrain the read/write activity of each tier. This would allow you to offer different levels of performance to those tenants accessing a shared storage construct. The other storage tiering model is more focused on offering tenants siloed storage. Figure 14-6 provides an example of how these different strategies might land in your SaaS environment.

For this example, I have shown a range of multi-tenant storage scenarios. Along the bottom of the diagram, I've defined different performance and scale policies that correspond to each of my solution's tiers. These settings include read/write IOPS, CPU, and memory as examples of the parameters that could be configured on a tier-by-tier basis.

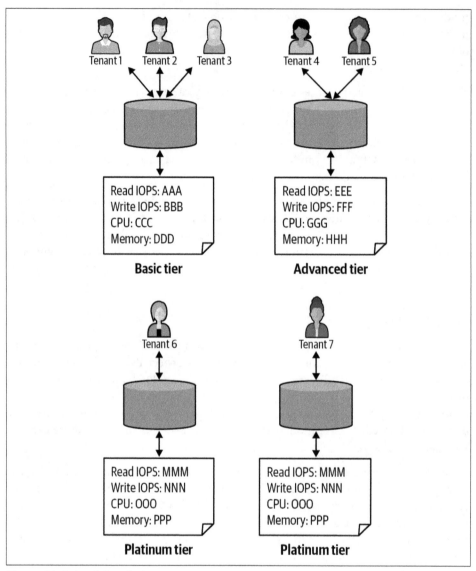

Figure 14-6. Applying tiering to storage

Now, if we walk through this diagram from left to right, you'll see that I have a basic tier that supports a pooled storage model for Tenants 1–3. The storage I used here will potentially be shared by a large collection of tenants and will need to be configured with settings that meet the requirements that you've agreed upon for the basic tier. As you move across, you'll notice that I have included an advanced tier that is also using a pooled storage model (for Tenants 4 and 5). In most respects, this tier is the same as the first tier we discussed; however, it is configured with settings that would offer better performance, scale, and throughput to the tenants.

For Tenants 6 and 7 in this example, you'll notice that they are using siloed storage. These tenants are offered the same scaling/performance configuration. While the data is stored separately for these tenants, they are still given the same performance and scale settings. In some instances, I have seen teams offer these siloed tenants separate policies. While this is possible, having one-off policies could, over time, undermine your operational efficiency. Any time you have to consider per-tenant configurations, it can add overhead to your operational footprint. Still, I have seen some teams take this approach.

Some SaaS providers will presume that the silo versus pool tiering strategy needs to be applied globally to a tenant's data, siloing all the data associated with a tenant. This is certainly a valid scenario, but it should represent the extreme case. In reality, you should look at the families of data that are in your system and figure out which categories of data may need to be siloed based on the nature of the data, the access patterns, and so on. You may find that you only need to silo a subset of the data. Taking this more granular approach to the silo versus pool tiering model allows you to keep some data in your system in a pooled model, which could reduce operational complexity and lower the cost footprint of your environment.

There are also other dimensions to the SaaS storage tiering story. Yes, performance and throughput are top of mind when we're thinking about how to partition and configure our multi-tenant data experience. However, you might also see SaaS organizations looking at how they might use tiers as a way to control the storage capacity of tenants. There are certainly domains and environments where the footprint of a tenant's data could have a strong correlation to value. In these scenarios, you'd likely impose capacity limits at different tiering levels. Storage retention represents another candidate for tiering. Here you might use tiers to differentiate each of your retention policies—especially for domains where retaining data could be impacting the cost profile of your SaaS environment.

Deployment Models and Tiering

In general, when you're thinking about tiering strategies, you may consider how the deployment model of your application might correlate to your tiering strategy. This already showed up in our discussion of compute and storage tiering models, where we deployed separate infrastructure for tenants and attached distinct scaling and performance policies to these resources. This is a classic theme that can apply to any of the infrastructure in your environment. You could, for example, have separate messaging infrastructure deployed and configured to support the message throughput you want to offer as part of different tenant tiers. The idea is that you should be looking at each element of your system and asking yourself how tiering could influence its deployment model.

This same mindset can also be applied to the microservices of your environment. For example, your solution may need to deploy some services as siloed and others as pooled. Figure 14-7 provides an example of how you might use tiering to shape the deployment of your application's microservices.

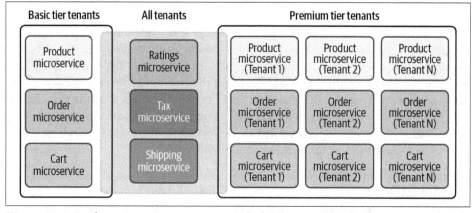

Figure 14-7. Applying tiering to microservice deployments

In this example, I have a set of six microservices that are used as part of an ecommerce SaaS environment. As part of our tiering strategy, I've determined that our premium tier tenants have requirements and workload expectations that have created the need to offer the Product, Order, and Cart microservices in a siloed model where each premium tier tenant would have its own deployment of these services (shown on the righthand side of the diagram). Our basic tier tenants, however, are willing to have these services run in a pooled model (shown on the lefthand side of the diagram). These resources are shared and scaled based on the combined consumption of the tenants in the basic tier.

Now, you should also notice that there are a group of services (ratings, tax, and shipping) that are not classified as belonging to any tier. These services are deployed in a pooled model and shared by both the basic and premium tier tenants.

There are two key points I'm trying to illustrate. First, it should be clear from this example that our tiering strategy does not have to correlate directly to some specific infrastructure resources and set of performance policies. The microservices in Figure 14-7 could be composed from compute, storage, messaging, and other infrastructure resources. Your tiering, in this mode, is a more coarse-grained model that uses the deployment profile of services to define the tiering experience of your solution. The other point is that the deployment model of these microservices is not an all-or-nothing strategy. You can create a tiering model that defines groups of microservices that are deployed based on your tiering requirements. Some may be pooled, some may be siloed, and some may be shared.

Throttling and Tenant Experience

Some of the tiering strategies that we've been talking about may employ policies that will impose limits on a tenant's experience. A basic tier tenant, for example, might intentionally have its experience degraded by these policies. It's fair to question whether limiting a tenant's experience is a good idea. You could easily argue that this approach is undermining the overall mission of delivering a great service experience to your tenants.

This is why you need to be especially strategic when defining your tiering model. Tiering is about finding that point of tension between giving all tenants a good experience and still acknowledging that it's impractical to allow tenants to impose load and consume resources without some form of constraints or limits. You have to presume that some tenants could put excess load on your solution and begin to impact the experience of other tenants. In fact, they could stretch the scale of your system and, potentially, create a scenario that brings down some or all of your system. So, in some respects, tiering is also part of a global performance and availability strategy that is used to prevent tenants from imposing loads that are deemed excessive and in line with their revenue footprint.

The other part of this tension is more related to keeping costs in line with consumption. If I have a basic tier that has explicit constraints and a new tenant opts into this model, it's my job to make sure the limits of that experience are clear. At some point, if you're really going to commit to a tiered model, you must also commit to having a model where tenants may encounter constraints based on the tier they've selected. The key is to establish constraints that make sense to your tenants and align with the experience that you've targeted for each tier.

Some SaaS providers rely purely on a consumption-based model that may only have tiered pricing based on your level of consumption. For example, you might have your tenants pay entirely based on bandwidth consumption. Here, though, you may still need to think about applying tiering policies that support limits that offer different levels of throughput. Generally, somewhere under the hood—even if customers can't see it—you may need to have policies in place that are more about maintaining operational health. The policies, however, may have no mapping to tiers.

Tier Management

Tiers, on their own, are a really basic concept. Somewhere in your solution you'll have some representation of the list of tiers that are supported by your system. These tiers may include some additional attributes, but there isn't much complexity to storing and managing this information.

The main question I get is: where should the management of these tiers live? In most cases, I think it makes the most sense to have these tiers managed as part of the control plane of your solution. This simply ends up surfacing as another microservice that has a basic set of operations to maintain the list of tiers in your system.

While tiers will land and be managed in your environment, you'll also have to consider how you'll manage any linkage that may exist between your management of the tiers and the representation of tiers within your billing system. Fortunately, this data doesn't change much. Still, you'll need to decide how to manage the linkage between these two and ensure that they remain in sync.

Operations and Tiering

I covered a lot of details about tenant-aware operations in Chapter 12. As part of that story, I also highlighted the role of tiering as part of the overall operational story. Yes, we certainly want to know what's going on with individual tenants in our operational view. However, there are also times where you're going to want to analyze your activity, scale, cost, and other attributes of your environment through a tier-based lens.

If you think about the role of tiering, it often has some mapping to the operational behavior of your system. When you define these tiered boundaries, you also need to have tooling and mechanisms that give you insights into how your tiering system is performing. Is it throttling tenants at the right time, and are the throttling policies effective? How often are tenants impacted by your tiering policies? Are your policies too aggressive or too lenient? These are just a few of the areas where you'll want to be tracking the operational profile of your tiering model.

The reality is, you should expect your tiering model to be evolving based on the insights and observations that surface through your operational experience. As new tenants come in and you develop a richer profile of tenant personas and their consumption patterns, you'll likely see opportunities to refine your tiering model. This further emphasizes the need to have a strong commitment to instrumenting your system with the operational metrics that will allow you to assess the tiering behavior in your system. In some instances, I'll see teams go the extra mile, introducing alerts that allow them to have more immediate visibility to when tenants are approaching or triggering tiering policies. In fact, some teams may use a phased tiering model where notifications are raised as tenants have reached the boundary without actually applying the throttling. Then, they'll have some internal level that's above this as the hard limit that actually applies the throttling. This allows you to have a bit more of a controlled experience that lets you notify tenants they are reaching a boundary. This isn't practical for all policies, but it's another approach worth considering. The key is adopting a more proactive approach that gives your operations teams visibility into tiering trends.

As we've seen throughout this book, tiering can also have a significant impact on the deployment footprint of your SaaS solution. As you offer dedicated resources to tenants as part of a tiering strategy, your deployment mechanisms will have to use these tiering configurations to determine how/where resources will land in your architecture (based on their tiering profile). Tiering can also be used as part of a staged rollout strategy. For example, you might choose to roll out a new version to a tier of tenants as part of a canary release. Then, based on the success of that release, roll it out to the remaining tiers. This might be used as a defensive tactic where you avoid rolling out to premium tier tenants. Or, you could argue the inverse of this, rolling out to premium tier tenants first as a way to avoid larger scale impacts that might be associated with deploying to a large collection of pooled, basic tier tenants. Both options are valid. The strategies here would vary significantly based on the needs of your environment.

Conclusion

My goal with this chapter was to give a broader sense of the value and importance of tiering, highlighting the role it can play in shaping the business and technical profile of a multi-tenant architecture. While tiering may not be a fit for every SaaS environment, for many it represents an essential tool that allows teams to construct an architectural, cost, and packaging construct that enables the business to target multiple tenant personas and market segments.

To drive this point home, I started the chapter by looking at broader tiering concepts and how they can be used to shape and control the experience of tenants. I went through some of the common tiering patterns and their nuances, exploring some of the key factors that might determine how you would employ these tiering constructs. Some of these strategies were more focused on defining value boundaries, whereas others put more emphasis on consumption and scale. The goal was to give you a glimpse into a menu of options that might be used to help define where you might consider introducing tiering into your environment.

From here, I moved into more concrete examples of how these tiering models might get implemented across the different elements of your SaaS architecture. I hand-picked a few core areas of the multi-tenant architecture (API, compute, and storage) and provided more specific examples of how these elements of your system could be configured to support tiering. I also looked at how you could come up a level from the infrastructure and use targeted strategies to package and deploy parts of your system based on the tiering of your different tenant personas.

I also touched, briefly, on the role that tiering plays in your operational experience, outlining the importance of having an explicit view into the tiering behavior of your system. The goal was to emphasize the importance of having proactive visibility into when tenants are nearing or triggering tiering boundaries.

I view tiering as one of the more valuable tools that architects can use to offer more options to their business counterparts. Part of this is about giving the business the flexibility it needs to address the current and emerging needs of tenant personas. Part of it is also about introducing constructs that put tighter control around how tenants can impose load on your environment. While we build a system to scale, we still want it to scale efficiently based on the pricing and packaging profiles of the different tenant personas you need to support. Giving all tenants free reign to consume as much of your system as they choose may sound appealing, but you can imagine the operational and cost efficiency burdens this could impose on the business. Tiering is often about striking a balance between the needs of tenants and the operational, performance, and availability profile of your overall environment. Even without tiering, you would still want to consider introducing controls that ensure that tenants can't consume resources at a rate that could bring down your system or impact the experience of other tenants.

For the next chapter of the book, I want to test the boundaries of how and where tenant infrastructure might land. Most of our discussion of multi-tenant architecture has been focused on environments where all of the components of your SaaS offering are running within infrastructure that is entirely under your control. While this is still the preferred model, we also need to consider what it means to support environments where parts of your system might be running in other environments. Here I'll look at some alternate deployment patterns and discuss how this more distributed footprint impacts the operational, agility, and architecture profile of your SaaS offering.

CHAPTER 15
SaaS Anywhere

Up to this point, I've presented a view of SaaS architecture that presumes that all of the system's resources are managed and controlled by the SaaS provider. In fact, so much of the value, scale, and efficiency of SaaS is achieved by hiding away the details of the system's underlying infrastructure. This is a cornerstone of the as-a-service mindset where tenants can only touch the surface (application, API, etc.) of your solution. Putting this wall in place allows teams to continually refine and optimize their environments, moving between technologies and designs without fear of impacting the tenants. At the same time, there are use cases where you may be required to stretch these boundaries, allowing parts of your SaaS architecture to be hosted in environments that may be controlled by your customer. This idea of having parts of your system running in multiple settings (in the cloud, on-premises, in a customer's account) is what I have labeled as SaaS Anywhere.

In this chapter, we'll start by looking at some of the fundamental factors that might have teams creating these SaaS Anywhere experiences. We'll explore some of the business and technical realities that drive this need to distribute resources to other environments, looking at how the choices you make here can influence the footprint of your SaaS business. I'll also review some of the core questions that you'll want to be asking yourself whenever you are considering adopting this model.

Next, I'll move into looking at specific SaaS Anywhere architecture patterns, identifying different remote infrastructure deployment strategies. The goal will be to outline the common models that are employed by SaaS providers and connect these models to the business, operational, and technical considerations that will come with adopting each pattern. You'll see that there are specific merits and potential challenges associated with these different configurations. As part of this, we'll also look at different approaches to integrating with the remote elements of your SaaS environment.

SaaS Anywhere, as you might suspect, has a significant impact on the operations experience of your solution. Deploying, provisioning, and operating resources that run outside of your environment will present teams a range of new challenges. Some of these challenges will have the potential to impact the agility, innovation, and efficiency of your SaaS business. The next part of this chapter will highlight some of the key areas you'll want to focus on and identify the complexities and trade-offs you'll need to weigh when enabling resources to run remotely.

I will regularly highlight the need to be cautious when considering a distributed SaaS model. While it can be a reality for some organizations, supporting it should not be taken lightly. The model and strategies you adopt here can have a significant impact on your ability to fully realize your full SaaS potential.

The Fundamental Concepts

At a high level, the basics of the SaaS Anywhere architecture model are relatively straightforward. The fundamental idea is that you'll be creating a multi-tenant environment that supports the *remote* provisioning, deployment, and operation of *parts* of your SaaS environment. For the purposes of our discussion, the idea of remote is pretty wide open, allowing for any environment that could be used to host some part of your system. Figure 15-1 provides a very simplified view of the most basic version of this concept.

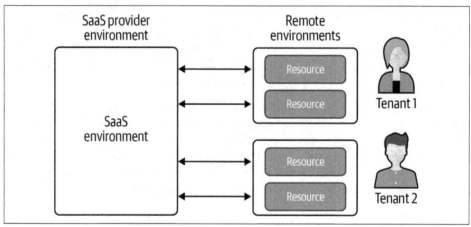

Figure 15-1. SaaS Anywhere conceptual view

While there's not much to this diagram, it gives you a sense of the basic moving parts of the SaaS Anywhere model. On the left is the environment where you host your SaaS solution. In a typical model, everything would be hosted in this environment. On the right are placeholders for the remote environments. Remote could be on-premises, in a tenant's cloud account, or running in the tenant's data center. The key is that these are per-tenant environments that are remote and generally tenant-owned. Within each environment, we have remote resources. These resources can be infrastructure or they could be code or services that are running on remote infrastructure. I'm generally going to refer to these as resources to be inclusive of whatever elements you run in a remote environment.

In looking at this, it may not seem like this should represent a significant shift from the strategies we've been discussing. The remoteness of a resource may not feel like it would have a significant impact on how you would approach designing, building, or operating your SaaS environment. However, as we get into the details, you'll develop a much healthier respect for the influence SaaS Anywhere can have on the design, implementation, and operation of your SaaS solution.

The sections that follow highlight some of the core principles that you'll need to consider as you set out to define the footprint and experience of any SaaS environment with remote resources. We'll get into more detailed examples later, but I want to start by ensuring that we have a clear mental model and foundation for this approach.

Ownership

When you have remote resources in a SaaS environment, you'll typically find yourself asking questions about who "owns" control in a distributed model. With this flavor of ownership, I'm less worried about who pays for these resources. I'm more focused on ownership through the lens of who configures, controls, updates, and manages these resources. To me, this is where all discussions about SaaS Anywhere must begin.

Part of the challenge with the idea of ownership originates from the fact that there are separate views of how you might describe ownership. Figure 15-2 provides a conceptual view of two distinct ways you could think about ownership.

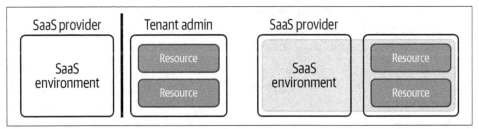

Figure 15-2. Ownership in SaaS Anywhere environments

On the left, the view of ownership draws a hard line between the SaaS provider and tenant environments. Here, the SaaS provider does not have control over the remote resources. In this mode, ownership is defined by who pays the bill for the infrastructure that is hosting the different resources that are part of your solution. If, for example, you have resources running in your tenant's cloud account or running in a tenant's data center, then the tenant or customer technically owns any parts of the system running in these environments. However, you can also think about ownership as being given to a SaaS provider. The SaaS provider is granted access and control to the remote environment, allowing them to provision, deploy, configure, and operate these resources—even though they're hosted on the tenant's infrastructure. This is shown on the right side of the diagram, which suggests that ownership is given to the SaaS provider who is then allowed to treat these resources as an extension of their current environment (with some caveats).

These views of ownership are at the epicenter of some of the key points of tension that you'll need to be thinking about when considering a SaaS Anywhere model. Up to this point, I've gone out of my way to describe an experience that put great emphasis on creating an environment where tenants have no visibility into the infrastructure used to implement that system. This foundational principle was at the core of retaining full control over the shape, operation, and configuration of all the moving parts of your SaaS environment.

So, what will it mean to adopt an architecture that has parts of your system distributed to other environments? Is it practical or a good idea to support this model or should this be considered a SaaS antipattern? To me, we can't always be quite that absolute. I think that you can best achieve the core values of SaaS when you are hosting all the moving parts of your architecture. At the same time, we can't ignore the realities of customer domains and business strategies that may present compelling use cases where parts of your system may need to be running in a remote model. This means we can't be so strict as to suggest that it's invalid to have parts of our system running in tenant-owned environments.

The more I looked at this problem, the more I realized that some flavors of SaaS Anywhere were inevitable. There are current and emerging business cases where SaaS providers will be required to adopt this approach. Latency, compliance, security, and a host of other domain-specific needs could all have some influence on how you may distribute the parts of your environment.

So, this brings us back to the fundamental ownership question we started with. I think it's fair to say that tenants might own these resources based on the purest definition of ownership. The real question we need to answer is: who controls these resources? That is at the heart of the ownership question, and it's also where this gets a bit sticky. In an ideal scenario, the SaaS provider would have complete and total control over any remote resources with privileges that allow them to provision, configure, scale, and manage these resources as if they were in the SaaS provider's environment. In this mode, the impacts of being remote would be much more manageable. At the same time, you're also right to be wondering if this is realistic. Would tenants really allow you to have this much control over these resources? If not, then you're going to likely live in some variation of a joint custody relationship where the tenant gives you selective control over the operations and accessibility of these remote resources.

This shared ownership model will likely require you to tackle a whole new range of challenges that will add complexity to the deployment, configuration, and operation of your overall SaaS environment. Now, you'll need to be thinking about how to orchestrate and synchronize changes with remote environments where you may not be able to dictate or control every aspect. You may find yourself working with tenant administrators to ensure that the remote environment remains in sync with the evolving needs of your architecture.

The more we drift down the path of distributed ownership, the more this can begin to undermine your broader SaaS vision. This is where you must play a critical role in helping the business understand how to navigate these challenging ownership questions. It becomes your job to figure out where and when it makes sense for your business to embrace the idea of having parts of your system run in a remote tenant environment. While you'll certainly want to listen to your customers and support their requirements, you also have to be protective of your SaaS environment. You have to go out of your way to ensure that you're surfacing and quantifying the potential impacts associated with adopting this approach, exposing your business and product leaders to the long-term trade-offs that could come with supporting this model.

The overall point I'm trying to drive home is that ownership is a delicate topic that requires careful analysis and consideration by business and technical teams. How you approach ownership may have a great impact on the future profile of your SaaS business.

Limiting Drift

My characterizations of what it means to be SaaS have included a heavy emphasis on having a single pane of glass that allows SaaS providers to onboard, deploy, manage, and operate all tenants through one experience—regardless of how tenants landed in their underlying architecture. This principle takes on even greater significance in a SaaS environment that must support distributed resources.

This, perhaps, could represent the biggest challenge of the SaaS Anywhere model. What level of compromise or bending of your SaaS fundamentals is too much? If you project this model out and consider its potential impact on your environment, you could imagine ending up with a long list of complicated constraints that are tying your hands. Ironically, the net effect of this could have you slowly drifting to a model that is more managed service than SaaS. Each little trade you make to support these resources could land you in a mode where you're constrained by all the operational complexity that is typically associated with non-SaaS environments.

So, how do you navigate this challenge? There are few absolutes. Foundationally, I think I would always start by asking myself how the presence of these remote resources is going to influence the success of the business. Will taking this approach allow us to target a clear customer need that's essential to landing and growing the business? I'd also evaluate how this approach would influence our ability to scale our operations, maintain our margins, and rapidly grow the business without feeling as though we've been penalized by the complexities inherited by supporting this distributed model. These are just examples of the parameters you have to evaluate as part of wandering into the SaaS Anywhere model. Think beyond the next few customers that may want this feature and consider a future where you may have many customers who are leveraging distributed resources.

Multiple Flavors of Remote Environments

I'm using remote as a general term here to describe any situation where some part of your system is running in another environment. In reality, what it means to be remote can still vary from one SaaS environment to the next. Each variation may influence the design and implementation of your SaaS solution.

Let's start with the simplest and most straightforward example of a remote model where your remote resources are hosted on premises. In this model, you may be running parts of your system in a tenant's data center or some other environment where the tenant has its own dedicated remote resources. In this model, your architecture will be heavily influenced by the nature of the on-premises environment. Here you might have to evaluate the available integration options and determine what level of control you'll have over the remote resources.

There's also another flavor of on-premises. In this model, the infrastructure that runs on-premises is provided by your cloud provider. This relies on remotely deployable hardware that supports a subset of the cloud provider's services, allowing tenants to meet their on-premises needs while still having access to cloud capabilities. AWS, for example, has AWS Outposts and Amazon EKS Anywhere that let you run versions of AWS services on premises. This approach can represent a good compromise for SaaS providers. This may also allow you to take advantage of cloud security and integration constructs to build the integration between your control plane and the remote services.

Finally, the last option we'll look at is one where everything is hosted in the cloud. The tenant's environment is only considered remote because it is running in a tenant's cloud account. This simplifies the remote model significantly, allowing you to leverage the built-in cloud constructs to integrate with remote resources. This tends to simplify the overall footprint of your SaaS Anywhere implementation and create more natural ways to control and manage the interactions between the control plane and the tenant environments.

These three distinct notions of remote resources highlight another layer of the SaaS Anywhere challenge. As you look at making any resource remote, you'll have to also think about how the nature of your remote environment might impact the integration, security, and performance of your solution.

Regional Deployments Versus Remote Resources

Some SaaS providers have a global footprint where they're hosting their offering in multiple geographies. In this model, you're essentially spinning up everything needed to run a full self-contained deployment of your solution within a geography or region. It might be tempting to think of this as a variant of SaaS Anywhere, but I don't equate these two models.

When your goal is to have multiple deployments of your solution, you're more focused on deploying entire copies of your application plane to each destination. The application plane you're deploying is meant to support all the tenants in that geography. This is quite different from hand-picking some specific resources of your application and selectively deploying them to a specific tenant's environment.

This discussion of SaaS Anywhere is focused more on experiences where your tenants would typically have no direct access to your underlying infrastructure. SaaS CRM or accounting solutions, for example, would not generally expose any of their underlying infrastructure to tenants. There are, however, scenarios where organizations might be offering infrastructure capabilities in an as-a-service model. In this mode, it might be less of a stretch for tenants to have exposure to infrastructure resources. This is more the byproduct of creating a service that is presented to builders, architects, and operations teams. My point is that the principles that guide how and when you might support remote resources could change based on the nature of your solution. The lines can certainly get blurrier as you factor in the realities of different domains and target personas.

Architecture Patterns

SaaS Anywhere is generally meant to characterize any environment where your SaaS architecture relies on remote resources. This means that there are plenty of permutations and configurations that fit into this model. At the same time, there are some distinct flavors of remote resources, each of which come with their own set of considerations. The goal is to highlight these fundamental SaaS Anywhere patterns and identify some of the impacts and considerations that are associated with each pattern.

Before we jump into these patterns, though, let's start by taking a high-level look at the core elements of the SaaS Anywhere model. Figure 15-3 provides a basic view of the most fundamental elements of a SaaS Anywhere environment.

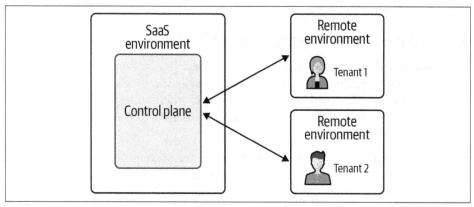

Figure 15-3. A centralized control plane

This diagram splits our SaaS architecture into two distinct halves. On the left, not surprisingly, is our control plane. The control plane continues to play its same key role, providing the central pane of glass that is used to manage and operate your SaaS environment. So, even as you move resources into remote tenant environments, you'll still need a control plane that can unify your approach to provisioning, managing, and configuring your remote resources. The goal is to require all the orchestration of remote resources to continue to go through the control plane, allowing you to avoid introducing one-off mechanisms to support any tenant-specific remote resource requirements.

On the righthand side of this diagram are our remote tenant environments. Across all these SaaS Anywhere patterns, you'll see that we're essentially landing services, databases, or other resources in a tenant owned environment. These tenant environments all have some flavor of integration with the control plane. In reality, this is often a two-way communication path where data is sent from the tenant environments and operations are triggered from the control plane. Much of how this works would depend on the nature of your technology stack and the types of resources that are deployed in each tenant environment.

It's important to note that all of these architecture patterns inherit a more complex availability model. The availability of your system and a tenant's experience is dependent on the availability of these remote resources. You'll have to consider how you might handle scenarios where these remote resources are unavailable. This could require a greater investment in creating the constructs and mechanisms that can gracefully detect and manage any failures that might occur in these remote environments.

In the sections that follow, I'll pick out some of the specific instances where teams see customer and domain requirements pushing the need to support remotely deployed resources. I'll outline the basic characteristics of each pattern and highlight some of the motivating factors that are driving adoption of each strategy.

Remote Data

Remote data is one of the most common SaaS Anywhere architecture patterns. There seems to be more companies, use cases, and business drivers that have organizations considering supporting a remote data model. Before we get into the details, though, let's start by looking at the SaaS architecture of environments that employ a remote data strategy. Figure 15-4 provides an example of a multi-tenant solution that's storing some of its data in a remote environment.

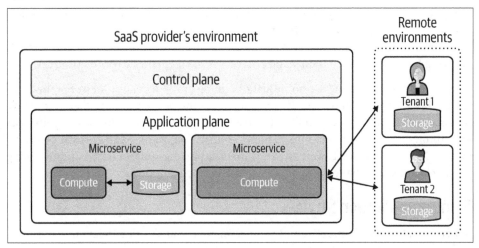

Figure 15-4. Remote data

In this diagram, you'll see that I've shown all the classic elements of a multi-tenant architecture on the left. In most respects, this environment conforms to all the same patterns and strategies that we've been discussing throughout this book. The one subtle difference is that one of my microservices is connected to remote storage (shown on the right). You'll notice that there is separate storage for each tenant in my system, and that my microservice must map each request to the appropriate tenant storage resource.

Moving storage out to the tenant's environment is usually motivated by a range of factors. Your domain could, for example, have some specific compliance or regulatory requirement that indicates that this particular data must be stored remotely. Tenants may also have specific security constraints that require portions of their data to be managed and stored in the tenant's environment. The source and size of a tenant's data might motivate some teams to have their data stored in a remote storage model. Here, the sheer volume of the data could make it impractical to move it into a SaaS provider's environment. The broader idea is that any number of factors (technical, performance, compliance, data size, etc.) could be at the root of steering teams toward a remote data model.

It's worth noting that supporting remote data does not mean that all of the system's data must be remote. Instead, you should try to identify the specific family of data that needs to be remote and retain control over the rest of the system's data. To highlight this point, the diagram in Figure 15-4 also includes a microservice that is storing its data within the SaaS provider's environment.

Whenever you're looking at supporting remote data, you'll also want to think about how this could impact the performance and security model of your solution. Certainly, with remote data, you'll have to think about how accessing the data remotely could impact the performance footprint of your solution. You'll also have to determine how you'll authorize access to these remote data sources. This will include applying tenant context to limit/control access to each tenant's storage resources.

While this need to support remote data is going to be a reality for some environments, I think you should be ready to challenge some of the thinking that might have tenants pushing for this capability. In most cases, the native capabilities of your SaaS environment should support most tenant's security, regulatory, and domain considerations. The key is I don't want to see teams supporting remote data without asking hard questions and challenging business/customer assumptions.

Remote Application Services

When you're thinking about remote environments, you shouldn't view this purely as accessing remote infrastructure. There may be instances where you move the services and code from your application plane to a remote environment. Figure 15-5 provides an example of how you might host your services in a remote tenant's environment.

On the left of this diagram, we have the foundations of our multi-tenant architecture hosted in the SaaS provider's environment. What's new here is that I've extracted full microservices from the application plane and hosted them in a remote environment. This means that my application plane now spans these two environments. The tenant environment essentially behaves as a logical extension of your application plane.

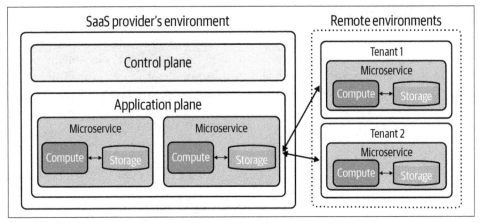

Figure 15-5. Running remote application services

Putting entire services in the remote environment is generally driven by a few factors. You may need to put the compute in the remote environment for regulatory reasons or you may have specific performance concerns that make it necessary to put these services closer to other resources in the remote environment. For example, I've seen stock trading solutions where the requirements for stock trade transactions made it necessary to host part of the trading solution nearer to the infrastructure and systems that were participating in the trade.

You could also see this approach applied in a scenario where you need the data to be remote and, as a result, you also move the application services to the remote environment to overcome latency or performance issues. Having the primary operations on the data performed via a remote service could limit the amount of data that would need to flow between the application plane and the remote services. How and when you might do this would depend very much on the nature of workloads and interactions between the data and the consuming services.

When you cross the boundary and move services to the remote environment, you take on yet another layer of operational, scale, and availability complexity. Your onboarding and deployment tooling, for example, will have to support provisioning and updating the services that are running in each tenant environment. Also, you'll have to determine how you'll approach scaling these remote services. You may have enough ownership of the remote environment to be able to configure the scaling profile of the services. If not, you may have to consider other strategies that will allow you to manage and configure the scaling profile of these remote services.

Remote Application Plane

There are some rare instances where you may find that your entire application plane needs to be hosted in a remote environment. In this mode, you're essentially saying that all of the tenant experience will be dependent on the scale and capabilities of the remote environment. Figure 15-6 provides an example of this model.

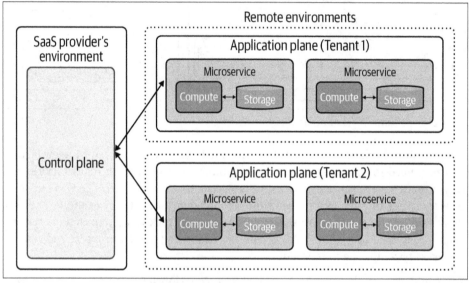

Figure 15-6. Remote application plane

With this approach, the SaaS provider's environment is trimmed down to a very small footprint. All that's here now is the control plane. Everything that was in our application plane is moved into the remote environment. When you take this approach, you're committing to a full stack silo model where each tenant is running their own fully dedicated set of application resources. Everything about this conforms to the same principles and considerations that come with adopting a full stack silo experience. The only unique twist is that the tenant silos are running in remote environments.

It's important to note that even in this model, our goal is to have a single version of the application that is run by all tenants. This may be more difficult to achieve when the tenant environments are remote, but it should still be the goal. A big part of the challenge here will be to identify a provisioning, configuration, and deployment strategy that can successfully span the two environments. You may find yourself introducing more fault-tolerance mechanisms to help overcome issues that might show up in individual tenant environments. For example, if you're deploying and something is down in a given tenant environment, can you create mechanisms that will handle these situations gracefully?

Adopting this model would represent a huge compromise for a SaaS business. It essentially eliminates any chance to achieve the economies of scale that come with having shared infrastructure. It also means that the scale, availability, and performance of your tenant environment would be directly shaped by the capabilities of the remote tenant environment. I've mostly included this to acknowledge that this can and will happen for some organizations. However, the business, technical, and operational trade-offs that come with this approach can be significant. So, if you're going down this path, you'll want to understand what this will mean to the growth, efficiency, and scale of your business.

Staying in the Same Cloud

The complexity of implementing the patterns I've outlined can change dramatically based on the nature of your remote environment. If you're running a cloud-based solution and the remote tenant environment is also running in that same cloud, the overall friction of this experience will be reduced.

When you're in the same cloud, your tenant environment will have access to all the same architectural constructs and services that are in the SaaS provider's environment. This simplifies what it means to run a remote resource. If, for example, I run an application service in the tenant environment that's running in the same cloud, that service can be scaled, built, and configured using the same strategies we would use if we were running it in the SaaS provider's environment.

To me, this is a critical nuance of the SaaS Anywhere story. Any time you're moving parts of your system to a remote environment, you're now dependent on the capabilities of that environment. This is why I think the spirit of SaaS Anywhere is best achieved when your remote services are running within the same cloud. The other flavors of remote environments are valid, but they add layers of complexity that are much more challenging to absorb.

Integration Strategies

As resources are made remote, you also have to consider how you will implement the integration between the SaaS provider and remote environments. There is no single solution that represents the preferred approach and the nature of your remote environment (on premises, cross-account, and so on) will certainly have some impact on the tools and technologies you can use to implement your integration.

For me, this discussion often starts with figuring out what kinds of interactions will flow between the two environments. Is this a chatty integration? Can the integration be asynchronous? How much data will flow between the environments? How will you secure the integrations? These are all just examples of questions you'll need to ask yourself as part of picking an integration strategy.

There's also a range of different technologies that are available to implement your integration. You might, for example, use a message-based integration model to connect the two environments or you might use a networking construct that allows the remote environment to fit more naturally into your overall infrastructure footprint. There's no right or wrong here. The path you choose will be dictated more by the realities of your remote environment and what it allows.

Operations Impacts and Considerations

If your solution is going to support remote resources, you should expect this to add a layer of complexity to your operations experience. Everything about how you provision, configure, onboard, and manage tenants can be impacted by the presence of remote resources. In fact, this is an area where ownership can complicate your architecture significantly. The fundamentals of how you access, configure, and manage remote resources may end up being dependent on what level of control you have over the remote environments.

Now that you have remote resources, you have to consider how this will influence the overall operational profile of your SaaS environment. You now have a dependency on a remote environment that has its own scale, availability, and performance footprint. The health of your solutions and the experience of your customers is, in some respects, dependent on this external entity over which you may have limited control.

The sections that follow highlight some of the key areas where supporting remote resources could impact the design and implementation of your architecture.

Provisioning and Onboarding

I've put a great deal of emphasis on the importance of having a fully automated onboarding experience. I've outlined sample architectures that had detailed onboarding flows that provisioned and configured all the resources needed to support each new tenant that's introduced into your environment. Now, as we look at the distributed resource model, we have to think about how the need for remote resources will impact the automation, efficiency, and durability of your onboarding experience.

There are lots of questions that come up here, most of which surround the ownership and lifecycle of your remote resources. In an ideal case, my tenant onboarding and provisioning process would have full control over its remote resources. This would mean that the onboarding constructs running in my SaaS environment would be able to directly provision, configure, and manage these resources. That would limit the impact of the SaaS Anywhere model, allowing me to create, update, and manage these resources as if they were part of my SaaS environment. There may still be performance and other concerns associated with the remote model, but having this level of control would certainly mitigate a fair number of the challenges associated with the remote resource model.

The issue is that it may be impractical for your tenant to allow you to fully control the lifecycle of the resources hosted in their environment. They could be entrusting you with a level of access and control that goes beyond what they're willing to support. It's here that everything can get much more complicated. If, for example, I have to create a remote database each time a tenant onboards, I'll need to have a much more staged onboarding experience that orchestrates the creation and configuration of that database. This could include requiring tenant administrators to run processing, scripts, or tools that you provide to provision and configure the tenant's new database.

Generally, the less control you have over a remote resource's provisioning, the more impact this will have on the agility and operational efficiency of your SaaS business. This is all part of the compromise that you have to consider when thinking about whether supporting remote resources is a good fit for your business. For some, the challenges may be offset by clear customer or domain needs. For others, it could have a stifling effect on your business and its ability to rapidly evolve based on its ability to own and control all of the underlying implementation.

Access to Remote Resources

Any time we move resources to a remote environment—even if it's in the same cloud—you have to think about how you are going to manage access to these remote resources from your SaaS environment. How this access is granted will vary based on the nature of the integration that you're performing. The key point is that, as part of your design, you'll need some mechanism or construct that grants you access to the remote environment. How and when this is done varies based on the nature of the integration and the resources you are accessing.

The security of your SaaS Anywhere model is also influenced by the type of remote environment you're accessing. If your remote resources are running on premises, for example, this could require a more specialized or targeted approach. Also, the services and tools you're using to integrate your environments (events, APIs, synchronous, asynchronous) will have a significant influence on how you secure the interactions between your environments.

There's one other consideration that may not be so obvious. There are scenarios where your remote environment may need to interact with your control plane. Remote services will likely need to send logs, billing events, and metrics and insights data back to the centralized control plane running in your SaaS environment. This means your remote services will need to be granted access to these aspects of your control plane.

Scale and Availability

Multi-tenancy requires teams to focus heavily on the scale and resilience of their solutions. Any outage in a SaaS environment has the potential to impact all tenants. Building a solid scaling and resilience strategy is hard enough when you have full control over all the resources of your environment; now imagine how supporting remote resources adds complexity to this story.

If your resources are running in a remote environment, you may now have less control over how those resources address scale and promote high availability. With SaaS Anywhere, you now have to put external dependencies into your overall scale and availability model. What if there's some outage in the remote environment? How will your system respond gracefully to this outage without impacting other tenants? How will you manage and detect these outages and surface them to your operations teams? These are just examples of the questions you'll need to take on when you consider supporting remote resources as part of your model.

Operational Insights

No matter where your solution is running, your solution will still need to provide a single, unified view of operational health and activity. This means that even if we have remote resources, the consumption, health, and operational insights for these resources must still surface alongside all the other operational data that we use to manage and operate a SaaS solution.

To make this work, we need our remote resources to publish metrics, logs, and any other operational data back to the control plane of our SaaS environment. If, for example, you have a remote microservice, that service should still publish all the operational data and insights that it would normally publish if it were running in the SaaS provider's environment. Having this data centrally accessible is essential to be able to detect and troubleshoot issues associated with any remote resources.

In general, the added complexities and challenges that come with the SaaS Anywhere strategy require a strong commitment to operational tooling that allows you to more proactively deal with the potential issues that can surface in these environments.

Deploying Updates

The use of remote resources has a direct impact on the deployment footprint of your SaaS offering. As you roll out updates, your infrastructure automation code will need to include support for deploying services, updates, and other changes to each tenant's remote environment. Your implementation of these concepts will depend heavily on how much control you have over the remote resources.

Imagine rolling out an update that requires an incremental change to your remote database schema. If you have full control, you can apply this change directly. If you don't, then you need to figure out how you'll coordinate this change with the owners of the remote environment. You also have to consider how you might handle scenarios where some part of the remote update fails.

The key here is that you're going to need to reevaluate the scope and nature of your multi-tenant deployments, accounting for some of the challenges that might come with deploying to any remote resource.

Conclusion

SaaS Anywhere is a topic that pulls me in two directions. The architect in me wants to maintain full control over all the moving parts of my architecture so that I have few constraints on how I construct a multi-tenant solution. On the other hand, I know that businesses and domains can impose requirements that force me to test my boundaries. The idea of introducing SaaS Anywhere in this chapter was to acknowledge these realities and begin to look at how you can build a distributed multi-tenant environment without completely compromising on the foundations of your SaaS architecture.

I started the chapter by outlining some of the core principles of the SaaS Anywhere model. The goal was to provide a high-level view into the core concepts that come with creating a multi-tenant architecture that supports a model where portions of your solution are running in a remote environment. A key part of this discussion centered around the role of ownership and how it influences the footprint of your SaaS Anywhere strategy.

From there, I moved more into architecture patterns, looking at different types and scopes of remote resources. The goal was to tease some of the typical patterns that SaaS providers may need to support. I looked at remote databases, remote microservices, and a fully remote application plane and highlighted some of the considerations that come with different types of remote resources. The idea was to expose you to some of the possibilities, realities, and motivations that could come with deploying parts of your system in a remote model.

I wrapped up the chapter by looking at operations, one of the most critical areas to evaluate when you're considering supporting remote resources. I highlighted a handful of areas where I saw SaaS Anywhere adding new dimensions to your overall SaaS operations story. We looked at its impact on scale, availability, deployment, operational insights, and security.

I see SaaS Anywhere as a bit of a balancing act. Teams can and should embrace this model where it makes sense. At the same time, adopting this approach should come with a healthy dose of introspection. Any move down this path needs to be weighed against the overall growth, agility, and innovation profile of the business. The more your business is counting on agility to fuel growth, the more you have to think about how supporting a remote resource model is going to complicate that growth.

As we move to the next chapter, I want to begin looking at what it means to build multi-tenant SaaS applications with generative AI (GenAI). With the emergence of GenAI, we now have a range of strategies to consider when determining how we'll use the power of GenAI to create value and differentiation for tenants and SaaS businesses. As part of this, we'll also have to look at how GenAI influences core SaaS concepts (noisy neighbor, isolation, tiering, and so on). The goal will be to give a good sense of the GenAI and SaaS landscape, highlighting some of the areas where multitenancy influences your GenAI implementation.

## CHAPTER 16

GenAI and Multi-Tenancy

The whole world of software development is asking itself how and where they can introduce generative AI (GenAI) into their offerings. GenAI has opened an entire new front of opportunity that has teams evaluating how and where they can introduce GenAI constructs into their architecture. If we look at the potential of GenAI, you can imagine that it could have profound impacts across applications from a wide range of domains and use cases. For our purposes, though, I wanted to identify areas where SaaS providers could mix GenAI constructs with multi-tenancy to deliver new experiences that could differentiate their offerings. With that in mind, I've focused this chapter on outlining specific GenAI architecture strategies that enable SaaS providers to introduce tenant contextual capabilities into their GenAI model. This added context would allow SaaS providers to have a single, shared multi-tenant GenAI footprint that applies tenant context to inference, yielding responses that are tailored to the needs of individual tenants. This also opens an entirely new landscape of multi-tenant considerations. Isolation, noisy neighbor, cost, and pricing are new territory that will require new approaches to applying these principles in a multi-tenant context.

To get started, though, we'll need to establish a foundation, reviewing some of the core concepts that come with building a multi-tenant solution that includes GenAI-enabled capabilities. The goal here is to bring more clarity to the overall GenAI and SaaS landscape by outlining the fundamental building blocks before considering what it means to integrate multi-tenant realities into your overall GenAI strategy.

With the basics in place, the chapter then begins to examine specific GenAI constructs and mechanisms that you can configure to support per-tenant GenAI functionality. The idea is to consider what it means to have a single large language model (LLM) that is shared by all tenants while still supporting the ability to surround that LLM with per-tenant configuration that enables unique tenant or domain experiences. The two constructs we'll examine are Retrieval-Augmented Generation (RAG) and fine-tuning, highlighting the nuances that come with applying these mechanisms to your multi-tenant architecture.

As I introduce these new GenAI capabilities, we'll also have to consider what it means to apply core multi-tenant principles to these constructs. For this part of the chapter, we'll look at how classic multi-tenant concepts like tenant isolation, noisy neighbor, and onboarding can be applied to these new mechanisms. How do you isolate GenAI requests? How do you ensure that tenants don't saturate your system? These are some of the new areas you'll need to be thinking about as you introduce GenAI into your environment. Finally, I'll wrap the chapter up by exploring how these GenAI strategies might influence the footprint of your pricing, cost attribution, tiering, and throttling strategies.

The broader goal here is to simply start the multi-tenant GenAI discussion, identifying some of the potential areas where GenAI and multi-tenancy intersect. It's essential that as GenAI is emerging and begins finding its way into more SaaS solutions, we continue to consider how and where it might influence the overall footprint of our SaaS architecture. It's also worth noting that this is a rapidly evolving space and the guidance is a bit of a moving target in the near term.

Core Concepts

Before we get into the specifics of multi-tenant GenAI, it makes sense to establish a bit of a foundation to better understand the landscape of technologies. Then, we can look at what it means to add layers of multi-tenant constructs and principles on top of these fundamental concepts. Figure 16-1 provides a highly simplified view of some of the core building blocks that are part of GenAI experience.

For this diagram, I've tried to create a bit of a hierarchical view of some of the key elements of the GenAI landscape, focusing on the elements that will play a bigger role in our review of multi-tenant strategies.

If we explore this view from the bottom up, you'll see that we start out with the most essential aspect of any GenAI experience. This is where we see the LLMs that represent the center of the GenAI universe. It's these models that have been trained to take all of our inputs, process them, and yield the responses that are needed to support the different GenAI features and capabilities of our SaaS solution. These LLMs have gone through significant training that allow them to take on a wide range of requests.

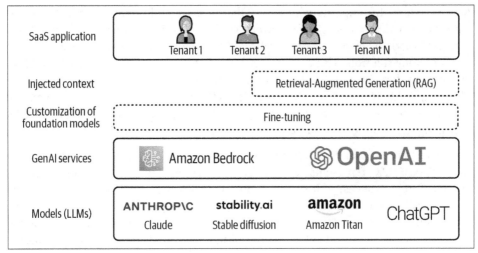

SaaS application	Tenant 1	Tenant 2	Tenant 3	Tenant N

Figure 16-1. Fundamental GenAI building blocks

There are, of course, multiple LLMs, each of which has its own nuances. Some may be better suited for certain domains or types of requests. For example, some may be targeted at image generation and others may focus on language translation. I've listed a handful here to give you a sense of the growing range of possibilities. Some of these are tied to the AWS GenAI service and some are bound to the OpenAI service. The key point is that, as part of bringing GenAI into your SaaS solution, you'll have to consider which LLM best suits your needs.

A level up from the LLMs are the GenAI services that sit on top of these LLMs. These services provide the APIs and constructs that developers can use to configure and invoke operations on the underlying LLMs. I've shown Amazon Bedrock and OpenAI, both of which bring their own unique wrinkles to the GenAI builder experience. For the simplest of use cases, this could represent the entry point for your SaaS application. Your solution could simply invoke requests on these GenAI services, get your responses, and be done. This would be a very simple scenario that doesn't really introduce many multi-tenant considerations. Still, for some solutions, this could be a valid path.

As we move further up, though, this is where we see additional capabilities layered onto the GenAI services. The first layer I've shown is fine-tuning. The basic idea is that an LLM, on its own, may need some additional level of refinement to support the needs of your solution. Think of this as extending the core capabilities of the LLM, introducing domain or other layers of context that can be used to supplement the LLM's capability in ways that will allow it to better target the specific requirements of your solution. I've shown this fine-tuning as a dashed box that sits on top of the LLM, indicating that it optionally builds on the full GenAI scope and experience.

Above fine-tuning, you'll also see a layer that represents Retrieval-Augmented Generation (RAG). RAG represents yet another way that you can augment the capabilities of your GenAI experience. It too is an optional construct that can refine and target your overall GenAI experience. It sits outside the GenAI services, augmenting the prompts that are fed into these services. We'll get into fine-tuning and RAG in much greater detail later in the chapter. At this point, I want to identify these basic building blocks and outline the role they play in the overall footprint of the GenAI solution.

Finally, at the very top of this diagram, you'll see a multi-tenant SaaS application. This is more of a conceptual placeholder that represents the interaction between your multi-tenant environment and its underlying GenAI constructs. This environment might interact directly with GenAI services with no tuning or augmentation, or it may rely on these tenant-focused refinements to target the needs of specific tenants and domains.

The Influence of Multi-Tenancy

With the basic building blocks in place, let's look at how the key moving parts of this GenAI puzzle are introduced into the design of an application. Let's start with the simplest possible flavor of how you might introduce GenAI into any environment. Figure 16-2 provides a conceptual view of the basic elements of a SaaS application interacting with a GenAI service.

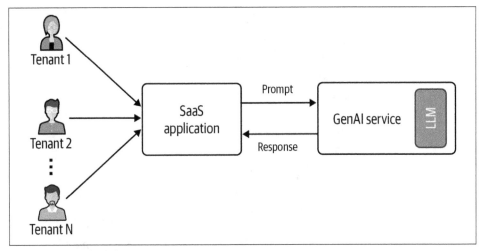

Figure 16-2. A simple GenAI integration

This is as simple as it gets. Our SaaS application simply takes requests from tenants, sends prompts to the GenAI service, and gets a response. In this mode, there's nothing here that would offer any of these tenants a distinct experience. In fact, if they all sent in the same request, they would all get the same response. There's simply nothing we're doing to apply any tenant context in a way that would influence the output of our GenAI interactions. In reality, the application that's invoking the GenAI service could be any application (multi-tenant or not). This could still be a valid model. It just doesn't connect to this idea of generating more contextual responses based on the profile of your tenants.

How, then, do we alter this approach and make it more inclusive of tenant context? What strategies can we introduce to inject tenant context into our overall GenAI experience? To better understand our options, let's look at another multi-tenant GenAI approach that begins to apply tenant context to our overall experience (shown in Figure 16-3).

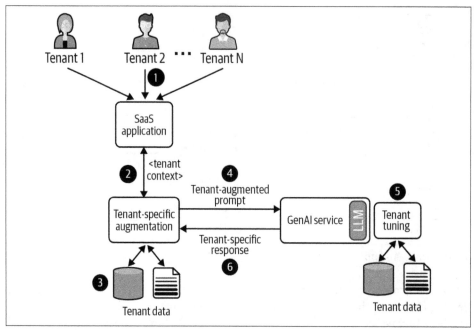

Figure 16-3. GenAI with tenant context

You'll see that I've extended the basic model shown in Figure 16-2, adding a few more elements that apply tenant context to this experience. If we work the diagram from left to right, you'll notice a collection of tenants that are interacting with my SaaS application (step 1). This part of the experience is no different than what you saw in the prior example.

What's new here is this notion of tenant-specific augmentation. This is where added a new construct that sits between the SaaS application and the GenAI service. The idea is that something sits between my application and the GenAI service that introduces tenant-specific augmentation context into the process. So, tenant context will be part of the GenAI invocation process (step 2), using tenant-specific data to augment the request (step 3). Now, the requests that will go to your GenAI service will be altered with our tenant context (step 4). In addition to augmenting our requests, you'll also see that we can add tenant-specific fine-tuning to the LLM (step 5), which may also be refined based on tenant/domain data. This combination of augmentation and fine-tuning will influence the output that is yielded for each tenant request (step 6).

There are two key dimensions of this model. First, and most obvious, is the idea that we're intentionally extracting and applying tenant context across our interactions with the GenAI service. The aspect of this that's easier to miss is the additional tenant data represented here (with RAG and fine-tuning). The key is that we're not just altering and generating prompts based on some static parameters. Instead, we're providing additional tenant data that provides a richer model for shaping the end-to-end experience.

As you can imagine, introducing these tenant-specific constructs opens up all kinds of questions. How these constructs are created, how they're isolated, how they're represented, and even how they're routed are all on the list of factors you'll need to consider when you add tenant context to your GenAI experience. So, while the diagram in Figure 16-3 is more conceptual, you can imagine how supporting multi-tenancy could influence the design and implementation of your GenAI architecture. The upside, though, is that this added complexity will also allow you to offer tenants unique, targeted GenAI experiences that can differentiate and target your SaaS solution.

Creating Custom Tenant AI Experiences

The idea of applying tenant context may still seem a bit abstract at this point. To help make this a bit more concrete, let's consider an example where we might use this approach in a specific domain where you could use the power of this per-tenant customization to create a powerful and distinct experience for different tenants. Figure 16-4 provides an example scenario that highlights how you might support per-tenant GenAI customization in an ecommerce setting.

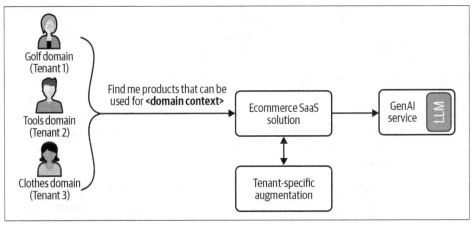

Figure 16-4. An example of per-tenant GenAI

For this solution, we have a general ecommerce platform that allows different tenants to create their own custom stores on the platform. The nature of the stores that are selling on this platform could span any number of different product categories. In this example, I've included three different tenants that sell products from three very different product categories (golf, tools, and clothes). Each of these tenants, as part of their onboarding, supplied data to provide more context about the nature of the products sold by their store.

Now, on the surface, it may seem as though these three stores are still just stores. They list products, process orders, and so on. It's true that there are core operations and capabilities that span these different stores. However, you can also imagine that the experience of shopping for golf clubs might be quite different from the experience of buying tools or clothes. As a shopper, I could ask the system to find me golf clubs that have attributes that are very specific to the type of club, the golfer's capabilities, and so on. Or, I might just ask it to recommend a club based on my preferences. It's here that I can introduce tenant-specific refinements into my GenAI experience that allow it to generate a more targeted response for the golf domain. The same would be true for the tools and clothes domains.

While this may be a bit oversimplified, you can see how a multi-tenant environment could take advantage of these GenAI refinement mechanisms to enable our LLMs to generate much more custom and tenant-contextual responses. The power of this model enables SaaS providers to build on the core capabilities of existing LLMs while still introducing constructs that allow them to create added dimensions of value and differentiation for their customers.

A Broad Range of Possibilities

I've focused most of my attention on creating more tenant-contextual GenAI experiences. However, it's important to note that there are a range of additional areas where SaaS providers may apply GenAI to their environments. The challenge in outlining these other applications of GenAI is that the solutions and strategies will vary significantly based on the nature of your environment and business model.

There are a few areas that are emerging as good candidates for applying GenAI to your overall SaaS business. For example, some teams are looking at how they can apply GenAI to their customer journey, using it to analyze, refine, and orchestrate the movement of tenants through the various stages of their overall life as a tenant. This can be applied to all phases of the customer lifecycle, touching everything from customer awareness to advocacy.

Operations is another area with GenAI potential. SaaS environments often track a wide range of insights and metrics that can assess trends, health, and activity patterns that can be valuable in both operations and business contexts. The assumption at this stage is that this data and GenAI could be combined in a model that enables operations teams to have richer, more dynamic, and more insightful views into the activity of their SaaS environment. This could include asking questions that have broader business implications. Why is time-to-value slowing down for customers? Is the agility of our release process improving? How frequently are we successfully rolling out updates? How did the most recent update impact performance? This is just a sampling of possibilities. In reality, I think the questions would eventually be more exotic, allowing teams to ask more difficult questions. Imagine a SaaS GenAI experience that suggested optimizations, made load predictions, identified potential isolation challenges, and so on.

The main takeaway is that the scope and role of GenAI in SaaS—like so many other settings—could be broader than you might expect. As you begin to explore the GenAI space, you should consider how and where it can be applied across more dimensions of your business.

SaaS and AI/ML

While GenAI seems to get all the buzz, it would be wrong to presume that GenAI is the one and only target for the experiences I'm outlining here. The reality is, there are lots of solid multi-tenant strategies that are a natural fit for artificial intelligence/machine learning (AI/ML) that should not get overshadowed by GenAI.

In the GenAI world, most of our multi-tenant energy is focused on augmenting the LLM with tenant context (where it makes sense). With AI/ML, however, this dynamic shifts. It's more likely that you may be creating and training ML models to support the needs of your SaaS solution. In that mindset, we open a whole new range of opportunities and use cases. Now, as we're deciding how and where we want to use AI/ML, we can think about what it would mean to offer individual tenants entirely custom ML models. The model itself and your ability to train and consume it for tenants can become a differentiating aspect of your SaaS offering.

This idea of having per-tenant AI/ML models ends up mapping pretty naturally to the tiering and economies of scale strategies that we've discussed throughout this book. I can, for example, have a single, pooled ML model that offers a baseline experience to my basic tier tenants. These tenants all share some pre-packaged model with no support for tenant specialization. Then, for my premium tier, I could offer a more custom experience where they would upload their training data and create a tenant-specific ML model.

You can see how this could represent a compelling strategy for some SaaS organizations, using the power of ML to drive targeted tenant experiences. There are also instances where organizations might build their own ML models and deliver them in a model-as-a-service offering. With this approach, SaaS providers would build their own models and monetize them as services that are consumed by their tenants.

This AI/ML space also introduces more knobs and dials that can control how your inferencing is delivered to tenants. If you're using Amazon SageMaker, for example, you could configure the consumption profile of your AI/ML inference requests. The service supports mechanisms that allow you to pool inferencing across tenants, using economies of scale for your inferencing. It also offers mechanisms for dedicated inferencing that can support the SLAs and noisy neighbor requirements of higher tier tenants. In general, AI/ML tends to be less of the black box that you see with GenAI, allowing you to have more influence over the configuration of your inference infra-structure.

The universe of SaaS AI/ML strategies is a bit better understood and maps more nat-urally to the general principles and strategies we've been exploring. I suggest that you take a closer look at your options in this space to figure out whether AI/ML might be better fit for aspects of your SaaS offering. For the scope of this chapter, though, I wanted to focus more on GenAI nuances since I believe so much of the multi-tenant GenAI landscape is undefined.

Introducing Tenant Refinements

I've highlighted the basic notion of tenant refinements. Now it's time to go a bit deeper and examine the mechanics and details that come with using these techniques in a multi-tenant environment. The goal is to give a bit more definition to the con-cepts to help crystallize what it means to augment the GenAI experience with tenant context, giving you a clearer mental model for where these constructs fit within the overall GenAI experience. In the sections that follow, we'll look at the two main tech-niques that can be used to introduce tenant-specific customizations. We'll start with Retrieval-Augmented Generation (RAG) before turning our attention to LLM fine-tuning. Both of these mechanisms, as you will see, represent very different approaches to creating a tenant-focused experience. I'll look at how they work inde-pendently as well as how they might be combined to support different needs.

Supporting Tenant-Level Refinement with RAG

RAG is a generalized GenAI mechanism that allows developers to apply targeted aug-mentations to your prompts. It allows you to pre-process and refine the nature of the inputs that are being sent into your GenAI service. To better understand the role of RAG, let's start by looking at a simplified SaaS environment that employs RAG to add tenant context to GenAI prompts (Figure 16-5).

In looking at this diagram, you'll notice this nebulous concept of tenant augmenta-tion at the bottom. Essentially, each of these images are meant to represent placehold-ers for the different tenant-specific constructs that you'd use to augment requests that are sent to the GenAI service. I've presented them this way to make it clear that how these RAG constructs are actually implemented can vary significantly based on the nature and needs of your SaaS solution. There are some well-defined mechanisms and tools that are often used in the RAG model. However, in reality, you could use any number of different technologies here to implement your augmentation model.

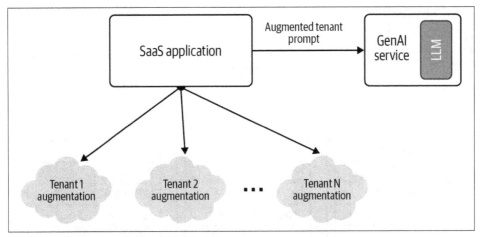

Figure 16-5. The basics of RAG and tenant context

It is tempting to think of these per-tenant refinements as somehow directly shaping the LLM or configuring the GenAI service. Neither of these are true with RAG, which is exclusively focused on augmenting the prompt that gets sent into the GenAI service. This means its impact is achieved purely through changing or refining the nature of the request.

This means that much of your focus will be on determining which combination of RAG mechanisms and tools best align with the multi-tenant needs of your solution. Will you be using a vector database, a search index, a relational database, or some other tool to define the shape of your multi-tenant RAG design? The list of options and design considerations here is certainly beyond the scope of this chapter. However, it will be an area you'll want to dig into to better understand the nuances that are associated with each of these different RAG approaches.

Given this backdrop, though, let's look at a slightly more concrete view of what it means to use a per-tenant RAG model in a SaaS setting. Figure 16-6 builds on our prior ecommerce example (Figure 16-4), providing a view of how you might refine the experience of individual stores within a SaaS ecommerce platform.

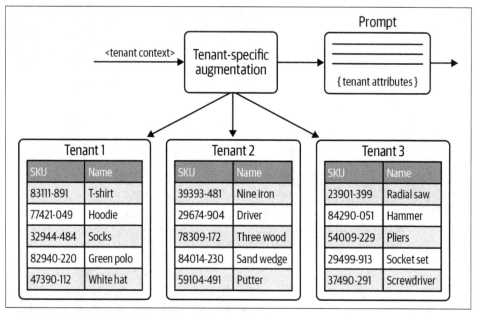

Figure 16-6. A SaaS ecommerce RAG example

In this diagram I have three different tenants, each of which is from a specific domain. For simplicity, I've shown the RAG data represented in a relational database that holds information about the nature of the different products that are available in a tenant's online store. Tenant 1, for example, represents a clothing store and includes data about different clothing items. Tenant 2, on the other hand, has product data about golf clubs.

While your actual RAG configuration and data would be much more exotic than this, this should give you a sense of how we're creating targeted, tenant-specific information that can determine how an LLM prompt will be augmented with parameters derived from this tenant-contextual RAG data.

The basic flow would be that, for each prompt that is being sent to our GenAI service, we'd have a mechanism that would use the current tenant context to augment a GenAI prompt with tenant-contextual information that yields a custom response for each tenant. The mechanics of how this would work would vary based on the tools you're using. There are libraries and helpers that connect all the moving parts of this experience, creating a more natural and seamless way to generate and submit augmented prompts.

As I noted, I kept this example intentionally simple. However, as you move into more complex RAG constructs, you'll have to consider how your tenant's specific RAG configuration will land in the different technologies that represent and store this RAG information. To highlight this point, I've included an example in Figure 16-7 that illustrates how you might use Amazon OpenSearch indexes to hold per-tenant vector information that can augment your GenAI prompts.

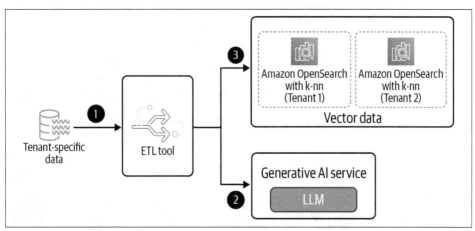

Figure 16-7. Create per-tenant OpenSearch indexes

For this example, you'll see a process that brings in tenant-specific data and processes it with extract, transform, load (ETL) tooling that extracts the data that will populate our tenant-specific indexes (step 1). The new wrinkle here is that this process also relies on the GenAI service and LLM to compute the vectors for each of the tokens that are processed (step 2). Once these vectors have been determined, they are inserted into our vector storage (step 3), which happens to be Amazon OpenSearch indexes. To get this to work, OpenSearch is configured with the k-nearest neighbor (k-nn) plug-in, which enables it to search for points in a vector space and find the "nearest neighbors" for those points.

Once these OpenSearch indexes are populated, our SaaS application can then use this data to augment our prompts. In this case, it will use the GenAI service to tokenize and get the embeddings. Then, it will use that data to execute a text-contextual similarity search against the tenant's OpenSearch index. The data from this search will be used to augment the prompt that is then sent into the GenAI service to get the final output.

The key is to highlight yet another model where RAG could be applied in a multi-tenant setting. You'll see lots of references to vector databases as part of RAG use cases, and I wanted to illustrate how tenancy can still be introduced into this model. Most of what you'd do here is very much in line with general vector database strategies. The main difference is that we need separate OpenSearch constructs to hold each tenant's vector data. Naturally, the vector storage tool you choose to apply will directly influence how you might partition each tenant's vector data.

With the RAG model, you have the option to determine how your data is represented for individual tenants. It's here that we have options to determine whether and how we want to have this data siloed or pooled for tenants. Figure 16-8 provides an example of a RAG configuration that uses a combination of silo and pool models for storing RAG information.

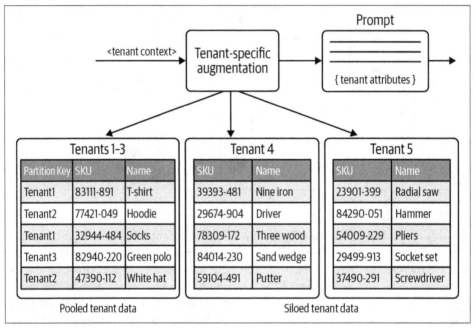

Figure 16-8. Siloed and pooled RAG data

In this diagram, you'll see RAG data for five different tenants. On the bottom right, I have two tenants with siloed data. Tenant 4 has RAG information for the golf domain and Tenant 5 has information for the tools domain. These tenants could be siloed for a variety of reasons, including performance and isolation.

At the bottom left of the diagram is where you'll see the pooled tenants. These tenants are all from the clothing domain and are placed in a table that is partitioned by tenant IDs. You could apply the pooling strategy here based on the specific operational or efficiency needs of the clothing domain. How or if you choose to pool this data would depend on the nature of your solution. The key is that the same data partitioning considerations that were part of our general multi-tenant data partitioning discussion can also come into play.

Supporting Tenant Refinement with Fine-Tuning

Fine-tuning provides you with yet another approach to refining and targeting the experience of your tenants. While RAG was more about pre-processing our requests outside the LLM, fine-tuning is more focused on altering the behavior of the LLM. This means that our fine-tuning is applied more directly to the LLM to extend and shape the experience it delivers. Figure 16-9 provides a conceptual view of the fine-tuning model that we'll be covering.

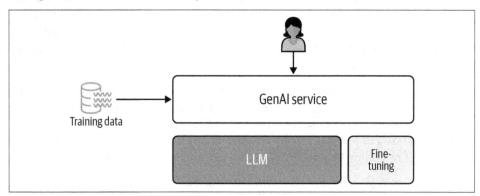

Figure 16-9. Basic fine-tuning concepts

In Figure 16-9, you'll see the fundamental concepts that are core to any GenAI experience. We essentially have clients that are sending prompts into our GenAI service and that service leveraging its underlying LLM to process your requests. What's different here is that we've also introduced fine-tuning into the environment, which will directly influence how the LLM will process requests (at the bottom right of the diagram). The assumption is that we're augmenting the behavior of the LLM, enabling it to provide more targeted and contextual responses that better align with the needs of our solution.

On the left of the diagram, you'll see that I've introduced the idea of training data. The idea is that as part of configuring and preparing your fine-tuning experience, you'll need to "train" your environment with this new contextual data. The nature and mechanisms that are part of this "training" process can vary based on the GenAI service you're using and the type of training that is being applied. For this particular example, I've shown a scenario that employs parameter efficient fine-tuning (PEFT), which augments the experience without changing the core LLM. This is conveyed by showing the tuning to be applied outside the scope of the LLM.

Once the training is done, the requests that are sent to our GenAI service will now include the added context that is provided by the fine-tuning. This approach to refining the LLM can be especially useful at creating a more targeted experience and enriching the overall capabilities of your SaaS offering. It's important to note that there are other fine-tuning strategies that take different approaches to augmenting the LLM. As you dig into fine-tuning, you'll want to explore the full range of fine-tuning options that are supported by your GenAI service.

Using global fine-tuning

Fine-tuning, as you can imagine, is a mechanism that you could apply with different strategies to support the requirements of a multi-tenant architecture. The first option I want to look at is the idea of using fine-tuning as a more global construct that can apply to all tenants. In this mode, we'd use fine-tuning to shape the overall footprint of the LLM without needing to handle or support any notion of tenant context. In this respect, global fine-tuning will be applied exactly as it would be in non-SaaS environments. It's just augmenting the LLM equally for all requests.

While this flavor of fine-tuning has few SaaS nuances, it still can represent a valuable tool for SaaS providers. Imagine, for example, that you create a SaaS solution for the healthcare domain and you want to refine the LLM, enabling it to more directly support the context and needs of healthcare-related tasks. This is where you would apply your global fine-tuning through PEFT or direct training of the LLM.

This can be an especially powerful construct for SaaS providers that are looking to hone the overall capabilities of their GenAI experience, allowing them to refine the core capabilities of the LLM and add the context of their specific domain. Yes, the LLM may be able to support the basic needs of your solution without requiring this global fine-tuning. However, for many, this level of fine-tuning could be seen as essential to creating an LLM experience that can target the unique needs and value proposition of their GenAI capabilities. In some cases, it could represent the core part of a SaaS organization's differentiating intellectual property.

Using tenant-level fine-tuning

Where fine-tuning gets more interesting is when we start thinking about how it can support tenant-specific refinements. The idea is that you could selectively apply fine-tuning on a tenant-by-tenant basis to enable custom LLM experiences for individual tenants. Figure 16-10 provides a conceptual view of the per-tenant fine-tuning strategy.

You can see how this move to per-tenant fine-tuning has influenced the design of the GenAI experience. At the bottom of the diagram, you'll now see that there are now logical pairings of the LLM and each tenant's fine-tuning configuration. There is still a single LLM, but the combination of the LLM and each tenant's fine-tuning represents a logical construct that can now be referenced separately when processing tenant requests. For example, the pairing of Tenant 1 and the LLM yields a logical model that is labeled ABC. Meanwhile the pairing of Tenant 2 and the LLM is now labeled XYZ. These labels are just conceptual placeholders. Each GenAI service will have its own way of representing and identifying these logical models.

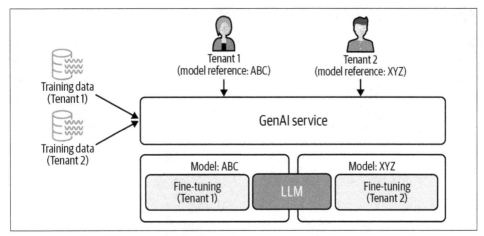

Figure 16-10. Enabling per-tenant fine-tuning

Of course, as part of introducing per-tenant fine-tuning, you'll also need to separate training data for each tenant (shown on the left). As each new tenant is onboarded to your environment, you'll need to include support for configuring the per-tenant fine-tuning and executing the training process. Naturally, there could be limits that you might approach based on the number of tenants that your system will need to support. You can also imagine scenarios where some tenants have per-tenant fine-tuning and other tenants are using shared fine-tuning (or they may have none). This comes back to how you might choose to package and tier the experience you're offering.

To use this strategy, you'll also need to consider tenant context as part of each invocation of the GenAI service. Somewhere within the code or libraries of your environment, you'll need to extract the tenant context for a given request and determine how it maps to a tenant's logical model identifier. Then, you'll need to use this identifier to invoke the GenAI service. This will allow your request to apply the appropriate, tenant-specific fine-tuning. This concept is shown at the top of the diagram where you'll see that Tenants 1 and 2 supply a model reference as part of parameters that would inject tenant context into their requests.

Combining RAG and Fine-Tuning

It should be clear at this point that RAG and fine-tuning take very different approaches to introducing tenant and domain context into your GenAI experience. While it's true that they are different, they should not be viewed as mutually exclusive. In reality, you could use both RAG and fine-tuning as part of your tenant-specific refinement strategy. Figure 16-11 provides one view of how you might combine RAG and fine-tuning to support the needs of your multi-tenant environment.

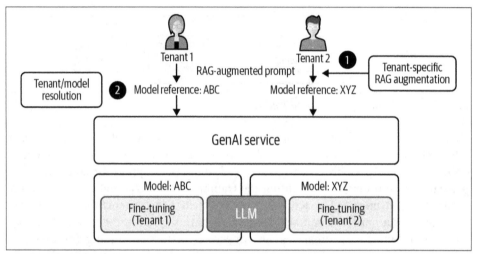

Figure 16-11. Combining RAG and fine-tuning

For this example, we are presuming there is some level of per-tenant customization that is best introduced through RAG and some additional level of refinement that would be best applied with fine-tuning. Combining them is about injecting and applying both constructs at the appropriate stage in the invocation process.

As each request is submitted, your solution will need to augment the prompt, using RAG to inject tenant-specific context into the request (step 1). Then, it will need to determine which logical model it will invoke to apply tenant-specific fine-tuning (step 2). This will send the augmented prompt to the appropriate per-tenant fine-tuned model for processing, ideally yielding a more tenant-targeted response.

Of course, this represents just one approach that you can use to combine RAG and fine-tuning. How you actually implement this would depend very much on the requirements and nature of your SaaS offering. Ultimately, this comes down to determining which flavor of tuning best targets the experience you need to support. There are no rules that dictate which combinations of RAG and fine-tuning are considered valid.

Applying General Multi-Tenant Principles

As you begin to introduce multi-tenant constructs into your GenAI experience, you should also consider how you will apply core SaaS principles to these new GenAI constructs. GenAI doesn't change any of the fundamentals, but it does open up some new areas where it may influence your broader SaaS environment. You still need to be thinking about how these GenAI elements will impact the scale, performance, agility, and efficiency of your SaaS environment. The sections that follow outline some of the key areas where GenAI can add new dimensions to your overall multi-tenant architecture.

Onboarding

As you introduce tenant refinements and other GenAI mechanisms into your SaaS environment, you are also introducing a range of new tenant-specific infrastructure elements to enable these refinements. Training data, vector databases, and fine-tuning add new elements to the footprint of your multi-tenant architecture. Of course, whenever you introduce any dedicated tenant resource, you must also consider how it will influence your overall onboarding automation. Figure 16-12 provides a glimpse of how GenAI configuration could be woven into your onboarding experience.

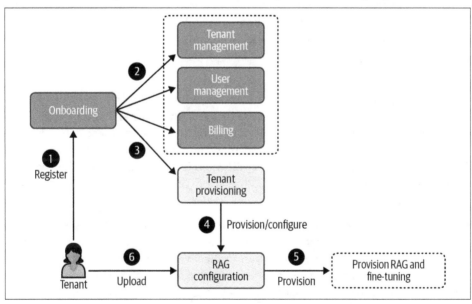

Figure 16-12. Onboarding with tenant refinements

For this example, I brought in some basics from our standard onboarding process. What's new are some additional placeholders that are meant to provide a flow to configure the moving parts of your tenant-specific GenAI refinements. If we walk through the steps, you'll see that we start with our tenant registering with our Onboarding service (step 1). This then goes through all the traditional motions to create a tenant, user, and configure billing (step 2).

The last bit of our onboarding flow invokes the Tenant Provisioning service to create and configure any required tenant resources (step 3). This is where I've added on a RAG Configuration service to capture the need to add support for creating the different GenAI tenant refinement elements (step 4). This would call the scripts and automation tooling that would create the storage and any other infrastructure needed to support and configure your tenant refinement model (step 5).

Now, once the tenant resources are provisioned, there's still some question about where the data for your refinements will come from. Is this data sourced from some existing part of your system or will it be provided by the tenant? Both scenarios could be valid. For this example, I included a scenario where the data would be provided by the tenant (step 6). This, of course, adds another layer of complexity to the onboarding experience. Your process may need extra logic or tracking to determine when the tenant can be considered active (based on when or whether they've uploaded their refinement data).

This only represents a sample of how these new GenAI mechanisms could shape your onboarding experience. The main point of emphasis here is that these GenAI refinement strategies come with new per-tenant resources that will certainly influence the design and implementation of your onboarding process.

Noisy Neighbor

The notion of noisy neighbor is a bit interesting with GenAI. In many scenarios, we naturally map being noisy to those tenants that are generating excess traffic. In a classic example, we'd tend to associate noisy neighbor with scenarios where one or more tenants are sending in a burst of requests that could be overloading your system and impacting other tenants. This concept is still valid in our GenAI model. You can certainly still have a tenant that is sending bursts of GenAI requests that are impacting the experience of other tenants.

With GenAI, however, there are other factors that can influence the noisy neighbor footprint of your environment. With GenAI workloads, the complexity of requests and responses also have some correlation to the level of load that is being placed on the service. This requires us to add another layer to our noisy neighbor model, introducing constructs that can evaluate the number of tokens and complexity of individual requests, ensuring that tenants aren't saturating your service with a stream of complex requests. This may also play into your overall tiering strategy, where tenants might be offered different SLAs for the parts of your system that rely on GenAI services.

This adds a new noisy neighbor wrinkle to your overall architecture, which now needs insights and tools that can track and assess the complexity load generated by individual tenants. You'll need visibility into this data to implement policies that can proactively detect and manage these noisy neighbor conditions.

Tenant Isolation

Any time you add data to a multi-tenant environment, you'll need to think about how that data will be protected from any cross-tenant access (intentional or unintentional). If I create vector databases, RAG data, or tenant-focused fine-tuning, I must also introduce the tenant isolation policies and strategies that can ensure that these resources are adequately protected. Figure 16-13 provides a conceptual look at protecting your tenant resources with isolation policies.

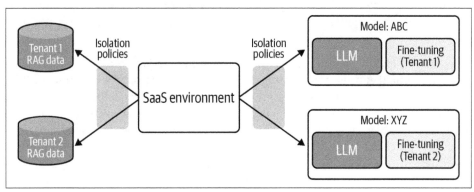

Figure 16-13. Isolating your multi-tenant refinement resources

This diagram includes examples of both RAG and fine-tuning tenant resources that need to be isolated from cross-tenant access. In the middle sits a placeholder for any code or mechanisms that might need to access the RAG and fine-tuning constructs. I've also included boxes to convey the idea that isolation policies need to be applied to any attempt to access these resources. These could be runtime-applied policies or they could be applied when the infrastructure is deployed (depending on the nature of the technology being used).

The challenge of this topic is that there are simply too many variations of technologies and strategies to implement multi-tenant refinement mechanisms. There are vector databases, search indexes, and a host of other technologies, each of which could require its own unique approach to isolating its data at the tenant level.

GenAI Pricing and Tiering Considerations

GenAI introduces a number of factors that can directly impact how you might choose to price, package, and tier your offering. While there is some guidance in this area, SaaS organizations are still searching for clear patterns and strategies that will help them create pricing models that incorporate the nuances that come with embedding GenAI into their SaaS environments.

The assumption is that pricing for GenAI capabilities will probably follow some pattern where the level of GenAI consumption will be woven into the overall pricing model of your SaaS offering. It might just be blended in, or it could be called out as a separate component of your billing model. There are simply too many permutations to make any sweeping generalities about what a preferred approach might be. In fact, while there are well understood pricing themes in the SaaS universe, the domain, market, and other realities of any one solution will often yield a mix of different pricing models.

If we start by looking at how GenAI services are billing today, we can get a good sense of how we might approach integrating these costs into our SaaS pricing strategy, Pricing for GenAI services tends to fit into a managed service model where the service exposes an API and hides away the details of its underlying infrastructure, enabling services to change in a pay-as-you-go model. The unit of cost for these services is derived from the complexity of the prompts that are submitted and the output that is returned. This complexity is metered based on the number of tokens in your prompt and the number of tokens in your output. There will be specific price points and tiers connected to these prompt and output token counts. You'll also see that these token price points can vary based on the LLM that you're consuming. This pattern is a bit atypical in that the cost is less about the volume of activity and more about the resources that are needed to process a prompt and generate its corresponding output.

There are plenty of other nuances that are part of the GenAI cost puzzle, but this notion of token complexity will likely be the primary influencer of cost in your system. You may also find that there are separate costs associated with fine-tuning your model.

Developing a Pricing Model

Given these GenAI pricing dynamics, we now have to figure out what it would mean to incorporate these costs into your overall SaaS pricing strategy. Your approach to pricing will likely be heavily influenced by how GenAI is embedded into your experience. Some may use GenAI in a model where its presence is entirely outside the view of tenants. Others may be surfacing GenAI in a way that more directly exposes the tenant to GenAI capabilities. Naturally, these two approaches could require very different pricing strategies.

Let's look at the embedded model first. Figure 16-14 provides a view of a SaaS environment that relies on GenAI as part of supporting some internal elements of your multi-tenant experience.

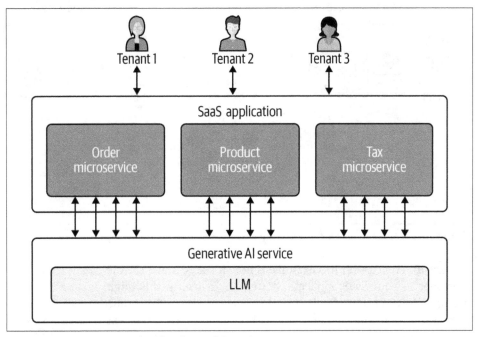

Figure 16-14. Pricing with a fixed set of GenAI interactions

In this diagram, you'll see three microservices, each of which has some level of interaction with the GenAI service. While the prompts and output for these interactions could include some level of parameterization, they would likely have relatively predictable tokenization profiles. This more controlled experience would likely allow you to have enough data to develop some reasonable estimate of the cost that would be associated with these different operations, enabling you to better predict how these workloads will contribute to the overall cost profile of your solution.

Pricing gets much more complicated when the interactions with a GenAI service are more open-ended. Consider, for example, a scenario where your SaaS environment more directly exposes elements of the GenAI experience to tenants (via a chatbot, for example). In this model, the nature and token complexity of the prompts and output could vary wildly. This would make it almost impossible to have any kind of fixed pricing since the variations in your tenant consumption patterns could cause significant swings in your infrastructure costs.

In these scenarios, you may choose to measure this consumption and integrate these costs directly into your overall pricing model. The question is: how will you capture those consumption events and correlate them to specific tenants? To get here, you'll need to introduce mechanisms that will analyze prompt and output complexity, connecting this consumption to individual tenants. Figure 16-15 provides a conceptual view of how you might capture and publish your GenAI-related billing metrics.

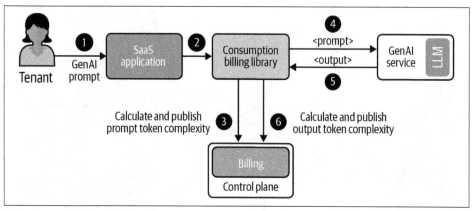

Figure 16-15. Capturing and calculating token complexity

The key difference with this example is how it starts. You'll see the tenant submitting a prompt to your SaaS application (step 1). In reality, this might not be an actual prompt. However, the idea is that the tenant is submitting something of unknown complexity into our system (instead of the more fixed example we saw in Figure 16-14).

When this request gets processed by the application, it is then ready to be sent to the GenAI service for processing. However, before it's processed, it is evaluated by a consumption billing library (step 2). This library is a conceptual placeholder that could be introduced via a microservice or some other construct that can intercept and process inbound requests. In this example, it calculates the complexity and sends a metering event to the billing service that resides in your control plane (step 3).

From here, the prompt is then sent to the GenAI service (step 4). When the output is returned by the GenAI service (step 5), our library will also intercept the output, evaluating its complexity and publishing a second metering message to the billing service (step 6).

The prompt and output consumption data captured by this process would be aggregated by the billing system and incorporated as one piece of your overall billing model. The key here is that, if the consumption is unpredictable, you're likely to surface this as part of your overall billing model to prevent a tenant from imposing unexpected infrastructure costs on your system.

It's worth noting that this same construct could have value beyond pricing and billing. I've outlined the general importance of having insights into per-tenant consumption activity and correlating that consumption to costs to arrive at a cost-per-tenant metric. The data from this mechanism could also be used to surface GenAI consumption that would contribute to analyzing the cost-per-tenant profile of your environment.

Creating Tiered Tenant Experiences

Tiering has been a big theme throughout our discussion of SaaS. And, not surprisingly, tiering is also likely to be part of your GenAI story. It would not be unlikely for SaaS providers to associate SLAs with their GenAI capabilities, using tiering to offer a range of throughput levels at different price points. This would also enable you to limit the level of consumption that is imposed by lower-tiered tenants, preventing them from imposing excess infrastructure costs and, potentially, impacting the experience of other tenants.

To make this a bit more concrete, let's consider a scenario where you have basic and premium tier tenants. Now, for the GenAI part of your system, you may want to introduce a throttling mechanism that could control the consumption activity of each of these tiers. Figure 16-16 provides a view of the moving parts of this strategy.

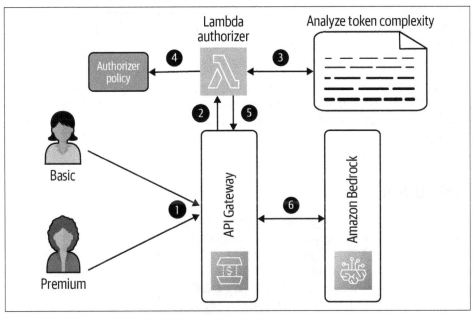

Figure 16-16. Tiering and throttling GenAI requests

This approach uses the same interception strategy that we used for pricing. In fact, this could be a shared concept that supports your tiering and pricing requirements. Essentially, we need some way to evaluate each inbound request to determine whether it may trigger a tiered throttling policy. On the left of the diagram, you'll see two different tenant tiers submitting requests (step 1). Now, to make this a bit more concrete, I've shown this example using AWS services. Specifically, you'll see that I've put an API Gateway in front of my GenAI service (in this case, Amazon Bedrock).

Each request that is sent to the API Gateway will be processed by a Lambda authorizer (step 2). This serverless function will evaluate the complexity of the incoming prompt (step 3). The output of this complexity analysis determines if the request should be allowed to proceed, configuring the authorizer policy with the allow/deny state (step 4). This configuration will then go back to the API Gateway (step 5) and, if allowed, it will all be sent to Amazon Bedrock for processing (step 6).

Admittedly, this is a relatively simple model that attempts to use the existing mechanics of the API Gateway throttling to control access to the GenAI service. While there may be more elegant ways to achieve this, the concepts are still valid. Essentially, this is all about evaluating prompt complexity and using it as part of a tier-based throttling policy. In some instances, you may also consider combining complexity with frequency data as part of your throttling model.

There is one additional approach to tiering that is less about the specific consumption activity of tenants. Since GenAI services generally support multiple LLMs (each with their own nuances), you could choose to offer access to different LLMs at different tiers or price points, so a basic tier tenant could get the lower cost LLM, while a premium tier tenant may have access to a presumably "better" and more costly LLM.

Overall, it's tough to really know which of these strategies might fit with your environment. There are simply too many variables to map this to any absolutes. A lot also depends on how the GenAI service is being used within your environment. If the service is entirely internal, this would have different dynamics than a solution that was exposing the GenAI service more directly.

Conclusion

This chapter was meant to give SaaS builders a glimpse of some of the tools and techniques they can use to introduce GenAI capabilities into multi-tenant environments. My goal was to identify some of the patterns and strategies that represent the intersection between GenAI functionality and the realities of SaaS environments, which included looking at how you could use targeted GenAI tenant refinements in a way that would bring more value to your offering and to your overall tenant experience.

This started with a review of core GenAI concepts where I outlined the basic elements of the GenAI architecture footprint. As part of this, I provided a view into how multi-tenancy could be folded into the GenAI experience. I then shifted into more concrete concepts, looking at how constructs like RAG and fine-tuning can create tenant-specific refinements. Understanding how and where these constructs enable you to create custom tenant experiences is key to understanding the range of multi-tenant possibilities within the GenAI landscape.

The chapter then shifted to exploring some of the broader implications that come with employing these constructs in a multi-tenant environment. Here we looked at how and where core SaaS concepts like tenant isolation, noisy neighbor, and onboarding are influenced by the presence of these new constructs. Finally, the chapter finished up by exploring how GenAI can influence the tiering, pricing, throttling, and cost model of your solutions.

It should be clear at this point that the notion of GenAI and SaaS is an emerging topic. My goal was to do what I could to surface some of the current possibilities knowing that this space is evolving rapidly and that new options will continue to surface new strategies and principles. It's likely that some of the techniques I covered here were not intended to be applied as per-tenant constructs. However, that's how most multi-tenant architecture finds its way into different tools, services, and environments. We have to begin to figure out what can be made to work with the tools we have right now and expect that the needs of multi-tenant providers will ultimately drive the evolution of these tools and services.

Now that we've covered GenAI and the broader SaaS strategies and architecture patterns, I want to use the final chapter of this book to explore some core guiding principles. The goal is to bring together a collection of some of the essential themes that I've touched on throughout this book. Bringing together and elaborating on these principles will give you a parting set of insights that can help establish a set of common values that will shape how you design and build your SaaS architecture and business.

## CHAPTER 17

Guiding Principles

Throughout this book, I've tried to surface a mix of SaaS technical and business principles, highlighting key concepts that have a direct influence on how you approach designing, building, and operating a SaaS business. In some respects, having a firm grasp of these foundational concepts is almost more important than knowing all the nuances of how multi-tenancy might land in your underlying implementation. It's these concepts that guide and help you determine which strategies you should be considering, which questions you should be asking the business, and which multi-tenant patterns are going to best align with the needs of your business. Given the importance of some of these principles, I thought it would be valuable to have one dedicated chapter that would focus exclusively on this guidance.

I've picked three areas that represent a good grouping of these principles. The first part of the chapter starts by looking at strategy, vision, and structure. So much of succeeding with SaaS is driven by having a clear, unifying view of what your SaaS goals are, what it means to be SaaS, and how you're organizing and measuring teams around a clear service-centric mindset and strategy. I outline a range of principles, all focused on areas where I often see organizations struggle to achieve top-down alignment.

The next part of the chapter focuses more on technical principles. Here, I'm looking more at strategies and mental models that can influence how builders and architects approach creating their multi-tenant environments. The last part of the chapter covers operations considerations, identifying a few foundational guiding principles that might help shape the footprint of your SaaS operational model. Getting operations right is fundamental to creating a successful SaaS business and teams need to be thinking about how they can give this area the priority it needs.

By no means is this chapter meant to represent some ultimate list of guiding principles. Instead, my goal was to simply surface themes that represent some of the common practices and approaches that play a big role in shaping the successful adoption of a SaaS delivery model.

Vision, Strategy, and Structure

When I engage SaaS companies and start helping them build their SaaS solution, I'm most interested in understanding how the business is driving its strategy, vision, and structure. I want to understand how the adoption of SaaS is influencing the way teams operate, what they value, and how they view it driving the success and growth of the business.

While having good alignment around SaaS principles seems like a pretty straightforward concept, you might be surprised to discover just how many companies struggle with this basic concept. I continue to find organizations where SaaS is viewed mostly as a new technical strategy that will yield some efficiencies for the business. In these instances, businesses tend to underestimate the importance of building a vision, strategy, and culture that weaves the as-a-service mindset into the fabric of the business.

Success with SaaS always starts at the top. You need executives that understand and value how SaaS changes the build, operation, sales, marketing, and support of their offering. Having leaders that know how to set the tone for your service will allow you and the teams around you to feel comfortable leaning into and incorporating all the nuances that come with adopting a SaaS mindset. This is essential to building a foundation that allows your organization to realize the agility, innovation, efficiency, and growth that's associated with the SaaS delivery model.

The sections that follow highlight some of the key areas that stand out as common challenges and opportunities for organizations that are trying to establish their vision, strategy, and structure.

Build a Business Model and Strategy

It's well understood that strategy and vision are always at the core of building a successful business. However, I've seen many instances where SaaS companies—very large companies—decide to adopt a SaaS delivery model without having a clear picture of where they're going, what values should shape their path forward, and what guiding principles will inform downstream execution. These organizations buy into the value of SaaS and set their teams off on a path without really asking themselves the hard questions that will give definition and detail to their strategy.

You can imagine how problematic this would be for any team. Now, consider the compounded impact this can have in a SaaS environment. There are too many variations and pieces to the SaaS puzzle to be vague about the strategy. Good SaaS teams will lean into vision and strategy, working hard to develop a clearer view of the flavor of SaaS that's going to be best aligned to the goals of the business. This requires a much deeper dive into understanding current and future market segments, the profile of the tenants, the workloads you need to support, the margins you're targeting, and a host of other insights that will have a profound impact on your SaaS strategy. This also includes thinking about how you expect the business to grow. Are we expecting to add 10 new tenants every year or 1,000? How do you expect to reach those tenants? Will you offer a free tier as part of your marketing model? I could fill this entire page with all of the different topics and data points that are needed to formulate a SaaS business vision and plan.

It's at this stage that you're establishing the core values that are going to directly impact your SaaS journey. Product, operations, architects, builders—they're all going to reference these goals and data points as they begin to turn this vision into reality. Without this data, teams may not have a clear view of what success looks like for their business. When the vision and strategy is vague, SaaS companies can end up with very loose definitions of what kind of SaaS experience they're trying to build, how it will need to evolve, the scale it will need to support, and so on. All teams need a well-defined North Star that defines what they're targeting and, more importantly, what they're *not* targeting.

The broader theme here is that you need to develop a vision and strategy that goes beyond traditional goals and metrics. For SaaS, that's not enough. Your vision and strategy must go further, developing a more complete profile of the tenants, segments, growth strategy, and so on. Without this, teams will be left to fill in vital gaps on their own.

A Clear Focus on Efficiency

The SaaS story is very much focused on economies of scale. This means that the overall strategy and day-to-day execution should always be thinking about how it promotes efficiency across all the moving parts of your business. The mental model is one where teams openly embrace opportunities to highlight their ability to scale and pivot based on the emerging needs of customers and the business. Your goal as a business is to leverage the efficiencies enabled by SaaS as the fuel that can drive growth, agility, and innovation. A key pillar of the SaaS model is that it thrives in environments that demand change. In fact, much of the effort and energy that goes into building a robust SaaS business is squarely focused on investing in the people, culture, constructs, and strategies that will enable efficiency.

So, given this broader goal, how should leaders approach achieving this efficiency? It's tempting to assume that efficiency is largely a technical problem. That, for some, is the trap of SaaS. Far too often, teams will view efficiency purely through the lens of infrastructure scale and costs. Technology is just one piece of the efficiency puzzle. When I am looking at a SaaS organization's efficiency, I take a much broader view of efficiency. I look at how teams are organized, how they sell, how they onboard customers, how product teams work, how customer success is plugged in, and a host of other areas. I want to know how efficiently the organization operates collectively, assessing how the structure and culture of the company is contributing to the overall efficiency of the business. I want to know if the company is set up to use this efficiency to scale. To stress this point, I'll pose a hypothetical question to SaaS providers, asking them how their business would be able to support the addition of 1,000 new customers—tomorrow. While this may be entirely unrealistic, it raises interesting questions about whether you've built your business to scale. It takes us beyond the technical and asks us how the different parts of the organization can scale to meet this load. How will this spike in load impact our operations team? Is our onboarding efficient enough to support this load? Will our customer success team be able to scale to meet this need? These are all examples of the stress points that may or may not indicate that your business is ready to scale efficiently.

Notions of scale and efficiency should be core elements of your organization's vision and strategy. The leadership of your organization, the product owners, the architects, and the operations teams should all be thinking about how they can achieve these efficiencies as part of their overall strategy.

Avoiding the Tech-First Trap

As teams set out on their SaaS journey, they often have a tendency to want to dig directly into the details of their multi-tenant architecture. These teams are hyper-focused on figuring out which combination of technologies can best address the requirements of their SaaS offering. Which identity model should we use? How can we isolate tenant resources? How do we store multi-tenant data? These are all examples of the kinds of questions these technology-centric organizations start with. In many instances, these discussions are happening mostly outside the view of the business teams. In fact, the business teams may also be comfortable assuming that SaaS belongs exclusively in the technical realm.

The challenge is that, with SaaS, there is a much tighter connection between the business and technology strategies. In many respects, the business and technical paths need to proceed in parallel. The reality is, many of the architectural choices you're going to make are entirely dependent on the vision and strategy of the business. Which markets are you trying to reach? What are the tenant personas? Will different segments have different requirements? How will you tier and price the offering? These aren't just high-level business data points. The choices you make here can impact the fundamental shape and strategies employed by your architecture. As a SaaS architect, you can't really move forward without some clear, jointly agreed upon view of the multi-tenant profile and experience that you're enabling. You can't bolt these concepts on after the fact.

Generally, formulating your technical footprint in a vacuum will often impose limits and assumptions that could undermine the success and growth of your SaaS offering. If you're the lone technical person championing the move to SaaS at your company, your first move needs to be focused on pulling in product, operational, and business strategists and beginning to ask the hard questions about the service experience, personas, and multi-tenant profile of your offering.

This may seem like a basic and even obvious point, but time and time again I come across companies that don't seem to see the strong connection between business and technology strategies. Builders want to build, and their fascination with the technology often creates blind spots that have them missing out on the importance of leaning into the full business view of what it means to be SaaS. I have dropped into countless SaaS projects where the technical teams and technical leadership have been developing their SaaS solution for months without having answered any of the key business questions about their offering. It's an easy trap to fall into. This is where you have to continually make an extra effort to ensure that the technical and business strategies remain aligned throughout the process.

Thinking Beyond Cost Savings

The move to SaaS, for some, is often influenced by a strong desire to reduce costs and maximize operational efficiency. These are entirely valid goals and often very important to organizations that are seeing their margins eroded by operational complexity and the burden of one-off customer installations.

The challenge is that this mindset suggests that the vision and strategy for your SaaS solution is mostly focused on making a multi-tenant version of your existing offering to get costs under control. It's true that SaaS will achieve cost efficiencies, but making this the focal point of your strategy and execution seems to miss the point.

Generally, the move to SaaS is a transformational event that goes well beyond cost savings. Adopting SaaS, for many, is about rethinking how you build, operate, market, sell, and monetize your offering. It's about using the economies of scale and agility of SaaS to fuel innovation and growth. Cost is just one parameter of the broader SaaS value proposition.

The point is that your vision and strategy for adopting SaaS should not be narrowed to cost savings. I'd prefer this to be viewed more through the lens of economies of scale where your multi-tenant architecture and operational model are built with cost efficiency and optimization being top of mind.

Be All-In with SaaS

With some SaaS providers, there's a real temptation to have it all. They see how SaaS can enable them to grow their business faster and achieve the efficiencies, agility, and innovation that comes with SaaS. When you ask if they're all-in with the fundamental principles of SaaS, you get a resounding yes. They want the goodness that comes with having one unified experience for all customers. They see the importance of having all customers running the same version. At first glance, they seem to have a vision and strategy that lines up with all the core SaaS principles.

Then, as I dig deeper into the vision, the caveats start to surface. Yes, these organizations want to be all-in with SaaS, but they also have some customers that are given exceptions to the rules. The needs of these few customers are viewed as being so vital that they end up offering them one-off configurations and environments. It's here that companies are at the crossroads of SaaS. Is it feasible to support these one-off exceptions without undermining the vision, strategy, and success of your SaaS business? Does supporting this approach slowly move you to a managed service provider model, limiting your ability to fully realize the economies of scale that come with having a single, unified environment for all customers?

I completely understand the business realities that teams are facing here. This can be especially challenging for companies that are migrating to SaaS. You may have stockholders, revenue expectations, and existing relationships that make it difficult to make the full commitment to SaaS. Also, when large customers make demands, it's often challenging to say no. The allure of a near-term, lucrative deal can also sway organizations.

To be fair, there are no absolute rights and wrongs here. Ultimately, the business is going to make compromises based on any number of market, business, and customer pressures. For me, this is more about having a clear vision of what it is that you're trying to achieve by adopting SaaS. If your goal is to maximize the value of SaaS to scale and use the fundamentals of that scale to grow your business, then you'll have to weigh the longer-term impacts of supporting a model where you support one-off customer experiences. Each one-off customer that you take on can slowly move you away from the core SaaS value proposition.

For some, there may be reasonable trade-offs that make this a viable option. For others, it could put you on an unintended path to lower margins, higher operational costs, and reduced agility. The key is to be aware of these trade-offs and clear about how the choices you're making will influence your long-term ambitions.

Adopt a Service-Centric Mindset

The "service" part of software as a service can get lost in the shuffle. Many teams that are moving to SaaS are rooted in the traditional product-centric mindset where their focus was mostly on features and functions. This, for some, makes the transition to an as-a-service model a bit more challenging. SaaS requires teams to think beyond functional aspects of software, expanding their scope to consider the broader service experience of their offering.

This shift reaches across all dimensions of the business. As a product owner, my backlog is now populated with all kinds of new operationally focused deliverables. How effectively are tenants onboarding? How are we measuring their time to value? What data do I have that gives me insights into the tenant experience? These are just a few examples of areas I'll want to watch as a product owner. They also have implications for builders that have to implement and measure this service experience.

You can imagine how this service mindset extends into all the roles in your organization. Customer success, sales, marketing, operations, and builders must alter their approach and give priority to the different parts of the service that will impact the customer experience. In some cases, organizations may even choose to adopt shared goals around service metrics. The idea is that you will adopt service-focused goals that span teams, encouraging them to come out of their silos, work more collaboratively, and put greater emphasis on the importance of building a rich service experience.

The key is that we're expanding our view of the experience, thinking about how and where the service footprint of our experience will impact the success of our business. Don't get caught in the trap of viewing SaaS as just another way to sell products.

Think Beyond Existing Tenant Personas

When you're building a SaaS business, you have to have a firm grasp of the profile and nature of the tenants that will be using your solution. Yes, with any system, you have to develop customer personas. With SaaS, however, there's another layer to this discussion that goes beyond the traditional notion of tenant personas.

In a SaaS world, tenant personas can have far-reaching impacts on how you design and build your system. We have explored different architecture patterns throughout this book, using tiers, deployment models, isolation strategies, and other techniques to create distinct experiences for your SaaS tenants. These are all tools you have in your tool bag that you can offer to the business. However, it's also the job of the business to think about how the market is segmented. Who are the customers you're trying to reach today, and what other segments might you be able to target by creating different experiences for your solution? Where might you introduce tiers and pricing strategies that allow the business to address a range of market segments without undermining the margins of the business? These are the kinds of questions that you need to be asking as a business to understand how you can best position your offering to maximize its reach, impact, and growth.

As part of shaping your vision and strategy, I want you to think beyond the customers that might be your most natural target and consider how you might be able to reach new segments of customers by offering a broader range of options. This exercise can directly impact how you choose to package and offer your solution. The choices you make here are also likely to influence key elements of your architecture and operations experience.

The nature of your tenant personas will also drive other key decisions. The number of tenants you plan to have in the system, the workloads of these users, their compliance requirements, and their performance requirements are all factors that can impact the architecture choices you'll make. The architecture I build to support 100 tenants could be quite different from the architecture I build to support 1,000 tenants. Some tenants may also value price over performance. There is a long list of variables you'd have to weigh as part of developing a rich tenant profile.

SaaS businesses need to push hard on assembling this data, pushing themselves to imagine a tiered experience that can support a more diverse range of tenant experiences.

Core Technical Considerations

As a SaaS technologist, it's your job to go beyond the basics and challenge yourself to identify new and creative ways you might be able to enhance the cost efficiency, agility, and operational profile of your solution. The organization will lean on you to build an architecture that balances a complex combination of competing goals that will test your ability to find technology strategies that align to a potentially shifting set of business, market, and customer goals. As a SaaS architect, you are at the center of creating the architecture, tools, and constructs that will enable the business to realize its SaaS goals.

For this section I want to highlight some of the key principles that can play a significant role in shaping how technical teams approach designing and building a SaaS environment. The objective is to simply focus on a few high-level areas that I believe need to be top of mind when you're creating a SaaS service.

No One-Size-Fits-All Model

Builders and architects often come to me looking for the blueprint for their SaaS architecture. They want that one, gold-plated multi-tenant architecture that can be universally applied to all domains, business problems, and use cases. That may be a bit of an overstatement, but that's often the sentiment behind the ask.

It should be clear at this point that there simply is no one blueprint for SaaS. In fact, this is part of why I find SaaS so compelling. Whenever I'm looking at the customer's proposed architecture, it's my job to find the mix of SaaS strategies that will best target the specific business, operational, technical, and timing realities of their environment. Yes, there are common themes and core principles that are global to all SaaS solutions. However, the actual mapping of those principles to a working architecture can vary significantly from one solution to the next. If you just look at the two architecture stacks we reviewed in Chapters 10 and 11, you can see how each technology brings its own set of constructs and mechanisms to the SaaS story.

For me, arriving at a target architecture starts with a long list of questions that are often targeted at the business stakeholders and product owners. Where you're starting, the nature of your domain, market pressures, tenant personas, the technology stack you're using, and a number of other factors end up providing the insights that I need to figure out which flavor of architecture is going to align your business, technical, and customer needs. This all comes back to having a clear vision and strategy that provides enough detail to help you make these choices. Without this data, I'm not sure how you would be able to pick an architecture. This may require you to go back to the business to get the data you need before you move forward. In some cases, you may serve as the forcing function that pushes the business to ask itself to further define its strategy.

Protect the Multi-Tenant Principles

Technical teams are directly immersed in the details of how the system is built, operated, and deployed. These teams are on the front lines of ensuring that the core values of SaaS are being applied in a way that supports the agility, innovation, and efficiency that the business is targeting. It's unlikely that other teams within your organization are going to be able to detect whether you've made some compromise that could impact the organization's ability to achieve its SaaS goals.

This means that the technical teams take on some added responsibility. They must be the ones to understand how the system can scale effectively, align to performance requirements, support tiering needs, provide efficient tenant onboarding, ensure that tenant resources are adequately isolated, and so on. Ultimately, the business is relying on these teams to adopt the best practices strategies that allow them to release quickly, achieve economies of scale, and provide a zero-downtime experience.

Delivering on this promise can be challenging in any environment. It's especially challenging when you are building a system that must support multi-tenant workloads where tenants are coming and going and their workload profiles are continually shifting. This is where I feel like SaaS architects must be especially diligent about protecting their architecture. In many instances, the business may entertain opportunities that will test your ability to adhere to the core values of your multi-tenant architecture. It's your job to be the ambassador and protector of these principles, helping the business find creative ways to deal with customer needs without making compromises that could slowly erode your ability to manage, operate, and deploy your tenants through a single, unified experience.

Whenever the business is steering down a dangerous path, point them back to the vision and strategy that is guiding your business. Highlight the slippery slopes that might lead you further away from fully realizing the SaaS value proposition.

Build Your Multi-Tenant Foundation on Day One

Across this book, I've outlined a number of multi-tenant strategies that I feel are core to building a robust, best practices SaaS environment. Generally, I think these concepts resonate with builders. They see the value. They understand how important it can be to apply these strategies in their solutions. While these core principles will resonate with teams, they don't always get the day one focus and priority they deserve. Instead, I'll see teams race off to start building their application services, focusing their initial energy on getting their solution up and running. For some, there seems to be this expectation that these core, cross-cutting concepts can be bolted on later in the process without much penalty.

From my perspective, the first steps in your multi-tenant journey must start with creating the shell of your control plane. The goal is to get the most fundamental bits of tenancy put in place, introducing the onboarding process that provisions tenants, the bits needed to establish tenant and admin identities, and the authentication of tenants, which will inject tenant context into your backend services. By starting here, you're creating the foundational building blocks of your SaaS environment, forcing teams to begin dealing with the nuances of supporting multi-tenancy across all the dimensions of your architecture. It also begins to surface the elements of your administration experience, exposing the basic mechanisms that are used to track and manage the lifecycle of your tenants. This may seem like a small step, but it creates a cascading effect that will set the stage for the rest of your multi-tenant journey.

You'll see this progression as you move into the application plane. Here, your application services now have access to tenant context. They are now forced to consider how this context will influence the implementation of their service. Will tenant context now be introduced into your logs and metrics? How will tenant context be used to implement data partitioning and isolation for your service? These are all examples of areas where the presence of tenant context forces teams to apply tenancy to the footprint of their application code. It will also create opportunities to introduce libraries and helpers that can be reused across your application services. Extracting tokens, logging with tenant context, getting scoped isolation credentials—these are all areas that become candidates for reusable code or libraries that can be shared across your application services.

Of course, now that our application services are multi-tenant aware and publishing logs, metrics, and billing data, we can consider how we might use this data to begin to exercise the operational side of our environment. Teams can now troubleshoot their code through tenant-aware logs that are centrally published and laced with tenant context, allowing builders to narrow their view logs to individual tenants. You can see how this begins to lay the early foundation for our operational tooling and experience. Early on, you want builders to simulate and exercise the operational mechanisms that will eventually be an essential part of your production experience. You also begin to open doors for the QA teams that want to validate the system's ability to add tenants and stress workloads. The ability to onboard multiple tenants means these teams can begin thinking about how they can automate their testing and validation based on different tenant profiles.

My hope is that this helps you see just how essential it is that you focus your initial efforts on introducing tenancy and a control plane, putting the team in a position where it's building and operating in a multi-tenant mode from day one.

Avoid One-Off Customization

In a SaaS environment, many of your agility and efficiency goals are achieved through your ability to have all customers running the same version of your software. Any divergence from this begins to move you away from what it means to be SaaS. So, with this in mind, it's fair to question what role customization should play in the SaaS universe. Is customization allowed? Is it prohibited? Where are the boundaries?

I think lots of this comes down to the intent and mindset behind how, where, and when you are introducing customization into your SaaS offering. Some teams will view customization as a tool to offer one-off capabilities to individual customers. Depending on your approach, this could end up having negative consequences. Any time we're introducing something into our SaaS environment to meet the needs of a single customer, we have to question whether it aligns with the overall goals of our business. At the same time, it's not wrong to expect that a SaaS system could have one version of your offering that uses customization techniques to offer tenants different experiences.

To better understand the nuances here, let's consider two separate approaches to introducing customization. For this discussion, let's presume that we're going to use feature flags to enable or disable capabilities within our solution. Now, in one scenario, you could view feature flags as a way to create distinct experiences for individual tenants. This often happens in organizations that are chasing deals and giving in to old temptations to offer whatever is needed to land a customer. The challenge of this approach is that it slowly erodes the fundamental goals of SaaS, often leading to a complex maze of code and configurations that are challenging to support and manage. The other scenario is one where we apply feature flags more selectively. Here, instead of viewing customization as a per-tenant concept, you would view customization as a global, shared mechanism that can be applied to any tenant. The key idea is that we use feature flags as a way to define distinct categories of experiences. A typical example might center around tiers where we would use feature flags to configure the different experiences of each tier. The fundamental difference is that we're applying customization to groups of tenants that fit a profile—not individual tenants.

There are no absolutes to this. The bigger takeaway is the mindset. Are you using feature flags to create a complex web of one-off tenant customizations, or are you using it to land groups of tenants in a well-defined set of customization profiles? The idea is to embrace feature flags as a way to offer customization without abusing the construct.

Measure Your Multi-Tenant Architecture

As we've seen throughout this book, SaaS architectures come in many flavors. Within one organization, you could be supporting a range of tenant workloads, deployment models, performance profiles, tiering strategies, and so on. Given these diverse and potentially competing needs, it can be difficult to assess how well your resulting architecture is going to react and respond to real-world tenant workloads. Even if your environment is working well today, there's no guarantee that your system will continue to perform as your mix of tenants and workloads shift over time.

This reality makes it especially important to have tools and mechanisms that can provide ongoing insights into the performance, scale, and efficiency of your multi-tenant environment. It's true that your existing technology stack might already provide some useful data that can help you profile the behavior of your architecture. However, it's likely that you'll still need to instrument your environment with additional metrics and analytics that will provide you with more targeted multi-tenant insights. You'll want to know more about how tenants and tiers are pushing your environment and have specific metrics that can help you understand how your architecture needs tuning. This data may also uncover potential areas where you're overprovisioned or where your tenants are saturating resources in ways you hadn't anticipated.

The key point is that multi-tenant architectures are in constant motion. This is to be expected—especially for SaaS businesses that have populations of tenants that are coming and going. The only way to stay ahead of the curve is to invest in surfacing the data that will allow you to analyze and profile the behavior of your architecture, correlating activity and consumption with specific tenants and tiers.

Streamline the Developer Experience

When you're building a SaaS solution, you're going find yourself introducing a variety of policies to support concepts like tenant isolation, data partitioning, tiering, and so on. As a SaaS architect, you're going to want to do all that you can to ensure that these mechanisms don't somehow hinder the productivity of developers. In an ideal world, you'd like to create an experience where builders can simply focus on the features they're building without being required to add traces of multi-tenant strategies all throughout their code.

In addition to simplifying code, you also want to centralize the build, deployment, and versioning of the multi-tenant constructs. The idea is that we'd move all the policies and code into a set of reusable libraries. This is really just about following the typical design best practices that are applied in anything you might build. However, it's also about having one place your teams turn to for any multi-tenant constructs that can be used across multiple services.

So, as you're building out the services of your SaaS application, you should be looking for opportunities to move tenant details outside the view of your developers. There are some obvious targets that you'll likely go after on day one. For example, many systems will introduce helpers to deal with token management, equipping builders with mechanisms that allow them to easily extract tenant context from incoming tokens. Logging is another area where you can add helpers that automatically inject tenant context. Tenant isolation also represents another area where teams want to move their isolation strategies and code into libraries. The goal is to make complying with these strategies as simple as possible.

The true measure of success here is found directly in the code of your application services. If you dive into some operation in one of your services and discover that it's laced with line after line of code to acquire, apply, and inject tenant context, then it will be clear that more work should be done here to move these concepts into helper libraries. It's important to note that I'm not suggesting that this approach will entirely remove any multi-tenant handling from your application code. It's more that I want to do what I can here to minimize complexity for developers.

Operations Mindset

SaaS businesses rely heavily on having rich, proactive operational tooling to drive the success of their business. Addressing this need can be particularly challenging in multi-tenant environments where you have a more fluid and potentially unpredictable range of tenant personas that are exercising and pushing the limits of your architecture. Multi-tenancy can also add new layers of operational risk to your environment. As you rely more on pooled resources, you also face the reality of having outages that can impact all of your customers. These are the kinds of outages that can make headlines and do lasting damage to your brand.

Supporting these sometimes challenging operational needs requires SaaS businesses to have a clear commitment to making operations a priority. We talked about this in detail in Chapter 12. However, in the sections that follow, I want to highlight some of the core guiding principles that are part of the overall SaaS operations mindset.

Thinking Beyond System Health

In many organizations, operations is seen as the team that's responsible for keeping the lights on. Their job is to monitor and manage the health of the system. This is a completely fair way to think about the role of operations in some organizations. However, with SaaS, I believe operations teams take on a broader role that goes beyond ensuring that the system is up and running. A SaaS operations team is, to me, at the epicenter of observing all the activities, trends, and experiences that are playing out via your multi-tenant architecture. They are seeing the various multi-tenant policies and architecture strategies being fully exercised by tenants with varying profiles and consumption patterns.

SaaS operations teams are at the hub of observing and interpreting the health, activity, and metrics data that provides a collective view into the overall operational health of the business. To me, this is where I see a bit of the divide. I see operations extending beyond bugs, outages, and failures, extending into insights that allow us to make broader observations about the evolving state of our architecture and business.

To make this more concrete, let's look at an example of an operations view into the tenant onboarding experience. At one level, the operations team will be monitoring and capturing any onboarding failures and working to troubleshoot any failures that are happening in this area. That's the more traditional role of operations. Now, in another context, I'm also watching metrics and trends around the onboarding process that give me insights into how onboarding is responding to load, whether it's meeting SLAs, and how efficiently tenants are moving through the process. In this mode, there's nothing broken. However, I still very much keep my finger on the pulse of onboarding to see if there are issues or inefficiencies that could be impacting the tenant's experience. The business would want to know this and be proactive about finding new ways to refine the onboarding process.

The main idea is that SaaS businesses ought to have an expanded view of the insights that are surfaced and acted on via the operations experience. Multi-tenant environments often have so many moving parts and strategies that are continually being pushed based on an evolving set of needs. Your team is going to want to know that the architecture and design strategies you've employed are successfully handling these needs.

There are so many multi-tenant details that you'll want observed and evaluated. For example, I may want to have views into how my throttling policies are being applied to my basic tier tenants. Or I might want to assess consumption trends for the siloed resources of my platinum tier tenants to figure out if they might be overprovisioned. Or I could want to see how tenants are imposing load on specific infrastructure resources. The overarching theme is that I'm not just reacting to health events—I'm assessing the runtime realization of the multi-tenant policies that are currently employed by my architecture. I'm looking around corners to see how, where, and when tenants may be testing my assumptions in ways I hadn't anticipated.

To some, this may just seem like an extension of what you already do. When I discuss this topic with teams, they'll often indicate that they understand the need and have it covered. However, when I dig into their operational tooling and approach, I often discover that they're mostly relying on some mix of off-the-shelf tools that have little or no awareness of tenant context. Yes, the tools can still be a valuable part of your environment. At the same time, it's likely you'll need to supplement these tools with your own custom-built or configured mechanisms that allow you to analyze the unique multi-tenant operational footprint of your system.

Overall, the real point of emphasis is that operations is at the epicenter of your service experience. It is one of the most foundational elements of successful SaaS businesses, equipping teams with the tools and mechanisms that allow them to anticipate emerging issues, quickly target tenant challenges, and prevent outages. Investing in the right tools here is critical to being able to deal with the challenging dynamics that come with operating a multi-tenant business.

Introducing Proactive Constructs

SaaS is generally intended to be a zero-downtime experience. If you're running an entirely pooled environment, for example, any outage could ripple across all of your tenants. The impact of any outage could have a significant impact on your business. This naturally puts added pressure on SaaS operations teams. They're continually looking at how they can ensure that they're maximizing their ability to head off issues before they impact tenants. To me, this also places greater emphasis on the need for proactive operational tooling that implements policies and mechanisms that can detect and surface operational issues before they have a wider impact.

In many respects, the mindset here is mostly an extension of general operational practices. Operations teams typically already have alerts and alarms in place that can be used to fill this need. With SaaS operations, it's more about figuring out how and where you should introduce these constructs. I may, for example, have tier-focused throttling policies that are preventing tenants from saturating some aspect of my system, or I might have metrics from my database that let me know when pooled tenants might be overloading a shared database. The idea is that there are all these different multi-tenant policies and mechanisms that span our architecture and you need to find the key points of operational tension in your architecture where you'll want to monitor activity and, potentially, surface alerts and alarms.

Using this proactive approach may uncover new opportunities to introduce constructs that will reduce the possibility for outages. The data that comes out of this might lead to changes in policies, deployment, partitioning, sizing, and other aspects of your architecture, allowing you to more proactively evolve the design of your environment.

Validating Your Multi-Tenant Strategies

You never really know how your SaaS system is going to respond to the varying needs of tenants. This unpredictability of workloads is a reality for SaaS teams. At the same time, it's also an obvious area of risk for the operational health of your system. What new things might a tenant try that you hadn't anticipated? How will their workloads shift and change over time? You do what you can to plan for this, but there are few certainties here.

To address this need, teams can and should look at how they can stress their systems and validate their ability to perform and respond as anticipated. Again, stress and load testing is nothing new. However, in a multi-tenant setting, we have new dimensions and considerations that need to be factored into our validation approach.

This idea of stressing and validating your SaaS environment is partly connected to some of the metrics discussions that we've had throughout this book. For example, I've talked about measuring the onboarding efficiency of your system and attaching a metric to this. The question: how do I know if my system will be able to achieve the levels of efficiency that we've agreed to target? This is where your load and stress testing should include tests that exercise the onboarding performance of your system. What happens if I add 100 tenants in a tight window of time? How will the system scale to handle this? How will it handle onboarding of tenants with different profiles (silo and pool, for example)? Could this degrade other aspects of the system? The only way to answer these questions is to simulate this activity across multiple use cases.

Onboarding is just one of many areas where you'll want to validate your multi-tenant strategies. You might simulate loads to test the tier-based throttling strategies of your system. You might simulate pooled scaling strategies of microservices. You might introduce tests to validate your tenant isolation strategies. The list of possibilities could be quite long. You can imagine just how valuable this can be to the operational profile of your organization. The more you can simulate these loads and validate your policies, the more confidence you'll have in your ability to limit the potential for these issues to surface in production.

In some respects, you could see this approach wanders a bit into the chaos testing realm, where you're essentially attempting to throw lots of challenges at your multi-tenant architecture and see how it responds to these challenges. As part of this, you should also think about the mix of tenant personas/profiles that could be part of these tests. You might have one load test that features a heavy dose of basic tier tenants consuming some key aspect of your system to see if this creates noisy neighbor conditions for your premium tier tenants. The overall goal would be to create a suite of tests that spanned a different mix of tenant profiles (tiers, workloads, etc.).

It's fair to question whether this testing discussion fits more in the quality assurance and development domains. Perhaps it does. However, I also see this as part of the operations universe. It is here that, as part of running these tests, we're also validating our ability to analyze and surface the side effects of the tests through our tenant-aware operational tooling. This validation isn't just testing the architecture—it's also about testing the efficacy of your operations model.

You're Part of the Team

Operations teams often view themselves as being downstream of the team's vision, strategy, design, and build. In some instances, operations teams might view themselves in more of a support-focused role. I see operations teams needing to be woven into all the moving parts of the development process. These teams bring a unique perspective to your SaaS vision and execution, weighing in on how different models or approaches might influence your ability to effectively manage and operate your SaaS offering.

I think part of the challenge is that operations can be incorrectly viewed as being somewhat static. In the mental model, there's an assumption that we're just applying a known set of tools and mechanisms to our system to monitor its health. This approach presumes that the operator requires minimal insights into the underlying strategies and policies that were used to construct the environment.

I believe that operations—especially for SaaS environments—need to be tightly integrated into the overall development decision making, playing an active role in shaping and understanding how the choices being made will impact the overall operational footprint of the service. This level of exposure and involvement will more directly influence the tooling and strategies that are used to assemble an operational experience that better aligns to the details of the underlying architecture. Teams will be in a better position to develop the insights, metrics, and operational views that will drive a richer operational experience.

As part of this, I'd also expect the product owners and architects to be looking at how and when they may need to put operations deliverables on the backlog of your service. If there's a change in the SaaS service that may also require changes to the operations experience, then those changes should be added to and prioritized in the backlog. Including these operations impacts in your backlog will better integrate the operational perspective into ongoing development efforts.

Conclusion

The path to creating a successful SaaS offering is not always so clear. Well-intended teams often struggle to find their way through the myriad of business and technical challenges that come with creating a SaaS business. The biggest part of the challenge is that SaaS is a business strategy that requires a high level of collaboration between business and technical teams. It's here that teams need a clear set of guiding principles that can help them align around a shared vision that maps their target SaaS service experience to a mental model that will cascade across all the moving parts of the business.

For this chapter, I assembled a list of some of the core guiding principles that represent areas where it's important to have strong alignment on your SaaS vision and principles. The first area we looked at was strategy, vision, and structure. The goal was to highlight some of the most common, cross-cutting themes that I see impacting the success of SaaS organizations. I outlined a few of the foundational areas where SaaS businesses need to have a unified value system and strategy that can cascade across all the moving parts of the organization. I wanted to highlight key areas where even small disconnects in the business could ultimately impact the growth, scale, and efficiency of a SaaS service.

I also looked at these guiding principles through a technical lens, focusing on common areas that can influence the direction and strategy of your SaaS architecture. Here, I wanted to review some of the fundamental principles that may have the biggest impact on how you approach your broader technical strategy. Finally, I finished by exploring some of the principles that can influence your operations mindset. The emphasis was on understanding the role that operations plays in a SaaS environment, outlining the areas where SaaS operations teams need to augment their approach to deal with the realities that come with operating a multi-tenant environment.

It's important to note that the principles outlined here represent a sampling of some of the key areas where I've seen organizations struggle. The hope was that, by assembling these core principles in one place, it would allow us to step away from the details and look at the basic themes that surround the development of your SaaS solution. Organizations that have good, top-to-bottom alignment around what it means to be SaaS are often in the best position to maximize the success of their SaaS offering.

Index

containers, routing and, 153-155
Content Delivery Network (CDN), tenant subdomains, 141
Continuous Integration/Continuous Delivery (see CI/CD)
control plane, 27-29
  administration console, 41
  application plane integration, 44
  application plane interaction, 30
  baseline environment, 84
    provisioning options, 87-88
  billing, 32-33
  deployment, EKS and, 255-256
  full stack pool deployment models, 67
  full stack silo deployment models, 56-57
  identity, 30-32
  legacy code in migration, 355
  metrics, 32
  migration and, 344
  onboarding and, 29-30
  Provisioning service, 94
  remote resources and, 392
  SaaS Anywhere, 392
  serverless computing and, 286-288
  technology choices, 45
  tenant management, 33
  tenant provisioning, 42
core tenant attributes, 117
cost
  full stack pool deployment models, 71
  savings, guiding principles and, 435
cost-per-tenant metrics, 318-321
custom claims, 102
  populating, 105
  tenant context and, 105
customer acquisition costs (CAC), 321
customer lifetime value (CLTV), 322
customization, one-off, 441-442
cycle time, 314

D

dashboards, operations console, 329
data access, tenant context, 176-178
data partitioning, 36, 189, 190
  (see also pooled data partitioning; siloed data partitioning)
  backup and restore and, 194
  blast radius and, 193
  data lifecycle and, 216-217

database partitioning, relational databases, 199-202
databases, object storage and, 208-210
  isolation and, 193-194
  management footprint and, 194
  multi-environment support, 196
  NoSQL data partitioning, 202
    pooled data partitioning, 203
    siloed data partitioning, 204
    tuning, 205
  object storage service and, 206
    pooled data partitioning, 206-207
    siloed data partitioning, 207
  OpenSearch service and, 210
    mixed mode data partitioning, 214
    pooled data partitioning, 211-212
    siloed data partitioning, 212-214
  operational footprint and, 194
  relational databases, 199
    pooled models, 200
    siloed models, 201-202
  security, 217
  storage
    selecting, 195
    SLAs and, 192
    workloads, 192
data sharding, 215-216
decommissioning tenants, 127-130
deployment
  applications, 39
  automating, 259-260, 330-332
    scoping, 332
    targeted releases, 332-334
  failed, 314
  frequency, 313
  tenant-aware, 264-265
deployment models
  conceptual, 48
  description, 48
  full stack hybrid models, 74-75
  full stack pool models, 67-73
  full stack silo models, 53-66
  full stack, onboarding and, 95
  Lambda and, 282
    mixed mode, 284-285
    pooled, 283-284
    siloed, 283-284
  mixed mode deployment model, 75-77
  pod deployment model, 77-80

I

IAM (Identity and Access Management), 267
IAM Roles for Service Accounts (IRSA), 267
identity
    authentication and, 101
    creating, 100-112
    federated, 107-109
    OIDC and, 102
    system admin, baseline environment, 86
    tenant identity, 100
        attaching, 102, 105
        control plane, 30-32
    Tenant Management service, 117
    user identity, 100
identity model, migration, 346
innovation, 18
integration, SaaS Anywhere and, 397
interception, runtime isolation and, 232-233
internal onboarding, 89-90
IRSA (IAM Roles for Service Accounts), 267
isolation, 35-36, 111, 178-181, 184, 219-223
    application isolation versus infrastructure
        isolation, 226-227
    application-enforced, 225
    authorization and, 225-226
    data partitioning and, 193-194
    deployment-time, 228-235
    EKS (Elastic Kubernetes Service) and, 247,
        265-271
    full stack, 224, 235-237
    full stack pool deployment models, 70
    GenAI and, 423
    item-level, 224, 239-240
    policy management, 240-242
    RBAC (role-based access control) and,
        225-226
    resource-level, 224, 237-239
    runtime, 228-235
        interception and, 232-233
        scaling and, 234-235
    serverless computing, 296
        deployment-time isolation, 298-299
        pooled isolation, 296-298
        route-based isolation, 301-302
        silo isolation, 299-300
    siloing functions and, 284
    tiering and, 368
isolation credential injection, 296
isolation models

full stack isolation, 224
item-level isolation, 224
layers, 227-228
resource-level isolation, 224
item-level isolation, 224, 239-240

J

JWTs (JSON Web Tokens), 34, 102-105
    bearer tokens, 172-173

L

Lambda Extensions, 186
Lambda functions, 284
Lambda Layers, 186
large language models (LLMs), 403, 405
layered migration, 348-351
legacy code, migration and, 355
LLMs (large language models), 403, 405
logging
    operations console, 329
    tenant aware, 174
    tenant context, 173-174

M

man-in-the middle, 145-146
Managed Service Provider (MSP) model, 14
mean time to detection/recovery, 314
metrics
    aggregation, 323-324
    agility metrics, 313
        availability, 313
        cycle time, 314
        defect escape rate, 314
        deployment/release frequency, 313
        failed deployments, 314
        mean time to detection/recovery, 314
    baseline metrics, 322
    business health metrics, 321-322
    composite metrics, 322
    consumption metrics, 315
        architecture layers, 317
        microservices level, 318
        resource level, 316
    control plane, 32
    cost-per-tenant metrics, 318-321
    instrumentation, 323-324
    operational metrics, 310
        tenant activity, 311-313

About the Author

Tod Golding is a cloud applications architect who has spent the last 10 years immersed in cloud-optimized application design and architecture. As a global SaaS lead within AWS, Tod has been a SaaS technology thought leader, publishing and providing SaaS best practices guidance through a broad set of channels (speaking, writing, and working directly with a wide range of SaaS companies). Tod has over 20 years of experience as a technical leader, architect, and developer, including time at both startups and tech giants (AWS, eBay, Microsoft). In addition to speaking at technical conferences, Tod also authored *Professional .NET Generics* and was a columnist for *Better Software* magazine.

Colophon

The animal on the cover of *Building Multi-Tenant SaaS Architectures* is the bat-eared fox (*Otocyon megalotis*). This small, friend-shaped creature is actually an ancient, basal species of canid—one of the earliest dogs, having first appeared sometime in the Middle Pleistocene age (between 126,000 and 770,000 years ago). It is the sole remaining species of the genus *Otocyon* (from the Greek *otus*, for ear, and *cyon*, for dog).

Bat-eared foxes are found in two distinct populations (subspecies *canescens* and *megalotis*) separated geographically by about 600 miles in eastern and southern Africa. Here they live in pairs or small family groups in the open grasslands, shrublands, savanna, and woodland edges, raising their young in dens, which are also used as shelter from the extreme temperatures of their arid and semi-arid environments.

Big ears are a fairly common adaptation among denizens of arid regions and often play a role in thermoregulation—their surface area allowing for more heat loss to the environment. Bat-eared foxes also leverage their large listeners to detect the underground movement of the termites, scorpions, and other bugs that make up the majority of their diet. Interestingly, bat-eared foxes are considered the only truly insectivorous canid, and as an adaptation to their diet, they have smaller teeth than those of other dogs.

Due to their stable populations, bat-eared foxes have been classified by the IUCN as of least concern from a conservation standpoint. Many of the animals on O'Reilly covers are endangered; all of them are important to the world.

The cover illustration is by Karen Montgomery, based on an antique line engraving from *The Natural History of Animals*. The series design is by Edie Freedman, Ellie Volckhausen, and Karen Montgomery. The cover fonts are Gilroy Semibold and Guardian Sans. The text font is Adobe Minion Pro; the heading font is Adobe Myriad Condensed; and the code font is Dalton Maag's Ubuntu Mono.

O'REILLY®

Learn from experts.
Become one yourself.

Books | Live online courses
Instant answers | Virtual events
Videos | Interactive learning

Get started at oreilly.com.

Printed in the USA
CPSIA information can be obtained
at www.ICGtesting.com
JSHW050806040524
62494JS00003B/6